AIRMEN OF ARNHEM

THE HEAVY LIFT CREWS OF OPERATION 'MARKET'

MARTIN W. BOWMAN

Pen & Sword
AVIATION

First published in Great Britain in 2020 by
PEN AND SWORD AVIATION
an imprint of
Pen & Sword Books Limited
Yorkshire – Philadelphia

ISBN 978 1 52674 611 5

Typeset in Times New Roman 11/13.5 by
Aura Technology and Software Services, India

Printed and bound in the UK by TJ International

Pen & Sword Books Ltd incorporates the imprints of Pen & Sword
Archaeology, Atlas, Aviation, Battleground, Discovery,
Family History, History, Maritime, Military, Naval, Politics, Railways,
Select, Social History, Transport, True Crime, Claymore Press,
Frontline Books, Leo Cooper, Praetorian Press, Remember When,
Seaforth Publishing and Wharncliffe.

For a complete list of Pen and Sword titles please contact
PEN & SWORD BOOKS LTD
47 Church Street, Barnsley, South Yorkshire, S70 2AS, England
E-mail: enquiries@pen-and-sword.co.uk
Website: www.pen-and-sword.co.uk

Or

PEN & SWORD BOOKS
1950 Lawrence Rd, Havertown, PA 19083, USA
E-mail: Uspen-and-sword@casematepublishers.com
Website: www.penandswordbooks.com

Contents

Acknowledgements

Airborne Assault; Paradata, The Living History of the Parachute Regiment and Airborne Forces website; The Pegasus Archive.

Chapter 1

From 'Neptune' to 'Market'

We seemed to be violating Napoleon's maxim about never fighting unless you are at least 75 per cent sure of success. Then, the other 25 per cent can be left to chance. The British were reversing the process - we were leaving 75 per cent to chance.
34-year old Major Jonkheer Jan van Blokland, Dutch Chief of Staff, Prinses Irene Brigade, whose parents lived in the village of Oosterbeek, only 2½ miles from the Arnhem Bridge.

In the summer of 1944 the sun shone over Southern England and success greeted the allied armies in France and Belgium. At airfields in south-west England and in Lincolnshire increased activity aroused suspicions but no-one really knew what was in the wind. In August WAAF Corporal Ruth Mary Parker was posted to RAF Fairford in Gloucestershire. 'This airfield had the longest runways in the country and had been used by the United States Army Air Force as a base. The billets where we slept and spent much of our off-duty time were built of corrugated metal shaped like long tunnels, with the door and only windows at each end. The bedsteads we used were made of iron and had previously been used by the Americans. The 'Yanks', as we called them, who were well known for their gum-chewing habit, had left dollops of this stuck all round the frames! Mind you, they also left us some delicious tinned peaches, pineapples and Spam, which were at that time unobtainable in Britain because of the rationing. When I arrived at Fairford everyone was immediately confined to camp and letters home were all censored. The phrase 'Careless talk costs lives' was used widely by the government during the war: it was an attempt to make sure that no-one let slip anything which a German spy might find useful. The reason we were not allowed to leave the camp was because Fairford was going to be involved in a top secret operation intended to shorten the war.'

Between 'D-Day', 6 June 1944 and the airborne landings in Holland in September that year, no fewer than sixteen airborne operations were planned, mounted and, often at the very last moment, cancelled. In the three months between 'Neptune' and 'Market' the First Allied Airborne Army was created and Lieutenant General Lewis H. Brereton relinquished his command of the 9th Air Force to head the new command on 16 July with headquarters at Sunnyhill Park near Ascot. Later in the month crews were instructed to add an 'Airborne' flash above their shoulder patch. Eisenhower had nominated Brereton to command the organization, based on his extensive and diverse combat command experience at the air force level over Lieutenant General Sir Frederick A. M. 'Boy' Browning, commanding the British 1st Airborne Corps, despite Browning being four months senior. Although Brereton was a distinguished tactical air force officer, he had never before commanded airborne forces. On 2 August Eisenhower asked Brereton to pay particular attention to improving troop carrier navigation. Two days' later Brereton accepted Browning as his deputy commander. A Grenadier Guards officer, Browning had a legendary reputation as an airborne theorist in some quarters but he had never commanded an airborne corps before and he lacked the battle experience of some of his British and American contemporaries. On the 5th the embryonic organization was plunged into the planning of Operation 'Market-Garden'.

The plan was for the Allied Parachute Army to seize three vital bridgeheads which would enable the main forces to break through the last three natural defensive positions left to the Germans. The 1st British Airborne Division had the job of securing the vital road bridge over the Neder-Rhine at Arnhem which would open up the way to the plains of Northern Germany. Brigadier General James M. Gavin's 82nd 'All-American' Airborne Division would jump ten miles below Arnhem at various zones around the city of Nijmegen and secure the big bridges across the Waal River. General Maxwell D. Taylor's 101st 'Screaming Eagles' Airborne would jump about thirty miles to the south at Eindhoven so that a British armoured spearhead (XXX Corps) could drive down this Airborne-held corridor to swing eastwards into Germany, outflanking the Siegfried line and sweeping on to Berlin. Brereton called for the bridges to be taken 'with thunderclap surprise' but his decisions were to achieve exactly the opposite. When Browning consulted Major General Richard Nelson 'Windy' Gale DSO OBE MC commanding 6th Airborne Division who had dropped on 'D-Day' so successfully, Gale was adamant that at least one brigade should be dropped next to the Arnhem road bridge to hold it until the remainder of the Division arrived. He told

Browning, 'Without such a drop, the chances of success were slim' and added that, had he been in command at Arnhem, he would have persisted with this demand to the point of resignation.

Airborne Army exercised command of the British 1st Airborne Corps under Browning and command of the American airborne through XVIII Airborne Corps, a new headquarters under the command of Lieutenant General Matthew B. Ridgway. It took over operational control of IX TCC from AEAF despite spirited protests from AVM Sir Trafford Leigh-Mallory. Inclusion of 38 Group and 46 Group was impeded by involvement of the former in special operations with resistance groups on the Continent and by the desire of the RAF to keep at least part of 46 Group for its own use in air supply. Ninth Air Force and USSTAF each had an American air transport group assigned to it and serving it almost exclusively. For these reasons the status of 38 Group and 46 Group was left open and Airborne Army was only given control of 'such RAF transports' as might be allocated to it 'from time to time.'

Crucially, the US Army Air Force was unable to fly the airborne forces in two lifts on the first day. The aircraft requirement for the airborne force (less 52nd Division) was 3,800 aircraft (parachute and glider tugs), but only 1,550 aircraft were available, thus the force would have to be landed in three lifts. The commander of 38 Group, RAF Transport Command, AVM Leslie N. Hollinghurst (and every division commander) requested two drops on the first day, the first before dawn, which would give time for a second lift the same day. But Major General Paul L. Williams of the IX US Troop Carrier Command did not agree. As air commander for 'Market' Williams had operational control not only of IX TCC but also of 38 Group, 46 Group and such bomber aircraft as might be used for resupply, presumably the RAF transport component, which could have flown two lifts. Williams had recently obtained extra aircraft for his units but still lacked the extra ground crew to service them and he was of the opinion that the task of servicing hundreds of transport aircraft in between two lifts would be beyond them; a view that was supported by Brereton even though two airlifts had been accomplished on the first day of Operation 'Dragoon' (the code name for the Allied invasion of Southern France on 15 August), albeit with 45 more minutes of daylight against negligible opposition. Browning does not appear to have queried the decision which resulted in having to carry out the lifts over two to three days; a decision which would ensure that any element of surprise was completely lost.

The RAF had allocated ten squadrons of 38 Group and six squadrons of 46 Group to Major General Royal 'Roy' Elliott Urquhart, Commanding

First Airborne Division to tow in his gliders and the USAAF were to make available the C-47s of the 9th US Troop Carrier Command for his parachutists but Urquhart calculated that he needed at least 130 aircraft for each of his brigades. On Friday 15th September Urquhart learned from Lieutenant Colonel Charles Mackenzie his Chief of Staff, that to enable Lieutenant General Browning to take his Corps HQ to journey to Nijmegen he had needed 38 transport aircraft and 32 Horsa gliders for administrative personnel and six Waco CG-4A gliders for US Signals' personnel (enough for an infantry battalion) on the first lift. Urquhart told Browning that he must have another forty aircraft but was told that even a proportion of these were impossible. Browning had already decided to use 36 of the badly needed gliders to take his personal staff to Holland when it was a questionable necessity.

Troop Carrier planning between 'Neptune' and 'Market' falls into three phases, one of inactivity from 13 June to 29 July, one of readjustment to a rapidly changing situation between 29 July and 17 August and a period of heavy and conflicting commitments from 17 August to 17 September. The only large airborne units available for missions up to the end of July were the First Airborne Division and the Polish Parachute Brigade, which was not fully trained. The consensus early in July was that none of the three airborne divisions committed in Normandy would be ready for another flight into battle until after at least seven days of training and refitting. The 101st Division had been kept in action until 27 June, the 82nd until 8 July. As for the British Sixth Airborne Division, it was not relieved until 26 August. The American divisions recuperated sooner than expected, but winter came before 6th Airborne was again fit for an airborne operation. Training was a major occupation for the all the troop carrier groups and the airborne units. Unfortunately, training for combat, like combat had its price. On 8 July 369 Polish paratroopers arrived at Spanhoe located between Leicester, Nottingham and Peterborough to participate in a training mission named Operation 'Burden'. At 2130 hours, 33 C-47s departed Spanhoe for a training DZ near Wittering. En route over Tinwell, Rutland one of the aircraft in the 309th Squadron collided with another in the formation. Both aircraft crashed to the ground killing eight crewmen and 26 paratroopers. Only one man survived, Corporal Thomas Chambers, 9th Air Force, leaping from the aircraft as it plummeted to earth.

On the evening of 3 September Montgomery asked for an operation by the 1st Airborne Division and the Polish Parachute Brigade to secure a crossing of the Rhine in the stretch between Arnhem and Wesel on the afternoon of the 6th or the morning of the 7th. Montgomery's staff selected Arnhem as the crossing point, largely because the flak around Wesel was considered prohibitively thick. Airborne Army began on the 4th to prepare for this operation, which was christened 'Comet'. The troops who were to take the bridge at Arnhem were to be flown in over a route very similar to the northern route later used in 'Market', to a drop zone and a landing zone five miles northwest of Arnhem which were practically identical with zones used on 'Market'. In these respects 'Market' was simply 'Comet', slightly revised. The rest of the troops were to be flown over a more southern route to zones south of Nijmegen to take bridges over the Waal at Nijmegen and over the Maas at Grave. While these objectives were retained in 'Market' the planning in relation to them was drastically changed.

By 7 September 'Comet' plans were complete and field orders were issued. The 52nd Wing called in its group commanders and their staffs at 1300 for briefing. However, storm warnings forced a 24-hour postponement. On the 8th Montgomery got word that German resistance along the Albert and Meuse-Escaut canals west of Antwerp was stiffening. He therefore asked another postponement. Further news of effective German resistance and even counter-attacks caused him to delay 'Comet' again on the 9th and to cancel it on the 10th. That morning Eisenhower flew to Brussels to confer with Montgomery on the strategy they would use in the coming weeks. In a stormy session aboard Eisenhower's aircraft Montgomery won his superior's approval for an expanded version of 'Comet'. This operation, 'Market', was to lay an airborne carpet, comprising not only the 1st Airborne Division and the Polish Parachute Brigade but also the American 82nd and 101st Divisions, along the road to Arnhem. To lift this force would require all available RAF and American troop carrier aircraft in a series of missions lasting at least two days. Montgomery also wanted ground operations outside Belgium brought to a standstill so that he could put maximum force into Operation 'Garden', a ground assault from his front along the Meuse-Escaut Canal up the Hasselt-Arnhem road.[1]

At 1430 hours on 10 September General Browning, who had just flown back to England with news of the Brussels conference, notified Airborne Army of the decision on 'Market'. At 1800 General Brereton held a conference of his troop carrier and airborne commanders and their staffs (except General Ridgway who was in France) at Airborne Army Headquarters in Sunnyhill Park near Ascot, Berkshire. There Browning sketched out Montgomery's conception of 'Market' and a short discussion was held on the main points of the operation. The commanders agreed that the British and Polish airborne should be concentrated for the Arnhem assault, that the 82nd Division should take over the Nijmegen-Grave area and that the 101st Division should seize crossings over the principal waterways south of Grave. This decision ensured that missions carrying the 82nd Division from the Grantham area would not cross the path of missions bearing the 101st from southern England. It also ensured that the less seasoned 101st would be the first to make contact with the Allied ground forces. Finally, it was decided that the 101st was to be responsible for the crossings in a sixteen-mile area between Veghel and Eindhoven and could postpone the taking of Eindhoven until two hours after its initial operations. Thus drops near Eindhoven would not be necessary and the division could concentrate its drops and landings further north. The Nijmegen-Arnhem area was more than fifty miles behind the German front and in between were seven canals and rivers at which, the Germans might be able to hold. If they did so the predicament of the airborne would be very dangerous; just how dangerous, events were to show.

Brereton ruled that 'Market' would be flown in daylight. Intelligence estimates indicated that the Luftwaffe would not be a serious threat, but that the flak around Arnhem was increasing to the point where it might. (Whatever the danger from flak, a night mission was virtually out of the question since 17 September - the date finally selected for 'Market-Garden') fell at the dark of the moon. Postponement would not help, since on the following nights the moon would not rise until about dawn. Both doctrine and experience warned against attempting airborne missions in total darkness and Brereton judged that flak could be avoided or neutralized sufficiently so that 'Market' could be flown safely by day. Even so, objectives in 'Market', deep in enemy territory and 200 miles from the nearest 'Gee' chain would be much more difficult to locate by radar than those in Normandy had been.

On 12 or 13 September 'H-Hour', the moment when the initial troop carrier serials, exclusive of pathfinders, would arrive over their zones, was set at 1300 hours. This timing gave ample opportunity for preliminary anti-flak operations between dawn and 'H-Hour'. It was also considered early enough to enable armoured units of Second Army to begin their attack after 'H-Hour' and still make contact with the airborne troops in the Eindhoven area before sundown.

On 11 September at a conference at Eastcote the troop carrier and airborne staffs met convened to decide on the selection of routes and zones and make preliminary decisions on the loading plan. General Paul L. Williams and his wing and group commanders considered two routes, a northern one that ran across the occupied Netherlands and a southern route that approached through Belgium. The northern route began at the seaside town of Aldeburgh ('Antigua') beside the Alde estuary, ran for 94 miles straight across the North Sea to the west end of Schouwen Island, a distinctive landfall point and on without turning for eighteen miles to the eastern tip of the island. From there it ran for 52 miles to the IP ('Ellis') about three miles south of Hertogenbosch and could be readily identified by several road intersections in its vicinity. The southern route started at Bradwell Bay ('Attu') and cut across the Thames estuary for 34 miles to the tip of the North Foreland. All serials going to Arnhem and Nijmegen on 'D-Day' would use the northern route. Those for the Eindhoven area would take the southern route. Because their objectives were relatively near the Allied lines, use of that route would cut their time over enemy territory by more than half. The British were convinced that the American troop carrier tactic of flying in serials was inferior to their own method of individual navigation. The glider-towing aircraft of 38 Group flew in loose pairs at twenty-second intervals and 46 Group flew in 'V's of three aircraft at thirty-second intervals. General 'Boy' Browning was so sure that the technique of 38 Group was better that he recommended that IX TCC adopt it. American paratroop formations would be the usual nine-aircraft 'V of V's in serials of from 27 to 45 aircraft which would each tow only a single glider. Double-towing gliders was difficult and dangerous, but single-towing meant stretching the glider lift out over four days and made it necessary to add a couple of glider serials to the original sequence and to schedule additional missions on 'D+2' and 'D+3' to bring in the displaced gliders. American glider formations again would be columns made up of pairs of pairs in echelon to the right in serials of from thirty to fifty. RAF tow-aircraft and gliders would proceed in a loose column of pairs at ten-second intervals, flying at 2,500 feet on the way to their zones and returning at 5,000-7,000 feet. After passing their zones the American troop carriers were to turn 180° to left or right, depending on the position of the zone and return by the way they had come. They were to fly at 1,500 feet on the trip out, descend to 500 feet to make the drop or release and return at 3,000 feet to avoid the incoming traffic.

Selection of drop and landing zones was owed much to the fact that the terrain was more favourable than that in the Normandy operations. In the north, especially around Arnhem, the land is rolling and in many places wooded. Between the Rhine and the Waal and everywhere in the Eindhoven sector it is flat, open and interlaced with rivers, canals and ditches, which could shield the airborne troops against attacks by enemy armour. Fields varied from very large to less than 200 yards in length but they were bordered by low, weak fences and small hedges instead of the formidable barriers encountered in the Cotentin.

The great prize was the single-span steel bridge which the road running north from Hasselt crossed the Lower Rhine into the city of Arnhem. The river at that point was about a tenth of a mile across. The south side was low-lying and scant settled. The north side was a thriving urban area, Arnhem being a modern city of over 100,000 persons with several good-sized suburbs. A second road bridge into the city had been destroyed but a railway bridge 2½ miles east of the road was still intact. At Heveadorp, a mile below the railway bridge, there was a ferry. The Germans were known to have built a pontoon bridge near the road.

To take and hold one or more of these crossings was the task of the First Airborne Division. Its initial paratroop drop was to be made in at DZ 'X' about six miles northwest of the centre of Arnhem, north of the village of Heelsum and just south of the Amsterdam-Arnhem railway. It was an irregular area containing about a square mile. The first British gliders were land on LZ 'S', a narrow strip over a mile long and about half a mile wide, a little way northeast of DZ 'X' and on the other side of the railway. The next contingent of gliders was assigned LZ 'Z', adjoining DZ 'X' and extending about half a mile east of it. All three zones were made up of fields, pasture and heath bordered by pine woods. All these zones were over five miles away from the road bridge which was the chief objective of the troops. American airborne doctrine, confirmed by Allied experience in Normandy, held that this was too far. Precious time would be consumed merely in marching to the bridge. The risk of delay by roadblocks was great. In addition, part of the force would have to be left behind to hold zones for use by other missions on 'D+1'.

The British airborne staff officers were not unaware of these handicaps but Major General Urquhart preferred good zones at a distance to bad zones near his objectives. North of the river there were no large open areas near the city, though some smaller ones might have been used. Dutch reports as to the topography of the south shore of the river were pessimistic, indicating that it was swampy, dissected by ditches and easily swept by gun fire from the opposite bank. Moreover, the area was said to be subject to flooding, a most unpleasant possibility to men who remembered British and American drops into swamps in Normandy. Another consideration was fear of anti-aircraft guns, great numbers of which were said to be massed near the bridge. Consequently no 'D-Day' drops or landings were to be made near Arnhem. The coup de main contemplated for 'Comet' was abandoned and nothing was put in its place. Lieutenant Colonel John Frost, commanding 2nd Parachute Battalion who were detailed to take the three bridges over the Rhine at Arnhem, regarded it as absurd to be ordered to capture a bridge without landing troops on both sides of the River, but he felt that the restrictions imposed on the locations of the Division's drop zones for the first day were unavoidable.[2] Colonel George James Stewart Chatterton (32), commanding the Glider Pilot Regiment recalled that he wanted 'a force of five or six gliders to land near the bridge and take it.' He saw no reason why he could not do it but apparently nobody else saw the need for it. 'I distinctly remembered being called a bloody murderer and assassin for suggesting it.'[3] The 82nd Division in contrast to the British placed its zones on an average about a mile from its initial objectives. Its staff spent the night of 10/11 September selecting zones and next morning after discussion and some revision to me troop carrier objections its choices were approved at the Eastcote meeting.

On 12 September more than 100 officers assembled in what had once been Lady Charlotte Ebury's bedroom in Moor Park, an elegant 18th-century Palladian mansion set within several hundred acres of parkland to the south-east of Rickmansworth in Hertfordshire. Earlier in the war the mansion had been a comfortable jail for German officers. Lieutenant General 'Boy' Browning and Major General Roy Urquhart, who were billeted in the mansion, stood up to face the men. They told their stunned audience that after a month's frantic and secret planning that an airborne assault by parachute and glider would be launched to seize bridges across the Rhine.

For the invasion of Normandy 17,000 airborne troops had been used but 'Market' would be the largest airborne operation in history; over 34,600 men of the 101st, 82nd and 11,900 men of the 1st Airborne Division and the Polish Parachute Brigade (*Samodzielna Polska Brygada Spadochronova*), who would be flown to Arnhem to capture the most northerly bridge. 14,589 troops were to be landed by glider and 20,011 by parachute. Brereton had been advised that the glider losses of Normandy had been made good with 2,160 Wacos, 104 US and 812 British Horsas and 64 Hamilcars available to land over 20,000 glider troops, 1,736 vehicles, 263 artillery pieces and 3,342 tons of ammunition and other supplies. However, the US had only 2,060 glider pilots available, so that none of its gliders would have a co-pilot but would instead carry an extra passenger.

To deliver its 36 battalions of airborne infantry and their support troops to the continent, the First Allied Airborne Army had under its operational control the 14 groups of IX Troop Carrier Command and after 11 September the sixteen squadrons of 38 Group RAF (an organization of converted bombers providing support to resistance groups) and a transport formation, 46 Group. The combined force had 1,438 C-47/Dakota transports (1,274 USAAF and 164 RAF) and 321 converted RAF bombers. IX Troop Carrier Command's transport aircraft would have to tow gliders and drop paratroopers, duties that could not be performed simultaneously. Major General Williams ruled that, for ease of control, all parachute drops would be made from USAAF aircraft. Ninety percent of the USAAF transports on the first day would drop parachute troops, with the same proportion towing gliders on the second day. The RAF aircraft on the first two days would be almost entirely used as glider tugs for the British Division, except a dozen Stirlings for their pathfinders. For the first day's landings the allocation of aircraft was: 101st Airborne Division: 501 (431 parachute: seventy tugs) 82nd Airborne Division: 530 (480 parachute: fifty tugs) 1st Airborne Division: 463 (147 parachute: 316 tugs) HQ 1st Airborne Corps: 38 (38 tugs). They would take off from 23 airfields (eight in Lincolnshire and Leicestershire, fourteen in Wiltshire and Hampshire and one in Kent).

The task of the 82nd was to take and hold bridge over the Maas outside the village of Grave five miles southwest of Nijmegen, at least one four bridges over the Maas-Waal Canal between Grave and Nijmegen and the bridge over the Waal at Nijmegen itself. Success in holding the crossings was dependent on possession of the Groesbeek heights; a ridge thirty feet high about two miles southeast of Nijmegen. This ridge was the only high ground for miles around and dominated the whole region. Nijmegen, a town of 82,000 population on the south side of the Waal was reported to have around it least 22 heavy anti-aircraft guns and 86 light pieces and was thought likely to contain a large garrison. South of the town between the canal and the ridge the country was wooded, so drops to take objectives other than the Nijmegen Bridge would have to be made west of the canal or south east of the ridge. Units put down near Nijmegen on 'D-Day' might suffer heavily from flak on the way in, would be quickly engaged by fairly strong enemy forces and would have to deal with those forces for many hours in isolation from the rest of the division. Furthermore, without the ridge and crossings over the Maas and the canal, the Nijmegen Bridge would be worthless. Brigadier General Gavin and his staff therefore determined to put first things first and leave Nijmegen to be taken by ground attack after the other objectives were secured. This decision was later confirmed in very explicit terms by General Browning.

Gavin chose to bring in most of the division in a belt of drop and landing zones between three and four miles southeast of Nijmegen on the far side of the Groesbeck heights so that he could attack the ridge as quickly as possible with maximum force and then set up a defensive perimeter including both ridge and zones. This seemed to minimize the risk of an enemy occupation of the landing area such as had happened in Normandy. At the northern end of the belt was DZ 'T', an oval 3,000 yards long from east to west and three-quarters of a mile wide, framed in a neat triangle by a railway along its south side and by two roads which intersected at the village of Wyler a few hundred yards north of the zone. Approaching serials would pass close to the bridge at Grave about seven miles short of the zone and over the Maas-Waal Canal about three miles before reaching the zone. Three thousand yards southwest of DZ 'T' was a slightly smaller oval, DZ 'N', bordered on its western and northern sides by the woods of the Groesbeek Ridge. The junction of the canal with the River Maas a mile and a half east of DZ 'N' made an excellent landmark on the line of approach.

Between and overlapping both DZs was a rough oblong averaging 3½ miles from north to south and 1½ miles from east to west, which had been selected for glider landings. This was split into a northern half, LZ 'T' and a southern half, LZ 'N'. The latter had small fields averaging 200 yards in some sections. However, there were few high obstacles and the Germans did not seem to be erecting any. Experts calculated that by daylight the two zones could receive between 700 and 900 gliders, all the 82nd would need. LZ 'N' was also selected as destination for parachute resupply missions to the 82nd Division. Its zones would have a particularly distinctive network of waterways, roads and railways south of Nijmegen. If a pilot could come within sighting distance of Grave, he would have an abundance of landmarks thereafter. One regiment had to be put within striking distance of the bridge at Grave and for this purpose DZ 'O', an oval drop zone over 1½ miles long from west to east and almost a mile wide, was marked out on flat, open land astride the Eindhoven-Nijmegen road halfway between the Grave bridge and the Maas-Waal Canal. The troops dropped there were to attack both the Grave Bridge a mile to their west and three bridges over the canal between one and two miles east of them. Having had the horror of men being cut off on an earlier mission, Gavin laid great stress on taking at least one bridge over the canal to ensure contact between this outlying regiment and the main force in the Groesbeek area. Convinced that the big bridge at Grave would be defended and prepared for demolition, Colonel Reuben Tucker, commander of the 504th Parachute Regiment, which was picked for the mission to DZ 'O', urged that the proper way to attack the structure was to drop men on the south bank of the Maas and rush the bridge from both ends. Just 36 hours before 'Market' began, Tucker's proposal was accepted and orders were given that a company of his paratroops be dropped on a special DZ on the south side of the river half a mile from the end of the bridge. The ground there was low, marshy and heavily ditched, a bad drop zone, chosen deliberately to achieve quick access to the objective.

The initial tasks of the 101st Division were to take a bridge over the Wilhelmina Canal at Zon five airline miles north of Eindhoven, a bridge over the Dommel River at Sint-Oedenrode four miles north of Zon and four bridges over the Aa River and the Willems Canal at Veghel, which was five miles northeast of Sint-Oedenrode and thirteen miles southwest of Grave. After that, but before nightfall if possible, the 101st was to take Eindhoven and four bridges there over the upper Dommel. Of these objectives the two canal bridges were much the most important, since the canals were sixty feet across and too deep for tanks; none of the rivers were over 25 feet wide and the Dommel at Eindhoven was a mere creek. Faced with the problem of taking objectives strung out over more than fifteen miles of road General Maxwell Taylor decided to bring in most of his division to a single area midway between Sint-Oedenrode and Zon from which he could strike quickly against both places and then move readily against Eindhoven. Available for his purpose was a large open tract on the west side of the north-south road about 1½ miles north of Zon. South of the open land lay a belt of woods, known as the Zonsche Forest, extending to the Wilhelmina Canal running east and west from Zon. A road and a railway running northwest from Eindhoven crossed the canal about a mile southwest of the tract and a mile southeast of the little town of Best.

On the open area the divisional staff marked out an oblong 4,000 yards long and 2,800 yards wide, which it split longitudinally into two equal drop zones, DZ's 'B' and 'C'. The long axes of these zones ran east-northeast. Troop carriers approaching them by the southern route would be on a heading of north-northeast. A landing zone, LZ 'W', was drawn to include most of the oblong but was slightly narrower from north to south and extended 1,000 yards further west. The zone was considered more than sufficient for 400 gliders and most of its fields were over 300 yards in length.

One parachute regiment would have to be dropped farther north for the taking of Veghel, at DZ 'A', a potbellied oval about two miles long from east to west, up to 2,000 yards wide and about a mile southwest of the town. North of the zone was a railway running east to Veghel. Southeast of the zone was the Eindhoven-Arnhem road. The bridges over the Willems Canal were only a few hundred yards northeast of DZ 'A', but the Aa River was a mile further on. Thus the paratroops would have to secure a crossing over the canal and move through a populated area before attacking the road and railway bridges over the river. Lieutenant Colonel W. O. Kinnard, a battalion commander, proposed that his unit be dropped north of the Willems Canal in position to move against the river bridges immediately after assembling and his battalion was given a new zone DZ 'A-1', a flat, open area on the northeast side of the canal about a mile north of DZ 'A'.

Even though 'Market' was to be flown by day previous experience indicated a need to provide navigational aids. 'Eureka' beacons and M/F (CRN-4) beacons for use with radio compasses were placed at the wing assembly points, 'Eureka's, M/F beacons and the aerial lighthouse known as occults were put at the points of departure from the British coast. About half way between England and the Continent on both the northern and the southern route were stationed marker boats code named 'Tampa' and 'Miami' with 'Eureka' beacons and green holophane lights. All the beacons except the occults were operated by troop carrier personnel. No beacons were to be provided on the northern route between 'Tampa' and the zones because that 150-mile stretch was all over water or enemy territory.

The American aircraft in 'Market' were equipped with radio compasses and 'Rebecca'. As in 'Neptune', only flight leaders were to operate 'Rebecca'. However, this time if formations broke up, the lead ship in each element would operate its set. IX TCC had asked on 18 June that half its aircraft be equipped with both SCR-717 and either 'Gee' or Loran. Its request for SCR-717 was considered excessive, but its quota was raised to two and then three sets per squadron. The command had also won authorization to install 'Gee' equipment on all its aircraft. However, so long as a serial held together only its leader would have much occasion to use SCR-717 or 'Gee'. The aircraft of 38 and 46 Group were equipped with both 'Rebecca' and 'Gee' (but not radio compasses or SCR-717) and all crews were authorized to use them. Under the RAF system of flying in column the risk of interference was small enough to permit such general use of sets. The bombers employed for resupply had radio compasses, but no 'Rebecca' sets.

The Americans planned to employ six 'sticks' (a number of paratroops carried in one aircraft) of pathfinder troops. A pair of teams with one officer and nine enlisted men apiece was to be dropped on DZ's 'O',

'A' and 'B-C' respectively. Each pair was to be responsible for setting up a 'Eureka', an M/F beacon, panel 'T's and letters and smoke signals. Each zone had its distinctive colour combination of panels and smoke. By the 16th the pathfinder drop was scheduled for 1245, 15 minutes before the main force arrived. The RAF were to dispatch a dozen modified Stirling bombers of 38 Group to drop pathfinder teams twenty minutes before 'H-Hour', half on DZ 'X' and half on LZ 'S'.

Eighth Air Force and Air Defence of Great Britain would fly escort and cover for the missions and protect them from anti-aircraft. If desired, Ninth Air Force would help with the latter task. Between missions the Second Tactical Air Force RAF, whose aircraft lacked staying power for escort work, would protect the airborne troops from enemy aircraft and be available for close support missions. At night Second TAF would be assisted by night fighters of ADGB. Measures were also prescribed to neutralize in advance, as far as possible, those enemy flak batteries and air bases which were in a position to endanger 'Market'. For this purpose Eighth Air Force was directed to reconnoitre the troop carrier routes to locate flak positions and to bombard those positions with its heavy bombers at the latest possible time before 'H-Hour' and RAF Bomber Command was to attack enemy airfields on the night of 'D-1'.

'Market' would be the first major test of resupply by air. Resupply by parachute avoided the difficulties of a glider tow and the hazards of a glider landing, but it was inefficient and wasteful. A C-47 capable of carrying about three tons could deliver little more than a ton by parachute from its pararacks (large cylinders containing supplies slung under the belly of the aircraft) or in bundles pitched out its side door. Installation of conveyor belts in the cabin was helpful in handling bundles but such conveyors did not go into production in the United States until the spring of 1945. Moreover, the bundles had to be small to get out the door or fit the pararacks. Even the 75mm howitzer had to be broken down into several parts to be dropped.[4] Approximately 200 C-47s were required to carry the 265 tons a day of automatic supply set up for the 82nd Division. Stirlings could carry three tons apiece, but 38 Group had scarcely enough of them to meet the needs of one British division. Plans were made for a resupply mission by about 250 B-24 Liberators of Eighth Air Force 2nd Bomb Division on 'D+1' after a request by the troop carriers to free their aircraft from resupply work in order that they might be devoted to bringing in more airborne troops. Though practicable, it would prove both inefficient and hazardous and beset with unsolved problems and the 8th Air Force felt its participation in 'Market' seriously interrupted its bombing programme and could not be expected to loan its B-24 groups frequently or for long.

On 15 September escort and flak-suppression on the northern route between England and the IP was entrusted to ADGB. Beyond the IP, Eighth Air Force would perform those tasks. On the southern route Eighth Air Force was to fly escort between the Belgian coast and the zones. It also agreed to provide perimeter patrols to intercept enemy air-aircraft approaching the 'Market' area from the east or north. Airborne Army asked that four groups of fighter-bombers be provided to neutralize flak and ground fire on the southern route between the IP and the DZ during the missions. That responsibility was given to Ninth Air Force. Another request by Airborne Army was for rocket-firing aircraft to break up possible attacks on the 82nd Division by tanks reported lurking in the Reichswald Forest, which lay two or three miles southeast of the zones of that division. On 16 September Ninth Air Force was asked to provide a group of rocket-equipped fighters, but it was unable to make them available in time for use on 'D-Day'.

At 'H-Hour' Eighth Air Force was supposed to deal with German garrisons in Arnhem and Nijmegen but objected to employing its high-level heavy-bomber formations over towns with friendly populations, so medium bombers of Second TAF were given the job of attacking German barrack in those towns on the morning of 'D-Day'. Dummy drops were to be made from forty aircraft of Bomber Command on the night of 'D-Day' at point west of Utrecht, east of Arnhem and at Emmerich to delay, if only momentarily, the movement of German ground reinforcement from Holland and the Rhineland against the air-heads at Arnhem and Nijmegen. Weather permitting, the resupply mission on 'D+1' was to be undertaken by 252 B-24s with ball turrets removed.

Almost without exception the troop carrier units in 'Market' had flown missions before. The Ninth Troop Carrier Command had the same three wings, fourteen groups and pathfinder unit that it had had in 'Neptune' and all wings and all groups but the 315th and 434th had participated in at least one other airborne operation, either in 1943 or during the invasion of southern France. The RAF had in 38 Group the same ten squadrons which they had used in June but had increased 4 Group from five to six squadrons. In most cases the troop carriers were located at good bases, at which they were well established and were teamed with troops which were stationed nearby and had flown with them before from those bases. The RAF had made no changes of station since June. Their squadrons were located in pairs at eight bases, six of which were bunched about eighty miles west of London and thirty miles northwest of Greenham Common. The others, Keevil and Tarrant Rushton lay respectively thirty and sixty miles south of the rest. From these eight airfields would fly the glider echelon of the 1st Airborne Division, which had been in readiness with gliders loaded since the marshalling for 'Linnet' on 2 September. The 53rd Wing and its groups still held the bases at and around Greenham Common that they had occupied during 'Neptune'. Once again they were to lift the 101st Division, which was in its old billets nearby. The 442nd Troop Carrier Group was attached to the 53rd Wing on 11 September for 'Market', moving that same day from Fulbeck to Chilbolton in Hampshire and making large-scale supply flights from there on the 12th. The 442nd were to tow 65 gliders containing 252 men, 32 jeeps and 32 trailers with platoons of the 326th Parachute Field Artillery Battalion engineers over the Groesbeek Heights.

The 52nd Wing and its groups remained at the same bases around Grantham which they had held since March. The only change needed was the addition of pierced steel plank for glider marshalling on muddy ground at Cottesmore, Fulbeck and Barkston Heath. Besides carrying the 82nd Division, the wing was also to lift the British paratroops of First Division and the Polish Brigade. The 50th Wing was to assist it in carrying the American troops. This Wing and the 439th, 440th and 441st Groups had been moved to Balderton, Fulbeck and Langar in the Grantham area in preparation for that operation. However, on 8 September, they had been ordered to France to concentrate on air supply operations for the ground forces. By 10 September the air echelons of the 439th and 441st Groups and a detachment of wing headquarters were actually in operation in the Reims area[5] and most of the wing's equipment and all its refuelling units were either already in France or in transit to France. At 2330 on 10 September the wing was alerted for 'Market' and ordered to be at its British bases ready to operate by 2400 on the 11th. The bases were then being closed out for release to the British. Strenuous efforts by supply and engineering officers of the wing and IX TCC set Balderton, Langar and Fulbeck functioning again and provided necessary unit equipment, including refuelling units borrowed from the 52nd Wing.

On 16 September IX TCC had 1,274 operational aircraft and 1,284 assigned and available crews. The RAF had 321 converted bombers in 38 Group and 164 Dakotas in 46 Group. The supply of gliders had increased despite the loss of almost all of those used in Normandy. On 1 July IX TCC had had 1,045 operational Wacos. These were only enough to lift the glider echelon of one division, so on 8 August in anticipation of operations involving several divisions a new glider assembly programme had been inaugurated at Crookham Common with the objective of producing at least forty completed Wacos a day. This time IX AFSC employed 26 officers and over 900 men under direction of the 26th Mobile Repair and Reclamation Squadron. Well organized and adequately equipped, they proved capable of assembling sixty (and once even 100) gliders in a day. By the end of August IX TCC had 1,629 operational Wacos and by 16 September it had 2,160 of them. Plans called for the employment of about ninety percent of these gliders in 'Market'. The British had 812 Horsas, the Americans only 104 of them. In addition to its Horsas 38 Group possessed 64 of the huge Hamilcar gliders, which were capable of carrying tanks. About 1,900 American glider pilots were on hand at the end of August, but the arrival of 200 more by air a few days later gave IX TCC a total of 2,060 on the eve of 'Market'. Since Williams and Brereton had decided not to use co-pilots on American gliders, they had enough glider pilots for the proposed missions, but they would have virtually no reserves. The British glider pilots, who were organized as ground troops in a special glider pilot regiment, would make a much better combat showing in 'Market' than the American glider pilots, who were simply an element within the troop carrier squadrons. Proposals were that the American glider pilots be put under the command of the airborne divisions to make good soldiers of them but Lieutenant General Ridgway decided that since the primary duty of glider pilots was to fly gliders, they belonged with the troop carriers.[6]

As in June, the aircraft of IX TCC were without armour or self-sealing fuel tanks. While in England on a tour of inspection in the latter part of June, Robert A. Lovett, Assistant Secretary of War for Air, promised that IX TCC would get at least enough for its pathfinders. However, the tanks were then very scarce; AAF Headquarters was unwilling to reallocate them; and the troop carriers got none. Some were shipped in September but did not arrive in time for 'Market'. Only about 400 of the Wacos had nose reinforcements of either the Corey or the Griswold type and only about 900 had parachute arrestors. Large orders for arrestors and protective noses had been sent to the United States long before 'Market', but delivery had been slow. One cause of delay had been disagreement and vacillation in the United States as to which type of nose should be produced.

'Market' is unique as the only large American airborne operation during World War II for which there was no training programme, no rehearsal, almost no exercises and a generally low level of tactical training activity. In the month before 'Market' only two paratroop exercises, totalling

288 sorties were flown and no glider exercises at all. Less formal tactical training was also on a very low level. Only 306 airborne troops were carried during the two weeks before 'Market'. From 12 August to 17 September there were only five days on which FAAA did not believe that an airborne operation was just around the corner. This belief made training plans seem superfluous and realistic exercises a rash commitment. On 14 September the troop carrier units were alerted and restricted and American airborne troops began moving into bivouac at the bases. Early in the evening on the 15th wing commander and key members of their staffs were fully briefed at Eastcote. On their return that night they briefed the wing staffs and the group commanders. About the same time field orders for the operation arrived at the wings from troop carrier head quarters. Early next morning rigid restriction and security measures, such as had been in force before 'Neptune', were imposed at all bases. During the day group staffs were briefed and win] and group field orders were issued. In the afternoon and evening of 16 September 'D-1', the groups briefed their combat crews. The briefings were generally regarded as well organized and comprehensive. However, detailed maps (1:50,000 and 1:25,000) were in such short supply that there were hardly enough for the group staffs and as usual there was an acute lack of low level photographs of the zones and run-in areas The final briefings, held on the morning of the 17th just before the crews went to their aircraft were short and were concerned mainly with weather conditions.

While General Brereton was the final judge of the routes and timing for 'Market', the verdict really lay in the hands of the Staff Weather Officer of IX TCC and the Senior Meteorological Officer of 38 Group, acting at Ascot as joint weather officers for Airborne Army. 'Market' needed three days in a row of good flying weather to give it a reasonable chance of success. Every day at 1630 the weather officers issued a four-day forecast for use by the commanders and their operations staffs at Ascot and Eastcote. They also issued daily 24-hour forecasts which were sent to all troop carrier wings and groups by teletype or telephone. Actual conditions over Belgium were checked before each day's operations by three flights by aircraft of the 325th Reconnaissance Wing of the Eighth Air Force, timed so that telephone reports could be made to Airborne Army and Eighth Air Force at H-8, H-6 and H-4. This was intended to prevent such unpleasant surprises as the cloud bank which upset operations in Normandy. At 1630 on 16 September ('D-1') the experts delivered a favourable report on the coming four-day period. A high-pressure system was approaching Belgium from the southwest and would be over it next day. Fair weather with little cloud and gentle winds would prevail until thc 20th. The forecast did predict fog on and after 'D+1', but only during the early morning. With auspices so favourable Brereton gave orders at 1900 hours that next day the airborne carpet would be laid along the road to Arnhem.

Twenty-one-year old Private Edward John 'Johnny' Peters, a sniper in the 1st Battalion, The Border Regiment, had been billeted with his unit in pig sty's on a farm close to Burford in Oxford since August. Born on 12 February 1923 in Liverpool, he had three sisters and one brother. His father served on the Western Front during World War I. Before he volunteered to join the army on his 18th birthday on 12 February 1941 'Johnny' had been an apprentice blacksmith. He remembers with distain, 'We were called the 'stillborn Army' because for three weeks nothing happened.

'Then it did.'

Chapter 2

'D-1'

'I was based at Ringway (now Manchester Airport). I'd just been made up to Sergeant in the RAF. One day we knew that something was happening and we heard a whisper about 'Market-Garden' but we didn't know what it was. We were fitting winches on an Albemarle aircraft used for towing Hotspur gliders training paratroopers when all hell let loose. Everyone was in a flap and we didn't know what was happening. We found out that one of the larger Stirling aircraft had an engine failure. It should have been towing two Horsa gliders. Because this meant the Horsas couldn't take off the troops were redistributed into smaller Hotspur gliders. We hooked up to take them round the perimeter of the airfield thinking it was a training exercise. We were fully suited up for high altitude flying and the paratroopers were fully equipped but we were a bit slow and the penny hadn't dropped! We found ourselves at the tail end of the Arnhem drop! We were only on training aircraft and we had no defence weapons. When we came back the aircraft looked like a lace curtain and the four of us were awarded a big meal!

Later we received the Aircrew over Europe Star and I didn't really know what it was for as I was in the Fleet Air Arm by then. It took a while for it to sink in.'

Ken Rose RAF. Albemarles of 38 Group took part in Operations 'Husky' (the invasion of Sicily) and 'Elaborate' (gliders to North Africa) and four Albemarle squadrons played an important role in Operation Overlord ('D-Day'). As more 'redundant' Stirlings and Halifaxes were released by Bomber Command two of these squadrons converted to Stirlings. Soon after 'D-Day' only two squadrons (296 and 297) still had their Albemarles.

As previously planned, 'H-Hour' would be at 1300, the 53rd Wing mission to the Eindhoven area would take the southern route and missions to Nijmegen and Arnhem would fly the northern route. Before the carpet could be laid, the ground had to be cleared. This work was begun by 282 RAF bombers which on the night of 'D-1' attacked airfields at Leeuwarden, Steewijk-Havelte, Hopsten and Salzbergen within fighter range of 'Market' objectives and formidable flak installations around a bridge at Moerdijk which menaced aircraft flying the northern route. Though the bombers were shielded from enemy interceptors by six RAF aircraft and five from Eighth Air Force with radar jamming equipment, two were lost, presumably to flak or fighters. About 1,180 tons of bombs were dropped during the operation and the effects were considered generally good.

On the morning of Sunday 17th September Eighth Air Force dispatched 872 B-17s to attack 117 installations, mostly anti-aircraft batteries, along the troop carrier routes. Scheduled to arrive at 0900, they were delayed for thirty minutes, but did their bombing between 0930 and 1130 and were clear of the Continent before the troop carriers appeared. In order to cope with their obscure, small targets, they flew in formations of four or six and relied principally on 260lb fragmentation bombs, which they dropped from altitudes of 10,000 to 22,000 feet. All told, 852 bombers dropped 2,888 tons of fragmentation bombs and 29 tons of high explosive. Analyses of the results indicated that about 45 percent of the bombs came within 1,000 feet of their targets and that good results were achieved in 43 of the 117 cases. Visibility was good; no enemy aircraft appeared; and there was little flak except around Arnhem, where it was reported as moderate but inaccurate. Two bombers were brought down and 112 damaged, only four seriously. They had been given area support during the operation by 147 P-51s. One of these failed to return.

Another operation that morning was an attack by 85 Lancasters and fifteen Mosquitoes of the RAF, escorted by 53 Spitfires of ADGB, against coastal defences on Walcheren Island. It was presumably intended to mislead the Germans into thinking that Walcheren, which lay between the two troop carrier routes, was the objective of the initial troop carrier missions.

The last preliminary operation on the morning of the 17th was the dispatch of fifty Mosquitoes, 48 Mitchells and 24 Bostons of Second TAF against German barracks at Nijmegen, at Arnhem and at Ede ten miles northwest of Arnhem. Six Mosquitoes made low-level attacks on the barracks at Nijmegen with four tons of high explosive. Thirty-four Mosquitoes dropped 27 tons of bombs on Arnhem at a price of three aircraft lost to flak. At Ede thirty Mitchells and thirteen Bostons bombed from medium altitude with 63 tons of high explosive. Because of cloud conditions and other difficulties 23 or more pilots returned without bombing and the remainder hit targets of opportunity. In retrospect it appears that these attacks on barracks did not have much effect on the enemy's power to resist.

At RAF Watton in Norfolk on the night of 16 September three American Mosquito crews in the 25th Bomb Group had been called in and told that they would go out early the next day at staggered intervals. No details. One Mossie was to take off at 0200, one at 0400 and one at 0600. Next morning, just before take off the crews were given the details. They were to fly to the Nijmegen-Arnhem area, find the base of the clouds - how thick and how low and go down to the deck if necessary – and then radio back that information. 'Jimmy' Speer and his navigator, 1st Lieutenant Claude Creath Moore, born 15 March 1916 in Des Moines, Iowa were the last flight. Moore wrote: 'The sky was already light when we left. It was only a matter of minutes from Watton to Holland. We skimmed across at 2,000-3,000 feet. Soon we were at the target area, which, I learned later, was where the parachute drops were made and the glider-borne assault troops were landed. There were large clouds, intermittently broken, so we descended. At around 500 feet we were finding the base of the clouds. Apparently High Command was not waiting for our information; there were planes everywhere. I had never seen so many fighters up close. Below us, above us, around us, on every side they were climbing, diving, milling like a swarm of angry bees. They were really beating the place up. We reported thick, low, occasionally broken, white clouds and smaller, grey puffs of clouds and gave the cloud base as approximately 400-500 feet. The smaller, grey puffs of clouds were spaced all around. Only, I finally realized, they weren't small clouds. They were shell bursts. We were being shot at!

'I was startled to see a plane coming off the deck, climbing straight at us and closing - a snub-nosed, radial-engined plane. From the markings and the silhouette I took it to be from Hermann Goering's own elite group - cowling painted in a distinctive yellow-and-black checkerboard pattern. 'Focke-Wulf 190' flashed through my mind. 'Damn,' I thought. 'This is it!' I'm sure that, mentally, I was frozen in space. But the next thing I knew, the snub-nose had zoomed past us. I did a double take. It was a P-47 Thunderbolt. We stayed in the area a little longer, made a few more weather reports and then headed back to Watton. At the base we were debriefed. We went over to the Combat Mess for breakfast and settled into the day's routine.'[1]

22

Flying Officer Nigel L. Gilson, a Mosquito fighter-bomber navigator on 107 Squadron at Lasham, had spent a day's leave in Winchester and was all set for an enjoyable evening to round it off at a dance hall in Basingstoke. Then a friend gave him the bad news that he had to return to base immediately as the squadron was confined to barracks overnight. The squadron shared Lasham with 613 'City of Manchester' Squadron and formed 138 Wing of 2 Group in 2nd TAF, which was also equipped with North American Mitchell and Douglas Boston twin-engined light bombers.

'My pilot, Flying Officer Phil Slayden and I were met by the usual expectant rumours, but could still learn nothing definite except that we were to be up for briefing at 0530. Ours was a quiet Mess that night, only admin officers were drinking more than lemonade and all air crews were in bed by about ten - most unusual for us!' Rising before midday was a bit of a strain, but 0530 on Sunday found us all milling around the briefing room with an exceptional complement of 'braid and scrambled egg' among us. The tense gaiety and laconic humour of briefing are something one remembers but can't adequately describe. I can recall only two things. The CO's description of the purpose of the Arnhem landing (for that was the cause of the trouble): 'If this one comes off the war will be over in 14 days'; and his description of the anticipated reception of the paratroops: 'They expect to slide down stocks of 40 millimetres.' A minor flap broke out while navigators struggled with maps, rulers, protractors and computers, working out tracks, courses, winds and other essentials to the successful combat of hostile gremlins, until at last there was a welcome break for a hasty bacon and egg breakfast. It was a hectic and hilarious meal and then we were back for a final route check and squadron briefing on formation and tactics.'

Shortly before H-hour (1300 hours) 32 Mosquito fighter-bomber crews on 107 and 613 Squadrons were detailed to attack in shallow high-speed dives at between 800 and 1500 feet two German barracks' complexes in Arnhem; the Willemskazerne in the centre of the town and the Saksen-Weimarkazerne in the northern outskirts. Eighteen Mosquitoes on 21 Squadron in 140 Wing at Thorney Island were to bomb three school buildings in the centre of Nijmegen, which were being used by the German garrison. Twenty-four Bostons of 88 and 342 Squadrons and forty-eight Mitchells would attack other targets at Nijmegen and the barracks complex at Ede, about ten miles west of Arnhem. All the bombers were to complete their missions at 25 minutes before H-Hour.

On 613 Squadron navigator Dudley Hemmings whose pilot, Squadron Leader Don Wellings DFC, 'a tall, unassuming man' had completed a tour on

Blenheims at a night-vision course, recalls: 'The attacks were scheduled to begin five minutes before midday Dutch time to soften the German defences ahead of the invading paratroopers. As was usual with all Mosquito daylight raids, low level flying and careful routing into the targets to gain surprise was essential for success. Whilst by late 1944 the Luftwaffe had diminished in the air, enemy anti-aircraft guns were still heavy around German held positions. The task given the Section led by Don Wellings and me as his navigator was to attack the barracks in the centre of Arnhem.'

At Lasham 'time for take-off was altered twice' recalled Nigel Gilson 'but at last we went to our aircraft where tired ground crews, who'd been working half the night, were just finishing bombing and arming up. Phil Slayden and I sat on the grass waiting for the signal to get into our aircraft. In the peace of a brilliant Sunday morning war seemed very far away. Only Dougie, who'd come to the squadron the day before, remarked on the incongruity of it all; the strains of *'Abide With Me'* from a nearby hangar service sounded too ominous to his unaccustomed ear to pass unnoticed! The ground crew gave us the usual strict orders to do a good job with their aeroplane and wished us a brief but sincere 'Good luck' and we taxied out. We took off into a clear sky already filling with squadrons of ungainly gliders and tugs, took up formation and set course. Soon the English draught board gave place to a sea of rippled blue and finally that to the deeply cut green flats of Holland.

'Arnhem identified itself for us - the natives, or their uninvited guests were distinctly hostile - but we rejoiced in our speed and ploughed in. At first one could watch things quite objectively; one gun team was firing explosive shells, with tantalizing persistency, right on our track and I wondered absent-mindedly by how much they would miss us. Then we dived to attack. I bent to switch on the camera, began to rise and then instinctively ducked again, only to be conscious of an explosion and a shower of perspex splinters. I jerked up, looking anxiously at Phil and heaved a sigh of relief when I saw that he was OK and that we were climbing again. At least, I think we were climbing - neither of us was quite sure what happened in those thirty seconds. A glance showed that the gun team had been robbed of their prey by the dive and the shell had burst above us, merely shattering our cockpit cover.

'Suddenly 'Phil' called, 'Hey, the bomb doors are shut, we couldn't have dropped the bombs!'

'I jammed them open and he pressed the tit to drop the bombs; we looked behind for the flash, but there was none and then we remembered that we'd opened the doors before the dive and must have closed them instinctively during the attack. But the look behind had shown us one thing - an aircraft with our markings suddenly catching fire in the starboard petrol tank. The flames spread rapidly to the port, covering the cockpit; the aircraft lost height and finally hit a house and overturned into the river. We shall not forget that quickly. 'Woody' and 'Mac' were in that mass of flame.

'It was only a matter of minutes before we were over the Zuider Zee again, flying below formations of gliders and tugs. We felt sorry for them - they hadn't our speed, they had to fly straight though the flak and their occupants had to go down on 'chutes or without engines or guns - no future in that.

'The CO called up to check formation. As we called 'Here' to our own call sign we waited anxiously to hear who was missing. Two failed to reply - two out of 14. 'Woody' and 'Mac', 'Ted' and 'Griff' had bought it - tough luck; we should miss them.'

At Lasham 'Vic' Hester and 'Ted' Moore were briefed for two tasks that day. 'First was to film the 613 Squadron raid, then after that, photograph the airborne drop at Arnhem. We took our usual four bombs in case we found an opportune target. Whilst in our aircraft sorting out our cameras etc just prior to 'engine start time' the Wing Intelligence Officer appeared and gave us an extra brief. 'Can you take off at once and attack an undefended telephone exchange in a disused barracks in the town of Arnhem?' He handed us a map of the town and the position of the barracks, adding that they had just found out that the German land-line communications would need to go via that exchange when the para drop began. What could be simpler? We loved undefended targets and were used to hitting small buildings.

'We took off about five minutes ahead of 613 Squadron. I think they probably thought my watch was wrong. Upon arrival over Arnhem we found the target. Good Boy. Good Boy. We made live one bomb only. The target was a haystack size building just inside the main gate of the barracks. Why not treat this attack as a practice bombing exercise and make four runs? We slowly descended for the first and when we were established in a shallow dive, 'Ted' Moore in the nose said, 'Jesus Christ, look at that!' Now 'Ted' was a very cool, quiet South African who seldom got excited about anything, so I realized that something was afoot. Taking my eye off the target, I saw that we were gently approaching twenty Tiger tanks - all manned and firing at us!

'We dropped our one bomb from an approach pattern we would not have used had we known the target was defended. As a result our aircraft was hit and I got three bullets in my left leg, which stopped my left foot from working. 'Ted' kindly fastened a field dressing around the outside of my trousers and we continued the exercise. Fusing the other three bombs, we made a further attack on the telephone exchange, but did not wait to see if we had hit the target. We were now too late to film the attack by 613 Squadron, so with regret, we continued to the Para dropping zone, found and filmed considerable German armour etc surrounding the dropping area and decided to head for home. There was no way I could break radio silence and even if I had, no single aircraft transmission could have put a stop to such a large operation as 'Market-Garden'.'

107 Squadron finally began taking off from Lasham at half-minute intervals at 1051 hours. 'After a few last minute hiccups' recalls Dudley Hemmings 'we formed up in tight formation and set course for Southwold on the English coast for the 750 miles round trip. Across East Anglia we had a marvellous view of the sky filled with the great armada of some of the 2,000 transports and gliders en route to their drop zones several miles west of Arnhem. Crossing the English coast at Southwold we soon left the brave Red Berets behind and skimmed over the North Sea at fifty feet and 250 mph - IFF off and bombs switched to 'Fire'. As lead navigator I was map reading each pinpoint every two minutes to keep on track knowing there were seven crews behind relying on our lead. Our routing into Arnhem was circuitous and required good timing, pinpoint map reading and the use of 'Gee' over the 130 miles of sea to the Dutch coast. Midway over the North Sea we turned slightly to port at a DR position in order to cross the Dutch coast one-mile south of Egmont, a position presumed undefended. Landfall without incident was made as planned and we swept across the lowlands of Holland, lifting up over some high-tension lines east of Alkmaar. At a headland on the Zuider Zee near Hoorn we turned south east to cross 32 miles of the Zuider Zee, making for a checkpoint at Nijkerk where a railway ran 90 degrees to our track. We crossed the town of Nijkerk at house top level and looking behind us it was good to see the flight still in close formation.

'We were now eight minutes to our time on target. About ten miles west of Arnhem we turned on an easterly course and climbed rapidly to 3,000 feet; the others breaking the box formation to line astern. I had an oblique photo of a model made from aerial photographs and knew that a white gravel road led straight to the barracks. We flew in a shallow dive down this road. I pointed out the target to 'Don' Wellings and we dropped our bombs from 1,000 feet. The Mossies behind us did likewise. We carried instantaneous bombs on this trip and could not bomb at low level for fear of blowing up either the following aircraft or ourselves. When really low level bombing was done, eleven-second delay bombs were carried. Pilot aimed bombing became quite accurate after much practice by pilots on the bombing ranges back in England. Up came some flak and with the bomb doors open Wellings opened up with the firepower in the nose as our bombs were released. The Section followed us in. Until now the crews had maintained radio silence but soon after flattening out past the target I heard one of our crews over the radio call out 'We've got it!"

One of the experienced crews on 21 Squadron who took part in the attack on the barracks complex at Nijmegen was Canadian Flight Lieutenant 'Ed' McQuarrie RCAF and his navigator Flight Lieutenant J. L. 'Les' Bulmer, who took off at 1045 and were flying their last operation as a crew. Bulmer recalls.

'It was intended to be another of 2 Group's pinpoint raids but it turned out to be a total cock-up. It was to be quite an exciting finish to our tour together. Both raids were to eliminate the opposition before the airborne forces of 'Market-Garden' went in later that day. We were still based at Thorney Island, so we would have quite a way to go to reach the target. As a result we had to carry wing tanks, which meant that our bomb load was confined to two 500-pounders in the bomb bay. At briefing we had the usual 2 Group model of the town so that we could familiarize ourselves with the target and the run-in over the town. There would be fifteen aircraft in five sets of three in echelon starboard. Wing Commander David F. Dennis DSO DFC DFM led with 'Jock' Murray as his No 2. We led the third echelon with Flight Lieutenant 'Bert' Willers as our No.2. To ensure that all fifteen aircraft would be clear of the target before the bombs exploded the leading aircraft (the first ten) had 25-second fuses, whereas the rear echelons had the normal eleven-second delay. To stay clear of trouble we planned to fly across the Channel and up to the front line at high level. Once over enemy territory we would drop down to the deck and head for a road that ran northwest from Cleve into Nijmegen. The road would give us an accurate run-up to the target, which consisted of three large buildings forming a semi-circle facing the direction from which we planned to attack, so it would be easy to identify.

'Somewhere short of the front line we shed our drop tanks - empty tanks could be lethal if hit by flak. Just after crossing the front line we came under heavy ack-ack fire near Weert. There was nothing we could do to avoid it, as this would have destroyed the formation. But this didn't stop No.2 in the second echelon from trying to weave. He was a bigger menace than the flak.

As far as I know nobody was hit, although a message came over the R/T calling someone by name - which we didn't catch - telling them that they were on fire. I think it probably came from some other formation because there were no signs of fire in ours. But I reckon it caused a mild panic among all our crews. On the deck it was hard work for the pilots trying to keep one eye on the ground and the other on the rest of the formation. Somewhere along the way there was a cry of 'Wires, wires!' and we had to climb to get over an electricity pylon. I was amazed to see that Willers on our right seemed to fly underneath! In fact, I found out afterwards that he'd taken advantage of the droop in the cables to stay low.

'Our turning point on the Cleve-Nijmegen road came up, which we planned to follow into Nijmegen but we carried straight on, then circled starboard to come up on Cleve from the east. I had no idea what was going on. Every navigator in the formation, except the leader, must have been wondering what the hell was happening. I could hardly believe my eyes when the leading aircraft opened their bomb doors. 'Ed' followed suit and I yelled at him that this wasn't the target and not to release our bombs. Poor 'Ed' was totally confused and probably thought I had gone off my head since the leaders were obviously intent on bombing whatever was coming up. After what seemed ages but was probably only seconds the leader's bomb doors closed and I breathed a sigh of relief as we shot over Cleve. On the straight road, with houses on either side and a larger building, which could have been a church or chapel, people were standing watching us go over. I looked back to check that the rear echelons had noticed that bomb doors had been closed and saw to my dismay a large cloud of black smoke. Some of the rear six aircraft had let their bombs go. (According to later official reports three aircraft bombed a barrack square in Cleve and machine-gunned troops.)

'Southwest of Cleve is the Reichswald, a large forest and we proceeded to career around this. By now there was not much formation left, just a gaggle of aircraft milling around waiting for someone to make a decision. Suddenly I saw two aircraft haring off in the right direction - one of them, I later discovered, was Jock Murray. I told 'Ed' to follow and we chased after them, with everyone else tagging along behind or beside us. We were now fifteen aircraft all flying individually towards Nijmegen. And we had no means of knowing whether any of the leading planes were the ones with the short fuses.

'We sped up the road to Nijmegen and I could see the bridge over on the right. Then we were over the town looking anxiously for the target. It seemed to be chaos, with Mosquitoes going in all directions, flak coming up and Mustangs milling around above us. I noticed one Mosquito climbing away to the north and wondered where the hell he was going. Then another Mosquito shot underneath us almost at right angles. I shall never know how we found room between the rooftops and I wondered why he was going in that particular direction. Then I realized that he'd seen the target and was heading straight for it. I yelled to 'Ed' to pull round and pointed to the target, by now almost on our port wing tip. He put us into a tight turn but we couldn't make it in time. We shot over the town and I recall the railway station with crowds waiting on the platform and what appeared to be a green-coloured train alongside. In a flash we were clear and out over farmland where we dumped our bombs and fled. On the way in and on the way out the farmers and their families were standing in their doorways waving like mad - probably cheering on 'the brave RAF' while we were thinking, 'what the hell are we doing here, let's get the hell out of it.' The element of surprise is essential on low-level attacks and there is no going round again unless you have suicidal tendencies so we found a convenient wood and jettisoned our load. In the confusion we forgot to put the arming switches to 'OFF' so I just hoped that no one would be passing that way within the next 25 seconds. (We weren't the only ones to blow holes in the countryside. At the subsequent inquest there were several photographs taken by rearward-facing cameras showing jettisoned bombs exploding. There were a few caustic comments from the flight commanders about this. Fortunately we didn't have a camera on board so we managed to conceal our misdemeanour.) We found another Mosquito, which seemed to be going in the same direction as us, so we joined him for the journey home. This was uneventful; we didn't even get shot at over Weert this time. Maybe the Germans didn't consider two aircraft to be worth wasting ammunition on. And besides, we were heading for home.'

'We returned to Thorney Island (one crew was missing) where the full story of the confusion over the target route unfolded. Wing Commander Dennis had a bird hit his windscreen just before reaching the turning point. In retrospect it might have been wiser for him to pull out and hand over to Jock Murray immediately but he chose to carry on, not being able to see properly and hence the mess we finished up in. Only five aircraft claimed to have located and bombed the target. Most of the rest did as we did and dumped them in fields, apart from those who had already got rid of theirs over Cleve. I've always felt that it was a mistake to have fifteen planes in one formation. The usual formation on previous raids of this sort was groups of six in two vics of three. Because each of the following echelons had to be stepped down on the one in front to avoid slipstream problems, it meant that the leader had to keep a reasonable height above the deck, otherwise the rear echelons would be ploughing a furrow across the countryside. In the event, it was impossible to avoid hitting slipstreams and we were being thrown all over the place and at treetop height this is not the healthiest of situations. It was only later that we learned that the German troops were not in their barracks anyway, so all we succeeded in doing was probably to kill a few innocent Dutchmen and some German civilians. Such is war. In wartime I suppose you can't very well admit to the world that you made a cock-up.'

An official reports concluded that 'In retrospect it appears that these attacks [by Bostons, Mosquitoes and Mitchells] did not have much effect on the enemy's power to resist.' Sixty-nine Dutch civilians died as a result of misplaced bombs; 37 of them killed when B-17s bombed a flak battery at Wageningen) and the Germans shot dead three more locals. In the vicinity of the railway siding at Wolfhezen forty-six patients in the psychiatric hospital and forty-four other civilians were killed and a home for the blind was burned to the ground. The *Willemskazerne* in the centre of Arnhem was completely burnt out along with some commercial premises nearby. At Ede thirty Mitchells and thirteen Bostons bombed from medium altitude with 63 tons of HE. Because of cloud conditions and other difficulties 23 or more pilots returned without bombing and the remainder hit targets of opportunity. The Bostons had scattered leaflets addressed 'To the Population of the Southern Part of the Netherlands, South of the Lek and the Rhine', announcing *'Het oogenblik waarop gij zoolang hebt gewacht is gekomen'* - 'the moment you have been waiting so long for has come' - in other words - the imminent liberation of the Netherlands. Though 'Market-Garden' had been delayed a week, it was only twenty-three days after the liberation of Paris.

On arrival back at Lasham, the AOC, AVM Basil Embry, was on base. With no food for several hours, Vic Hester 'hobbled' into de-briefing. 'Noting my state, Basil Embry handed me a half-pint glass full of issue rum and proceeded to take our report. 'Ted' Moore went off the process the films, which were flown to Monty within hours.'

Dudley Hemmings and Don Wellings made it safely back at Lasham after three hours in the air. 'Then' recalls Hemmings 'it was a debriefing, some discussion of the other Sections' experiences (two aircraft failed to return), a beer at 'The Swan' in Alton nearby clouding the knowledge that tomorrow was another day, another 'op'. As to whose bombs hit the barracks or went astray I do not know. It is best not to know as a number of Dutch civilians were killed during the raid. For navigator and pilot on such missions it was purely a test of one's navigational and flying skills, a hope of survival under fire, a task completed as ordered and a mental isolation from the outcome on the ground. When my CO told me my operational tour was completed and to take Rest Leave Wellings said to me that the CO had told him the same. While he insisted I go Wellings stated that he would ask to stay on because he wanted to 'see out the war'. Sadly, when I was on leave he took a new navigator and went missing on 9 October 1944.'

Chapter 3

'Market' Sunday 17 September
'D-Day' - The British Lift

We are a step away from freedom. Any moment now the English will rush over the Amsterdamsestraatweg to free us and Arnhem. What a beautiful day. This morning, after breakfast, Father Ammerlaan had told us that the Allied had broken through the Siegfried Line in two places at Aken.

Diary entry by Father H. C. Bruggeman, a resident at the Mill Hill Fathers' House, a mile east of the Johannahoeve Farm and three miles north-west of Arnhem.

At the forward airfield at Manston in Kent during the night of 15 September soon after falling asleep aircrew officers and any army officers billeted in Nissen huts on rows of two tier bunks were rudely awakened by some 'happy' characters that had obviously had a 'few' calls of *Put out the bloody lights* and other less polite additions, resulting in the late comers taking unsteady aim and eventually shooting out all the lights. Needless to say the bunks had emptied on to the floor at the first shot! Frustrations had been building at the airfield for some time and letting off steam now was not surprising. Such was the strain upon the resources of the airfield that on 8 September, an Armstrong Whitworth Albemarle and a Horsa was flown back to Brize Norton to return with a load of WAAF waitress reinforcements. Despite Manston's long runway and large dispersal area, the airfield was at bursting point with men, supplies, a dozen RAF and Fleet Air Arm squadrons, mostly fighter squadrons operating against the V-1 flying bombs, or standing by to either escort the air armada to Holland. The situation was not helped when fifty-six Albemarles, towing their Horsa gliders flew in. Kenneth Frere, who joined 296 Squadron at Brize Norton in August 1944 and spent the month practicing mass glider tows, parachute dropping and navigational exercises with gliders, recalls: '38 Group squadrons were based in the southern counties of England where they were well placed for operations into France, including the support for the SAS and for the French Resistance which was another part of 38 Group's tasks. However, when the front line moved into Belgium and beyond it was out of range for Albemarles towing loaded gliders. From 2 September onwards in readiness for Operation 'Market' we spent our time moving Horsa gliders over to Manston, as near to Holland as it was possible to get.' The Albemarle was one of the RAF's least well-known aeroplanes. With a tricycle undercarriage and large 'dive-bomber' flaps it was quite a contrast to its predecessor, the well-tried but out-of-date Armstrong Whitworth Whitley. Like the Whitley, the Albemarle was one of the 'redundant bombers' which Winston Churchill urged his Air Staff to provide for his orphan child, the Airborne Forces. Though under-powered, it had one advantage for glider towing. Its tricycle undercarriage put it into a flying attitude even before it began to roll. The nose-wheel allowed full power to be applied rapidly because there was no torque to offset. It also prevented an over-enthusiastic glider pilot from putting the tug into a nose-down attitude on the runway if the glider went into high-tow before the Albemarle was airborne. Its jump-hole in the floor was almost as bad for the noses of parachutists as that in the Whitley.

At Manston also was 'B' Squadron, The Glider Pilot Regiment. It would carry infantry of Lieutenant Colonel W. Derek H. McCardie's 2nd Battalion, The South Staffordshire Regiment and Battalion Headquarters and elements of 1st Airborne's various artillery units over two days in 62 Horsas from Manston and Broadwell and a Hamilcar from Tarrant Rushton. On 7 September, heavy rain the night before forced the troops to evacuate their tents for dry accommodation. Rain continued until well after midday and created difficulties being able to marshal gliders and tugs. On 10 September, after a church parade at 1100 hours, word was received in late afternoon that 'Comet' had been cancelled and at 1730 hours, the South Staffordshires were allowed out of the camp, although few took up the offer down to having plenty of foreign currency, presumably ready for the operation, but no English money. Next day McCardie and his Intelligence Officer returned to Brize Norton. At Manston, a field cashier arrived in the afternoon to exchange the foreign currency leading to a larger influx of airborne troops into the local towns. From the 12th to the 16th, the men of the South Staffordshire were either on leave or carrying out PT and games. McCardie and his Intelligence Officer returned on the 16th by Albemarle from Brize Norton.

At Fairford Sergeant 'Ron' Kent, a 23-year-old section commander in the 21st Independent Parachute Company, said, 'The suspense was killing us and action was the only antidote. We were tired of fighting the 'Yanks' in the pubs in Salisbury, Newark and Huddersfield. We were like boxers in danger of becoming over-trained and afraid of passing our peak. It was time we went. We could not have the war end with 6th Airborne getting all the glory for its 'D-Day' operations.'[1]

'We were raring to go' recalls 24-year old 'Bill' Higgs of 'D' Squadron, 1 Wing, The Glider Pilot Regiment at Keevil. A PT instructor and a champion boxer, 'Bill' had taken part in Operation 'Tonga' when he and his co-pilot, Sergeant Major Oliver, took part in Operation 'Tonga' during the early hours of 6 June 1944, carrying a jeep, 6-pounder anti-tank gun and three men of the 4th Airlanding Anti-Tank Battery. Some 1,378 members of the Glider Pilot Regiment would be needed to carry out the 'Market' operation and it was considered to be essential that they be used only in defensive roles once on the ground and withdrawn as soon as possible as this number represented 90% of the entire regimental strength. Heavy casualties were therefore to be avoided; quite apart from the fact that further airborne operations might be carried out in Europe, South-East Asia Command was in need of glider pilots.[2] 'It was not a case of saying 'I hope we don't have to' says Higgs; 'we were ready to go;' this despite having questioned the merits of the plan at a briefing. 'General 'Boy' Browning was there - immaculate, of course. I didn't like him. We had the 'spiel' about what we were going to do. 'Any questions?' he asked. I was acting squadron sergeant major and the boys were pushing me, saying, 'Bill', ask him why we are landing seven miles away when we landed next to the Orne bridges in the dark and amongst Rommel's glider posts on D-Day.' So I opened my big mouth and I said: 'Excuse me, sir. Why are we landing seven or eight miles from the bridge in daylight when we landed ...' And he stepped down half a step off the dais he was on and he put his finger out, upright and he said, 'That is the plan.' And I never said another word. I was frightened to say any more than that. But what a plan it was.'[3]

On Saturday afternoon and early evening of 16 September the glider pilots at Down Ampney loaded and checked their dozen Horsas, which would carry the 137 men of Lieutenant Colonel Arthur Marrable's 181 Airlanding Field Ambulance RAMC which had been billeted at Stenigot House in the Lincolnshire Wolds and Martin, a small village in North Kesteven, to LZ 'S' west of Arnhem. Sam Issacs and 'Bill' Perry loaded and checked Horsa 448 - chalk number '289' that would carry 21 men, two handcarts and two lightweight motorcycles and then they checked the tug plane towline with the pilot of their Dakota tow aircraft (KG411) on

48 Squadron captained by Warrant Officer F. F. Felton. The load was of key importance as it included Major Simon Fraser, second in command of 181 Field Ambulance; the dental officer, Captain P. Griffin, who acted as anaesthetist; half a section and several members of the surgical team. Corporal George Aldred an Operating Room Assistant in 181 who flew on 'Chalk 289', recalled: 'We were briefed two or three days before the op. Walking out we were all of the same opinion; no confidence in the Americans getting the previous three bridges (Eindhoven, Grave and Nijmegen) as we had been let down badly by them in North Africa and Sicily. The day before takeoff we were getting kit ready; afterwards writing letters. We missed tea, got to bed in our tents about midnight, ravenously hungry. I remembered I had a Mars bar in my pack. I took it out in the dark and bit it. Ants had eaten the soft interior. I struck my lighter. I had to spit out a mouthful of ants and hundreds more (were) everywhere. We went to Down Ampney next morning and saw many fellows from other units that we had not seen from North Africa and Sicily - all saying the same thing. 'Hi Tom' or 'Jack' or whatever, 'We're in the shit!' And we knew it!'[4]

Flight Lieutenant 'Jimmy' Edwards, one of the Dakota pilots on 271 Squadron at Down Ampney who would tow a glider, was equally succinct: One day we were briefed for another major airborne assault, ahead of the front, but that evening I went down with severe tonsillitis and waited miserably in the sick-bay to hear the others taking off. But nothing happened and soon Squadron Leader 'Joubie' was beside my bed to tell me that the whole thing had been cancelled because General Patton had reached the dropping zone before the gliders had even taken off. As soon as I was well again, it was back to the almost daily re-supply trips. The whole thing was building up to a tremendous climax, when suddenly we were all grounded for a whole day and we saw the ominous signs of those long-range fuel tanks being dragged out and refitted in the fuselage. What had the moguls thought up now? It wasn't long before we knew. As we filed into the briefing room there on the wall was the usual large map of Europe and on it a thick line of red ribbon stretching from Down Ampney right across the North Sea and deep into Holland. At the very end of the line, written in large blue letters, was the word 'ARNHEM'.[5]

Born in Barnes, London (then Surrey) on 23 March 1920, the son of a professor of mathematics, James Keith O'Neill Edwards was educated at St. Paul's Cathedral School, at King's College School in Wimbledon and at St. John's College, Cambridge, where he acquired a taste for comedy and the stage while performing in the 'Footlights Revues'. His aptitude for the footlights was confirmed with the staging of concert parties at Down Ampney. He had also his own personal Dakota which rejoiced in the serial number KG444 and which he had nicknamed *The Pie-eyed Piper of Barnes*. This had been painted in large yellow lettering on the nose. 'This was a wheeze that Wing Commander Booth had borrowed from the Americans and it certainly gave one much more interest and pride in the job'.

'Arnhem began with the best intentions. More men were going to be dropped than ever before and were going further into enemy territory than ever before. The first glimpse of that map in the briefing room brought whistles of incredulity from many of us. Clearly, the moguls had gone mad. It seemed too many of us that the generals were determined to use this massive airborne force simply because it was there and all their previous plans had been thwarted. It was all made to sound so simple at the briefing. 'You will take off and fly in pairs to Aldeburgh on the Suffolk coast, where all the other aircraft involved will join you in a steady stream as you set course for the Dutch coast. It has all been worked out with split-second timing so that a continuous flow of gliders will arrive at exactly the right time over the dropping-zone the other side of the river at Arnhem.' All well and good. But it didn't happen like that. For one thing, the 'other aircraft' involved were not all Dakotas. By this time, the lumbering, stolid Stirling bomber had been relegated to this humble task of dragging three-ply and piano wire through the sky and so had the Albemarle, a medium-sized bomber that had done very little to commend itself up to now. The snag was that they all flew at different airspeeds, so that even with the most immaculate precision flying, the 'steady stream' was just a briefing officer's pipe-dream. In the event, it was more like a dog's dinner... Treble Four's days were numbered.'

The plans for taking the 1st Airborne Division to Holland had been laid by the joint planning staff of 38 Group RAF and the US IX Troop Carrier Command at Eastcote where it had been decided that the base airfields for the complete operation should form two distinct groups. At eight RAF and fourteen American airfields, stretching from Dorset to Lincolnshire, the troops were waiting to climb aboard the aircraft. From airfields in Oxfordshire, Dorset, the 1st British Airborne Division, 1st Airlanding Brigade and the 1st Polish Parachute Brigade were detailed to be delivered to Arnhem by 38 and 46 Groups RAF and the US 9th Troop Carrier Command's 61st and 314th Troop Carrier Groups[6] at Barkston Heath and Saltby. All told, 625 Troop Carrier Command C-47s and fifty more in the 52nd Troop Carrier Wing towing gliders were to carry the men of the 82nd Airborne and the paratroop elements of the 1st British Division. On 16 September the American combat crews had been given a short lecture on 'Escape and Evasion in Holland' and Escape purses and kits were issued. They received the final briefing for the air invasion of Holland the following morning.

The use of two routes, each with three or four lanes for traffic and the closer spacing of serials, 1,055 planeloads of paratroops and 478 gliders were to be delivered in the initial lift within 65 minutes. A noteworthy innovation was the massing of serials in three parallel lanes 1½ miles apart. In addition 38 Group and 46 Group were to fly gliders over the northern route at a level 1,000 feet above the Americans, making that a four-lane skyway.

The two groups of airfields were each assigned a forming-up point. Aircraft from bases in the south western group would form up over Hatfield in Hertfordshire north of London and those in the north over March near Peterborough in Cambridgeshire. From the rendezvous over Hatfield the aircraft were to continue their flight, in three parallel streams one and a half miles apart, towards the North Fenland and then due east across the Channel to Gheel, turning north there for Eindhoven. From the rendezvous over March the aircraft were to fly to a second rendezvous over the Suffolk coastal town of Aldeburgh beside the Alde estuary and then east-south-east for 94 miles straight across the North Sea to the west end of Schouwen Island at the Dutch coast and on without turning for eighteen miles to the eastern tip of the island. From there the route ran for 52 miles to the IP, about three miles south of Hertogenbosch where the streams would diverge and make for the respective targets at Grave, Nijmegen and Arnhem.

Owing to the 'reasonable hour fixed for take-off at Saltby' where 34 C-47s waited patiently to take the 2nd Parachute Battalion to Arnhem, there was no need for its commanding officer, 32-year old Lieutenant Colonel John Frost to hurry over breakfast and he read the papers as usual while eating the last plate of eggs and bacon he was to have for some time to come. The Battalion, which had been billeted at Stoke Rochford and Grantham, was to take the three bridges over the Rhine at Arnhem in vehicles which would arrive in seven Horsas from Keevil and a Hamilcar from Tarrant Rushton. Frost's equipment, weapons, food and parachute were all ready. Earlier that morning he had hopefully asked his batman Wicks to put his shotgun and cartridges and dinner jacket and golf clubs in the staff car which with his heavier baggage, would eventually reach him in Holland in the 'Sea Tail'. Having fed, Frost wandered along to the mess 'to find everyone else reading and smoking, all in the best of spirits and no worries anywhere. Quite a contrast to some of the operations we had done before! I don't think any of us had any doubts as to the ability of any part of the forces engaged to fulfil their role. I certainly did not anticipate much difficulty as far as our task was concerned and was thinking ahead to the time when we would fight as infantry again, well supported by adequate artillery, with our own tanks never far away and the comforts that are always at hand when the heavy transport is available. As for us, we always had a few miscreants who absented themselves, but they had a sort of grapevine which seemed to tell them, wherever they were, that an operation was pending, so they ought to turn up. In fact, one party of men arrived at Saltby in a taxi from London - morale was terrific.'

At Fairford, General Urquhart had breakfast alone in the mess. He had been wide awake since dawn. Captain Charles A. Pare, padre of the Glider Pilot Regiment conducted a communion service on the airfield. The Reverend had also taken part in the Normandy landings and the Regiment was justly proud of him.[7] On the airfield, the men were clustering round the 'positive jam of aircraft'. Walking among them Urquhart recalled General Horrocks' somewhat strange words during the planning of a previous operation. 'Your men are killers,' Horrocks had said. In their battle smocks and crash helmets Urquhart could not help thinking that they looked now 'like a force that would be capable of big things against the enemy. Every team was thoroughly shaken down. The men of the glider units now stood alongside their Horsas and the more bulky and vulnerable looking Hamilcars with their loads of heavy gear ranging from 17-pounder anti-tank guns to Bren carriers.'

Urquhart wished Major Bernard Alexander 'Boy' Wilson MC DSO* commanding the pathfinders of 21st Independent Parachute Company good luck. Wilson, who at 45 was the oldest parachutist in the division was 'positively boyish now that he was about to set off in the van of the armada' Urquhart wrote. 'His appetite for a fight had enlivened many a discussion in the months of waiting'. Wilson was rather possessive about his hand-picked unit, who had captured the Italian port of Bari. The six officers and 180 men of his unusually large company were pathfinders and as such were due to spend half an hour in the Arnhem area on their own marking four dropping zones and five glider landing areas before the rest of the division started to come in. Browning had decided that gliders would not be able to land without the aid of men on the ground using 'Eureka',[8] smoke and coloured panels as signals for the pilots and mark out a landing path. The

Independent Company were highly confident that 'Market-Garden' would be a resounding success and many had packed metal and boot polish for the liberation celebrations.

Alex McCallum, a Halifax crewmember on 298 Squadron at Tarrant Rushden recalled: 'On Sunday morning the NAAFI canteen supplied us as we waited, not the usual mugs of tea - but with rum. We could feel the heat rising from it.' Halifax crewed aircraft on 298 and 644 Squadrons at Tarrant Rushden returned to their Airborne Forces role on 17 September when they participated in the lift of the 1st Airborne Division to Arnhem. Their aircraft were not particularly suited for supply drops and so the Halifaxes were used in a glider-towing capacity only. 'We had been heavily engaged in supplying the French Resistance and others throughout Occupied Europe. This fact must have caught the attention of Hitler, for he authorised us to be executed if captured, regardless of wearing a British uniform. In addition to Arnhem, I suppose we were a slight source of annoyance to Hitler. While waiting to tow the first glider to Pegasus Bridge we had dropped secret agents into Europe from the French Alps to Norway also dropped supplies and arms to the Resistance Workers and had also dropped in the SAS complete with jeeps.'

Staff Sergeant Gordon Jenks, a Londoner who once played the trumpet in a dance band, had woken with a thick head and a strong suspicion, as he told his second pilot, that 'They're not kidding this time - we're really going.' Jenks had once played the 'Last Post' and 'Long Reveille' at the funeral of two of his fellow glider pilots who were killed in a Halifax that crashed just after take-off at Holmsley South while en route to Hurn to collect a Horsa. It was an experience he would never forget. As RAF and glider pilots stood in silent ranks by fresh graves as the coffins rested three volleys were fired and Jenks began to play. 'Never had I played with so much feeling at that moment' he said. Birds were singing, an aircraft droning overhead and Jenks noticed that the relatives of the victims were softly weeping. For the first time he was conscious of the bond that had formed, despite disparate attitudes, between the crews of the tugs and the glider men. Later in North Africa Jenks witnessed another Halifax crash. In a repetition of the disaster at Holmsley South, smoke poured from an engine, the aircraft lost height and crashed in flames as 2,400 gallons of high-octane fuel ignited. The rear turret was thrown clear on impact and the rear gunner lived. He was the only survivor. After a wash and a shave Jenks stuck his head under a cold water tap for two minutes and felt better. Dressing, he picked up his flying helmet and went for a much needed coffee. He began to wish that he had not drunk so much beer the night before. At Great Dunmow, Essex Derrick Shingleton, a fair-complexioned young man, tall and powerful, fixed his strappings beside co-pilot Raymond Percival. Some time earlier Shingleton had proposed to his WAAF fiancée, Celia and she had consented to marry him. Shingleton promised himself that it would be the first thing he would arrange when he returned from Arnhem.[9]

'We left our tents, which were just three fields away from the runway, for a drumhead service with the padre' recalls Corporal Tom Smithson, 'then some sandwiches and tea. After that we lined up ready for the off. The planes were all marked off with big chalk marks and you were allocated your number. We'd got our parachutes fitted and kitted and were allocated our seats and we sat there and tried not to look frightened.

'At around mid-day we were taken to Saltby airfield' recalled Private 'Bill' Gibbard - 'Operation 'Market-Garden' had begun! At 1pm I boarded a Dakota aircraft, with no idea where we were going, other than it was an operation. When were up in the air I realised it was something pretty big because the sky was full of aircraft, all heading in the same direction. During the flight the padre, Captain [Bernard Mary] Egan [who had been awarded an MC for his role in 'Husky'] gave us each a copy of the New Testament and I wrote my name and address in it.'[10]

The 1st Battalion, The Border Regiment and Battalion HQ flew in 56 Horsas towed by Albemarles and Halifaxes from Broadwell and Blakehill Farm and a Hamilcar from Tarrant Rushton. Lieutenant Edmund Filford 'Bob' Scrivener commanding 10th Platoon, 'A' Company, 1st Battalion wrote: 'When I looked down and saw the North Sea beneath us and the fighters buzzing around us ready to beat off any enemy attacks, it began to sink in that very soon action was going to be the name of the game. Even then I wasn't really worried, for had we not been told that we would meet no opposition to speak of. All we had to do was to secure the landing zones for the paras and then belt off to Arnhem and the bridge and keep an eye on it till the Guards Armoured Division arrived to take over. 'Piece of cake'. Better take a field dressing with you in case somebody scratched themselves on a bush. What a load of bullshit that was! In reality we were flying into the biggest shambles of the war, for which 17,000 men would pay the price for the stupid incompetence of those in authority.'

'The huge airfield at Saltby' continues Lieutenant Colonel John Frost, 'swarmed with Dakotas and convoys of lorries were moving slowly round the perimeter track. I went to the Air Liaison Officer's place. 'Nothing to worry about, sir,' he said. 'Met report couldn't be better and everyone seems to have arrived on time. Your plane is No.16. You'll find a mark on the tarmac beside it. Times for enplanement and take-off unchanged. Tea and sandwiches will be round shortly...My pilot was a reassuring type of man who exuded confidence and his crew were feeling fine...The time of waiting for the aircraft to take off is, for the parachutist, the transition from peace to war. For him there is no gradual, growing consciousness of battle that other Arms must feel. There are no enemy positions to study with binoculars. No preliminary bombardment to wait for, no careful moving up in dark or wet with fingers crossed against the enemy's defensive fire...This time, in the light of our past experiences, I felt that we had trained, prepared and planned well and was sure that the battalion had reached its highest peak of readiness. We had been chosen for the most important task, but I was sure we should succeed. In fact, I found that I was happier at this stage of going into action than I had ever been before.' Suddenly, the Dakota's engines roared into life and seemed to blow away all of Frost's thoughts of death. Another thought persisted, a more strident, vigorous one - 'Come on! Let's get away. We've been too long already'.'

Lance Sergeant Harold Padfield and his stick commander in 'B' Troop in Major Douglas Murray's 1st Parachute Squadron RE at Donington boarded one of nine C-47s in the 61st TCG at Barkston Heath airfield which carried this unit and Squadron Headquarters, with four tugs and their Horsas joining the flight from Keevil. 'We checked straps and hooks on the plane' recalled Padfield 'also that the door opening was taped and that the bomb rack switches worked, before getting the stick to fit up the containers. It was a lovely sunny day and we laid around until we were told to enplane at around eleven o'clock. The plane eventually taxied into position at the head of the runway, lining up for take-off, which in our case was around midday.'

Tugs and their gliders with names like *Scrounger's Roost* and *The Flapper* hurriedly chalked on their sides rolled down runways and rose in the air at a launch rate never before attempted: one combination per minute. The weather over England was far from ideal with the cloud base ranged from 500 feet to 2,000 feet and before the English coast was reached 23 gliders had parted from their tugs. Forming up was especially intricate and dangerous. Climbing slowly to altitude, the planes headed west over the Bristol Channel. Then, speeds synchronized, the tugs and gliders echeloned to the right in pairs, turned back, flew over the take-off bases and headed for the marshalling point above Hatfield. In southern and eastern England thousands of people looked up at the spectacle and gaped in amazement. Road traffic came to a halt. Passengers in speeding trains crowded one another to stare out of windows. One passenger recalled: 'The sky was dotted as far as one could see with tugs and gliders; hundreds and hundreds of them; right away towards the clouds in the east. Looking away south towards the engine, there they were, pouring eastwards across the track. Looking back to the guard's van, more hundreds of them, still flying over the station we'd passed through a few minutes back. And, overhead, a constant roar of two- and four-engined tugs with their silent gliders; the slender cables between them sometimes flashing in the sun. Sometimes dozens of Dakotas - twin engines and up tilted wings - and then a group of Halifaxes. Then more Dakotas and more Halifaxes; endless it seemed, passing low over the train and away to the east. A seasoned aircraftman, with four service chevrons, standing next to me in the corridor struggled hard to look blasé; but he gave it up in the end, put his paper away and stared, as excited as the rest of us, at this simply tremendous display of airborne strength.'

A Red Cross worker, Angela Hawkins, from the window of a train, stared up, astonished, as wave after wave of planes flew over like 'droves of starlings.' She was convinced that 'this attack, wherever bound, must surely bring about the end of the war.' In churches and cathedrals special commemorative services were being held to remember the 'few,' who four years' earlier had defeated the Luftwaffe in the Battle of Britain. The steady drone of the troop carriers flying at low altitude over London drowned out the service in Westminster Abbey where the sound of the organ during the *Te Deum* could not be heard. In north London, a Salvation Army band overpowered by the din gave up, but the bass drummer, his eyes on the sky, thumped out a symbolic beat in Morse code: three dots and a dash - 'V for Victory'.

Troops could not help but look out of the window at England and think that they probably might never see it again. Looking down from his Dakota, 27-year old Major Anthony John Deane-Drummond MC, second-in-command of 1st Airborne Signals, thought how peaceful everything looked. 'It was midday when we crossed the coast and flew out across the North Sea, which for once was like a mill-pond with scarcely a ripple to disturb its brown-looking water. The men in my plane were nearly all asleep. We could see the streets of the villages we passed over thronged with people looking upwards and an occasional handkerchief could be seen waving a farewell.'

Even as the first British glider serials were forming up above the Bristol Channel, twelve big black Stirling bombers on 190 and 620 Squadrons at Fairford and six US C-47s filled with American and British pathfinders began taking off at 1025 for Holland for the drops scheduled for about

1240 hours. Both of the Stirling squadrons provided six Stirlings carrying six airborne officers and 180 enlisted men of the 21st Independent Parachute Company, whose job it was to mark all three drop and landing zones for the First Lift due to begin arriving half an hour later. The teams were to set up 'Eureka's, panel letters and smoke on both zones, put out a panel 'T' on DZ 'X' and fire Very lights on LZ 'S'. On the following days they would use the same set of aids on the other British zones, reserving Very lights for landing zones and 'T's for drop zones and drop points. A further nineteen Stirlings on 190 Squadron were involved in this lift, each towing a Horsa glider.

'Stick' commanders like 'Ron' Kent made the acquaintance of the navigator and crew. 'The plan for us was to drop about twenty minutes ahead of the main body. The navigator and I compared notes over maps and air photographs taken the week before. I pointed out the roof of a farm building not far from the centre of our DZ and asked if he could drop us within a hundred yards or so. He saw no problem.'[11]

Flying Officer Reginald Lawton was a navigator on one of the 190 Squadron Pathfinder Stirlings to drop sixteen paratroops at Arnhem. 'The day was cloudless and we had no difficulty in finding our DZ and the men jumped successfully. We had to circle then at about 500 feet while we tried to release some parachute containers that had 'hung-up' in the bomb bays; and while doing so we could see Dutch civilians waving and starting to cycle towards the paratroops. On the way back we flew over the main force of tugs and gliders and parachute aircraft, supported by fighters, who were shooting up the few ack-ack batteries which opened up. All these aircraft made a continuous stream 280 miles long.'

Some flak was met and one Stirling was damaged, but none of the troops were injured. Every 'stick' was dropped successfully on its proper zone even though three of the Horsas had to be cast-off prematurely. The teams assembled quickly, accepted the surrender of fifteen Germans and had their equipment functioning several minutes before the main serials arrived. On the following day, twenty-two Stirlings on 620 Squadron towed Horsas to the same landing zones, all but one of which arrived successfully. This latter glider was brought in by the Squadron with the Third Lift on the following day, accompanied by a further seventeen aircraft which dropped supplies.

Twenty Halifaxes on 298 Squadron towing thirteen Horsas and seven Hamilcars and twenty-one of 644 Squadron's Halifaxes towing fourteen Horsas and seven Hamilcars were airborne in 23 minutes ten seconds. Engine trouble forced a 298 Squadron combination to return after twenty minutes while a 644 Squadron Halifax lost its Hamilcar through tow-rope failure but the glider managed to reach the coast. The remainder reached their appointed zones without incident though two of the Hamilcars turned overturned on the soft ground, causing the loss of their 17-pounder guns.[12] Flight Lieutenant 'Jimmy' Stark, a 298 Squadron Halifax pilot, who in May 1943 had twice attacked U-528[13] while on 58 Squadron Coastal Command, recalled: 'The air in a glider train can be exceedingly disturbed unless you are in the leading aircraft and if you hit the slipstream of the aircraft ahead, your wing stalls and you sweat like a pig pulling it up again. To avoid that, the dodge was to move out slightly to one side of the train and thereby fly in clear air. As we approached the front line, a friend of mine called Ensor was just ahead of me, well out to the left of the train. All of a sudden, his aircraft was surrounded by black puffs of bursting flak. I am afraid that I started laughing and shouting, 'Get into line, you silly clot.' Then my own aircraft was hit. It was a most unusual sensation and a most unusual noise. It sounded like someone running an iron bar along a corrugated iron fence. I immediately tried all the controls and they worked perfectly. However, the glider pilot in the Horsa saw the whole incident and started calling me up on the intercom. 'Are you all right?' I replied, 'Yes, I am all right; are you all right?' We kept this up for a few minutes; we were like a couple of old 'dolls' at a Women's Missionary Association. Our conversation was brought to a halt by my tail gunner, a laconic Canadian, who said, 'There is a f—ing great hole in your tail.' Part of the starboard fin had been blown away, but we got to Arnhem safely.'[14]

Because the unwieldy gliders and tugs flew at 120 mph and the C-47 paratroop carriers at 140 mph these immense serials had to be launched first. Some 4,700 aircraft - the greatest number ever used on a single airborne mission took part. At 0945 and for two-and-a-quarter hours more, 2,023 troop-carrying planes, gliders and their tugs swarmed into the air and headed east. Winds were light, visibility was good and the few patches of stratus cloud had lifted by 10 o'clock. At 0950 the first of 482 C-47s started taking off from the Grantham area. Those not towing the fifty gliders carried parachutists. Gliders carried elements of the headquarters of the 82nd Airborne Division and the XVIII Corps. It took fifty minutes for them all to get into the air. By the time the last of the planes had lifted its wheels, the lead-plane was almost a third of the way to the landing and drop zones near Groesbeek in Holland. C-47s carrying paratroopers flew in seemingly endless 45-plane formations and more Dakotas and Halifaxes, Stirlings and Albemarles with 300-foot-long tow ropes pulled 478 gliders carrying troops and equipment. The smaller

Horsas and Wacos were dwarfed by the huge Hamilcars each with a cargo capacity of eight tons that could hold a small tank or two 3-ton trucks with artillery or ammunition. Above, below and on the flanks, protecting these huge formations, were almost 1,500 Allied fighters and fighter-bombers and low-level dive bombers. There were so many planes in the air that Captain Neil Sweeney of the 101st Airborne thought that 'it looked like we could get out on the wings and walk all the way to Holland.'

The British glider forces, who were further north on the 'Market-Garden' corridor than the Americans and with different requirements, were the first to take off. Urquhart needed the maximum numbers of men, equipment and artillery, especially anti-tank guns, to capture and hold his objectives until XXX Corps could reach them so the bulk of his division was glider-borne; 320 gliders carried the men, transport and artillery of Brigadier Philip H. W. 'Pip' Hicks DSO MC of 1st Airlanding Brigade. They were due to reach the landing zones west of Arnhem just after 1300. Thirty minutes later Brigadier Gerald 'Legs' Lathbury's 1st Parachute Brigade, in 145 troop-carrying planes, would begin dropping.

General Urquhart's Horsa glider would be flown by Colonel Iain Arthur Murray DSO, commander of No.1 Wing and his co-pilot. Urquhart found it 'difficult not to feel excited that we were off at last' but he felt a pang of conscience. He thought of his paratroopers, crowding into heavy transport planes, who were to be seen hobbling with gear which included leaden-looking leg-bags containing heavier weapons - Brens, mortar parts and Vickers machine-guns. Others, looking even more weighed down, had valises across their chests containing weapons and ammunition. The general carried only a small shoulder pack, containing his shaving gear, a map-case, one map of the Arnhem area, a notebook and inside his smock, two grenades and chocolate. Hancock had made a practice of giving him his chocolate out of the ration in exchange for the general's cigarettes, as he was a non-smoker. Urquhart rummaged finally through his pockets to check that he was carrying no information which could be of use to the enemy and strapped himself in, exchanged a word with Hancock and glanced around the inside of the glider. As well as Urquhart, Graham Roberts and Hancock the other passengers were Charles Pare, a signaller and two military policemen whose function was to escort the general. In the glider also was his jeep where Urquhart had another shoulder pack with a clean shirt, a change of underclothes and a bottle of whisky; and the MP's motor-cycles. Several test landings had been completed without mishap.

Urquhart felt the slight jolt as the 300-foot-long tow-rope took the strain. This was his first operational trip in a glider and earlier he had taken a couple of air-sickness pills. His throat was dry and he had difficulty swallowing. He was conscious, too, that Hancock was watching him, a look of concern on his face. He knew, as did so many members of the division, all about the general's capacity for airsickness but Urquhart did not oblige. Idly he watched 'squadrons of fighters flashing past the glider trains.' 'We were in a huge stream of aircraft and I concentrated on impressions. We were committed. We had made a good plan. I still wished we could have got closer to the bridge, but I did not brood on it.'

At Down Ampney 'Chalk number 289' took off at 1012 hours 'All the way across the North Sea' wrote George Aldred 'we kept getting messages from the tug crew, 'We might have to go back'. Apparently the Dakota kept having engine trouble. We hit the coast of Holland. It was flooded. I was surprised to see some lights spiralling up to us. When one flashed by about 20-30 yards from the wing, I realised it was anti-aircraft fire. We landed on LZ 'S' at Reijers Camp, far corner; the glider was tipped on its left side, tail in the air and we had trouble getting the tail off and the motorcycles and hand carts out. I remember pulling a handcart with our surgical kit in down the long lane to Dautsekampweg, the site of a 1st World War German prisoner of war camp and some Dutch people with apples. We opened an operating theatre in an outhouse of one of the houses…' Chalk number 289 would have landed on LZ 'S' at approximately 1400 hours. Sam and 'Bill' dug in on the south east corner of the zone as part of the defence for the landings on Day 2. 'E' Squadron were involved in a fairly heavy confrontation with the enemy NCO Training School Battalion at about 1800 hours, but fought them off. On day seven (24 September) 'Bill' Perry, who was listed as 'lightly walking wounded' was handed over to the Germans in the truce arranged between the medical officers of both sides. During the night of the withdrawal, a particularly abysmal, rainy night, Sam Isaacs his fellow glider pilot swam the Neder Rijn after the DUKW amphibious craft he was in developed engine trouble and he decided he had to swim from half way across the Neder Rijn rather than drift toward enemy lines on the far side. Of 184 men in 'E' Squadron, 46 were killed, seventy were PoWs and 68 crossed the river. On Sam's arrival back at Down Ampney on 29 September, he was the only member of his hut of eighteen men to return.

C-47, C-53 and C-46 aircraft of the 313th Troop Carrier Group at Folkingham carried British paratroops to the Arnhem area. Private James W. Sims of the mortar platoon in Lieutenant Colonel John Frost's 2nd

Parachute Battalion 'should not have been on Arnhem, only for a trick of fate' as he recalled. 'There were three us - a fellow called 'Brum' Davies, myself and a young Geordie, we were all only nineteen; and Colonel Frost said, 'You're too young to go in the battle, but if you follow the Second Army with the baggage train, you'll see something - what war is all about. When we're victorious you'll meet up with us north of Arnhem.'

'At the last minute, however, three old sweats went absent thinking it was just another false alarm and they couldn't be found. They went round the fleshpots of Nottingham shouting their names out through loud-hailers trying to get them to surface, but they didn't want to know. So we got roped in and had to go. Not that either 'Brum' or myself minded for at nineteen this was an adventure not to be missed. We had already been briefed on the German opposition. The qualities of the Panzer Grenadiers and the Herman Goering Regiment, the vicious 88 mm 'flak' all purpose gun, the zip-fastener fire of the MG 34 machine gun. The fearsome multiple-mortar with its six rocket projectiles and its unnerving sobbing-moaning sound, which the Allies had nicknamed 'The Sobbing Sisters.' Also the 9 mm schmeisser sub-machine gun - perhaps the finest weapon of its class during World War II and our greatest dread - The Tiger Tank. Although it was slow - in fact the Germans themselves called it the 'Furniture Van' - it carried the 88mm gun and also HMGs and was heavily armoured with tracks nearly a yard wide and weighing almost seventy tons. To the parachutist, with nothing larger than a six-pounder anti-tank gun or a PIAT it was a formidable opponent. Well this is what you wanted' I told myself. 'It all goes together with the red beret, the wings, the jumping pay and the reputation.'

Having always flown with the RAF - whose attitude, Sims recalls, was: 'Don't worry, lads, whatever it's like, we'll get you through' - he received quite a shock on seeing his American pilot. 'He was a lieutenant-colonel with one of those soft hats. His flying jacket was hanging open and he was smoking a big cigar. Our lieutenant saluted him quite smartly and asked if the men should move up to the front of the plane on take-off.' The American grinned. 'Why, hell, no, lieutenant,' Sims remembers him saying. 'I'll get this goddamn crate off the ground if I have to drag its ass halfway down the runway.' Sims' officer was too startled to speak.'[15] Now, although he was fond of his colonel, Sims, watching Frost go by, had reached the limit of his patience. Surrounded by his equipment, he sat on the ground and muttered, 'There goes old Johnny Frost, a .45 in one hand and that bloody horn in the other.

'The increasing roar of the aircraft engines blotted out our thoughts and reduced our speech to mime. Dakota transports taxied along in Indian file to the head of the runway. The American pilots handled their charges with a mixture of seeming indifference and skill born of years of experience back home on their many trans-American airlines. One after another the aircraft turned into the wind and commenced to take off and the noise became a howling storm of sound as we bumped and bucketed along the runway. It seemed as though we would hurtle on until we smashed through the boundary fence but a sudden subtle change in the motion of the Dakota told us we were airborne. My stomach turned over as I realised that this time there was to be no 'stand down'. Now we were finally on our way, this time to Holland, enslaved since 1940. It was 1130 hours. We regarded ourselves as the vanguard of the liberating force which was even then thrusting up through Belgium to join up with the American parachutists who were to seize the Dutch towns of Eindhoven and Nijmegen. After this the armour would make a final drive to link up with us.

'We looked out of the small windows of the Dakota and watched the friendly soil of England drop away as we rose heavily into the air. The aircraft headed for the coast in flights of three where we picked up our fighter escort, mostly Hawker Typhoons and Tempests. The imposing Air Armada swung out over the North Sea and we settled down for the journey. We sat eight a side down the round-ribbed fuselage. Men from all parts of the British Isles, 'Geordies', 'Scouses', 'Jocks', 'Cockneys', 'Norfolk dumplings' and the inevitable sophisticated 'Townie'.

'Our Platoon Officer, Lieutenant Reg Woods, sat by the open door - he would lead us out. I was number fifteen and the last man out was number sixteen, Sergeant Maurice Kalikolf. Maurice was a Russian Jew, born in Kiev and his family had fled to England when he was just a small child because of a pogrom. He still retained a sad almost fatalistic streak in his nature and was quietly spoken, for a Sergeant. He was a first class soldier and one of the finest human beings I've ever met. Most of the men in our Mortar Platoon were veteran paratroopers who had seen action in North Africa, Sicily and Italy.'[16]

The slower glider combinations had begun taking off at 0940, towing 304 Horsas, thirteen Hamilcars and four Hadrians. The weather was unkind and of the 321 gliders which were towed off 26 parted company with their tugs either over England, over the sea or over Holland. 296 and 297 Squadrons made the largest contribution in aircraft numbers, dispatching 28 each. No other RAF squadron managed more than 25. 296 Squadron towed 26 Horsas and two Wacos to Arnhem without loss. 297 Squadron towed twenty-five Horsas to both of the landing zones at Arnhem, with a further three to Nijmegen with Waco gliders carrying sections of 1st British Airborne

Corps HQ. The Manston glider loads were anti-tank and light artillery, part of the 2nd South Stafford's infantry and four Waco gliders with two teams, each of five Americans from the 306th Fighter Control Squadron with two British jeep drivers brought forward from the second lift and towed by four Albemarles that flew in the morning from a reserve unit. Five reserves actually flew in but were told they would be in the way so were told to return, with only one taking up the offer before the other four were found to be required.

WAAF Corporal Ruth Mary Parker at Fairford wrote: The combination of glider and bomber was very heavy and took a long time to get into the air which was why they needed the very long runways at Fairford. The first wave was an unbelievable sight: four squadrons, each of over 100 aircraft, each towing a glider: the sky seemed full of aircraft! The same number of aircraft also took off from nearby RAF Brize Norton.'

'We were all thrilled at hearing the news that we were about to take part in what was clearly going to be quite a special operation' wrote 24-year old Birmingham-borne Lieutenant Michael Donald Keen Dauncey, who had been assigned to 'G' Squadron of the Glider Pilot Regiment in January. 'The whole thing was kept terribly secret and our first briefing was on the Saturday before we set off from Fairford. This informed us that our mission involved going to Arnhem. A few maps were shown to us and I was given a little photo showing exactly where he and his first pilot, Staff Sergeant Alan Murdoch were to land. 'On one side there was a farm with a little triangular copse in the middle of it and to the east of that was the local lunatic asylum.'

Lieutenant Colonel 'Sheriff' Thompson's 1st Airlanding Light Regiment RA and Regimental Headquarters at Boston flew in 57 Horsas from Fairford, Blakehill Farm, Down Ampney, Manston and Keevil on the first lift; No.2 Battery and remainder flew in 33 Horsas from Manston on the second lift. Lieutenant Dauncey was encouraged to see that an MC and an MM were worn by two of their passengers. 'Apart from seeing one Horsa down in the sea there were no mishaps on the flight. Murdoch made an excellent landing in the fields not far from the lunatic asylum. The gliders poured into the area without opposition, but it was sad to see a Hamilcar turn completely over on to its back, having burrowed into the soft earth on landing.' The eight-ton Hamilcar carried a jeep, trailer and six gunners from an artillery battery. Weight and ground speed had driven it deeper until the huge tail rose up in the air and the Hamilcar had flipped over. 'It was useless to try to dig them out' wrote Dauncey. 'A Horsa's flat on top but a Hamilcar's got a hump where the pilots sit and we knew the pilots were finished. The gunners' vehicle and trailer were soon taken from the tail of our Horsa, which came off more easily than I had expected.'

As 'Sheriff' Thompson's glider approached the Dutch coast saw that the low, broken clouds had completely dispersed and 'it was easy to see: first the air-sea rescue craft; then the coast defences of Holland, apparently abandoned and the flooded land at the mouth of the Scheldt. William Francis Kynaston Thompson, born in Greenwich, London on 12 November 1909, was described as 'an extremely able gunner whose light-hearted manner and un-soldier-like appearance concealed an urgent seriousness of purpose.' Quite suddenly Thompson noticed that 'the air photographs we had so carefully studied came to life and we were fast approaching our landing zone. My pilot pushed down the release lever and we were off, slowing down to gliding speed, beginning to lose height. I kept a sharp look out for other gliders crossing our path. There were none. As we made a half circuit, I waited for the first shots to be fired at us, but none came. We swung into another turn, half flap down, the nose dipped; 400 feet. Full flap, we were standing on our nose. Surely someone down there had his sights on us; we seemed to hang in the air. We flattened out, bump, jolt, rolling a few yards, stop. Down in one piece, we had landed unopposed. We sweated for half an hour before the load was off. Still there was no opposition.'

Lieutenant Dauncey meanwhile watched 1st Parachute Brigade drop; 'a marvellous sight'. On landing, his role was to act as close protection for The Light Regiment and while in command of a party of men defending the guns of the Regiment at Oosterbeek, Dauncey did this throughout the whole week of the battle. During the action his position was continually attacked by superior forces of enemy tanks and infantry. On three occasions the enemy overran the sector necessitating a counter attack. Dauncey, on his own initiative, organised and led each sortie with such determination that the positions were regained with heavy loss to the enemy. In the face of heavy small arms and mortar fire he personally attacked machine-gun posts, showing remarkable coolness and complete disregard for his own personal safety. During these attacks he was wounded on three occasions but refused to be evacuated from the area. On 24 September a more determined attack was made by the enemy using tanks and self propelled guns. Dauncey, whilst leading his men in a further counter attack, was wounded again - losing the sight of one eye. In spite of pain and handicap of defective vision, he continued to lead his men in a fearless manner thus recapturing the lost ground and inflicting heavy loss to the enemy. On 25 September the position was subjected to intense fire from an enemy SP gun. The houses were set on fire and the order was received to withdraw. By now no anti-tank weapons were available and there was imminent danger of the enemy SP gun penetrating the gun positions. Realising this fact, Dauncey, who had remained alone, assaulted the enemy vehicle single-handed with gammon bombs. By his action the critical situation was averted but he received further injuries which resulted in his capture by the enemy. The high morale of the men, who had been drawn from many units, was undoubtedly due to the fine example of this officer. Had the enemy broken through this sector, the gun positions would have become untenable and thus unable to support the Airborne Division. Despite being blinded in one eye, he fought on, but was taken prisoner. With another officer he escaped from a Dutch hospital on a rope of knotted sheets and hid in the Utrecht English Parsonage for four months. For extreme bravery shown during this battle Dauncey was recommended for the Victoria Cross, but this was reduced to DSO by General Montgomery.

'By now' wrote Private James Sims 'we were flying over huge billowing masses of fleecy cloud tinged with pink and blue and shaded with grey. The Dakotas droned and we even dozed off for a bit, but soon we neared the Dutch coast and braced ourselves as the aircraft dived down through the cloud to about 2,000 feet. Now we saw the North Sea glistening below and suddenly a German naval craft opened fire at us. Our plane took evasive action and we held on to each other and braced ourselves with our boots as we banked alarmingly. Through the window we could see the enemy patrol boat on a sea which was now at a 45° angle and watched fascinated as the tracer curved up towards us slowly at first then whipped by the door like a line of angry hornets. Typhoons peeled off and the German ship disappeared from view in a storm of rockets and cannon fire. Luckily we had escaped damage and renewed our position and those not immediately being sick witnessed the frantic efforts of the German captain to save his ship zigzagging all over the place whilst the sea was churned up all around him.

'Suddenly we saw a ridge of earth projecting from the sea like the spine of some extinct creature. This marked the coastline of Holland for there was extensive flooding in this area. We flew on and gradually the water gave way to ribbons of soil then whole fields as we flew further inland and we were not sorry as few of us had much faith in the issued life-jackets. We crowded at the windows to see the country below and saw that the RAF had marked the route to Arnhem for us with one blazing flak tower after another. One of the American crewmen came back to inform us that we were descending to 700 feet for the run in. We started to fasten our helmets and checked our parachutes just that once more. Then we heaved the cumbrous kit-bags onto our right boot and fastened the straps around the leg. These kit-bags contained six 10lb Mortar bombs, a pick, rifle and small pack - nearly 80 lbs of kit. On our person we carried forty rounds of .303, bandolier fashion, 2 x 36 grenades, a 75 anti-tank grenade and a phosphorous bomb. We were sure of a quick descent with this lot on and it certainly dampened down the oscillation of the 'chute.

'We stood up and closed up in single file behind our platoon officer, Lieutenant Reg Woods. Our right hand held the kit-bag grip and our left hand was on the shoulder of the man in front. This was to ensure a rapid exit and, therefore, a compact section on landing or, in the trade - a 'tight stick.' If one man hesitated in jumping at that speed it might mean him being separated from his section by a hundred yards or more on the deck.

'Suddenly the aircraft throttled down almost like a bus changing gear and we seemed to slew around slightly to the right and the floor of the plane seemed to rise and fall much more than before.

'The Red light winked on - 'Action Stations.'

'It was strangely exhilarating now it was here and I felt fine and wanted to go. We all watched the Lieutenant as he stood framed in the open doorway, the slipstream plucking at the scrim camouflage on his helmet as though eager to drag him out.

'The Green Light came on - GO!

'The Lieutenant disappeared and we shuffled one after another along the heaving deck of the Dakota, 3, 4, 5. One of the Americans had a Cine-camera filming our exit, 8, 9, 10 through the open door I could see a huge familiar glider on fire, but going on regardless, 12, 13, the man in front of me hunched slightly as he went out. Almost before his helmet disappeared I jumped but the slipstream caught my right leg and spun me round. The sound of the aircraft engines was cut off abruptly and one could distinguish other sounds.

'Overhead Dakotas were still disgorging their loads of parachutists and canisters. Wave after wave of multi-coloured 'chutes in a blizzard of silk. It was a tremendous thrill and a never-to-be-forgotten experience. However, I was in trouble as my rigging lines were twisted and I had to let go of the kit-bag grip and quick release in order to try and stop the twisting getting worse.

'My parachute had opened all right, but the twisting rigging lines made me sweat, luckily they didn't twist all the way up and slowly I began to unwind but still couldn't reach down to my kit-bag.

'Down below figures like ants scurried about and the sound of shouts and shots came up punctuated by bursts of machine gun fire. The Americans had dropped us 'spot-on' and it was like looking down on the sand table back at HQ. Battalion rallying points were marked by coloured flares and I picked the yellow for the 2nd Battalion. Everywhere order was developing out of seeming chaos as the men hurried to their rendezvous. The ground which hitherto had seemed so distant suddenly started to spin towards me at an alarming rate for with the kit-bag still on my right leg I had descended more rapidly than was normal.

'I grounded with quite a jar but was all right and got out of my para-harness and sliced through the cords of my kit-bag. I wrenched the rifle out, cocked it and looked around but there was only my own side still landing all around me. As I tore open my kitbag to get out the 3-inch mortar barrel and pack, I noticed a rifle pointing at me: it was one of the Independent Company holding the DZ. He wished me luck.

'I heaved out the bombs and other gear and eventually staggered off towards the yellow flare like a walking Christmas tree. Luckily two of my mates appeared with a collapsible barrow and on went the bombs, picks, shovels, small packs, etc. We sweated and swore as we pulled and pushed the barrow over ploughed fields. A Dutch Resistance man ran up: 'Hurry the SS are coming in armoured cars' and indeed we could hear car engines in the distance.

'At last we joined the rest of the Mortar Platoon amid ironic jeers and whistles. They already had some prisoners, nearly all in their Sunday best uniforms. For a moment we rested by the side of the road as Colonel Frost spoke to our Lieutenant. Well we had got to the outskirts of Arnhem with the help of the American and British Air Forces. Now it was up to us.

'All right lads - on your feet' came the voice of Sergeant Jackman the Platoon Sergeant.

'The 2nd Battalion began to move off into history.'[17]

Chapter 4

The British Lift Continues

Everything is going too well for my liking.
**Twenty-two year old Lieutenant Denis Jackson Simpson,
'B' Troop commander, 1st Parachute Squadron. Between
17 and 20 September he was in charge of four positions
covering Arnhem Bridge, was wounded and taken
prisoner on 20 September. On the night of the 21st/22nd
he formed one of a party of four who broke out and
joined the main British forces after moving through
Germany and German-occupied Holland for two nights
and a day. He was awarded the Military Cross for courage
and complete disregard for his own personal safety
in leading the break out from Arnhem Bridge which
otherwise would have been impossible to evacuate the
wounded from a burning house.**

'At the time we did not know that disaster loomed for our Squadron' recalled flight mechanic Alan Hartley on 271 Squadron at Down Ampney. 'The whole of our 46 Group comprising 271 and 48 at Down Ampney, 512 and 575 at Broadwell and 233 at Blakehill Farm[1] supplemented by a newly formed Canadian Squadron, 437 RCAF, took the Horsa gliders full of troops, jeeps, guns etc on a bright Sunday morning. It was a very impressive sight to see all of the Dakotas towing their Horsa gliders rising under an hour, forming up in huge columns and roaring eastwards. Unfortunately we did not have enough Dakotas, Albemarles and Stirlings to drop the whole 1st Airborne Division, so a second lift had to be planned for the next day. When my skipper, Pilot Officer 'Len' Wilson returned I asked him how the operation had gone. 'Fantastic sight - the gliders flying in; the different coloured chutes to indicate ammunition, food, clothing, medical supplies as well as thousands of paras'. Wilson and the other pilots had been briefed to go in at 120mph at 500 feet in a straight line for two minutes because the squadrons were short of parachutes and many unbreakable supplies were dropped freefall in wickerwork panniers. Without any guns to fire back, no fighter escort and in broad daylight, the aircrews had flown into a horrendous curtain of bursting anti aircraft shells and small arms fire. It was the 'most spectacular sight' he had ever seen. John Leonard Wilson was 32 years of age, married with a one-year-old baby and came from the village of Cottingham on the eastern fringe of the hills of the Yorkshire Wolds.

At the outset Flight Lieutenant 'Jimmy' Edwards was in trouble. 'Halfway down the runway one of 'Treble Four's engines decided to play up, developing a thing called 'boost surge' which meant that the power fluctuated like mad and was gathering speed far too slowly. My glider, which had about six soldiers and 5,000lb of ammunition stuffed into it, got airborne okay but by the time we had reached the end of the tarmac we were still going pitifully slowly. 'We'll never get up,' shouted 'Tiger' nervously. 'Pull the bloody wheels up and we will,' I roared back and up they came. We sagged into the air and inched our way up, passing the tower of Cricklade church lower than the red light on top of it. Somehow or other I managed to coax the combination up to our allotted altitude and gradually the faulty engine righted itself and we joined the stream on the way to the east coast. Aldeburgh was easy to pick out on such a fine day and we settled down for the crossing of the North Sea.

'A few miles out we saw a 'Dak' floating helplessly in the sea beneath us, with its glider not far away. The chump of a pilot had chosen that place to switch over to his overload tanks and got himself an airlock in the pipeline. Both engines stopped and down he went, but we could see launches speeding on their rescue mission. We made the Dutch coast and tightened our backsides in preparation for the long daylight flight over enemy territory. Fighter Command was doing their stuff, but most of them were so high up you could scarcely see them.

'We drew comfort from our brand-new flak suits. I had draped mine over my uniform as instructed, but Tiger had decided to sit on his. 'That's the part of my anatomy I want to protect,' he said. 'If I get that damaged, I might as well be dead anyway.' There was a very occasional puff of smoke in the air to show us that the Jerries were extending a welcome, but below us the Typhoons were taking care of their gun emplacements as soon as they opened fire. Then, with a whoosh, all hell broke loose. Not German fighters; not ack-ack. The Stirlings came up from behind with their superior speed and flew through the lot of us. We rocked and swayed in their slipstreams, but there was nothing we could do except hang on to the stick and swear. Then it was the Albemarles' turn and soon the sky was a huge jumble of aeroplanes and gliders - but I didn't see one collision.

'We were getting nearer the target now and there was an increase in the ack-ack. In front of us, a tow-rope was severed by the flying shrapnel and down went a glider all on its own, while the Dakota turned and headed for home, the shredded length of hawser still dangling from his tail. 'If he's got any sense,' I thought, 'he'll take that back to England with him.'

'We plodded on. The Stirlings were well out of sight now. They were dropping the chaps who would set up small radar transmitters for us to home on to. Hertogenbosch passed under us, then Eindhoven - and eventually Arnhem. As we crossed the river, the ground was already littered with crashed gliders and the air full of many more on their way down. I bade farewell to my pilot Captain 'Joe' Mills, with whom I had supped many a pint, got rid of the rope and climbed away at full throttle. Some two hours later I was back at Down Ampney, comparing notes and swapping yarns with the others. I don't think we lost anybody that day. I had been in the air exactly six hours.'

The glider missions to LZ's 'S' and 'Z' began inauspiciously with one glider grounded by damage before take-off and 23 gliders breaking loose over England. The RAF, flying at 2,500 feet, had run into clouds which the Americans a thousand feet below them had not encountered. Beyond the English coast the clouds were mostly above 2,500 feet, but even under these improved conditions one more glider broke loose over the Channel and seven over Holland. Engine trouble caused one combination to turn back and forced the release of three gliders, two of them over the sea and one over Schouwen. All occupants of the ditched gliders were rescued. A total of 39 gliders were unable to reach their zones.

In their flight over the northern route the two missions suffered even less from enemy action than did the American paratroop mission to Nijmegen, which accompanied them much of the way. Nearing the coast they encountered some flak from batteries and a barge. They saw very little flak thereafter, although there was considerable small-arms fire near Arnhem. No aircraft were lost and only six were damaged.

The level of route accuracy was high. No pilot is known to have lost his way. The RAF attributed this success mainly to excellent visual navigation. 'Gee' was unable in most cases to give a good target fix. This failure of what all the RAF pilots relied on as their primary radar aid was only partly due to jamming and partly to unspecified factors, one of which may have been distance. Less than half the fliers elected to use 'Rebecca'. Good results were reported by most of those interrogating the 'Eureka' on LZ 'S', but barely half of those attempting to pick up the one on LZ 'Z' got satisfactory responses. American experience indicates this poor performance may have been due to imperfect calibration.

At Broadwell near Brize Norton Private 'Johnny' Peters and his compatriots in 14 Platoon B' Company, 1st (Airborne) Battalion, The Border Regiment boarded Horsa Glider chalk number '161' in 2nd Wing, Glider Pilot Regiment and were introduced to the pilots, Lieutenant Colonel John Place and Lieutenant Ralph Alexander Maltby the second pilot. Maltby, who turned 26-years old on this very day served with the Royal Artillery and in 1942, as an expert in anti aircraft fire he had been one of sixteen officers who volunteered to fly as air gunners in bomber crews over Germany in order to study German anti-aircraft defences at first hand. He was mentioned in despatches and received an Order of the Patriotic War from the Soviet Union for this work. His cousin was Flight Lieutenant David Maltby DSO DFC who is credited with breaching the Möhne Dam. Ralph became attached to No. 2 Wing, The Glider Pilot Regiment as an Intelligence Officer and started piloting gliders.

'Only fourteen of our platoon emplaned' wrote 'Johnny' Peters. 'I was sent out with a Corporal Heaton to search for two of our company who had absconded during the night. Needless to say our search was fruitless.'

With the weather moderately bright but overcast, Horsa Glider chalk number '161' was towed off at 0945 by a Dakota on 575 Squadron piloted by Wing Commander T. A. 'Jeff' Jefferson AFC the commanding officer. All told, nineteen of 575 Squadron's aircraft were used to tow Horsas to their landing zones near Arnhem, each carrying men and equipment of the 1st Border.

'We crossed the North Sea and broke out into singing the hymn *Lead us Heavenly Father Lead us* wrote 'Johnny' Peters 'possibly as a result of remembering those 300 glider troops who were drowned during the invasion of Sicily. At least we could look down below us and see the Air Sea Rescue boats in attendance, which was a sobering thought.'

At the controls of 'Chalk number '161' Place and Maltby witnessed a V-2 missile launch en route to LZ 'S'. Then Wing Commander Jefferson reported a power fault on the Dakota which prevented the crew taking their intended dog-leg and only joined the formation thirty minutes from Arnhem.

'Upon crossing the flooded part of Holland where there was no flak in evidence and being the leading glider in the armada, it was different' continues 'Johnny' Peters. 'We reached drier ground where heavy ack-ack fire was brought to bear on our glider. It was good to see the rocket firing Typhoons of the RAF bearing down in front of us and firing their rockets.'

Both the glider and the tug aircraft suffered heavy fire crossing the Dutch border. John Bradbury, one of the members of 14 Platoon, recalled: 'All of us must have thought, 'What if Colonel Place should receive a fatal injury? Who would pilot the glider then?' Not that it made any difference, as by that time the glider would probably be in a deep dive and spinning like a corkscrew, which nobody would be able to get it out of, so the outcome was inevitable - we would all die. Soon we were turning over the LZ, nose down, diving almost vertical towards the ground to get away from the flak and machine guns.'

'Shortly after that a cry went up from the rear of the glider: 'The tail's coming off!' This message was relayed up to Bradbury, who was sitting just behind the cockpit: 'Sergeant Alan Watson and the platoon commander had not heard what was said, so I leaned over and yelled the message to Lieutenant Colonel Place, who sent Lieutenant Maltby to investigate. He returned from the tail end with a cheerful grin on his face as all he found was fabric flapping in the wind and yelled to one and all that it was only flak and that no serious damage had been done. He had just returned to his seat when there was a massive explosion right next to the cockpit that shook the whole frame and he slumped sideways in his seat. The side where he sat was a complete shambles and couldn't possibly be used again. Both Sergeant Tom Watson and I immediately rushed to help the lieutenant, despite the fact that Watson had also been wounded in the head. [Watson was killed in action four days later]. Regrettably, Maltby was dead before any of us could reach him; his face was an unrecognisable pulp and his chest looked like a huge claw had dug its way into him. Everyone, including me, realised what the outcome was and a sudden fear gripped each of us.'

The glider started to do all sorts of twists and turns. Maltby was actually at the controls of the glider when he was shot and killed, with Lieutenant Colonel John Place map-reading at the time. Alone at the controls, Colonel Place asked Wing Commander Jefferson to 'weave a bit' to help avoid the flak, but was told that the tug lacked the power to manoeuvre. 'Johnny' Peters' immediate thought and that of the others was, 'what if the pilot should be killed or wounded?' Needless to say that on approach to our landing zone, we were met with small arms fire, with bullets ripping through the floor of the Horsa, but miraculously only one soldier, Private Hughes our Bren gunner was hit in the leg.'

'His loud scream did not help anyone overcome their fears one little bit' says John Bradbury, 'especially as more rounds ripped through the side of the glider at the same time.'

Parting company with his tug and flying solo without his flying panel operational, Colonel Place took the glider down almost vertically and performed a copybook landing. 'Chalk 161' was the first glider to land. John Bradbury recalled: 'At the last minute the nose lifted and the landing was fast and furious and we bounced around like a rubber ball before we came to rest jammed between two trees with the nose inside a wooded area - our prayers had been answered! All we had to do now was get out without being shot and fight a battle against an enemy who were waiting for us.'

On landing the platoon debussed shaken and formed a defensive perimeter around the glider, whilst two wounded platoon members were tended to, the platoon equipment removed and the body of Lieutenant Ralph Maltby placed beneath the wing, for later burial. At this point a young private approached Colonel Place and said 'Sir, I just want to thank you.'[2]

Several gliders were forced to cast-off during the flight. However all the Dakotas on 575 Squadron returned to base without incident. 'As the remaining gliders were landing on LZ 'S' continues 'Johnny' Peters 'some were overshooting and crashing into the woods that were adjacent to the LZ causing deaths and serious injuries to the pilots and the glider troops. 'B' Company took up immediate defensive positions on top of the railway embankment to guard the drop zone X, as we waited for the arrival of the Parachute troops. They landed and 'B' Company under the command of Major T. Armstrong proceeded along the road towards Renkum. We met no opposition until we reached the outskirts where we bumped into a German armoured vehicle. It is hard to say who was the most surprised. After an exchange of fire we proceeded to our objective which was the local brickworks, which is still standing to this day.

The position for 'B' Company again became un-defendable and we were not that same fighting force who held the position three days earlier. The order was again given to withdraw, and the remnants were sent to different companies as reinforcements. I went to 'A' Company for a short while. It seemed that we were always digging in, not knowing where we were; no food and we were always in the open. We watched the supplies being dropped by our own aircraft, but sadly straight into the Germans hands. 14 Platoon had several of its members killed during this time. We kept hoping - when is the Army coming? The officers - they didn't know - but as a morale boost they said, 'They'll be here tomorrow. Tomorrow never came.' Only two of us returned home: me and Private Brooke, having successfully escaped across the Rhine to safety, which was out of a total of 25.'

When his mother in Liverpool was shown a picture of her son in the *Daily Express* which was captioned 'They Fought Like Lions' she promptly collapsed.

After the war John Bradbury found out that the estimated life expectancy for bomber crews over Europe during the war was approximately one hour 46 minutes. For fighter pilots it was nineteen minutes and for glider pilots it was seventeen seconds. 'Luckily nobody had ever told us, as I would have transferred immediately out of the air-landing brigade and gone to the RASC bath unit.'[3]

One other glider mission to the 82nd Division's sector was made by the British to take the Headquarters of 1st Airborne Corps to LZ 'N'. Dispatched were 38 aircraft of 38 Group towing 32 Horsas and six Hadrian (Waco) gliders which contained 105 airborne personnel and great quantities of equipment. One Horsa aborted over England, one over the sea and one broke loose over Holland. The other 35 gliders had a rather uneventful trip and landed safely in the Groesbeek area shortly after 1400. Photographs later established that 28 of the Horsas had landed on LZ 'N'. The first attempt to fly a corps headquarters into combat had succeeded.

The British troops assembled quickly and by 1530 hours had a corps CP functioning on the wooded slopes of the Groesbeek ridge near the northern edge of DZ 'N'. Unfortunately corps communications functioned very badly. Although radio contact was soon made with rear headquarters in England and with Second Army, no effective communication with First Airborne Division or with the 101st Division was achieved that day. Some improvement occurred on the 18th and some information was obtained by telephone, since Dutch patriots operated the exchanges in Arnhem and Nijmegen. Nevertheless, Browning's first full and reliable information on the situation at Arnhem was a Sitrep received at 0800 on the 19th and until that day he had little knowledge of or influence on operations outside the Nijmegen area.

The British airborne troops were to be delivered in four missions, three to Arnhem and one to Nijmegen. First, 130 aircraft of 46 Group and 23 of 38 Group were to release Horsa gliders on LZ 'S' beginning at 1300 hours. Then 167 aircraft of 38 Group would loose 154 Horsas and thirteen Hamilcar gliders on LZ 'Z'. Thirty Horsas at Manston (mostly) and Blakehill Farm would bring in troops of 1st Airlanding Brigade Group based at Heckington and Helpringham, including a newly formed anti-tank battery with 17-pounder guns aboard eight Hamilcars at Tarrant Rushton.

Next in line were the 38 aircraft which were to turn aside at Nijmegen and deliver British Corps Headquarters to LZ 'N'. Finally, 143 C-47s in the 52nd Troop Carrier Wing would fly to DZ 'X' and drop 1st Parachute Brigade there at 1355. The paratroop mission to Arnhem, flown by two serials of the 314th Troop Carrier Group and two from the 61st Group, began its take-offs from Saltby and Barkston Heath at 1121 hours and had all its aircraft in the air by 1155. In the 61st TCG the first serial of 36 C-47s dropped 559 paratroops and the second of 35 C-47s carried 609 men; all aircraft returning safely. They assembled smoothly and had a rather uneventful trip over the northern route. Slight and ineffectual flak greeted them as they reached the continent and there was some flak from near Elst and Wageningen in the Arnhem area. However, not an aircraft was shot down and only five were damaged. The formation leaders reported their 'Gee' sets were badly jammed, but 'Rebecca' guided them well. The white panels on the zones showed up clearly and the blue smoke was particularly effective in the still air.

At 0945 Stirling IV 'K-King' piloted by Pilot Officer 'Les' Bellinger on 'A' Flight in 295 Squadron in 38 Group lifted its huge bulk, plus a fully laden Horsa glider, clear of the Harwell runway and climbed slowly over the green Berkshire downs turning on course. 'The weather was superb' he recalled. 'Below, smoke curled lazily from village chimneys, tractors ploughed the stubble fields and people were strolling to church. It was difficult to remember we were at war and the Airborne were on their way to very serious fighting. The trip over to Holland was for us, uneventful. We saw aircraft with engine trouble dropping out of the main stream, casting their gliders clear, turning and heading for land or the North Sea not too far below. Waiting below was a small armada of boats. Some were stationary with beacons to keep us dead on course, but the majority were air-sea rescue craft. (Later at briefing we found some of the cast off gliders carried vital equipment and its loss helped to change the balance between success and failure). In crowded company, we reached our dropping area and over the intercom line wished our glider boys the best of luck. Once they recognized their nominated landing zone, they released, 'K-King' surged forward and we knew our lads were on their way. Following the main stream we dropped our towrope at a prearranged spot and set course for base. The flak had been light but persistent.'

'Ken' Bowman, who had joined 298 Squadron in September, was piloting a Halifax towing a Horsa glider from Tarrant Rushden to the drop zone near Arnhem. It was his first operation. Two years earlier he had been called up and went to Lords Cricket Ground which was the aircrew reception centre. The next two years, including seven months in Canada were spent mainly training and the airborne operation to Arnhem was his first operation.

'We were flying in loose formation and there were many dozens of aircraft in the sky. Lots of incidents occurred during the flight to Holland which involved mishaps to several of the aircraft. I witnessed some of these including a glider ditching after its rope had broke and also a glider being shot down due to anti-aircraft fire. I assumed the occupants of the ditched glider would have been picked up by an Air Sea Rescue Launch. As we flew towards Arnhem we experienced anti-aircraft flak, some of which shot the tail off the glider flying immediately in front of us. The occupants of that particular glider stood no chance of survival whatsoever. As we approached the drop zone more flak was noticed. I observed the many parachutes and gliders on the ground which indicated that many of the troops had arrived at the intended destination. We dropped the glider about ten miles from the centre of Arnhem then we turned around to head back to our base.'

A reporter from the *Daily Herald* reported the Dutch people, in their Sunday best, coming from church with their mouths open at the sight above them. The gliders went down parking up, wing tip to wing tip in straight lines; just like cars in a garage. Michael Moynihan of the *News Chronicle* flew in Halifax 'M for Mike' that towed a Hamilcar known as *The Undertaker and his Stiffs* flown by Staff Sergeant Hill and Sergeant Openshaw to Arnhem. William Troughton of the *Daily Express* flew in Stirling 'P for Peter' piloted by six feet tall, sandy-haired Canadian Flight Lieutenant 'Bill' Gardner from Vancouver.[4]

Sergeant Walter Simpson, sitting in the turret of a Stirling watched a Horsa glider carrying twenty-one men of the 9th Airborne Field Company, Royal Engineers come apart when 'the back end just dropped off the front.' Simpson shouted to the captain, 'My God, the glider's coming apart!' The tow rope broke and the front of the glider sank 'like a rock falling to earth.' The Stirling left formation, gradually lost height and turned back to locate the wreckage. The front half was spotted in a field near the village of Paulton near Weston-super-Mare in Somerset. The tail was nowhere to be seen. Marking the spot, the crew returned to Keevil and drove by jeep to the crash location where Simpson saw what appeared 'like a match box that had been stepped on.' The bodies of the men had remained inside. 'It was just a mass of arms, legs and bodies.' There were no survivors.'

By the time the last serials reached the English coast - the northern streams passing over the checkpoint at Aldeburgh, the southern columns flying over Bradwell Bay - thirty troop - and equipment-carrying gliders were down. Tug engine failure, broken tow ropes and in places, heavy clouds, caused 23 gliders to part from their tugs.[5]

Although by military standards the operation had begun with eminent success - casualties were light and many of the men and most of the downed cargo would be flown in on later lifts - the losses were sure to hurt. On this vital day when every man, vehicle and piece of equipment was important to General Urquhart, twenty-three of his glider loads were already lost. Not until the Arnhem force reached its drop and landing zones would commanders discover just how crucial these losses would be.

Now, as the long sky trains swarmed out over the English Channel and the land fell behind, a new kind of expectancy began to permeate the armada. From the marshalling points at March and Hatfield, the airborne columns were aided by various navigational devices: radar beacons, special hooded lights and radio direction-finding signals. Over the North Sea, beacons on ships began to guide the planes. Additionally, strings of launches - seventeen along the northern route, ten below the southern flight path-stretched away across the water. To Flight Sergeant William Thompson, at the controls of an aircraft towing a four-ton Horsa glider, 'there wasn't much navigating to do. The launches below us were set out like stepping stones across the Channel.' But these fast naval vessels were much more than directional aids. They were part of a vast air-sea rescue operation - and they were already busy.

Staff Sergeant Godfrey Freeman, a glider co-pilot recalled: 'It was my first operation, I didn't know what to expect. The intercom crackled. 'OK, tug,' said the pilot, 'leaving you any minute now. Thanks for a lovely ride.'

'Don't mention it, it was a pleasure.'

'He pushed down the release lever and we were off, slowing down to gliding speed, beginning to lose height. I kept a sharp look out for other gliders crossing our path. There were none. As we made a half circuit, I waited for the first shots to be fired at us, but none came. We swung into another turn, half flap down, the nose dipped; 400 feet. Full flap, we were standing on our nose. Surely someone down there had his sights on us; we seemed to hang in the air. We flattened out, bump, jolt, rolling a few yards, stop. Down in one piece, we had landed unopposed. We sweated for half an hour before the load was off. Still there was no opposition.'

In immense triple columns, together at least ten miles across and approximately 100 miles long, the vast armada swept over the English countryside. The 82nd Airborne and 1st British Division, en route to Nijmegen and Arnhem, flew along the northern track. A special serial of

63

38 gliders carrying General Browning's Corps Headquarters bound for Nijmegen travelled with them. In his younger days, Browning had been an Olympic class athlete. Now, with his glider down on the US LZ just yards from the Reichswald forest marking the German border, he used his speed for a very personal purpose. Returning a few minutes later, he explained that he 'wanted to be the first British officer to pee in Germany.' Browning also unfurled a pennant bearing a light blue Pegasus against a maroon background he wanted placed on his jeep. When he was appointed commander of the 1st Airborne Division on 3 November 1941, in this new role he was instrumental in parachutists adopting the maroon beret and assigned an artist, Major Edward Seago to design the Parachute Regiment's now famous emblem of the warrior Bellerophon riding Pegasus, the winged horse.

On the southern route, passing over Bradwell Bay, the 101st Airborne headed for its drop zones slightly north of Eindhoven. In the thirty-minute trip across the North Sea, gliders bobbed on the water as low-flying amphibious planes circled to mark their positions until rescue launches could reach the spot. From his Horsa, Lieutenant Neville Hay, of the 'Phantom' fact-gathering liaison unit, watched 'with complete detachment two downed gliders and another ditching.' He tapped his corporal on the shoulder. 'Have a look down there, Hobkirk,' Hay shouted. The corporal glanced down and, as Hay remembers, 'I could almost see him turn green.' Hay hurriedly reassured the man. 'There's nothing to worry about. Look at the boats already picking them up.' Hay's Horsa was one of two carrying 'Phantom' sections that were towed from Manston by Albemarle aircraft. In the other was the 'Phantom' section led by Lieutenant Colonel Derek Heathcoat-Amory. He had taken two days' leave to come on the operation, having talked his old friend Brigadier John Winthrop 'Shan' Hackett DSO MBE MC commanding 4th Parachute Brigade into taking him with him as a 'special liaison'.

Staff Sergeant Joseph Kitchener, piloting a glider saw an air-sea rescue launch that came alongside a floating glider and pick up the men so fast I don't even think they got their feet wet.' Another glider pilot, Staff Sergeant Cyril Line, saw one combination drop slowly out of position. The Horsa cut loose and descended almost leisurely towards the sea. A ring of white foam appeared as it hit the water. He wondered 'who the poor devils were.' Then the starboard propellers on the Stirling pulling his glider slowed and stopped and Line found himself 'in the embarrassing position of overtaking my own tug.' He immediately released the tow line and his co-pilot called out, 'Stand by for ditching!' From behind in the cabin, they could hear rifle butts crashing against the side of the glider's plywood fuselage as the frantic passengers tried to open up an escape route. Rapidly losing altitude, Line looked back and was horrified to see that the desperate troopers had 'cut through the top of the glider and the sides were just beginning to go.' Line screamed out, 'Stop that! Strap yourselves in!' Then, with a heavy thud, the glider hit the water. When Line surfaced, he saw the wreckage floating some thirty feet away. There was no sign whatever of the cabin, but within minutes, all were picked up.

Apart from some long-range inaccurate shelling of a downed glider, there was no serious enemy opposition during the Channel crossing. By the time the convoy passed the Dutch coast thirty gliders had been lost in the clouds, mainly through broken tow ropes. But flak was not nearly as heavy as had been predicted and the enemy fighters that were seen attacked the high fighter cover but did not interfere with the main formations. It was, one of the Stirling pilots said afterwards, 'no trouble at all - a piece of cake'.

On release short of Nijmegen, General Browning's pilot, Colonel George S. Chatterton, began circling down. Chatterton's glider had flown in an American serial carrying the staffs of operation 'Market'. They included Wing Commander John Laurence Brown MBE who was in charge of two mobile radar units or LWUs (Light Warning Units). Radar surveillance and control coverage of the pocket at Arnhem was not good enough to provide effective fighter protection for the troops on the ground. All the Fighter Direction Posts (FDP) and Ground Control Interception (GCI) units were behind the main front line in some cases by several miles, so at the beginning of September 6080 and 6341 LWUs were transferred from 60 Group to 38 Group and attached to Headquarters 1st British Airborne Corps.[6] Brown was a veteran controller of the North African campaign and arguably the first fighter control 'ace' with over 100 'kills' to his name. Originally it was intended that the LWUs would go on the first lift but a lack of aircraft tugs meant that 6080 and 6341 LWUs would fly on day two in four Horsa gliders. In fact their participation had been in doubt right up until the last moment. A meeting at Bentley Priory on the 15th the representative of the First Allied Airborne Army stated that the transportable ground radar equipment would not be required for the operation but on the 16th Brown had met with Browning at RAF Harwell and the decision was reversed. Little did Brown know that he had become the architect of his own death.

Chatterton created a great imaginary funnel and ended his downward flight in a skid that brought the glider abruptly into a small cabbage garden behind several farm cottages. A few Dutch people wandered up and watched almost disinterestedly as Browning and others in the glider got out. Brown had apparently forgotten his sleeping bag and decided to retrieve it. On his way to do this the DZ was strafed by a Me 109 and he was hit. He died of his wounds the next day.

Twenty-eight other gliders had landed in the same zone. One piloted by American pilot Arthur Kaplan landed in a field near Chatterton's glider under sporadic mortar fire. He helped unload his cargo and set off with his passengers towards their RV. Passing a barn, they heard suspicious noises from inside and burst in. 'There - in one of the stalls' recalled Kaplan 'a paratrooper was making love to a very willing Dutch girl. He was quite profane at being interrupted, so we apologized and left ... The guy couldn't have been on the ground more than an hour.'

Up to now the immense armada had mesmerized the German ground troops into inaction, but they awakened and reacted, lobbing artillery rounds on to the area. Shortly, German forces assembling nearby began to fire at Chatterton. Then in the distance Chatterton and his passengers heard a great roaring like a waterfall and they ran out into the open, disregarding the German fire. Coming towards them overhead they saw a vast armada of aeroplanes, each towing two gliders. It was the American transport column looking like a swarm of angry bees. The sight staggered the British, as well as the Germans. They stopped firing and watched with awe.

During high mass Father H. C. Bruggeman at the Mill Hill Fathers' House heard sirens and constant planes flying over. 'After mass we saw even bigger formations fly over. After eleven they came back in formations of six, accompanied by fighters. Deelen Airport was bombed, bombs fell in Arnhem, also in Wolfheze. From the back path we saw the smoke clouds above Wolfhezen. The air remained crowded with planes. The English fighters dived down without stopping to see if there were hostile targets. During lunch a couple of fighters flew that low over the Amsterdamsestraatweg that we all hid under the tables or in cupboards. All this activity was beautiful, but bizarre. We didn't understand what this action meant, but that didn't last long.

'After dinner the overwhelming sound of planes increased. From the west we saw planes diving down in two's but only one came up again. Then we realised that they were gliders and our liberators had landed. We were dancing and jumping around like madmen. Most of the fathers came out to witness this rare spectacle. Most of the brothers found it sad that it was holy hour at three, because now it was happening. Later, on behalf of the rector, Father van de Laar said we all had to sleep outside and prepare a suitcase to be ready in case of an emergency. I didn't get permission to sleep in the farmer's chicken house. At around five a German tank came from the direction of Arnhem and it was positioned facing the Dieckman family's house, at the entrance of Warnsborn. Father Rombouts, who lived with the family, thought it would be safer to move in to the brother's house. Gerrit Dieckman, the youngest son, came to sleep with the fathers on the yard. We brought food, water, knives and butter into shelters. In the lounge we spoke only about the coming liberation. We didn't think of danger, not even with a tank 100 metres' from us with the barrel pointing in our direction, ready to fire. Everybody thought and said: tomorrow, when we wake up, we will wake up free.'

The first lift from Harwell had gone well with 25 gliders assigned to transport the First Airborne Corps headquarters and the Light Warning Units force commander, Wing Commander Laurence Brown, arguably the most successful interception controller of the war was on this lift. Originally it was intended that the LWUs would go on the first lift but a lack of aircraft tugs meant that 6080 and 6341 LWUs commanded by Squadron Leaders Wheeler and Coxon respectively would fly from Harwell on day two in four Horsa gliders. The pathfinders of Major 'Boy' Wilson's 21st Independent Parachute Company that had taken off in twelve Stirlings at 1015 were now firm in its positions, guarding sixteen prisoners and quite content with its acquisition of a German staff car, though Wilson admitted that it was a lonely period for them until the drone of the airborne armada could be heard approaching in the distance. Immediately they began putting out more markers. Presently the first lift came in and 130 Dakotas and 23 Albemarle and Halifax aircraft released their 152 Horsa and Hamilcar gliders, carrying elements of 1st Airlanding Brigade (less two companies of South Staffs and some Brigade vehicles). Nineteen minutes' later they were followed by 181 Stirling, Halifax and Dakota aircraft who released 156 Horsa, six CG-4A Waco (carrying USAAF air support teams) and eleven Hamilcars carrying other elements of 1st Airlanding Brigade and Urquhart's vehicles and artillery on LZ 'Z'. As the gliders began to come down all over the landing zones 'Boy' Wilson saw one such craft undergoing some drastic manoeuvring to avoid overshooting the zone, but one of its wings hit the ground, causing it to swing violently and skid along, tearing up earth as it went until the glider itself broke apart under the strain. Men from the Independent Company rushed to help and found men getting out with a number of bruises and cuts, though not a single serious casualty. By chance Wilson recognised an old friend in the glider pilot, an ex-Guardsman now with a blackened and a grazed face and he invited him to his Company HQ in the farmhouse for a drink of water. He poured the man a glass of whiskey and upon tasting he remarked 'My God, this Dutch water's good!'

The Independent Company had been told that any they might see or hear would be friendly; but as they were completing their task, they looked up and saw a number of Messerschmitt Bf 109Gs diving on them. They leapt hastily for cover as the 109s began strafing the glider landing zone. Wing Commander Brown had apparently left his sleeping bag in his glider and was on his way to retrieve it when he was hit by the strafing Messerschmitts. He died of his wounds the following day and is buried in the Groesbeek Canadian War Cemetery. Thirty-two of the 1,914 parachutists who jumped were killed by German ground fire or in accidents and eight men died as a result of pile-ups when the gliders landed with the rest of the division's guns and vehicles and the part of the 2nd Battalion South Staffordshire Regiment that had not been flown in on the previous day.

With their path finding role successfully completed and few casualties sustained, the Independent Company spent the initial days of the battle in the Divisional reserve, setting out to mark the drop zones for subsequent lifts as they came.

In one of the Dakotas approaching the LZ west of Arnhem Colonel Frost noticed the 'transparent insincerity' of his troop's smiles and the 'furious last-minute puffing at their cigarettes' and felt acutely conscious of their tension and their fear. 'While the red light glowed I peered anxiously ahead at the dropping zone', he remembers. 'At ten minutes to 'H-Hour' I stood in the doorway and tried to compare the country with my memory of the map. I was surprised to see no sign of any activity on the ground and thankful for the lack of opposition of any kind. The stick had travelled well, but as usual one could feel the tension among them all. The transparent insincerity of their smiles and the furious last-minute puffing at their cigarettes reminded me that the flight and prospect of jumping far behind the enemy lines was no small test for anyone's nervous system and I remembered that this was my first jump since Sicily fourteen months ago. We passed the Waal and finally the Lek, for whose bridges we were to do battle, while the red light glowed. I peered anxiously ahead at the DZ for any signs of trouble. In front and below parachutes were falling and then I was out. Once again the thrill of falling, the great relief of feeling the harness pulling and that highly satisfactory bounce as the canopy filled with air. The rigging lines were slightly twisted, needing a vigorous pull on the lift webs to bring me round and leave me free to enjoy the feeling of floating down. Following this came the fear of injury on hitting the ground; a last feverish pull as I touched down and then a resounding bang on the back of my helmet told me that all was well. There was no sound of enemy action, just the steady continual drone of aircraft approaching, leaving rows and clusters of parachutes in the air, followed by the fiercer note of their engines as they wheeled for home at increased speed. I felt grateful for the way they had done their task. A few kitbags broke away from the men as they were released, making it wise to keep a good look-out.'

'Saturday morning, 16 September, we had been given our final briefing and issued with ammunition and rations' recalled 26-year old Lance Corporal Arthur Hendy in 'B' Troop, 1st Parachute Squadron. 'The majority of the Squadron had served in the campaigns in North Africa, Sicily and Italy. The three Troops, 'A', 'B' and 'C' were usually detached to work with the 1st, 2nd or 3rd Battalions. We had been together before they were designated as The Parachute Regiment and we were referred to as 'The Battalions' or 'Bat Boys'. For this operation our role was different. 'A' and 'B' Troops were to make for the Bridge, with 'C' Troop to remain in the DZ area. Before we set off we were able to obtain the Sunday newspapers. Our morale was high at the good news we read of the latest Allied advances. Most of us carried Sten guns and in our kit-bags we had a rifle and extra ammunition. As we boarded the plane we were given extra bandoliers of .303 ammunition and hand-grenades.

'The flight was uneventful. Lieutenant Dennis Simpson emphasised that we get one of the containers, which the aircraft would drop and congregate by it. As the green light went on everyone appeared to be making a quick exit, but I was not able to move forward. It appeared that number 16 in the stick had caught his rigging line up on one of the seats and number 17, Lance Corporal 'Joe' Malley, was trying to push past him. The jammed rigging line finally cleared but in doing so his kit-bag had become released from his leg. He had no time to strap it on again and threw it out of the plane before jumping. The jump master shouted 'Good Luck' and I followed 'Joe' out of the door. We both landed in a small copse. As Malley had lost his kit-bag which contained his rifle and only had a Sten gun, I gave him the extra grenades and Gammon bomb from my kit. We were now some distance from the DZ. The drop must have finished as we could not detect any aircraft. We were not sure which direction the DZ was so started to go in what we thought was the right direction. The first contact we made was with a young Dutchman, about sixteen years of age, driving a horse and cart. As we approached him he thought we were Germans as our uniforms were similar. I opened my smock to reveal the English signs on my tunic and his attitude changed immediately. He indicated to us to get on the cart and then took us to a farmhouse which was the home of his family. They gave us food and wine, but we were unable to make them understand that we wanted to get to Arnhem. The lad finally indicated to us to board the cart. I don't know if it was luck or what but we feared for his safety if he was caught with us. We later picked up another heavily laden man; he was an American who like us had got lost. He dropped with the Brigadier's party. When we finally arrived at the DZ everyone had moved on except for a small Medical Unit which was treating those injured during the drop. Amongst them were 'Ted' Laker and 'Geordie' Plunton, two of my section. They had damaged their ankles so decided to board the cart and come with us. The Medics were able to tell us that the Brigadier had gone with the 3rd Battalion, so Malley and I decided to take the American to find Brigadier Lathbury whom we knew well by sight. We made good progress and the Dutch lad was still keen to take us. We met up with the Brigadier's party, which had another American officer with it; also a Dutch Captain who had dropped with the Brigadier.'

The flight taken by Lance Sergeant Harold Padfield in 'B' Troop, 1st Parachute Squadron commanded by Lieutenant Dennis Simpson his stick commander in their C-47 in the 61st TCG had been quite smooth and had 'plenty of fighter escort'. 'When we had crossed the North Sea we heard gunfire, but nothing to worry about. When we saw the dykes and windmills of Holland, we knew that time was getting close. The butterflies had risen from their slumbers and were playing havoc with my stomach. Lieutenant Simpson told us to hook up and it was then 'Red On, 'Action Stations', 'Green On', 'Go', time 1407 hours, or to the uninitiated, seven minutes past two. A good exit, no twists, not a lot of oscillation, but there was a tree in my way. I could see I wasn't going to miss it, so I took evasive action to cover my face. The 'chute was caught was caught in the branches and I just hung there. I hit my release box, pulled out the leg straps and lowered myself onto a branch and climbed down. The scene was bewildering, gliders were coming in thick and fast, many with a horrible 'crunch' and there were hundreds of parachutists, at any other time it would have been a sight to behold. I spotted blue smoke for my rendezvous and ran over to join the rest of my stick. We collected our weapons and stores and moved off in the direction of Wolfhezen. In battle we carried our explosives and grenades on our person, so you made sure that the detonators were stored where you wouldn't fall on them. As we moved off the dropping zone, we came across a German vehicle and a German General and his driver who had been killed, which brought you to the reality of the situation we were in. We marched in single file with our rifles at alert, but it was all quiet. Then we were welcomed by the Dutch people like conquering heroes. As we left Wolfhezen and came to the outskirts of Oosterbeek, we saw a lot of men dressed in white, they were quite strange looking and eerie, they were apparently from an asylum down the road.'

Lance Corporal Jack Bird of the 2nd Battalion, The South Staffords was in a glider that left from Broadwell aerodrome. 'I think all the RAF personnel turned out to give us a good send off - personally wished they had taken our places in the gliders and we had been doing the waving off. As we rose into the air and made for the Channel I said to myself: 'This is it!' and got stuck in to my haversack rations. The sky seemed full of gliders on either side of us and we swept along in formation; the weather being perfect. I saw rescue launches cruising about in the Channel waiting to pick up anybody who had the misfortune (?) to come down - needless to say our luck was out. Then we were over the Dutch coast (the time being about one o'clock) and below could be seen the flooded areas and of course down went one or two gliders - wonder where they finished up! We were encountering flak and it could be seen coming up at us, but luckily our glider was not hit. We carried on to our DZ which we reached at about two o'clock and after being cast off by our tug plane we sailed down to make a perfect landing, although there was not much room and gliders lay all over the place - many had come to grief and some were on fire, but the majority seemed to have come down OK. Out we jumped and took up defensive positions around the glider whilst the kit was unloaded. Then we moved off to the battalion rendezvous at Reijers Camp Farm. There we picked up the rest of our Machine Gun Platoon and then waited for the battalion to form up for the move to our objective - Arnhem'.

Twenty-four year old Sergeant Ernest 'Sim' Simion and Staff Sergeant 'Ron' Gibson, two 2nd Wing glider pilots had a smooth flight over Holland after taking off from Tarrant Rushton with a jeep, an anti-tank gun and two of the gun crew from the Border Regiment. 'At Aldeburgh' says 'Ron' Gibson 'we turned south east over North Sea. As we passed over the dunes on the Dutch coast we ran into some flak. Our tug pilot pulled us into some cloud to avoid it and then we went below cloud over flooded Lower Holland. As we approached the landing zone at Arnhem we could see some big fires blazing in the town and along the railway line on one edge of the ploughed field where we had to land. We released from 3,000 feet and had to weave our way through a host of gliders that all seemed to aim for the same point. We touched down in a ploughed field on the side of a pine wood and unloaded the gun and jeep, hacking the tail off. There were few enemies in the woods at that time and it was eerily quiet. Then we drove off to our rendezvous at 1330.'

There had not been enough glider space for Lieutenant Derrick Randall RAMC and his medical section, so had he hitched a lift for himself with two medical panniers and a precious 'Tilly' pressure lamp in an Artillery jeep loaded in a Horsa glider that set out from Tarrant Rushton airfield. The rest of his team were in the 'seaborne tail'. 'After a pretty quiet flight we landed about 1330 hours and I established a temporary aid post, i.e. my panniers and myself, by some bushes on the edge of the Landing Zone. An interesting casualty was a sergeant from my own anti tank unit. On landing, his Hamilcar glider had somersaulted and he had been doubled up under his 17 pounder. I was fairly sure that he had sustained a crush fracture of a lumbar vertebra. The standard treatment of this at that time was total immobilization in a full length body plaster. Obviously this was out of the question. As he had managed to get himself over to me and seemed to be reasonably comfortable I suggested that he 'carried on very gently with minimal activity'. Naïve perhaps, in view of subsequent events! I was very relieved when a long time later in England I heard that he had done very well! It is interesting that such 'mobilisation' treatment became standard some years later!

Sergeant 'Ron' Kent waiting for the Brigade on DZ 'X' recalled: 'Above us the Dakotas began disgorging the men who in North Africa had earned us the nom de guerre, 'the Red Devils' [Roten Teufel]. The sky blossomed with hundreds of parachutes bearing the tough and exuberant men of the 1st, 2nd and 3rd Parachute Battalions. I had a number of old comrades with these battalions. I saw one of them before he led his section off the DZ. We wished each other luck and promised we would meet for a beer in Arnhem once we got to the bridge and Second Army linked up. Watching those battalions forming up and streaming off the DZ in the direction of Arnhem, I had no reason to doubt that we would do just that in a few days' time. So far there had been no shooting, but as the battalions moved away from us, sporadic shots could be heard from about half a mile away. Our job was done and we had orders to RV about a mile away to the north.'

Sergeant Neville George Griffin of the Adjutant and Quartermaster Branch, Headquarters 1st Airborne Division landed at LZ 'Z' near Heelsum from RAF Fairford in the Horsa glider which carried Lieutenant Colonel Henry Preston and the Assistant Adjutant and Quartermaster General with a jeep and trailer. Griffin was not particularly happy about going by glider. As a trained parachutist he would have preferred to be 'jumping in' on the operation. 'Lieutenant Colonel Preston insisted I go with him in his glider as he wanted me to take his little black leather office box. We were the second glider out of Fairford and I did not enjoy the ride!' Colonel Preston's Horsa encountered some flak as they crossed the Dutch coast and upon landing another glider cut across their front causing the pilot of their own glider to veer away. Although no one was hurt the nose was dug-in and the tail high in the air, with Bill's typewriter lost in the crash. Once on the ground the situation from Bill's point of view did not improve as he witnessed other gliders landing. 'Hamilcars had a problem landing. I saw a glider pilot screaming from his injuries following a bad landing. I gave him morphine and left him. It was all I could do for him.' Later when the HQ came under sustained German mortar fire they had to move back amongst the gliders and set up under the wing of a Hamilcar.

Making his approach in his Hamilcar with the words *Bun House* - the name of Staff Sergeant Jenks' local pub - inscribed in large chalked letters on it, Gordon Jenks saw a Horsa crash. Everyone inside died when the 75 mm howitzer broke from its chain mooring and crushed the gun crew and decapitated the pilot and co-pilot. He knew that the ground ahead was too soft and he decided against landing in the field. Below in the great hold of his Hamilcar he carried a 17-pounder gun and trailer, eight men, a 3-ton lorry and a supply of high explosive shells. 'I reckoned that if we went into a dive right then we would have enough speed for me to hold her off the deck until we had cleared the fence and got safely into the next field' said Jenks. He pushed the control column forward, dived, then levelled out a few feet above the ground. Easing the huge aircraft gently over the fence, Jenks 'put her down in the far field, as lightly as a feather.'

Derrick Shingleton and 'Ray' Percival landed their Horsa east of Wolfhezen. As the glider touched down, the tail section, which had been hit by enemy bullets, failed to respond to the controls and the glider swung violently sideways before breaking in two. Incredibly, no-one was hurt and the crew performed the swiftest unloading of a jeep and gun that Shingleton had ever seen.

When they had neared the Dutch coast Private 'Bill' Gibbard in the 2nd Battalion heard the order to hook up and get ready to go. 'As I looked out of the open door I could see acres of open ground with gorse bushes. The red light came on, followed by the green and out we went. There was an amazing sight - the sky was completely filled with parachutes! I landed safely and we gathered ourselves together on a road, guided by our Commanding Officer, Lieutenant Colonel John Frost blowing his hunting horn.

'There was no difficulty in finding the way to the rendezvous' recalled Frost. 'En route some Dutch people greeted us... Just as I was beginning to feel that on the whole things could not be going better, the sound of firing broke out in the woods not more than three hundred yards from where I was standing and I moved to a track junction in the middle of the wood, which was where we had planned to set up Battalion Headquarters. A battle at our rendezvous in the woods was one of the things to be feared most of all. It was vital that we should be able to move off without delay and equally vital that our ammunition should not be expended unduly early when we had so much to do.'

All over the drop and landing zones, where 5,191 men of the division had arrived safely, units were assembling, forming up and moving out. General Urquhart 'couldn't have been more pleased. Everything appeared to be going splendidly.' The same thought occurred to 36-year old Sergeant Major John Clifford Lord, a six foot two inches ex-Grenadier Guardsman, who had appointed himself as General Urquhart's bodyguard. John Lord was born on 26 April 1908 in Southport, Lancashire. He was enlisted into the 3rd Grenadier Guards in 1933 and then posted to Egypt, where he remained for three years. He left the British Army in March 1937 and two days later joined the Brighton Police Force, serving with them until 3 December 1939 when he rejoining the Grenadier Guards on the following day. Lord qualified as a parachutist on 30 November 1941 and was posted, as Regimental Sergeant Major, to the newly formed 3rd Parachute Battalion. With them he participated in the operations in North Africa, Sicily and Italy. The veteran paratrooper recalls that Arnhem 'was one of the best exercises I'd ever been on. Everyone was calm and businesslike.' But the reservations he had had before take-off still bothered him. As he looked about, seeing the men assembling rapidly, with no enemy to contend with, he remembered thinking, 'It's all too good to be true.'

Major Ian Jodrell Toler DFC, Commanding 'B' Squadron, No.1 Wing, Glider Pilot Regiment and his co-pilot, 25-year old Staff Sergeant Arthur 'Shack' Shackleton (who acted as the former's bodyguard), flew the lead glider - a Horsa carrying Lieutenant Colonel W. Derek H. McCardie of the 2nd South Staffords with his command radio crew and jeep. The glider landed on LZ 'S', just fifty yards from the Battalion rendezvous at the Reijers Camp Farm. The four hundred and twenty men of the Battalion were assigned the task of clearing Wolfhezen of enemy troops and then securing LZ 'S' by digging in around the north-eastern area of the zone. Toler recalled: 'We were towed by an Albemarle from Manston. Over the

North Sea we sighted the rest of the force, stretching as far as the eye could see. We crossed the Dutch coast and flew on over the flooded fields, as our escort Spitfires and Typhoons appeared. Shackleton, my co-pilot, now flying the glider, fought the slipstream, leaving me to read the map. I easily recognized the three rivers and our last pinpoint - the bend on the River Lek. Soon I saw my LZ 'S' and our release point. Then up into high tow and with a 'cheerio' to my tug pilot, I released the tow rope and we were off. Speed back to 90 knots: half flap until almost up to the LZ; then full flap and nose down. The stick was fully forward but still the speed kept at 80: terrific juddering as if stalling, but we dropped fast going straight for the LZ. The landing was OK but well short of the overshoot boundary. I took off full flap and ran on, but halfway across the LZ we ran into soft plough and this pulled us up rapidly. I undid my straps, clambered out and lay panting on the ground, as the other gliders swished in and landed all around us amid plumes of dust; but some crashed into trees or collided with other gliders. I helped unload the glider, by removing the tail section - not always an easy task. We got the jeep out and I drove with Colonel McCardic to the RV where I organized my pilots for the defence of the LZ.'

'Shack' Shackleton who had transferred to the Glider Pilot Regiment after initially joining a heavy artillery regiment in Derbyshire, was to recall: 'At dawn we started the attack. But they were waiting for us with Panzer tanks. Three hundred and fifty of us were killed in one hour.' Toler and Shackleton established a command post in a cellar close to the Hartenstein Hotel. By 25 September, after days of relentless shelling and mortaring, mounting casualties and no sign of reinforcements, it was clear that the position was hopeless. Toler, by then in command of the regiment, was ordered to make a strategic withdrawal across the river during the night. He put Shackleton in charge of a file of airborne troops who were leaderless. At about 2200 hours Toler and Shackleton set off towards positions in a forest where they acted as guides during the evacuation to the south side of the Rhine. They spent two or three hours directing men along a safe route and when there were no more arrivals they decided to go to the river. They came across a small group of stragglers and Toler told Shackleton to stay with them while he found a way to the river. 'Shack' recalled: 'Suddenly I heard a burst of machine gun fire and I felt like someone had hit my arm with a sledgehammer. When I turned I saw that the others were dead. Then I felt my hand was sticky and blood running down my sleeve.' He set off in the direction of the river and there he met Toler again. Toler helped

Shackleton into a boat but while crossing the river it was hit by a mortar shell and Shackleton was thrown into the water. He was a non-swimmer and resigned himself to the inevitable. 'Suddenly I was in the river on my back. I felt my leg bump down into some mud and I heard someone say 'here's a body washed up' and I shouted, 'I'm not a body, I'm alive.' His rescuers were probably Canadian engineers, who took him to a field dressing station. The medics first attempted to remove the bullet and pieces of shrapnel from his shoulder and the rest of his body. At Toler's insistence, 'Shack' was evacuated with other wounded. From then on he was admitted to successive hospitals, finally being put on a hospital train to St. Elizabeth's hospital in Birmingham to recuperate.

'As we flew on that memorable Sunday' recalled Trooper John Bateman 'from the ground, thousands watched the great winged armada; an unforgettable sight winging its way towards the coast after many standbys for operations and cancellations. We flew for Holland and as we crossed the Dutch coast, we flew through the anti-aircraft gunfire. It was pretty nerve-racking. We got the green light to jump and landed on the dropping zone of Wolfhezen.'

The 1st Airlanding Brigade (the 7th Battalion King's Own Scottish Borderers, the 1st Battalion Border Regiment and half of the 2nd Battalion South Staffordshire Regiment) landed safely, the only casualty on their LZ being a pilot who was killed as he crashed into a tree. The cargoes were quickly unloaded and the men rallied to a piper playing *Blue Bonnets over the Border* so that by 1500 the battalion was fully formed and began securing and preparing to defend the landing areas for the second lift.

General Urquhart had landed at Renkum Heath. He too was struck by the stillness. 'It was,' he recalls, 'incredibly quiet. Unreal.' While Colonel Charles Mackenzie set up the division's tactical headquarters at the edge of the woods, Urquhart headed for the parachute dropping zones, four hundred yards away. The gliders carrying the 1st Air Landing Brigade and Divisional Headquarters swooped down to their appointed places, followed almost at once by the billowing parachutes of the 1st Brigade swinging down in hundreds. The drop and the glider landings were almost completely successful, 95 per cent of the troops reaching their rendezvous at the right place at the right time. The only serious loss was two of the Hamilcars which overturned on the soft ground, causing the loss of their 17-pounder anti-tank guns. Of 320 gliders, 35 failed to arrive, of which 21 landed in England and flew to Holland the next day. Scores of excited, friendly, talkative and pressing Dutch people came out of their farmhouses in their best church clothes and came running down the roads from Wolfhezen and Renkum and Heelsum and from villages even further distant, some carrying trays of food and jugs of water and baskets of fruit and flowers. At 11 o'clock that morning some of them, on their way to church, had looked up at the formations flying over their heads. 'They were low, very low,' a Dutch girl, Mejuffrouw Hogerzeil, remembered, 'unusually low. But the people were quite used to the sight and did not take much notice.' Even when the firing started, they stayed in church, loudly and defiantly singing the Wilhelmus, their national anthem. They thought it was another air-raid. And after church, in the early afternoon, when an old farmer called through the Hogerzeils' kitchen window that 'thousands, millions of Allied paratroops' were dropping from the sky, nobody believed him.

Most men who came in by glider recall a strange, almost eerie silence immediately after landing. Soldiers on the edge of Renkum Heath saw Dutch civilians wandering aimlessly through the woods or hiding in fright. Lieutenant Neville Hay of the Phantom unit remembers that 'it was a sobering sight. Some were in white hospital gowns and seemed to be herded along by attendants. Men and women capered about, waving, laughing and jabbering. They were obviously quite mad.' Victor Miller was startled by voices in the woods. Then, 'groups of weird white-clothed men and women filed past.' It was only later that the troopers learned the strangely behaved civilians were inmates from the bombed Wolfhezen Psychiatric Institute. Out of the woods from a bombed mental hospital, already filled with Dutch civilians wounded in the preliminary air-raids, came groups of bewildered patients, smiling and lost and their nurses, smiling with a bewilderment so similar that a glider pilot thought it was 'rather hard to tell who were the loonies and who were the nurses helping them'. And across the railway lines, screaming in excitement scampered gangs of little boys. The holiday mood was so infectious that some soldiers, waiting for the others to land, had already lit fires and were making tea. 'We were violently attacked by hordes of Dutch children who gave us dozens of apples', says the glider pilot, Alexander Johnson. 'Peter [Major Peter Jackson] and I were invited to tea by an elderly Dutch couple and we accepted - so far, everything had been very gentlemanly and unwarlike.'

The man with the most urgent task on landing was Major Charles Frederick Howard 'Freddie' Gough MC. Gough commanded the Air Landing Reconnaissance Squadron, which, assisted by 9th Field Company was to speed ahead to the Arnhem road bridge with his four-troop squadron in heavily armed jeeps equipped with Vickers K guns. Though commander of a group of men whose rationale was speed, Gough was notorious for being highly unpunctual when it came to attending conferences and the first briefing for 'Market-Garden' on 12 September was no exception. Major General Urquhart wrote: 'After the briefing had started, Freddie Gough, a cheerful, red-faced, silver-haired major, turned up with the air of a truant playing schoolboy and I laid into him afterwards for his unpunctuality. It was not the first time he had been very late for a conference.'

Since the air planners refused to allow a coup-de-main assault upon the bridge by means of an Airborne drop, the Reconnaissance Squadron was charged with the task of racing to the bridge in their jeeps the moment they were unloaded from their gliders and holding it until the 2nd Battalion arrived on foot. It was a role for which the Squadron was not suited, for they had been trained to act as scouts and Gough was known to find this part of the plan somewhat distasteful. 1st Parachute Brigade would follow on foot at best speed. Lieutenant Colonel John Frost's 2nd Battalion was to push on as fast as possible through the village of Heelsum and thence along the southern route, a road running close to the north bank of the Lower Rhine, until it reached the bridge, which it was to capture and hold. Major General Urquhart knew that 'Frost of all people would press on rapidly if it were humanly possible'. 'A six-footer with an anxious moon face and permanent worry lines across his forehead, he relished a fight and had become one of the most capable battalion commanders in airborne forces. Despite a deceptively slow-motion air, Frost had developed a very fine tactical sense.'

The 1st Parachute Battalion was to remain with Brigade Headquarters in immediate reserve, ready to be used wherever and whenever the necessity arose. As soon as the 2nd and 3rd Battalions had completed their immediate task, the 1st Battalion was to occupy the high ground just north of Arnhem. Thirty-six of the 320 gliders scheduled for Arnhem had been lost and twenty-two of the missing gliders failed to make the LZ, mainly because of broken tow ropes but on the landing zone 28 of the 1st Reconnaissance Squadron's 31 jeeps had survived the flight. One of the Squadron's troops had an unusually large number of bad landings that complicated vehicle recovery and some of the Squadron's personnel arrived by parachute so Gough and his men were delayed for two hours and did not begin to move from its forming-up area at the north east corner of LZ 'Z' until 1540. 'I went by glider with 'A' Troop vehicles', Lieutenant J. Stevenson of the 1st Airborne Reconnaissance Squadron said afterwards. 'We got down about ten minutes before the parachute party. It took us four-and-a-half hours to unload and when I looked round for the remainder of the troop vehicles I found that, besides the jeep from our glider, only two others had got down so far.'

Frost had selected 'A' Company to spearhead the 2nd Battalion's march to Arnhem Bridge because he regarded Major Allison Digby Tatham-Warter as a thruster and not one to hang around - thereby making him the ideal choice to lead in an operation that depended on speed. Frost and his men pushed on along the six miles of road which separated them from their objective, first encountering and overcoming opposition in Doorwerthsche Wood. Once it became clear that the paras had seized the north end of the Arnhem Bridge, II SS Panzerkorps HQ immediately began organising a counter-attack as soon as possible.

As attacks on the British perimeter increased in several sectors, particularly from the west along the river line, the ring was becoming dangerously weak as enemy tanks and infantry inflicted heavy casualties on the defenders. When the Border Regiment was driven off the high ground at Westerbouwing the loss of this commanding position seriously endangered the Division's hold on the waterfront and Urquhart ordered a company of the Border Regiment to retake it. Major Cousens's men, however, were so exhausted that the attack was not put in for fear that, if it were not successful, a disastrous gap would be opened upon that vital corner of the perimeter. Urquhart did not feel that he could reinforce them by taking units away from the northern lines which were under increasing pressure from hour to hour. And German reinforcements were on their way. At noon 45 of the long-awaited Konigstiger tanks from Panzerabteilung 503 had arrived in Arnhem. Later came units of another Panzergrenadier battalion from Germany under command of Captain Bruhns, several hastily-formed companies of Luftwaffe ground staff fighting as infantry, the 171st Auffrischung liegende artillery regiment with over thirty guns from Zutphen and the Landsturm 'Nederland' of the Dutch SS. By 1600 all of these units were in action. An hour later sixty Luftwaffe aircraft arrived over Arnhem and Nijmegen and all the German anti-aircraft units joined in the attack.

Urquhart's men's most pressing need was for water because the enemy had cut off the main supply to Oosterbeek on the first day of the battle. There was little for drinking, none for washing and precious little for the wounded. Storage tanks, central-heating systems, even fish bowls were drained. One enterprising company filled a bath half full of water before the tap failed and used this for cooking, even after a piece of the ceiling had fallen into it and made it look like thin, unpleasant porridge. When they moved to a new position on the north-side some of 'Boy' Wilson's men had taken over a house belonging to a far-sighted doctor who had taken the precaution of filling his bath before the Germans cut the water supplies. 'We cooked a goat and we have enough water for brewing up for some nights to come' he told Urquhart. 'My God I only just managed to save it though. I found two chaps about to use it for their ablutions'. The daily supply drop on Thursday included canisters of water but most of the supplies landed outside the perimeter and German sniper fire and lack of jeeps made it difficult to recover some of the containers that did land within the defences.

As night fell and the rain added to our discomfort, we moved to a position near a mortar group, with houses in the vicinity. The night passed with very little activity on the part of the enemy and we were able to snatch brief periods of sleep.

Twice in the afternoon the RAF tried to get supplies to the men in the perimeter. The first supply mission, at 1245 was a disaster. 'A new sound intruded on the sound of battle, the throb of approaching aircraft' recalled 'Fred' Moore 'and then the sky was suddenly filled with Dakotas. They started dropping desperately needed supplies, but too far away from us. We stood up, waved our yellow triangles, our arms, anything to attract their attention, but all to no avail. We watched, in horror, as planes were hit, caught fire and spiralled downwards to destruction. Then they were gone. Before long our position was being pounded with mortar shells, from dreaded Nebelwerfers, which were multiple-barrelled. We withdrew to the tree lined ditch at the rear of our position to wait for the barrage to cease. I was one of a close group of three, with a 1st Battalion Sergeant in the middle. A salvo straddled our position, two live shells bursting, one to our front, the other to the rear and another landing between the Sergeant and the other guy, which unbelievably failed to detonate.'

The aircraft were shot up by enemy fighters and there was some evidence to suggest that the Germans were using British signals to attract some of the supplies and that they were operating at least one of the Eurekas. Corporal Smithson recalled 'There was no way of saying 'not there, we're down here. We did everything we could, like waving, but it didn't make any difference. I watched one afternoon - seven Dakotas came in slow and low. And the Germans had God knows how many 88mm guns and they shot the first five down - bang, bang, bang. Down they came. Missed the sixth one and shot the seventh one down. They were all dropping their stuff towards what is now the cemetery but you just couldn't get it. So we had no supplies whatsoever.'

'Hell is Thursday' wrote Private Walter Boldock. 'Supply planes were still coming in, dropping their precious supplies into German hands. Sometimes 'Dummy' running, some at tree-top level, in flames from flak, courageous but futile; crashing in flames from concentrated flak pounding like devilish pile drivers. In a hopeful attempt, Lieutenant Clarkson lit a yellow smoke candle; a recognition signal to the planes. Almost immediately he was hit by a well directed mortar bomb. The yellow cloud drifted slowly over our lines. 'Anybody gotta fag? When's the Second Army coming?'Look to your front'. We repelled an advancing company of Germans, reeling and scrambling for cover. The Germans were quick to react. Bombs showered among our positions, spewed by the multi-barrelled mortars, splinters splattered through the stinking smoke. Death stalked two-handed to his harvest. Amid this hell, pinned down, deafened and weary, I dozed off. Asleep in the inferno. When I awoke (a hundred years later?) an astonished comrade exclaimed, 'I thought you were dead'.

'Four pm. we must withdraw. The remnants of our unit fell back along the base of a dry ditch. Me, Corporal 'Stan' Lunt and Private 'Frankie' Thompson covered them with Brens. We went back, through the smoke, eyes peering. An oath. Lunt had been hit. In the thigh from the flank, we couldn't see where. We ran back. 'Nothing serious'. He pushed us on.'

The second mission, at 1600, was much more successful. Because of the bad weather, the later waves of supply aircraft had to fly in without fighter protection and the force of 117 aircraft of RAF 38 Group met heavy flak and for the first time enemy fighters were in full evidence. Some aircraft were intercepted by ten FW 190s which broke through the fighter screen again. They took a heavy toll, shooting down seven out of ten aircraft from one squadron in the third wave.

Ralph Fellows, from Winnipeg, Manitoba was navigator on a DC-3 on 271 Squadron at Down Ampney in Gloucestershire flown by Major Pierre Simond 'Joubie' Joubert.

'We were detailed to drop supplies to our troops on the ground. But, due to faulty communications and unknown to us, the designated drop zone was held by the Germans and our fighter cover, so essential to protect us on the way in and out, was back on the ground in the Brussels area, rearming and refuelling.

'The line of Daks received a terrible battering during the slow low-level drop, but 'Joubie' held on grimly straight and level and eventually we were through. We climbed away and turned for home. 'Joubie' put in the auto-pilot and wandered back to the cargo cabin to speak to our wonderful army dispatchers.

'I was busy at my navigation table when a shout from our wireless operator caused me to glance outside. FW 190s had got among our unarmed Dakotas and the sky seemed full of burning aircraft and parachutes. We, meanwhile, flew on unconcerned - on auto-pilot. Joubie scampered back to his position and, with a fair measure of skill, coupled with his usual luck, got us home safely. It could only have happened to Joubie.'

'When we got out to our Stirling and started up' recalls 'Bert' Turner a flight engineer on 196 Squadron at Keevil, 'we could not get revs and boost on one of the engines so the aircraft was U/S and we had to take the spare, which entailed rushing across the airfield with all our kit and paraphernalia which all takes time. Consequently we were about thirty minutes behind everyone else. We cut every corner to catch up with rest of the squadron but it was hopeless and we arrived just as the rest of the lads had come out. There was nothing for it but to go on our own.'

In August 1942 when Herbert A. Turner was eighteen and a half and living in London he went to Penarth for induction into the RAF. From Penarth 'Bert' was posted to Blackpool where he did his 'square bashing' and in December he was posted to Halton where he completed a flight mechanics course. In February 1943 he volunteered for aircrew as a flight engineer and was accepted for training. Posted to St. Athan for a flight engineers course, he completed this in September and was promoted Sergeant. He then went to 1657 Conversion Unit Stradishall and it was here that 'Bert' met his new crew. The twenty-two year old pilot, Flying Officer Mark Azouz, was born in Glasgow to parents from Istanbul and Manchester and grew up in Chiswick in West London and had joined the RAF in 1941. The navigator was George Douglas 'Ginger' Greenwell, the air bomber, Leo Hartman, wireless operator/air gunner John McGuiggan - all flight sergeants - and the gunners were Pete Findley and 'Teddy' Roper. 'We were posted to 90 Squadron at Tuddenham' says 'Bert' Turner 'where we did five ops, which included mining trips and bombing runs on the rocket installations in France. An operational day was pretty consistent; you were usually told that you were on in the morning and normally you took the aircraft for a flight test to check everything out which would take about half an hour and on landing would report any snags to the ground crew, who would prepare the aircraft for ops. Sometime, usually in the evening we would be briefed as to the target. Met conditions, emergency drill and take off times could be any time depending on the distance but most of our ops took place at night. We joined 196 Squadron at Keevil and lost our mid-upper gunner 'Teddy' Roper as we were flying Stirling IVs which did not have a mid upper turret and so there was no need for a gunner. We were now in 38 Group TAF and started to tow gliders and drop paratroopers whist operating at night taking arms and supplies to the resistance in Europe. It was at Keevil that I met Elsie Bettany a young WAAF who came from Fenton who was to become my wife.

'On 6 June we were briefed to part in the Normandy invasion and took twenty paratroopers to France on 'D-Day' minus six hours after the drop we were flying back across the Channel when the fleet opened with the initial bombardment of the beaches; it was a marvellous sight. About this time our rear gunner 'Pete' Findley was taken ill and had to go into hospital we were given a spare gunner to replace him another 'Pete' - Peter Harold Bode (21), who was from Birmingham. By the time 'Pete' Findley was fit to return 'Pete' Bode had done as many ops with us and both gunners want to stay with the crew, because we could only have one of them, Mark told them both to sort it out between themselves, eventually they tossed for it, who won and who lost I never found out but 'Pete' Bode stayed with us. On 14 September I married Elsie Bettany in Warminster.'

The zones were clearly recognized and the landings were good. The coloured panels, smoke and Very lights displayed by the pathfinders were quite visible, but the glider pilots do not seem to have paid much attention to them. They came down all over the zones, showing some tendency to overshoot in the light and variable breeze. Of 134 gliders which reached the Arnhem area on their way to LZ 'S', 132 certainly landed on or very near that zone. Of the 150 remaining gliders headed for LZ 'Z', 116 landed on the zone and 27 were located very near it. The most serious accident was the loss of two guns when the Hamilcars carrying them stuck in soft ground and turned over.

Between 1353 and 1408 all but four of the 2,283 paratroops in the aircraft made their jump at altitudes of 700 to 900 feet and all but 35 of the 680 parapacks carried were released. One of the packs had fallen earlier and the other 34 stuck, although several of the pilots made extra passes in attempts to get them loose.

The accuracy of the paratroop drop was almost perfect and the troops were assembled and ready to move by 1500 hours. The plans had provided that a glider-borne reconnaissance squadron would race ahead in jeeps and seize the road bridge. The 2nd Battalion of the Parachute Brigade would follow on foot to reinforce this advance party. Unfortunately, so many of the gliders carrying the reconnaissance squadron failed to reach the landing zone that the unit was unable to operate. However, the paratroop battalion set out from Heelsum at 1530 and headed east down the Utrecht road toward the road bridge six miles away. During the first four miles throngs of cheering Dutchmen were the greatest impediment encountered. On the outskirts of the city 'C' Company was detached to turn right along the railway and seize the railway bridge over the river. Some men had actually sprinted onto the bridge when the German guards set off their charges and the main span curled skyward.[7] The company then moved into Arnhem, attacked German positions near the railway station, was cut off and a day or so later, destroyed.

Soon after 'C' Company left them, 'A' and 'B' Companies were halted by fire from an armoured car and from machine guns and mortars on a rise called Den Brink. An antitank gun was brought up to deal with enemy armour; 'B' Company was detached to neutralize-Den Brink and 'A' Company pressed on as quickly and unobtrusively as possible. On reaching the bridge about 2000, it seized the north end unopposed but an attempt to send a platoon to the south end was driven back by fire from SS troops supported by two antitank guns and an armoured car. The Germans had just arrived. A Dutch constable who walked across the bridge at 1930 stated after the war that the guards usually placed there were not on duty and that no one was there to defend it when he crossed. Never was the value of a coup de man more evident. A force landed or dropped near the south end of the bridge that afternoon could have secured it without a blow.

The company at the bridge was reinforced soon after arrival by battalion headquarters and later by part of brigade headquarters. Radio failure thwarted attempts to summon 'B' Company to the bridge, but it got there at dawn on the 18th, having lost one platoon in the dark. About 100 men of other units also marched in about that time after bypassing German strongpoints during the night. Their arrival raised the force at the bridge to approximately 550 men.

The struggle of this little band, led by Lieutenant Colonel John Frost, holds a place in British history like that occupied in American tradition by the battle of the Alamo, but in both cases the result was inevitable unless substantial reinforcements reached the defenders - and no help came. The paratroops held a perimeter around the bridge until driven from it by tanks on the 19th. On the 20th tanks and mobile guns moved to within a range of thirty yards and shelled the houses still occupied by the battalion until all were burning and only one was standing. Then German infantry began infiltration of what remained of the paratroops' positions. Less than 100 men were still able to fight and their ammunition was almost gone.

Early on the 21st the survivors were ordered to split up and escape by hiding or filtering through the German lines. Hardly any succeeded.

What had happened to all the other troops landed and dropped outside Arnhem on 17 September? The answer is that most of the glider-borne troops had to stay where they were to guard drop and landing areas for the next day's missions and that the rest of the paratroops had been stopped short of the bridge. Divisional Headquarters had opened at 1430 on 'D-Day' and by 1600 1,400 troops of 1st Airlanding Brigade had assembled to the strains of a bagpipe and moved into position around the zones. Although opposition had been negligible during landing, they were harassed during the night by aggressive patrols and mortar fire, indications of hard fighting to come. The 3rd Parachute Battalion had followed the 2nd down the Utrecht road but had been slowed by strong resistance. At dawn on the 18th it was still on the western side of Arnhem, heavily engaged and unable to advance. The 1st Battalion was supposed to take high ground on the north side of the city. Therefore, after a splendid drop 200 yards from its rendezvous, the unit moved north from the zone onto the Ede-Arnhem road and started down that road at practically full strength. Slowed by heavy sniping and by a halt to take defensive positions after sighting German tanks, it was unable to reach the city before nightfall. About 0100 the commander decided to push on into Arnhem and join forces with the other battalions, but the night advance proved costly and at first light his troops were at a standstill somewhat north of the railway station with the road in front of them effectively blocked.

At the end of 'D-Day' 'Market-Garden' seemed to be going well. With powerful air support to clear their path the American and RAF troop carriers had been successful beyond all expectations. The airborne commanders' were unanimous and fervent in their praise of the accurate and efficient delivery of their troops.

The ground thrust by the Guards Division had failed to reach Eindhoven; the Zon Bridge had been blown; and no bridges over the Waal or the Rhine had yet been taken. On the other hand, the Guards delay did not seem serious; the span at Zon would soon be usable; and paratroops had driven close to the still-intact road bridges at Nijmegen and Arnhem. Except at Best and in Nijmegen resistance to the American airborne been limited, as expected, to feeble attacks by small, nondescript groups. The plight of the British at Arnhem was desperate, but as yet they did not know it.

What made their situation so bad was the presence of overwhelming numbers of German guns and tanks near Arnhem. The Germans had recently moved both the 9th and 10th SS Panzer Divisions into that area to refit. Dutch agents reported their presence to the Allies but, although the 82nd Division appears to have received and to some extent accepted the report, British intelligence experts dismissed it as incredible. They judged that the Germans could muster at Arnhem no more than 3,000 disorganized men with very few tanks and guns.

The Germans were further favoured by the presence of their commanding general, Field Marshal Walter Model, who had his headquarters at Oosterbeek within three miles of the British landing zones. Without lingering in his ringside seat Model leaped into his car as soon as the landings began, drove full speed into Arnhem and summoned his panzers into action. Thus before the British had finished assembling, superior German forces were deploying against them.

It has been suggested that the Germans were able to plan a trap at Arnhem because the plans for 'Market' had been betrayed to them. Betrayal there certainly was, but it probably made little difference. A Dutch leader, Christian Lindemans, had been sent by SHAEF to Eindhoven on 14 September to warn the resistance group there of an Allied attack. Lindemans however had turned informer six months before to save his brother from the clutches of the Gestapo and he told all he knew of the operation to the head of German Army Intelligence at Driebergen on 15 September. He was also questioned at Vught by staff officers of General Kurt Student's First Parachute Army, which was defending that sector. Post war Student stated that he was completely surprised by the airborne operation by assuming that Lindemans' message merely referred in general terms to an attack through Eindhoven. A ground attack up the Eindhoven road had seemed quite likely to the Germans and the reconnaissance activity which they observed along the Eindhoven-Arnhem road tended to confirm such hypothesis. Apparently they even mistook the preparatory bombing and strafing on the morning of the 17th for an interdiction operation in support of a ground assault. Student, Germany's leading airborne expert, could hardly fail to see that the Zon bridge was a logical objective for an airborne mission, but since he is said to have regarded deep airborne penetrations as inconsistent with Allied policy and Montgomery's cautious character, he probably did not expect such an operation north of the Wilhelmina Canal.

All the German dispositions are consistent with the view that they anticipated an attack but had no specific knowledge of an airborne operation. Steps taken in accordance with that expectation would account for the stiff resistance facing the Guards on their way to Eindhoven; the promptness with which the Zon bridge was blown and the ferocious fighting around the bridge at Best. On the other hand, if the Germans had had definite knowledge of the 101st Division drop plans, they would surely have had a reception committee on the drop zones and if they had realized that Arnhem was in danger, the all-important bridges at Nijmegen and Arnhem would not have been left intact and almost unguarded. As for the two panzer divisions at Arnhem, they had been ordered to that area as far back as 8 September. The evidence, then, points to an Allied blunder rather than a German trap. German intelligence had not discovered the 'Market' plan. Allied intelligence had disastrously erred in ruling out the presence of the panzers at Arnhem.

The course of the battle in the first 24 hours might have been different, had Urquhart been able to use the 1st Battalion of the Border Regiment and the 7th Battalion of the King's Own Scottish Borderers, both of the Air Landing Brigade to reinforce the comparatively lightly armed parachute battalions which were unable to overcome the fierce German resistance on the high ground west and north of Arnhem. Had the whole Division been carried in one lift, these two battalions could have been used in an offensive role and when the South Staffords went into action they may have been at full strength but Urquhart had to hold and defend the landing zones so that the second and third lifts could land safely. Throughout the afternoon and the night the Borderers and the Border Regiment held the drop zones and repelled three attacks by the Germans.

Chapter 5

'Market' Sunday 17 September 'D-Day' - The American Lift

The C-47 troop carrier, workhorse of the Air Corps always got us where we had to go!

We left England at about 1000. We had been flying for some time now, it seemed forever, but I knew it had been less than three hours, and then, after the red light, it was time to stand up and hook up, and check everyone; the green light came on and there was no turning back now ...everyone was going out the door, like going for a walk, I would follow last as always, just to make sure, all troopers had left the plane and as my chute opened, I noticed some small arms fire coming from the ground and some big black puffs of smoke in the distance near the bridge. I then hit the ground, rolled forward, and then to my right to get out from under the collapsing chute.

21-year old John H. Self, a member of the Demolition Platoon, 505th Parachute Infantry Regiment, 82nd Airborne Division.

'Approximately two weeks before the start of 'Market-Garden' the first hint that we were going to drop in Holland was when we suddenly were ordered to attend a speech by General Eisenhower' wrote Second Lieutenant Eldon Sellers, a C-47 pilot in the 309th Squadron in the 315th TCG at Spanhoe about four miles east of Uppingham in Northamptonshire. Sellers was born in Aurora, Illinois on 9 March 1921. 'Ike' told us that it wouldn't be long before we were involved in an important mission. He didn't say where we were going then, but we had a good idea that it was probably an invasion of some sort across the Rhine. Up to that point our duties had consisted mainly of supplying gasoline and oil to forward positions in Belgium and transporting back to England, ex-prisoners of war who were being liberated as we advanced toward Germany. In between these missions, we practiced dropping paratroopers and towing gliders.'

'On 14 September' recalls Captain Aubrey L. Ross, a pilot in the 310th Squadron at Spanhoe 'we once again had 'guests' move onto our base.' The troopers in the 504th Parachute Infantry Regiment (PIR), 82nd Airborne Division that Ross and his fellow pilots would take to Holland had been billeted at Braunstone Park in Leicester. It was at Braunstone Hall that the 82nd 'War Rooms' were set up and the 'D-Day' planning for the Normandy drop took place. The 504th had not jumped on 'D-Day' but had been held in reserve. Lieutenant James 'Maggie' Megellas from Fond du Lac, born on 11 March 1917, the son of Greek immigrants, had an empty feeling in his stomach as he had watched those C-47s heading for France without him. 'I felt like a bride left at the altar' he wrote.[1] On 8 July the 82nd Airborne returned to England after 33 days of combat without relief or replacements and recuperated. 'Maggie' Megellas had been wounded during action in the Italian mountains near the Anzio beachhead. No one expected that they would remain in England for long but several missions into France, Belgium or Holland were planned and then cancelled. Then, on 15 September the 504th and 505th Regiments had moved to Spanhoe from their billets at Quorn and Shady Lane, Evington on the outskirts of Leicester. This town had everything to suit everyone's interest, from cinemas and dance halls to boxing matches between American and British paratroopers and at 'Louise's Doughnut Dugout' there were tea parties and even two-minute shampoos. After leading the 'good life' for so long (aside from ten mile runs each morning) the troop carrier bases must have seemed to the paratroopers basic in the extreme.

The 82nd and the 101st 'Screaming Eagles' Airborne Divisions were 'sealed in' at a cluster of five airfields around 100 miles north of London in Lincolnshire, Leicestershire and Nottinghamshire. Robert Murphy in the 'All American' Division's 505th Regiment recalled: 'The word about the operation was passed down to the other soldiers on the twelfth or thirteenth.' On 15 September Pfc Gordon A. Walberg and his buddies in the 80th Airborne Anti-Tank Battalion, 82nd Airborne had packed up their equipment at their garrison on the Race Course at Oadby five miles south east of Leicester where, instead of horse racing during the war it had became a home for various military units. Just across the road was Glebe Mount House, the Headquarters of General Matthew Ridgway who had commanded the 82nd Airborne Division prior to Brigadier General James Gavin. The 313th and 316th Troop Carrier Groups in the 52nd Troop Carrier Wing at Folkingham and Cottesmore were to deliver the 82nd Airborne's first lift. Brigadier General 'Jim' Gavin would fly in the lead plane ('Chalk 44'/43-15324) flown by Major Ben Kendig the 44th Squadron CO in the 316th TCG at Cottesmore. It was one of the duties of Walberg's Battalion to supply guards for the Divisional Commander while he waited to fly in a Waco CG-4A combat glider and land near Groesbeek. 'Our glider crew included Flying Officer G. W. Fuller as pilot, Corporal 'Ernie' Seddan, Pfc Robert Hayden and me. Our cargo was our 57mm anti-tank gun and the A-7 jeep was to follow in another glider, which with luck, we would locate at the same Landing Zone.'

Walter Cronkite, CBS News Correspondent had been picked as pool correspondent to drop into Holland with the 101st US Airborne Division under the command of General Maxwell D. Taylor. 'I was either one of the luckiest or among the unluckiest correspondents in World War II, depending on one's point of view. Prior to the air drop at Arnhem, the Allied Airborne Army had been scheduled to go into action on sixteen different occasions. Each time the correspondents would draw to see who would be pool man. I was winner thirteen of the sixteen times. From July until September I was constantly on alert. Awakened at night (it always happened at 3 o'clock in the morning), I would be driven out to some secret base in England, there to wait...Sometimes my drop-mates were Poles and Czechs, desperate men, blackened faces and all. One time we actually were in the planes, propellers spinning, when a soldier in a jeep came tearing across the field to tell us the drop had been called off. The reason the airborne operations were called off was General Patton's swift advance across France, securing the areas before the airborne troops could drop into them. On 17 September we finally made it - 20,000 men in 1,544 planes, 478 gliders.

'When I arrived at 101st headquarters the night before the mission, I was told that I was to go in by glider and not by parachute as I was led to believe. I came close to disgracing myself by turning down the mission...I didn't want to go by glider. I had seen what had happened to the gliders in Normandy. The wreckage of hundreds of them was scattered across the countryside. Many were impaled on the spiked posts the Germans had planted to defeat them. My fellow correspondents advised me not to go by glider. It was much more dangerous than dropping by parachute they told me. But on this drop I was assigned to glide and glide I did. Unfortunately, no one had told me the technique used in glider landings. I later learned that the pilot, after being cut loose from the tow-plane, puts the nose down and dives, thus making a fast-moving, hard-to-hit target. In short, the glider drops like a stone. Then after levelling out and touching down, the pilot slams the nose into the ground, bringing the craft to an abrupt halt - usually with the shattered tail waving in the air. In this correspondent's opinion, glider pilots were among the war's most courageous men. But I decided that the only thing worse than going to Holland in a glider would be the ignominy of not going at all on a mission for which I had volunteered.'

On 16 September a heavy fog enveloped most of England and a light rain would make takeoff difficult so the paratroopers returned to their tents. However it would be 'go' on the morrow, regardless of weather conditions.

'17 September had dawned clear and sunny and fairly warm' wrote 'Maggie' Megellas. 'We began the morning with a big breakfast of pancakes, chicken and pie, which was not our normal, everyday fare. It was as if the condemned were being served a hearty meal. After breakfast we loaded onto trucks and headed for the tarmac and the waiting C-47s. My platoon assembled around two aircraft. In my stick there were sixteen men; I was the jumpmaster and would give the jump commands and go out the door first over the DZ...'

Robert Murphy in the 'All American' Division's 505th Regiment recalled: 'When we were on our way to the airfield everybody knew where we were going and what we were doing. 85 percent of the men were seasoned combat troops at that time, having fought in Sicily, Italy or Normandy. Some did all three. We all were very excited about this jump. For all the men veterans and rookies this was to be the first daylight jump. Another 505th Regiment trooper, Private Howard Swartz, wrote: 'It was my opinion that the officers didn't tell us much about the operation that was coming. I don't think that we knew where we were going before we were taken to the airfield. I guess they figured that the less we knew, the less we could give away in the event that we were captured.'

The first pair of American pathfinder aircraft had taken off from Chalgrove at 1025 hours on 'D-Day', followed at ten-minute intervals by the other two pairs. A final briefing had been held at 0830 after which crews and troops reported to their aircraft. Both fliers and airborne had been working as teams for almost six months and nearly all were veterans of the Normandy drops. They knew their business and they knew each other. From Chalgrove the pathfinder serials flew eastward to the coast and appear to have followed the southern route from there on. They had a P-47 escort over the Channel but none over the Continent. The pathfinders of the 82nd Division, flying in the lead, had an easy trip as far as Grave where anti-aircraft batteries opened up on them. They were under intense fire as they made their drop on DZ 'O', but fighters of the 78th Fighter Group, which were in the area on a flak-busting mission, dived on the guns and silenced them. The drop was made at 1247 from an altitude of 500 feet. The two pathfinder teams landed side by side in open fields about 500 yards north of DZ 'O'. While the second team stood guard, the first set up its equipment. Except for a sniper or two there was no resistance and within three minutes the team had spread its panels and put both radar and radio beacons in operation.

The pathfinders of the 101st Division had a harder time. Their two serials made landfall together, but over the Belgian coast the rear pair circled to re-establish its time interval while the lead pair flew on to DZ 'A'. Both pairs sighted the orange smoke set out near Gheel to mark the front and both ran into heavy fire over the German lines Evasive action being forbidden, all the pilots could do was to speed their lumbering aircraft to 180 mph. Near Ratie one of the pair bound for DZ 'A' was hit in the left engine and wing tank and crashed in flames. The loss shows the particular value of leak proof tanks in pathfinder work. Had anything happened to the other aircraft in that pair, DZ 'A' would have gone unmarked. Fortunately the surviving aircraft flew safely and accurately to Veghel, sighted the railway which bounded the zone on the north, turned parallel to the tracks and made its run right over the zone. At 1247 it dropped its troops on DZ 'A' from standard altitude at minimum speed. The paratroops met no resistance and were able to put 'Eureka' in operation in a minute and to lay out the panels in 2½ minutes. They had trouble with the radio antenna but had that set working within five minutes. The smoke signals were not set off till the main serials were sighted.

The pair of aircraft tasked for DZ's 'B' and 'C' dropped their teams side by side with pinpoint accuracy at 1254. They had slowed to less 90 mph for the jump and the men landed so close together that no assembly was necessary. The 'Eureka' was in action in less than a minute and panels and radio were ready within four minutes. Although a few enemy troops were in the vicinity, they were readily disposed of without affecting the pathfinders' work.

The 101st Airborne Division was to anchor the British Airborne Corps' southern-most flank and secure a 15-mile sector between Eindhoven and Veghel. Taking this into consideration, General Taylor had decided that the three parachute infantry regiments would jump on the 17 September; the 327th Glider Infantry was to arrive on D+1 and the artillery units were scheduled for D+2, the 19th. The 'Screaming Eagles' took off from six airfields in the 50th (442nd TCG) and 53rd Troop Carrier Wings (434th, 435th, 436th, 437th and 438th TCGs) around fifty miles west of London, in the area of Basingstoke and Reading. The Southern Route was reserved exclusively for the 101st Airborne and this started at Bradwell Bay and cut across the Thames Estuary for 34 miles to the tip of the North Foreland. This involved a detour for the 53rd Wing, but a more direct course would have brought the wing over the anti-aircraft batteries and barrage balloons of the London metropolitan area. From the North Foreland the route dog-legged for 159 miles to the IP in Belgium where it crossed the Albert Canal and then ran east to Antwerp and then north over the British lines and on to the landing zones north of Eindhoven. The Eindhoven group of zones was slightly over thirty miles northeast of the IP. An approach on this heading would cut neatly between known flak concentrations around Eindhoven and Tilburg.[2]

Navigation was assisted by 'Eureka' beacons and occults at all rendezvous and turning-points; by further 'Eureka' beacons and coded Holophane lights[3] on ships in mid-Channel; and by ground strips, coloured smoke signals and Very lights, as well as 'Eureka' beacons, on the dropping and landing zones. Air cover was to be provided during the flight by VIII Fighter Command, which, assisted by fighters of Air Defence Great Britain, would also attack all flak positions along the route both before the operation and in the course of it; while, after the landings, cover would be maintained over the target areas by US IX Fighter Command by day and by fighters of Air Defence Great Britain by night. Coastal Command aircraft would fly diversionary sorties beyond the operational area and 2nd Tactical Air Force would carry out armed reconnaissance around the dropping and landing zones. Bomber Command even dropped dummy parachutes west of Utrecht, at Emmerich and east of Arnhem. Both the Northern and Southern routes were planned to fly between the densest concentrations of enemy flak but losses of up to 40 per cent of the gliders and transport aircraft involved were predicted.

The troop carriers had to keep column time-length short so that escorting fighters could give them greater protection and so that their time over enemy-held territory was the shortest possible. Formation intervals could be tighter than those used in night operations and troop-carriers might fly in three streams - the right and left each separated from the centre by one and a half miles. The formations had to allow a certain amount of manoeuvrability as well as giving good concentration for paratroops and gliders on the ground. The C-47s were to fly in nine-ship elements in a 'V of Vs' in serials of up to 45 aircraft, in trail, with four-minute intervals between the leading aircraft of each serial. Glider columns would form into pairs of pairs echeloned to the right, in serials of up to 48 aircraft towing gliders, in trail, with seven-minute intervals between heads of serials. The altitudes flown were chosen to avoid small arms as well as heavy anti-aircraft fire, to dropping troops and releasing gliders at minimum safe altitudes and to assuring clearance of incoming aircraft with those returning from the target area.

At 0615 hours the men in the 315th TCG at Spanhoe had gulped down a breakfast of hotcakes, syrup and cereal, fried chicken with trimmings, butterscotch pudding, hot coffee and apple pie. Then they had attended church service before a last-minute briefing 'Several missions were flown dropping paratroops on 'D-Day', 6 June without significant losses, but it would be a different story in 'Market Garden' wrote Aubrey Ross, in the 310th Squadron. 'At the first mission briefing, we learned that the 315th's first destination was DZ 'O' about three miles southwest of Nijmegen and a half mile north of the Maas River. Two serials of 45 aircraft each were to be used to transport 1,240 paratroopers and 473 parapacks. We did not do any specific training for this operation, nor was there a dress rehearsal. We were very happy to learn once again that our group would not have to tow gliders on this mission. This chore fell to one of the less fortunate groups. No Troop Carrier pilot ever wanted to tow gliders especially into combat. A normal cruise speed for the C-47 was 145 to 155 mph, but with a glider you would be slowed to 90 to 95 mph with increased power. It was also more work for a pilot when a glider was in tow with airspeed hovering near stalling speed. Our route to the target was to the east coast of England at Aldeburgh, then 94 miles across the North Sea to Schouwen Island in Holland. From Schouwen Island it was approximately ninety miles to the drop area.'

Captain Richard E. Bohannan of Mount Vernon, New York the flight leader of the third element was piloting *Bette* a brand-new C-47A (43-15308) in the 34th Squadron in the 315th Group, which carried fifteen paratroopers from 'H' Company in the 504th Regiment led by 1st Lieutenant Isidore D. Rynkiewicz, the jumpmaster. George Willoughby, who was only 18 years old and the youngest trooper in the plane, had, by using devious means, been able to enlist in the army before Pearl Harbor at the age of fifteen. 'After visiting buddies at their plane and taking a picture with them, I told them I would see them on the ground. Little did I know that the Germans had other plans for our plane.' He carried a land mine in his left leg jump suit pocket and a Gammon grenade in his left leg pocket; two fragmentation grenades in his jump jacket pockets, K rations, sniper rifle, an ammo bag with 200 plus rounds of ammo, gas mask, pack and other items. Private Richard Reardon recalled that he, like the others, was loaded down with heavy equipment. He wore two parachutes, main and reserve, a Thompson

M1928A1 sub-machine gun with a loaded magazine plus four extra double magazines, a Colt M1911A1 .45-calibre pistol plus two loaded seven-round magazines, an anti-tank mine, a Gammon grenade and four fragmentation hand grenades. To add some more weight, he carried 300 rounds of .45-calibre ammunition, a nine-inch steel jump knife, wool blanket, canvas shelter half, first-aid packet, compass, entrenching tool, several boxes of K-rations, a mess kit, canteen, carton of cigarettes and several chocolate bars. Before struggling out to the plane, Reardon found a scale and weighed himself: 392 lbs. His normal weight was 185 lbs! All the men also wore Mae West life preservers that ballooned in front of their chests.

Rynkiewicz gave the order to harness up and the men helped each other attach their parachutes. Then the order was given to load up and the men started to climb the steep ladder into the C-47. Being so heavily laden, the men had difficulty getting aboard, but helping hands from fellow troopers and crew chief Sergeant Thomas N. Carter of Winston-Salem, North Carolina enabled them to board the plane. The men took their positions on wooden benches on both sides of the plane's cabin and strapped themselves in. Like a mother hen, Carter had been hovering around his plane since the early morning, checking every inch of it. He had arrived in England in June 1944 and was assigned to the squadron as a replacement; the Holland mission would be his first operational mission.

Walter Cronkite the CBS News Correspondent had loaded up with members of a headquarters company into a glider just before dawn the next morning. 'I took my seat on the wooden bench that ran down the side of the glider. My two musette bags with my typewriter and paper in one and toilet articles in the other were in my lap and my heart was in my mouth' he wrote. 'The takeoff was not so bad. The C-47 towing us attained just the right speed down the runway to take up the tension on our tow line with unexpected smoothness and I began to relax. Well, actually, I didn't relax. What I did was take a deep breath for the first time that morning. And I began to find a few flecks of silver in my clouds.

'Well,' I thought, 'at least this ride will be quiet compared to those raids in the bombers with the deafening roar of their engines.'

'Wrong!'

'When the aircraft started to move on the tarmac, the noise was deafening' wrote 'Maggie' Megellas. 'Approximately two and a half hours after takeoff, 45 minutes of which was over enemy-held territory, we would be over our drop-zone and jumping out the single door of our C-47s. It was goodbye England; Holland here we come.'[4]

The mission bearing the paratroops of the 82nd Division began its take-offs at 1019 hours. Six groups of the 52nd and 50th Wings based in the Grantham area contributed 480 aircraft organized in eleven serials. Aboard the aircraft were about 7,250 paratroops. Take-off and assembly went smoothly and without serious mishaps. At the same time 424 C-47s of the 53rd Troop Carrier Wing with 6,695 paratroops of the 101st Division aboard had begun taking off from their bases around Greenham Common. The 435th Group got a 32-aircraft serial into the air and into formation in fifteen minutes. One serial of the 442nd Group in the 50th Wing got its 45 aircraft in the air in five minutes and a quarter hour later swept over Chilbolton in formation on its way to Hatfield, the wing assembly point. By 1039 hours the first of two serials of 45 aircraft in the 315th Group led by Lieutenant Colonel Donald G. Dekin were airborne and heading for DZ 'O'. The second serial led by Lieutenant Colonel Robert J. Gibbons followed at 1101, both serials with 1,240 paratroopers and 473 parapacks following the northern route to the DZ. 'We formed the usual 'V of V's formation and joined a stream of troop carrier traffic moving toward the coast of Holland' recalled Aubrey L. Ross. 'Our planes climbed to an altitude of 1,500 feet, then levelled off.' The 52nd and 50th Wing serials flew for twenty miles to March in Cambridgeshire, then 69 miles to Aldeburgh in Suffolk on the east coast of England for the 93 mile trip across the North Sea to Holland.

From Hatfield, where the serials swung into line at four-minute intervals in a column eighty miles long, the 53rd Wing flew 49 miles to Bradwell; from there it proceeded over the revised southern route, including the detour to Ghent airport. 'Delos' was reached accurately and approximately on schedule by means of visual navigation assisted by 'Rebecca' and 'Gee'. The 'Rebecca' beacons at the turns and on the marker boat were received at distances of thirty and even forty miles. 'Gee' was used occasionally by formation leaders to check position, but there were some who reported it unusable because of jamming. The aids at the IP were not in operation in time for the first serials and perhaps not for any, but the 'T' and yellow smoke set out near Gheel by the ground forces were clearly visible.

The weather was almost exactly as promised. Fog, present in the early morning, had cleared by 0900. A little thin, low stratus persisted longer but had dissipated by take-off time. That part of England was enjoying a warm, hazy autumn morning. Only at Langar did weather present any difficulties. There, overcast forced the 441st Group to climb above 2,500 feet before assembling. After reassembling over the bases the serials flew to March, the assembly point and swung into line at the appointed intervals. From

March they proceeded for 71 miles to Aldeburgh, the starting point on the northern route and over that route to the IP south of Hertogenbosch. The 'Eureka's in England and on the marker boat worked well and so did the 'Gee' sets of the leaders. All of the 480 aircraft made an accurate landfall on Schouwen Island.

As they were flying over the English coast 'Maggie' Megellas could see crowds who had gathered in the streets waving flags. 'They were witnessing history in the making, the largest airborne fleet ever assembled; taking off for the greatest airborne invasion ever conceived. Looking out of my plane at this vast armada left me with a feeling of insignificance, except for the fact that I was part of a historical occasion... The men in my stick knew they were part of something big, but the combat-hardened veterans of the Italian campaign took it in stride. For the most part they showed no emotion, just waited in sombre anticipation.'[5]

Over the North Sea the visibility was between six and eight miles and over Belgium and Holland it was generally good with visibility of from three to seven miles. In places masses of cumulus clouds gave as much as 8/10ths cover at 3,000 feet but, since their bases were at altitudes of 2,500 to 3,000 feet, they presented no obstacle to the Americans. Along the route, cloud cover varied from 4/10ths to 8/10ths with the base of the clouds between 2,000 and 3,000 feet and there was a slight haze, thickest at the Dutch coast, where it limited visibility to three or four miles. Conditions at the destination were favourable with cloud bases above 2,500 feet and visibility of seven miles or more.

'The sight from aloft was incredible wrote Walter Cronkite: '...other C-47s and their gliders filled the sky, it seemed from horizon to horizon.'

Cronkite had discovered that his glider was just a tubular steel frame over which canvas was stretched for the fuselage. 'Once in the windstream, the canvas beat against the frame with enough decibels to promise permanent deafness. Conversation was impossible, but a sergeant sitting across from me kept hitting me on the knee and mouthing some words that were totally incomprehensible. He might have been trying to comfort me, but, having learned something of the macho nature of the airborne soldiers, I suspect he was telling me something intended to scare me out of my wits.

'As we approached our landing zone we became aware that we were encountering ground fire. It wasn't heavy flak as I had seen from the bombers, but there was tragic evidence that it was there. A C-47 not far off to our left apparently was hit. One of its two engines burst into flames, the glider cut loose and the C-47 turned slowly on its side and fell to earth.

'Entranced with that horror I suddenly became aware that my glider mates were bracing and our pilot was tense. And then he pushed the lever that released us from our tow. We dropped like a stone - plunged straight down, it seemed to me. 'I knew it, I knew it, I knew it,' I was saying to myself. 'I knew these things couldn't fly on their own.'

'We dived like that for an interminable time - probably counted in seconds. The ground was fast approaching. I don't recall my life flashing before me. I only remember thinking that I knew better than to be there. I don't think we were more than a hundred feet from the ground when our pilot pulled back on the elevator controls. It seemed that we were pulling enough 'g's', enough force of gravity, to push us all right out of the bottom of the glider. The pilot levelled off and made a 180 into the wind and I was aware then that other gliders were landing just ahead of us and that there were still others to our sides also going into the same large field.

'We touched down and bumped across a roughly ploughed field and I was breathing again when suddenly our pilot yelled, 'Here we go!' The nose of our glider ploughed into the soft black dirt, the tail flew up into the air, the dirt came piling into the crushed nose and all was still.

When I landed near Eindhoven our pilots proved to be a classicist. Men, helmets and gear flew like shrapnel around the interior of our deliberately crashed glider. I grabbed a helmet from the debris and ran across the field to where I saw others heading. Stopped by enemy fire, an officer pounding along next to me, shouted, 'Major, are you sure that is the rendezvous point?' I told him I wasn't sure at all and in addition, wasn't a major.

'Then why are you wearing that helmet?' he yelled indignantly. I had picked the wrong one.'[6]

As he approached the coast of Holland 'Maggie' Megellas could see black puffs from exploding German anti aircraft fire. 'As the muzzle flashes were spotted, escorting fighter planes dived toward them with guns blazing. Fortunately in all of this, we encountered no signs of the Luftwaffe. Although our fighter escorts silenced most of the anti aircraft batteries, they did not get them all. As we approached the Walcheren Islands off the coast of Holland, enemy ground fire hit one of the 'H' Company planes, setting the belly of the plane on fire.'[7]

An anti-aircraft battery, consisting of an 88mm and two 37mm guns, was positioned on and near a bunker at Dintelsas and began blasting away at the incoming formation. The C-47s were also fired upon by heavy machine guns. Pfc's Walter Leginski and Everett Rideout had been sitting just opposite the door of Bohannan's aircraft next to Lieutenant Rynkiewicz and all three were slightly wounded by shrapnel in their legs and buttocks when the C-47 was hit. Several other paratroopers also received minor injuries. George Willoughby, who was so uncomfortable with all the equipment on, had got down on the floor of the plane and had fallen asleep. When they reached the coast he was awakened and immediately got off the floor and sat in his seat across from the door of the C-47. 'I could see out' he wrote. 'It was only a short time before I could hear the crack of small arms fire and hear and see puffs of anti-aircraft gunfire. Shortly after, the plane started filling with smoke.'

One of the six parapacks beneath *Bette* had been hit by flak and was on fire. The container held Composition C, a highly dangerous and combustible material used to make explosives. The 'Comp C' was burning and flames were spreading to the other parapacks under the fuselage, which also caught fire. The fire was so intense that it melted holes in the floor of the aircraft. *Bette*'s left engine was also ablaze. The plane's crew chief, Sergeant 'Tom' Carter informed the pilots of the fire over the intercom. Willoughby looked across the plane. 'I noticed that Lieutenant Rynkiewicz had been hit in the left knee and Hatfield, the BAR man, was hit on the back of his hand. To my right, a trooper was on the floor. I remember saying, 'let's get the hell out of here' and we started standing up. The Air Force Sergeant dived out the door. Within seconds, the plane was so full of smoke you could not see anything. Some men near the cockpit started coughing and pushing for the door. At that time, others and I fell through the floor. We were hooked up and when my chute opened, I could smell flesh and see the skin hanging from my face and hand. I had released my rifle when the flames burned my hands.' Willoughby would observe his nineteenth birthday in a German PoW camp.

In another C-47, 1st Lieutenant William M. Perkins was flying 600 yards behind Bohannan at an altitude of about 1,000 feet. Seeing flames trailing behind *Bette*, Perkins broke radio silence and called Bohannan: 'Bo', your parapacks are on fire!' Since Perkins did not receive a response, he repeated the same call several times. Then he saw paratroopers starting to bail out of the burning aircraft. Leginski and Rideout, who had noticed the crew chief jump from the plane and that Rynkiewicz was slumped forward in his seat, did not hesitate and out they went. Someone must have thrown Rynkiewicz out of the plane, since he survived the crash. Everyone was tumbling out now. While trying to get to the door, Pfc Reardon fell onto the burning floor. Suddenly, the floor gave way and he fell out through the bottom of the burning fuselage. Miraculously, his parachute opened. He looked up and checked that the canopy was okay; he did not have to pull his reserve.

On Bohannan's right wing was a C-47 piloted by 1st Lieutenant Jack B. Olds and 2nd Lieutenant Robert L. Cloer. They also witnessed Bohannan's flaming plane. Cloer took the radio microphone and tried to contact Bohannan but, like Perkins, got no answer. Engulfed in flames with full throttle *Bette* ploughed into a field that had been flooded by the Germans near the Postbaan of the Stadschendijk in the Heiningse Polder, near the farm of A. van Sprang. It was approximately 1230 hours. Bohannan and co-pilot Lieutenant Douglas H. Felber of Chicago, Illinois were trapped inside the cockpit and could not escape. They held the C-47 up by superhuman effort while the paratroopers jumped. Navigator, Lieutenant Bernard P. Martinson of St. Paul, Minnesota and radio operator, Staff Sergeant Arnold B. Epperson, Omaha, Nebraska were killed, as were Bohannan and the co-pilot.

The 17th chute carried crew chief, 'Tom' Carter, coming down after his harrowing escape from *Bette*. He noticed water below him except at a crossroads around which were clustered several houses. It was the village of Heiningen. Carter was able to guide his parachute and landed on a roof of one of the houses. The paratroopers splashed down nearby in the water and five Dutchmen wearing orange armbands that symbolized that they were in the Dutch Resistance helped them. The American had a map in his escape kit and pulled it out. One of the Dutchmen pointed out where they were, fifty miles short of the intended drop zone at Overasselt. They then informed the troopers that they had to leave but would return soon with other underground members who would guide them to safety. The paratroopers set up defensive positions in two of the houses but a squad of Germans from the 719th Infantry Division soon surrounded them and after a brief fire-fight the Americans were forced to surrender. Sergeant Carter was separated from the paratroopers and held in Stalag Luft IV in Tychow, Poland, arriving there in the middle of October 1944.[8]

The sight of Bohannan's C-47s burning had a terrible effect on 'Maggie' Megellas and his stick of men who still had about forty-five minutes of flying time over enemy-held territory before they reached the drop zone. At the altitude and speed the lumbering C-47s were flying, they were easy targets. The further the C-47s penetrated into Holland, the more intense the small-arms fire from the ground became. The C-47s levelled off at an altitude of about 500 feet as they approached the DZ. 'From the bridge at Eindhoven, a 101st Airborne Division objective, the enemy fired at us' wrote 'Maggie' Megellas. 'As I stood in the door of the plane looking out, I could see many tracers. From my vantage point, it seemed that every bullet would hit me between the eyes. A considerable amount of small-arms fire did zip through my C-47. There was nowhere in the fuselage or the cockpit that could provide any kind of cover from the enemy line. Nor was there any way we could return fire.

'Shortly before reaching the drop zone, two men in my stick were hit by ground fire and crumpled to the floor still hooked up to the static line. There was nothing that could be done for them. It would be only a matter of minutes before we were over our drop zone. I called back to Sergeant Rice at the rear of the stick to unhook the two wounded men and move them out of the way. It would be important that we all got out as quickly as possible in order to avoid a scattering of the men on the ground. In jump school, we had trained exiting a stick of sixteen men in thirteen seconds or less and to assemble rapidly once on the ground ready to fight.

It was a sobering introduction to the Netherlands for us.'[9]

In a rare, quiet moment, his co-pilot doing the flying, Aubrey Ross stared out through the windscreen of his C-47 and reflected. 'It was 28 May 1943, one of the happiest days of my life for I had successfully completed pilot training satisfying a dream from early childhood and also receiving a commission as a second lieutenant in Army Air Forces.' His fond memory was short lived '... the ground fire increased as we neared the drop zone and seven of our aircraft were hit before we reached the DZ even though fighters were keeping the pressure on the gun batteries all the time. Most of the planes dropped their troops on or near the drop zone. As soon as the last man cleared the plane, we would dive to the deck to provide a lesser target and avoid the heavy ground fire.'

Seventy-eight of the C-47s in the 315th successfully dropped their paratroopers near the target, but most of the eleven sticks whose jump area was south of the Maas River landed 500 to 1,200 yards beyond their zone, possibly because the pilots were concerned the men might land in the river. The 504th Regiment and 'Charlie' Company in the 307th Parachute Engineers landed on the drop zone at Grave at 1205, 34 minutes after the pathfinders had landed. 'Easy' Company in the 504th was dropped south of the Maas River and the rest of the 2nd Battalion moved toward the Nijmegen Bridge from the North side. There were fire fights in the vicinity for several hours before the 504th had secured the bridge.

Eldon Sellers recalled: 'The German fighter planes couldn't get near us because of the protection that was provided to us by our fighter aircraft. Before we arrived at the IP (initial point - before the DZ) most of the shooting at us had been directed toward the gliders that were being towed at a higher altitude than we were. Over the drop zone the flak was thick and it seemed impossible to fly through the smoke from the 88th shells exploding all around. Once over the drop zone we were too busy flying and giving signals for the drop to commence that we didn't think about the flak or anything else. We carried supply bundles as well as paratroopers. A lot of paratroopers were dropped in the wrong place, but we had been told forehand that it was better to drop everyone in the same place, regardless of it being wrong. However I did noticed that across the road from the field where the paratroopers were dropped, that there was a field with more open spaces. The field on which the paratroopers were dropped had many trees. I thought it made more sense if the stuff didn't got hung up in the trees, so I released the parapacks containing supplies and ammunition over the open area. During the drop we had flown at a slow speed of about 105 mph and an altitude of about 325 feet. As soon as everything was released we 'hit the deck'. We dived the plane just above treetop level and accelerated as fast as we could. We had been flying formation up to that point. From there we went completely our own way. Some climbed as fast as they could while others dived like us. On our way back I could plainly see the Dutch civilians waving at us from the ground. Some seemed to be crying.'

Thirty-five year old Winnipeg born Canadian war correspondent Stewart Myles Macpherson, better known to forties radio audience as 'Dare-devil Stewart, the man behind the headlines', had taken off in a scout plane from Belgium to meet the Airborne Army as it came in: 'As we drew near the area where we expected to sight the air armada, swarms of fighter aircraft swooped and dived from all directions, but we could not see any sign of the transport aircraft. For a few minutes we dodged in and out of the fighters, which were everywhere and then my pilot suddenly shouted, 'Look, straight ahead!' I looked and if there ever was a sight that defied description, there it was. The sky was black with transport aircraft flying in perfect formation. They were completely surrounded by Typhoons, Spitfires, Mustangs, Thunderbolts and Lightning fighters. It was an aerial layer cake. The transport planes were in the middle with their fighter cover flying at three different heights. From the ground below coloured smoke suddenly belched up and the whole armada banked to the left. Not one single aircraft one inch out of position. My pilot signalled to me that he was going to try and get up higher and for the next five minutes or so we tried to squirm our way through hundreds of fighters that continually whistled by on both sides of us. They raced overhead and roared up from under us, it was like the Glass House in the Fun Fair - there just seemed to be no way out. One fighter immediately above us whined its way down and flew straight at us, he came so close I could see the pilot grin as he waved and rushed by, followed by the rest of the squadron. The armada flew on and everywhere you looked were aircraft - Allied aircraft. As my pilot shouted to me, 'No room up here for Jerry!'

Sixteen USAAF fighter groups escorted aircraft of 1st Allied Airborne Army. Besides perimeter patrols, which protected both routes, the northern route had heavy protection of its own. Escort and area cover from England to the IP was provided by eighteen squadrons of Spitfires from ADGB. Between the IP and the Nijmegen area two P-51 groups sent by Eighth Air Force handled cover and escort duties using the same tactics as the groups on the southern route. From the time they arrived at the Belgian coast the troop carriers were given area cover by six groups of P-51s from Eighth Air Force. These flew in two layers, half at 2,500 feet and half at 5,000 feet, flying lower in cloudy areas to keep below the cloud-base. To the east between Hasselt and Wesel a P-51 group was sweeping back and forth on perimeter patrol and another was patrolling along a semi-circular line between Wesel and the Zuider Zee. No enemy aircraft came in sight of the troop carriers or their escorts. The only efforts by the Luftwaffe to penetrate the 'Market' area on 'D-Day' were met and turned back by the two groups on perimeter patrol. Pilots of the 4th Fighter Group, patrolling northwest of Wesel intercepted fifteen uncommonly aggressive and persistent Focke Wulf 190s near Bocholt and claimed to have destroyed five of them and probably a sixth while losing one aircraft. The 361st Fighter Group southwest of Wesel had a brush with fifteen Bf 109s and shot down one.

Flak suppression from the coast to the IP was purview of eight Tempest, three Mustang and two Spitfire squadrons of ADGB and two Ninth Air Force fighter groups. Their P-47s and P-38s were considered more suitable than the P-51 for anti-flak operations because of their heavy striking power and their ability to take punishment and carried two 500lb general purpose bombs apiece. One Mustang was lost during sweeps against armed barges, pillboxes and batteries. A total of 142 fighter-bomber sorties were made, four fighter groups arriving in the Eindhoven area at 1230, 1300, 1330 and 1350 and staying slightly under an hour apiece. Thus during the period of the main paratroop drop between 1300 and 1340 there were generally two groups in action between the front and the drop zones. The 474th Fighter Group, first to arrive, was much the most effective. It reported the destruction of seven gun positions and the probable destruction of eighteen more. The next two groups claimed only nine positions destroyed or silenced and the last group arrived as the last troop carriers were leaving. Because of hazy weather, low clouds and the inconspicuousness of the targets, dive-bombing of anti-aircraft guns was almost impossible. In fact any bombing was so difficult that the first three groups used only 61 bombs and relied largely on strafing. Two P-38s were reported shot down or missing.

Beyond the IP the Nijmegen column had only the 78th Fighter Group to sweep flak out of its path. This group went into action about half an hour before the troop carriers arrived. By flying low to draw anti-aircraft fire and then strafing and dive bombing, it knocked out an estimated eight guns and silenced six more. It also hit other targets including a flak barge and a Messerschmitt on the ground at Gilze-Rijn. Most of this work was done in fifteen minutes. Then the German gunners stopped firing. Unable to find targets, the 78th flew out to meet the troop carrier formations near the IP and accompanied them to the drop zones. The group lost one aircraft and had a dozen damaged during mission.

Paving the way for the parachute drop in their assigned area, fifty P-47s of the 78th Fighter Group at Duxford bombed and strafed flak positions and other ground targets, encountering intense flak and about thirty fighters, sending a flight down to between 2,000 and 2,500 feet to draw enemy flak while others strafed and dropped 260lb fragmentation bombs on the well-fortified flak and 88mm gun emplacements. After this the P-47s returned to the Dutch coast to escort the first glider towing transports to their landing zones. One of the fighter pilots, Captain Dick Hewitt, a 24-year old New Yorker from Lewiston, recalls. 'We came in around 8,000 feet, armed with two 250 lb frag bombs and a full load of .50 calibre ammo. Our plan, which sounded like we were to be the flak gunners' 'clay pigeons,' was to 'tool' along at 8,000 feet, getting them to fire first. Once we spotted their gun flashes or the flak bursts, we'd go after them, firing as we dove and then drop our fragmentary bombs right up their gun barrels as we pulled out. After expending our two bombs, we would continue to rake them until our ammo was gone. If successful in knocking out their flak emplacements, a lot of paratrooper lives would be saved. Well it sure did not work out as planned. Those flak gunners must have been experts at playing possum.[10] The C-47s and C-46s came in with gliders in tow, all loaded with paratroops. Several were hit and knocked down with their gliders still in tow. It was another one of those totally helpless feelings, to watch the gliders cut loose and then see men and planes go crashing to the ground. We did try to retaliate but with paratroopers, equipment planes and gliders all over the sky and ground, it was hopeless cause. We lost five 78th pilots in two days of this 'hide and seek' tactic. A total of eighteen men and planes were lost in the twenty day period during 'Market-Garden'.

Total claims included eight aircraft and 107 flak positions destroyed. Sixteen of the US fighters failed to return. The troop carriers reported that the fighter-bombers had done an effective job against enemy positions in the open but achieved little in wooded areas. As the serials crossed the German lines near Rethy they were met with intense flak and small-arms fire. The eighteen miles from Rethy to the Wilhelmina Canal were fairly free of opposition, but several flak installations along the canal were still sending up moderate to intense fire as the first few serials went over. Intense and persistent flak came from the village of Best, a mile southwest of DZ's 'B' and 'C' and from the woods surrounding the drop zones there was light flak and small arms fire which even the last serials rated as moderate to intense. After their drop the troop carriers made 360° left turns. These turns brought some of them over intense flak from the villages of Boxtel and Schijndel, causing a few losses and considerable damage. Probably the best measure of the work done by the flak-busters is that of sixteen aircraft destroyed on the mission only two came from the last four serials, although the number of aircraft damaged in those serials was greater than in the early ones. The inference is that, while small arms and machine-gun fire may actually have increased as the Germans mobilized their forces, most of the anti-aircraft guns had been silenced.

From Serial A-7 flown by the 316th TCG, 685 paratroops and 270 parapacks were dropped on the DZ. This Serial carried war correspondent, Edward R. Murrow of CBS and Mr. Maselle of the Blud Network, his technician. Murrow reported his experiences on the BBC: 'By now we were getting towards the dropping area and I sat looking down the length of the fuselage. The crew chief is on his knees back in the very rear talking into his intercom, talking with the pilots. The rest of the men have folded up their yellow Mae Wests, as there is certainly no possibility of our ditching in the water on this trip. They're looking out of the window rather curiously, almost as though they were passengers on a peacetime airliner. You occasionally see a man rub the palm of his hand against his trouser leg. There seems to be just that - oh - sort of a film over some of their faces, as though they were just on the verge of perspiring but they aren't. Every man the whole length of the ship is now looking down at this Dutch countryside. We see a few stacks down there that seem to be wheat. There's a small factory off to the right, about half of it demolished. The country is perfectly flat of course; a little while ago we saw some of those big thirty-passenger

British Horsa gliders being towed in and it looks much better glider country than it did in Normandy.

'Suddenly the pilot called our attention to the parapacks coming out from the aircraft in front of us.

'There go the parapacks from the formation ahead of us - yellow, brown, red, drifting down gently, dropping their containers. I can't see, we're a little too far away -1 can't see the bodies of the men - yes, I can, just like little brown dolls hanging under a green lampshade they look....

'Just before our men dropped we saw the first flak.

'I think it's coming from that little village just beside the canal. More tracer coming up now, just cutting across in front of our nose.

'They're just queued up on the door now, waiting to jump. Walking out of this aircraft with no flak suits, no armour plating on the ship, we're down just about to the drop altitude now - there are more tracers coming up - nine ships ahead of us have just dropped - you can see the men swinging down - in just about thirty seconds now our ship will drop and those fighting men will walk out on to Dutch soil - you can probably hear the snap as they check the lashing on the static line - there goes, d'you hear them shout 3-4-5-6-7-8-9-10-11-12-13-14-15-16-17-18 - there they go - every man out - I can see their 'chutes going down now - every man clear - they're dropping just beside a little windmill near a church - hanging there very gracefully - they're all going down so slowly it seems as though they should get to the ground much faster - we're now swinging about making a right-hand turn.

'As we came out there was the blue-grey haze of battle smoke. The parachutes dappled the green fields. And more planes and more gliders were going in. Only a few minutes after the drop we looked down and saw parachutists moving along the road towards a village. They had formed up, were properly spaced and were moving on their first objective.'

From Serial A-9 flown by the 316th TCG, 677 paratroopers and 270 parapacks were dropped on DZ 'O'. The C-47 (42-100517) piloted by 1st Lieutenant John H. Fulton in the 36th TCS had landed at Feltwell thirty miles from Cottesmore to discharge one paratrooper that had gone out of his mind. The private was removed and taken to hospital and Fulton immediately proceeded to DZ 'O' where the troops were dropped successfully. Near Tilburg a C-47 crashed into the rear of Fulton's aircraft, tearing off the roof of the fuselage from the pilot's bulkhead to the tail and completely destroyed the hydraulic system and VHF equipment. Despite this Fulton managed to fly the C-47 on one engine. The other C-47 was seen to veer off to the left with its port engine smoking; one parachute was seen to open.

Fulton's plane suffered hits by flak but the C-47 remained airborne and helped by a P-47 in the 82nd Fighter Squadron, 78th Fighter Group, Fulton was able to reach the safety of the open sea. But the tail section began to vibrate and spotting an ASR launch, Fulton decided to ditch. He landed into wind at about 90 mph and the plane came to a stop about 100 yards abeam of the launch. None of the crew was injured in the ditching. They were conveyed to Felixstowe and spent the night at Martlesham Heath airfield before returning to Cottesmore the next morning.

In the leading C-47 flown by Major Ben Kendig the 44th Squadron CO in the 316th TCG, John Dolan jumped with Brigadier General 'Jim' Gavin and he landed close to the woods. 'The losses were small at the landing. The Dutch were coming out of the church at that time and some rushed over to offer their help. The Germans were completely taken by surprise. The greatest advantage of the dropping by day proofed to be the fact that the troops could now operate within their own units. In Normandy many men had fought the first few days alone or in small groups, before they found their own unit. This time the men landed together and everybody could find his own unit and could fight with his own weapons. In the drops at night, there were much more problems collecting the supplies, so you fought with the first thing that came to hand. If you where a BAR-rifleman and found a bazooka instead, you would fight with that. You would swap it at a later time.'

In another C-47 in the 316th Robert Murphy recalled: 'It was a beautiful Sunday afternoon; there were no clouds, so we had a great view on the Dutch landscape from our position near the door in the C-47. We had extensive fighter cover this time. We could see these fighters diving down on the flak towers and that was a marvellous sight. The dropping at daylight had opened the possibility for a much higher casualty rate than a night drop. Some estimates ran up to a loss of fifty percent of the aircraft. There was some flak when we came in over the drop zone, but it had been a peaceful trip for the biggest part.' Fellow trooper Private Howard Swartz wrote: 'After takeoff I remember seeing the white cliffs of Dover, as we came over them. Then when we came over Holland I remember that parts of the country had been flooded by the Germans. We had cover from our fighter planes. There were many aircraft in the air. There as a lot of fire coming from the ground, rifle fire and flak. The plane directly to our right wing took a hit and we saw it go down. None of the paratroopers were able to leave the plane before it crashed. It was quite a relief when the order came to stand up, hook up and stand in the door. We were all anxious to get on the ground and retaliate. When we got to the ground there was quite a bit of confusion trying to locate the other members of our squad. But we managed to do so. My squad's first mission was to secure the drop zone and hold it until the arrival of the gliders on the next day. There was quite a bit of ground fire when we landed, but that receded after an hour or so. We moved up for a mile and then the officers apparently decided that the area was secured, so we went back to the drop zone and dug in for the night.'

Besides the sixteen troop carrier aircraft shot down, fourteen were badly damaged and 84 received moderate or light damage. Of the badly damaged aircraft, four had to make emergency landings in Belgium and several others barely reached England. The 53rd Wing had 26 men dead or missing and wounded or injured.

This time enemy fire had almost no effect the delivery of the paratroops. The formation held tightly together and the pilots of the damaged aircraft coaxed them along with a skill and a cot age which had the paratroops open-mouthed. One colonel was so absorbed in watching the struggle of a badly damaged aircraft to reach its zone that he almost forgot to jump.

'Don't worry about me,' the pilot of a burning aircraft told his flight leader. 'I'm going to drop these troops in the DZ.' He kept his word' - a crashed in flames immediately after the drop, least three other pilots stayed at the controls burning aircraft and gave their lives to give the paratroops an accurate drop. Every one of 1,424 sticks was dropped and, except for those two aircraft shot down near Rethy, not one dropped prematurely.

The 434th TCG spent the summer of 1944 mainly in carrying freight, fuel and troops to France. It was not involved in the invasion of southern France (as were several of the England-based C-47 groups) and its next combat operation was `Market'. Two serials of 45 C-47s each dropped paratroops of the 101st Airborne Division in the Veghel sector. Heavy flak shot down four aircraft and damaged ten of the first serial and another plane was lost from the second serial plus nine damaged. Next day, eighty of the group's aircraft towed gliders to a landing zone in the Son area. Seven gliders landed prematurely, two of them in the sea and flak brought down two C-47s and damaged 33.

The first three serials, ninety aircraft of the 434th Group and 45 in the 442nd were to deliver the 501st Parachute Regiment and a few other troops, about 2,050 in all, to DZ's 'A' and 'A-1' near Eerde and Veghel on what was soon to be known as 'Hell's Highway'. They began their run-in at Oirchot on the Wilhelmina Canal about twelve miles southwest the zones. The flak at Oirchot was particularly thick, which may account for the one bad drop given the 101st. The lead serial, which was carrying the 1st Battalion of the 501st to DZ 'A-1' swerved west of its true course and at 1301 dropped 42 sticks of troops in fields about three miles northwest of the zone. No pathfinders were to operate on DZ 'A-l', but it seems as though a 'Rebecca' on DZ 'A' should have shown the serial its error. The lapse in accuracy was offset by an excellent drop pattern. The battalion was able to assemble ninety percent of its men and materiel inside 45 minutes. It then marched, down a straight, open road to Veghel, preceded by an advance guard in requisitioned trucks and on bicycles, overcame token resistance by about thirty rear-echelon troops and by 1600 had taken its objectives, the two bridges over the Aa river just southeast of the town. The second serial dropped at 1306 in an excellent pattern at the western end of DZ 'A' and at 1311 the third serial put its troops in an equally fine pattern centred about 1,500 yards west of the zone. Three stragglers from the first serial also dropped near DZ 'A'.

Serial A-8 comprised 45 C-47s in the 304th and 305th Squadrons of the 442nd Troop Carrier Squadron who were transporting the 3rd Battalion of the 501st Regiment and the 3rd Platoon, 'B' Company of the 326th Airborne Engineers from the 101st Airborne. The C-47 named *Sonya* (43-15111) piloted by 2nd Lieutenants Herbert E. Shulman, who was born in Puerto Rico and Omar Kampschmidt most probably took a direct hit over the DZ which set the aircraft on fire but Shulman radioed his flight commander and told him, 'Don't worry about me. I'm going to drop these troops right on the DZ'. (Shulman probably said this in reference to the drop in Normandy when the paratroopers landed over a wide area because of heavy anti-aircraft fire and a cloud bank that made formation flying impossible). James Guthrie, who was a witness to the events, recalled: 'The paratroopers and the parapacks were dropped normally. The Dakota continued north and then made a wide turn to the left. It lost a lot of altitude and was below the formation. The last I saw were three men jumping from the burning plane by parachute, of which one parachute did not open.'[11] Sergeant Charles A. Mitchell watched in horror as the plane streamed flames from its port engine. As the pilot held it steadily on course, Mitchell saw the entire stick of paratroopers jump right through the fire. *Sonya* crashed near Erp on the banks of the Aa river below the Vogelenzang road. Shulman and his co-pilot, whose parachute failed to open, died in the crash. Both men were buried temporarily on the cemetery in Erp and later repatriated home. Shulman was awarded a posthumous DSC.

The 501st Regiment assembled 95 percent of its men and material in 45 minutes without any opposition and dispatched its battalions to their assigned objectives. By 1515 the 2nd Battalion had secured the road and railway bridges over the Willems Canal and the 3rd Battalion had taken Eeerde and set up positions south of the drop zone on the Eindhoven-Arnhem road. Within another hour contact was established with the 1st Battalion and Veghel was occupied. About 1800 the 3rd Battalion made contact with patrols of the 502nd Regiment moving up from DZ 'C'.

The 501st Regiment had taken all its 'D-Day' objectives intact and 32 prisoners besides at a cost of ten jump casualties and apparently no battle casualties. It was in touch with airborne units dropped south of it and had encountered very few of the enemy. No operation could have begun more auspiciously.

The next three serials, 45 aircraft of the 442nd Group and ninety in the 436th, were to deliver the 506th Regiment and a platoon of engineers, about 2,200 men in all, to DZ 'B', the southern member of the pair of drop zones a mile northwest of Zon. Except for one aircraft which was shot down early, those serials dropped their paratroops with great accuracy from tight formations at 1312, 1315 and 1324.

The regimental CP was set up at 1345 and within an hour after the jump assembly was eighty percent complete. Only 24 men had been hurt in the drop. The journal of the 506th calls it 'an ideal jump, better than any combat or practice jump [we] executed' and its after action report likewise described the drop as 'the best the unit ever had.'

The 1st Battalion had the urgent task of taking the road bridge and two small bridges over the canal at Zon before they could be blown up. Guided by experience in Normandy, it made a quick assembly on the south side of the DZ and started. Troops too late for the initial assembly formed groups of fifteen to 25 under an officer and set out after the rest. Thus most of the unit was well on its way within 45 minutes. In hopes taking the bridges by surprise the battalion moved due south through the woods from the drop zone to the canal and then turned left along the can bank to Zon, but it was observed and its advance was halted by fire from two 88 mm guns.

The 2nd Battalion, which was to assemble at the east end of the zone and advance down the big way against Zon an hour after its jump with t rest of the regiment following, was half an ho late in getting started. It had lost some time because of confusion with assembly signals of the 502nd Regiment on the neighbouring zone and more in assisting the glider serial which landed after it and in waiting for its commanding officer, who was missing. The battalion met no opposition on the road. Of at least four German tanks which might have attacked it, Allied fighters had destroyed two and driven off the rest. The 2nd Battalion like the 1st was held up temporarily by German fire in Zon. By 1600 resistance had been broken, but as the two battalions converged on the road bridge it blew up in their faces. The other bridges had been destroyed a day or two before. Some paratroops swam across and secured the far side of the canal while engineers built a footbridge across it. This was ready by 1730 but was small and weak that the 506th did not get completely across until 0100 and then had to halt for the night about 1,500 yards south of the canal.

The regiment had been supposed to take Eindhoven and its bridges by 2000, but its inability do so did not matter, since the British Guards Division which was to use those bridges had stop for the night six miles short of them at Valkenswaard. The division had jumped off at 1435 behind a rolling barrage from 400 guns with close support from 100 Typhoons working in relays but had had to fight its way past anti-tank weapons set near the road in swampy woods into which tanks could not go and pilots could not see. Somehow the Germans had gathered five battalions of tough troops to man those positions.

In any case, the crossings at Eindhoven were not difficult. What was essential was to have a crossing over the wide Wilhelmina Canal ready for the British tanks. For that purpose the airborne engineers dropped with the 506th worked frantically all night on the centre trestle of the Zon road bridge, the piers and underpinnings of which fortunately had not been much damaged by the blast.

The last parachute serials flown by the 53rd Wing were two of 36 and 28 aircraft respectively from the 435th Group and two of 45 each from the 438th Group bearing the 502nd Regiment, the advance echelon of Divisional Headquarters and a company of engineers, a total of 2,434 men, to be dropped on DZ 'C'. The lead aircraft of the 435th was flown by Colonel Frank J. MacNees the Group Commander with General Maxwell D. Taylor and the regimental commander as passengers. These serials kept the prescribed formation, route and timing all the way to the drop zone. When they were between ten and twenty miles away they picked up the signals of the pathfinders' 'Eureka' set. They reported seeing a 'B' of white panels spread out on one of the zones but no 'T'. As the first serial of the 435th approached the zone, the last serial of the 436th, slightly off course and four minutes late, cut across its path forcing it to climb to avoid a collision. As a result the 435th had to make a high drop from between 900 and 1,200 feet. Otherwise the drops were orthodox and very successful. Between about 1324 and 1338 the four serials dropped 2,391 of their paratroops on or very near DZ 'C'. One stick had been dropped near Rethy when its aircraft was fatally hit and another overshot slightly because a trooper was slow to jump. Ten men were returned for various reasons.

The 502nd Regiment considered its jump fully as good as that of the 506th. It was able to assemble within an hour. The 3rd Battalion, which rated its drop as very good and its assembly as excellent, had gathered 85 percent of its strength by 1440. The function of the 502nd Regiment was to act as a connecting link between the 501st on the north and the 506th on the south and to act as divisional reserve. Its 1st Battalion marched north up the road, easily captured Sint-Oedenrode, halfway between Zon and Veghel and about nightfall made brief contact with the 501st north of Sint-Oedenrode. A bridge over the Dommel in the town was taken intact.

One company of the 3rd Battalion was sent to seize a bridge over the Wilhelmina Canal nearly a mile southwest of DZ 'C'. It set out at 1440 and took the bridge without much trouble, but German forces counterattacked out of Best, drove the paratroops from the bridge and almost cut them off. The rest of the battalion moved to their aid at 1845 but was engaged by an approximately equal force of Germans and had to dig in short of the bridge. The rest of the 502nd Regiment spent the night near the drop zone.

Following the paratroop formations to the Zon area came two serials (A-29 and A-30) in the 437th Group at Ramsbury with 35 aircraft apiece towing Waco gliders. The gliders contained 43 jeeps, eighteen trailers and 311 airborne troops, mainly from the 101st Division's signal company and reconnaissance platoon plus some headquarters, artillery and medical personnel and a 'Phantom' (British liaison and combat communications unit) detachment. The large number of vehicles and the complete lack of artillery pieces showed that the 101st expected to need mobility more than firepower. Also, its planners had supposed that British artillery would very quickly come within supporting distance.

Glider pilot Flight Officer James Larkin who flew 'Chalk 62' (43-39784) which was towed by a C-47 (42-100805) flown by 1st Lieutenant Melvin B. Fredette and 2nd Lieutenant Darrah L. Roberts recalled: 'Our glider carried a jeep and three 101st Airborne guys and a bunch of other stuff including land mines, ammunition and boxes of other 'stuff'. A sergeant sat in the co-pilot's seat and we flew single-tow across Belgium and crossed over the line where the fighting was going on. I let the sergeant manipulate the wheel, turn it back-and-forth to see what the rudder would do in case I got wiped out he would have a half-way decent chance in getting that thing down. That was the best I could do and we had a lot of fun talking about it. The

British were all poised ready to roll and as soon as we got over the Belgian border, why of course all hell broke loose as far as flak was concerned. Holland was a real 'flak' mission. There, everybody was shooting at us. We were low, 500 feet above the trees and so it was crazy. A number of gliders did not get through of course, but my glider did. As a matter of fact, my whole flight got through.'

Three of the gliders aborted over England; one ditched safely in the Channel; and two broke loose or were released over friendly Belgium. The Germans, who found the glider formations a splendid target, brought down six of the 64 aircraft which crossed their lines and damaged 46 more, six so badly they were fit for nothing but salvage. The troop carriers had eighteen men missing and three wounded. Aircraft losses of nine percent (nineteen percent counting salvaged aircraft) and a damage rate of seventy percent contrast painfully with the corresponding ratios of four and 23 percent in the paratroop serials. Glider missions had flown in daylight with impunity in 'Neptune' on 'D+1' and in the invasion of southern France. 'Market' was a different story.

Seven gliders came down between the IP and LZ 'W'. At least three and perhaps five of these premature releases were made because the tug aircraft was hit and about to crash. One of the seven gliders plummeted into the ground; one was unaccounted for. The rest landed safely and all the men and materiel aboard them reached the division in a day or two with the help of friendly Belgians.

The first serial released its gliders at 1348 and the second did so at 1355. Three Wacos, two of which had collided in flight, crash landed on the zone, killing a pilot, injuring five men and damaging the cargoes. The remaining 53 gliders found ample room on the zone and landed safely with 252 troops, 32 jeeps and thirteen trailers. In one instance a soldier took the controls after the pilot was wounded and steered the glider down. The glider operation had been costly, but it had successfully delivered to the landing zone about eighty percent of the personnel and about 75 percent of the heavy equipment and vehicles carried.

When James Larkin's glider got to the landing zone there were a number of German tanks on the landing zone. 'Some of the fighter bombers were trying to take those out at the time, so, that was a little bit of excitement and they did take them out finally. We landed at the southern end - there were some bridges to be captured. Ok, so we land, get out of the glider and as always, we knocked our window out, pilot and co-pilot; we had plastic windows on the side. Before we took off we always knocked those out.

It made a lot of noise in the cockpit but it worked OK. And then when we landed we didn't have to climb back over that jeep, we could just go out that hole where that window was. It was big enough we could get out of there in one leap. And then, after things settle down, go back to your glider and get the stuff you needed out of it. Our glider was in a ploughed field and the furrows ran up to where a German tank was. Four P-51s were circling that tank. They went around it and as they came in they shot at it with their machine guns and whatever else ordnance they had - those guys were really good. Then came another guy from the side shooting at the tank's undercarriage and those airplanes buzzing around finally knocked that tank out. In the meantime, we were lined up with that tank and those airplanes and as the pilot pulled up the machine gun would still be on you. As they pulled up there were two or three occasions when the bullets were just a few inches of us hitting that black dirt but none of us got hit us. They hit the glider with the machine gun, but it didn't matter. When that tank was taken out - somebody else had taken out the other tanks there - and then about an hour or hour-and-a-half things calmed down except for the artillery.

'The Germans had now dragged their artillery out of the landing zone and were sending shells in, which they did more or less continuously and so that was that. Another pilot from my outfit named Johnny Murphy who had been flying a glider next to me and I palled up and went over to a farm and made friends. We gave them some cigarettes and the girls a bar of soap. That night we stayed in the farm house. The Sweeres had a room upstairs where I stayed and Murphy stayed somewhere else. The next day, some more gliders came in and the landing zone was starting to get cluttered up with gliders which would come in every which way; some of them shot up and some when their pilots panicked, tipped upside down or whatever. On the second day, Colonel Robert Sink, a moustached, good looking guy who was in command of the 503rd Parachute Infantry Regiment that was there came by in a jeep and saw that we were glider pilots and he said, 'Hey, what are you guys doing?' We said, 'well sir, we were just waiting for the British come up and get over that bridge, we going back to Brussels.' He said, 'we got six lifts coming in here; I need you guys to stay here and keep some landing lanes open.' He said gliders were scattered 'from Hell to breakfast' and was going to send over an Airborne bulldozer, a jeep and four infantrymen so we could pull the gliders out of the way or push them out of way to keep the landing lanes open. And he said 'after a lift comes in, you guys get back out there and keep this whole area (about a mile or so) open so that the new gliders would have a place to go and turn off if they wanted to. So, we did.'

The troop carriers had a quiet trip until they reached Grave. The route proved to have been well-chosen and effective preliminary bombing combined with splendid work by the flak-busters to reduce ground fire over most of the route to a negligible quantity. However, one aircraft was shot down and a few damaged by gunners near Zevenbergen and Oosterhout. As the mission neared its drop zones enemy fire began to thicken. The most intense and accurate light flak and small arms fire came up from bridges and wooded areas, especially the Reichswald Forest, over which passed the eight serials which made left turns after completing their drops. One aircraft crashed and another crash-landed shortly before reaching their zones but all their troops had been able to jump. Soon after leaving DZ 'T' four more were shot down by guns near that zone or in the Reichswald. On the way back two aircraft went down over Holland and one had to ditch, but two of these losses were caused primarily by collision rather than by flak. All aboard the ditched aircraft were rescued and fifteen other troop carrier men landed or parachuted safely and reached the Allied lines. Most spectacular was the case of Lieutenant Colonel Frank X. Krebs, commander of the 440th Group and Major Howard W. Cannon, piloting a C-47 named *Miss Yank*. Born in St. George, 'Utah' in 1912, Cannon became intrigued by the budding aviation industry while attending Dixie Junior College in the 1930s. He was more than just a little impressed by the glamour of flying in those days. 'Lindbergh had recently made his epic ocean-crossing flight and that added to the pilot mystique that dominated that era.' He later recalled the Arnhem mission:[12]

'Just as we passed Breda [The Netherlands], we were hit. I heard a terrific explosion in our left engine. The left propeller vanished, there was a huge hole in our side and companionway and the cockpit was a shambles of broken glass. With the controls gone, the ship began to nose down in a spiral. I rang the signal bell ordering the crew to bail out. Hydraulic fluid from the shot-out lines spurted all over us, almost blinding me. I groped for my parachute but slipped on the fluid and fell on my face. When I regained my balance, I had a hard time getting out of my flak suit, but I finally hooked on the chute pack and managed to reach the cabin door with the aid of Colonel [Frank] Krebs. The rest of the crew had already bailed out. I had never jumped before. Hardly able to see, I dived. When my parachute billowed out, I was at an altitude of 800 feet.'

Once Cannon and Krebs were on the ground, they were greeted by a Dutch farmer, Piet Withagen, who helped them bury their parachutes and gear. Cannon said local policemen who were part of the Dutch underground helped them evade German troops in the area. 'With the policemen slowly riding their bicycles ahead of us, we started the longest walk I've ever taken,' Cannon wrote. 'The Germans would have shot without warning anyone out after curfew without special identification. Three times we encountered enemy patrols, but the policemen tipped us off and we kept out of sight until the patrols passed.'

Cannon and Krebs eventually reached a farm, where they were hidden in a shed. They were greeted by a Dutch 'reception committee,' neighbouring farmers who brought them bread, cheese and hot milk. 'Everyone there wanted to shake hands with us,' Cannon recounted. 'It gave me a singular feeling of brotherhood that I had never before experienced.' Cannon and Krebs initially hid in a department store, where they slept in the upholstery department. They would escape to the store owner's house via a tunnel or climb through a trap door and hide on top of the elevator when the Germans would barge into the store. They were joined by other downed Airmen, including British and Canadian flyers, until there were thirteen of them - too many to safely hide in the store. The Dutch Resistance provided Cannon and Krebs with civilian clothes, ration books and forged identification papers for their escape. Cannon's Dutch alias was a city clerk, while Krebs posed as a school teacher. They travelled for miles, staying in the homes of sympathetic Dutch families. They spent a period of time living under the floor of a Dutch officer who had spent eighteen months in a Nazi prison. Because the house was routinely searched by German soldiers, Cannon and Krebs felt they were endangering the lives of the officer and his family. They decided to move on and were issued new identities - Krebs as a farmer and Cannon as his hired hand. Cannon and Krebs rendezvoused with two teenaged Dutch boys who were munching on apples, the recognition signal. The Dutch boys guided Cannon and Krebs to the American lines and a few days later they rejoined their unit after spending 42 days behind German lines.

Captain Don Orcutt, of Poulsbo, Washington, one of the pilots in the 95th Troop Carrier Squadron, 440th TCG: Orcutt had enlisted with the 104th Engineers of the National Guard in 1940. He was promoted to 1st Lieutenant and joined the Army Air Corps in 1943 and married Marion Dorothy Wille on 15 September in Seattle that same year. Donald Orcutt, flying a C-47 with eighteen men of the 82nd into a drop zone 500 yards from the edge of the forest, dropped to fifty feet for a fast turnaround. 'It was only then I spotted a German 88mm anti aircraft gun crew up ahead and only five hundred yards from the edge of the drop zone. The 88 was slightly off to my left and pointed directly at us. I distinctly remember the image of the gun crew. One man was naked from the waist up, the second guy had on only his long johns and boots and the third guy, a sergeant who was completely dressed as though about to answer roll call, pulled the lanyard just a moment before we roared over. I didn't see the muzzle flash. The three Germans looked directly up at us as we barrelled by. They must have taken a hell of a blast from our prop wash and wing down wash. The shot missed, obviously, or I wouldn't be here to talk about it.[13]

Elsewhere, a flak shell tore through the floor of a plane carrying paratroopers of the 101st. 'Now they give us a latrine!' one shouted to his fellow passengers. Private Robert Bryce, braced in the door of a low flying C-47, saw Dutch civilians 300 feet below making the 'V-Victory' sign. 'They're giving us two to one we don't make it!' he told the men behind him.

Total losses on the mission were ten aircraft destroyed and 25 troop carrier men dead or still missing at the end of October. Six men were wounded or injured and 118 aircraft were damaged, about twenty badly enough to require salvage or lengthy repairs. About eighty percent of the damage was concentrated in three serials which dropped on DZ 'T', evidence that the area around that zone was the most hazardous traversed on the mission.

The first drops were to be made on DZ 'N' by two 45-aircraft serials of the 313th Group and one of the same size from the 316th Group. Aboard them were 2,281 paratroops of which 2,151 were from the 505th Regiment and in their pararacks were 756 containers with seventy tons of supplies and equipment. In accordance with plan, DZ 'N' and DZ 'T' were unmarked, but the pathfinders had their beacons and signals in full operation on DZ 'O'.

Through an error in marshalling the 313th Group's second serial had exchanged places with the first. This formation, accidentally in the lead, appears to have sighted the smoke and panels on DZ 'O'. Nevertheless, it swerved north of course and under intense fire dropped almost all of the second battalion of the 505th between 1½ and three miles northeast of DZ 'N'. (Probably because of this heavy fire the drop was made from between 800 and 900 feet above sea level instead of about 600 feet as specified in the orders). Only six pilots carrying regimental headquarters and signal men did locate their zone and drop their troops on or near it. This performance in broad daylight shows the folly of economizing on pathfinders. Had radar and visual aids been functioning on DZ 'N' such a mistake could hardly have happened. The first seven aircraft in the 313th Group's other serial followed the lead of their predecessors and dropped half of regimental headquarters between two and three miles north of DZ 'N' at 1308. The rest, carrying the 3rd Battalion, gave it an excellent drop. The third serial, which brought Division Headquarters and the 1st Battalion of the 505th, had gotten so far south of its course that it actually passed over the lead serial of the 53rd Wing while the latter was making its drop northwest of Veghel. It quickly reoriented itself and by careful observation of landmarks achieved a perfect drop on DZ 'N' at 1312.

The 2nd Battalion of the 505th was supposed to occupy the west side of the regiment's perimeter, make contact with the 504th along the Maas-Waal Canal, reconnoitre a railway bridge over the Maas between Molenhoek and Mook and occupy high ground west of Groesbeek. Although their drop was neither accurate nor compact, most of the battalion had come down fairly close together near the village of Kamp about a mile northeast Groesbeek. Using an observatory as a rally point, they assembled a strong nucleus within half an hour and at 1415 set out to take their objectives. Against feeble opposition they pushed through the northern part of Groesbeek and seized the hill beyond it without a struggle at 1545. The battalion then sent a strong patrol south the railway bridge, which it found destroyed. Two patrols were dispatched westward to the canal make contact with the 504th. At 1930 one of these reached Bridge 8 over the canal near Malden. The bridge had been blown, but the men could see elements of the 504th on the far side. At 2100 the other patrol made contact with the 504th at the southernmost canal crossing, Bridge 7 between Heumen and Molenhoek, which the 504th had taken intact.

The 3rd Battalion of the 505th had assembled and set up its CP by 1345. Two companies then marched on Groesbeek, which was less than mile north of the zone and took it easily about 1500. The other company patrolled south-eastward toward the Reichswald Forest. The enemy halted its probing in several sharp encounters ne the edge of the forest but showed no aggressive tendencies. The tanks rumoured to be in the fore did not appear.

The 1st Battalion, which was to hold the division's southern perimeter from the rail bridge to the Reichswald, assembled about ninety percent its strength on DZ 'N' before 1330 - in less than twenty minutes. It proceeded to occupy positions the southern end of the Groesbeek ridge and the sent detachments west to Mook and the rail bridge south to Riethorst and east to the edge of the Reichswald. They took thirty prisoners at Mook and found the enemy in the Reichswald much weaker than expected, but at Riethorst on the main road running along the Maas to Gennep the Germans attacked with motley forces of somewhere more than company strength. By nightfall they had been beaten off with heavy losses and the front was quiet.

Thus by 2100 the 505th Regiment had taken all its objectives and held a strong semi-circular perimeter extending from the canal on the west to Rieihorst in the south and Heikant in the east, A summary of battalion strength reports at 2200 gave the 1st Battalion 43 officers and 614 men, the 2nd, 42 officers and 552 men and the 3rd, forty officers and 592 men. The regiment had at its disposal over 95 percent of those who had made the drop. Jump casualties from accidents and wounds combined had put only 14 of its men out of action and battle losses had been very small.

The second trio of serials, also of 45 aircraft apiece, carried 2,031 troops of the 504th Regiment. One aircraft load carried by the 315th Group went down over western Holland. Three soldiers refused to jump and two wounded were brought back. The rest jumped in the vicinity of DZ 'O'. The first of these serials, flown by the 316th Group, was to put down the 1st Battalion of the 504th at the east end of DZ 'O', a mile northeast of the village of Overasselt and 1½ miles west of the Maas-Waal Canal. The battalion had the task of taking the bridges over the canal and its drop point had therefore been set as close to them as was feasible. The drop was good, though about five minutes late. At 1315 32 sticks landed on the prescribed spot and the rest within a mile of it.

The 315th Group, flying the other two serials, was to drop all but eleven sticks a short distance northwest of Overasselt. Doing what the 504th's commander called a splendid job, it put all 78 sticks within 1,500 yards of the pathfinder beacons. In this area landed all of the 504th Regiment except the 1st Battalion and 'Easy' Company. That company had been detailed to drop in heavily ditched fields on the far side of the river to take that end of the Grave Bridge. The road, river and bridge marked the spot unmistakably, but ten of the eleven sticks landed between 500 and 1,200 yards south of the zone, possibly because the pilots feared they might drop the men in the river.

Eldon Sellers remembered flying back to England with a terrific headache from the tension. 'The sun was in our eyes most of the way, making it unpleasant. When we had returned to our home base in England we realized that we had several holes in the wing from 20 mm tracer shells. We had flown so low that these shells had to have come from people shooting at us from the flak towers. The shells had gone through the plane in a downward angle. We had seen the tracers on our way, but thought that we had escaped un-hit. We were debriefed and given a shot or two of whiskey. I sure could use one this time.'

At the end of the day the 504th was established securely on all its objectives at about 95 percent of full strength. Enemy action and jump injuries had produced 57 casualties. A slightly larger number of men, all of whom were later accounted for, were still missing.

The seventh serial in the 82nd's mission, thirty aircraft of the 439th Group, arrived at its destination, DZ 'N', at 1321, slightly ahead of schedule. The group gave a near perfect drop to 47 headquarters artillery personnel and 388 men of the 307th Engineer Battalion. All the troops landed on the zone with only six injured and one man wounded. There being no immediate call for engineers, the 307th was used initially to provide security for divisional headquarters and later to guard the 82nd's CP, which was set up at 1700 about 1,000 yards west of Groesbeek.

Next to drop were 1,922 men of the 508th Regiment and forty pathfinders of the 325th Glider Regiment, transported by two 45-aircraft serials of the 441st Group and one of 42 aircraft in the 440th Group with DZ 'T' as their destination. Charles Everett Bullard, a crew chief in the 440th observed: 'The place was bustling with activity. Looking out over the flight line at ninety C-47s lined up nose to tail with the spaces between the aircraft cluttered with paratroopers and their equipment was a sight more impressive than that of the morning of 'D-Day' June 6th.'[14]

One stick had to jump near DZ 'O' and another went out half a mile short of the zone because the aircraft carrying them were about to crash. Two or three other sticks jumped between DZ 'O' and DZ 'T' because of over-eagerness. Two pilots overshot the zone by 1,000 yards and dropped their loads east of it near Wyler. About 25 paratroops, a majority of whom had been wounded, were brought back to England.

The zone was unmarked and hopes that the first troops to land could set off smoke signals for later serials were not fulfilled. Nevertheless, although the fire around DZ 'T' was severe, headquarters and two battalions of the 508th were put down in excellent tight patterns just outside the northern edge of the zone and the 3rd Battalion, also well massed, was placed within its eastern end. The drop had begun at 1326 and by 1500 the regiment was ninety percent assembled. The commander of the 3rd Battalion wrote: We could not have landed better under any circumstances.'

The 376th Parachute Field Artillery Battalion was sent in the eleventh and last of the division's paratroop serials, a 48-aircraft formation of the 440th Group at Fulbeck, to drop on DZ 'N' at 1340. This gave the 505th about half an hour to clear enemy from the vicinity and to mark the zone with smoke as insurance against the inaccuracy and heavy losses which had plagued artillery drops in the past. The serial carried 544 troops and 42 tons of materiel, including twelve 75 mm howitzers. It reached the zone at 1333, about seven minutes early. This time every stick landed on or very close to the zone. In slightly over hour the battalion was assembled and had ten of its howitzers ready for action. Another gun was firing before nightfall. According to General Gavin these weapons were of very great assistance in breaking up attacks by low-calibre German troops thrown against his division in the 24 hours after it landed.

After the paratroops of the 82nd Division came a single glider serial from the 439th Group bound for LZ 'N' with fifty aircraft towing Wacos. In the first 22 gliders were 86 men of 'A' Battery; 80th Airborne Anti-tank Battalion, with eight 57 mm guns, nine jeeps and two trailers of ammunition to provide some insurance against attacks enemy by armour. In the rear were elements divisional headquarters, divisional artillery headquarters, the divisional signal company, the reconnaissance platoon and an air support party, which all together numbered 130 men and eighteen jeeps. The serial began its take-off from Balderton, just south of Newark in Nottinghamshire at 1112 hours and began assembling at low altitude while the 439th's paratroop serial was still circling overhead. Soon afterwards the serials of the 440th Group swept over the field causing some confusion. Two gliders broke their towropes at take-off and had to start over and another, brought back because its load started to shift, was towed to Holland alone some time after the rest. One Waco carrying a jeep began to disintegrate over the Channel, was released and ditched safely. Anti-aircraft guns on Schouwen Island brought down one aircraft and its glider, putting six troop carrier men and two of the airborne in the missing column. Five aircraft were damaged by anti-aircraft fire. With these exceptions the flight was successful and comparatively uneventful. Release was made at 1347 about a mile short of the proper point. This error probably prevented some losses by enabling the serial to make its turn without going over enemy positions in the Reichswald Forest. Only some of the gliders reached LZ 'N', but forty came down within a mile to the west and the other one in the formation landed about 1½ miles west of the zone. The terrain, on which they landed, though hillier than that within the zone, was otherwise favourable. Two of the gliders were destroyed in landing and fourteen were damaged, but only seven of the airborne troops were injured and four of the jeeps seriously damaged. All the guns came through intact.

American newsmen who interviewed the C-47 pilots on their return produced some exciting snippets for their readers back home. 'We carried paratroopers', recalled Lieutenant Kenneth McKim, a pilot in the 303rd Squadron, 442nd TCG from Hackensack, New Jersey; born 8 December 1922 in the Bronx, NY. 'It hardly seemed a war was going on as we crossed Belgium where farmers waved to us from fields below. Some were pitching hay while others tried to herd the cattle which ran around like mad as hundred after hundred of C-47s and pursuit escorts roared overhead. The first I knew of enemy attack was when the lead plane of the formation ahead of us burst into flames in mid-air and spiralled downward. We could see the Drop Zone then, but it seemed as though we would never reach it. After an eternity we hit the DZ and dropped our sticks of paratroops.

Direct ack-ack hits knocked off two pararack bundles, set both gas tanks aflame as Flight Leader Captain Melvin J. Parker, Blackwell, Oklahoma, approached the target area. Pilots on both sides advised that the fire was spreading, suggested that he drop his troops short of the objective and abandon ship. But he held his position in formation, made the drop over the DZ. He remained at the controls while his crew bailed out and then crash-landed the burning craft. Rather than drop the men in the midst of the enemy Captain Parker sacrificed his life to fulfil his mission.

When both engines were knocked out after dropping his troops, Lieutenant Albino Dell, Antonia, Allentown, Pennsylvania was forced to land. But he was accustomed to landing without power. He had learned to fly in one of Mussolini's glider schools as a student in Italy from 1935 to 1939.

Most flew from twenty to 75 feet above water all the way across the Channel. Flying above an overcast meant glider pilots would fly blind. One pilot recalled seeing a plane and glider at house-top level skimming so low over Antwerp they actually flew between - not over - a pair of church steeples.'

Unprecedented numbers of gliders followed into the Nijmegen and Eindhoven areas behind the 'chute soldiers, continued to reinforce the drop at Grave for several days.

Now a new enemy arose to harry the aerial thrust - fog. An unpredicted weather front over the North Sea rolled a blanket of mist across the Low Countries, at times more than 1,000 feet higher than the prescribed course.

C-47s in the 62nd Troop Carrier Squadron, 314th Troop Carrier Group loading
British paratroopers at Saltby.

A paratrooper and air crew in the 88th Troop Carrier Squadron, 438th Troop Carrier
Group check their watches.

Lieutenant General Lewis Hyde Brereton poses for the camera at Andrews Field (Great Saling) in Essex, home base of the 322nd Bomb Group, in front of *Mild and Bitter*, the first B-26 Marauder to complete 100 missions. The Group remained at Great Saling until September 1944 when it moved to France.

C47A 42-100766 *Lilly Bell II* in the 89th Troop Carrier Squadron, 438th Troop Carrier Group at Greenham Common, Berkshire in June 1944, which was named by the 28-year-old pilot, 1st Lieutenant Mercer Wilson Avent in honour of his wife's maiden name Lillian Bell. On 17 September *Lilly Bell II* dropped men of the 101st Airborne near Eindhoven and on 18, 19 and 23 September, towed gliders to the same location. On the morning of 25 October *Lilly Bell II* was one of a formation of four C-47s that took off from Greenham Common for the flight to Denain/Pouvry airfield south east of Lille loaded with 5,120lbs of signal equipment. *Lilly Bell II* crashed into a field two miles north of Guildford, Surrey. Avent and his crew were killed.

Turf and Sport Special in the 61st Troop Carrier Squadron, 314th Troop Carrier Group at Saltby.

C-47 in the 92nd Troop Carrier Squadron in a hangar at Upottery.

C-47s and Waco gliders in the 316th Troop Carrier Group at Cottesmore.

C-47s and Waco CG-4a's in the 436th Troop Carrier Group at Membury in September 1944.

British paratroopers in front of a C-47 at Barkston Heath.

The scene on the runway at Spanhoe with C-47s and CG-4A gliders in the 36th Troop Carrier Squadron, 316th Troop Carrier Group being prepared for takeoff at Cottesmore. Note the towing ropes, that also contain an intercom cable, spread out in such a manner that they cannot tangle.

C-47A 43-15663 in the 434th Troop Carrier Group at Aldermaston.

C-47A 42-92865 in the 306th Troop Carrier Squadron, 442nd Troop Carrier Group.

Paratroopers in the 101st Airborne Division apply the finishing touches to the artwork on their Waco CG-4A glider before leaving for Holland.

Major C. L. Schmid, CO, 80th Troop Carrier Squadron in the 436th Troop Carrier Group at Membury in the cockpit of *Caunt Miss Itt*. (Peter Schmid)

C-47 'Chalk 62' (42-100499) in the 316th Troop Carrier Group at Cottesmore with paratroopers of the 1st Battalion, 504th Parachute Infantry Regiment.

C-47's 'Chalk 44' 43-15317/R and 43-15671/W in the 316th Troop Carrier Group with 'C' Company, 505th Regiment, 82nd Airborne preparing themselves for the mission ahead prior to boarding their aircraft at Cottesmore.

S-2 Platoon (Intelligence) including Staff Sergeant John F. Tiller (far left) and Sergeant William R. Canfield (centre) in the 501st Parachute Infantry Regiment waiting to board their C-47 in the 73rd Troop Carrier Squadron, 434th Troop Carrier Group at Aldermaston.

British paratroopers wave their farewells to Stirling crews on 295 Squadron and other troopers in their Horsa gliders at Harwell on 17 September 1944.

C-47s setting off.

Stirling crews on 295 Squadron at Harwell on 17 September 1944.

Stirlings on 620 Squadron returning from their drops at Arnhem.

A Stirling IV towing off a Horsa during a training sortie.

An Albemarle VI on 297 Squadron in flight in September 1944. Due to the short range of the Albemarle aircraft, 296 and 297 Squadrons at Brize Norton temporarily moved to Manston on 15 September 1944, so that they could play their part in Market Garden. Both squadrons flew fifty Albemarle sorties, all glider towing, without loss.

Lieutenant Michael Donald Keen Dauncey of the Glider Pilot Regiment receiving his award of the DSO.

RAF ground and air crew on 620 Squadron at Fairford.

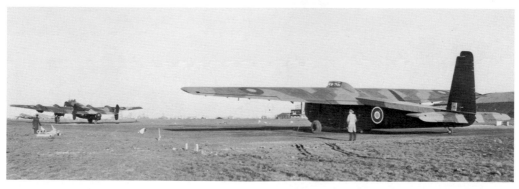

Halifax tug and Hamilcar glider.

Left: C-47 43-15617 in the 37th Troop Carrier Squadron, 316th Troop Carrier Group at Cottesmore crossing the coast at Aldeburgh in Suffolk en route to Holland with CG-4A glider 43-37328 in tow.

Below: Paratroopers of the 82nd Airborne parachuting from their 48th Troop Carrier Squadron, 313rd Troop Carrier Group C-47 over Groesbeek.

British paratroopers in front of C-47s in the 14th Troop Carrier Squadron, 61st Troop Carrier Group at Barkston Heath.

British troops loading a jeep into a Horsa glider.

General Maxwell D. Taylor commanding the 101st Airborne Division salutes for the camera before taking off for Holland.

General 'Jim' Gavin commanding the 82nd Airborne Division and his paratroopers at Cottesmore getting ready to fly to Holland. Gavin flew in the lead plane ('Chalk 44'/43-15324) flown by Major Ben Kendig the 44th Squadron CO in the 316th Troop Carrier Group.

Only momentary breaks permitted hasty orientation. For pilots, each day was a veritable classroom in weather.

With tight formation flying a near impossibility, individual navigators assumed a new value. One of these, Lieutenant Paul McPherson of Sigourney, Iowa carried on although a piece of shrapnel had pierced his leg. The painful wound hastily dressed by emergency first aid, he continued to navigate from a prone position.

'I'm going to find that LZ if I run out of gas looking' said 2nd Lieutenant Vincent Ruby, Rome, New York as he started for Holland, towing a glider. The glider load shifted in mid-air following take-off on schedule and Lieutenant Ruby returned to the field. After the load was readjusted and secured in place, he took to the air again but couldn't catch up to his formation. Finding the landing area, he released his glider safely over the target but was wounded by intense AA fire on the return trip. Plane and crew eventually were flown to the home base.

Lieutenant Thomas Mantell, born 30 June 1922 in Franklin, Kentucky was piloting *Vulture's Delight* in the 96th Troop Carrier Squadron, 440th Troop Carrier Group. Mantell was nicknamed 'Shiny' by his comrades. This was because of his 'constant well-scrubbed look.' He was also described as 'able to think fast and act quickly', attributes he needed when he came under heavy anti-aircraft fire. All but one of the rudder and elevator controls were disabled and the C-47's tail was set on fire. The crew chief fought the fire with live ammunition detonating. Rather than release the glider, Mantell decided to continue with his mission. The glider was released at the correct location and the C-47 returned to Fulbeck. Upon inspection, his aircraft was so damaged that it appeared to be unable to fly.[15]

Hostile fire knocked one engine, hydraulic system and all the flight instruments on the C-47 piloted by Captain James Brown [the 304th Squadron Operations Officer]. After cutting the good engine, he was told to move the ship elsewhere. Brown, who was from Montgomery, Alabama, nursed his aircraft back across the Channel and made an emergency landing [at RAF Manston in Kent with a wounded navigator]. After landing he remarked, 'I never saw a more beautiful runway in my life than the one we landed on.'[16]

It was the first combat flight for co-pilot Lieutenant John Alday, Cuyahoga Falls, Ohio and the sight of anti-aircraft shells swimming up toward the plane was new. Suddenly, just short of the release, a burst of flak penetrated the ship. The first pilot slumped forward. There wasn't time to determine the extent of his injuries. His aircraft and glider were a hazard to the rest of the formation. Alday took over while the navigator held the limp pilot away from the controls, but they were losing altitude fast. Instruments no longer registered. The left engine began to vibrate dangerously. Skilful handling brought the glider near the assigned drop area where it made a successful landing. Meantime, the C-47 staggered back to occupied Belgium with the vibration growing steadily worse. In spite of greatly reduced power, Alday made an emergency landing on a small strip without further injury to the plane or crew. When asked about the flight, the only comment of the crew chief, Tech Sergeant John A. Dean, Breckenridge, Texas, who administered first aid to wounded buddies on the hazardous flight, was: 'Bud'; scared ain't the word!'

In the 442nd Troop Carrier Group, Lieutenant Edward Hufnagle from Pittsburgh had a close call. During a run, a machine gun bullet struck his left knee but failed to pierce the skin. It fell harmlessly to the cockpit floor. He carries the bullet now as a souvenir. Hufnagle said, 'When the bullet hit, I had the co-pilot take over. I grabbed the bible that Chaplain 'Bob' Tindall had given me and read all the way back. I prayed all the while I was in that corridor of flak and feel our safety was a result of prayers.' (Robert W. Tindall, known affectionately as 'Chaplain Bob,' was an ever-present force within the Group in the run up to D-day and throughout the remainder of the war in Europe. 'Chaplain Bob' had a unique view of the human factor in the Group's participation in 'D-Day'. He greeted each crew upon their return after the mission, mourned those who did not and buoyed the spirits of those who faced future missions.)

As Lieutenant Gerald Arons, Peoria, Illinois, put it, 'I think most of our squadron had more sympathy and concern for the glider pilots they were tugging than for themselves. All they thought about was keeping the glider boys in the clear.'

'One strange, but true story happened on the night of the 17th' recalls Flight Officer George E. 'Pete' Buckley in the 74th Troop Carrier Squadron, 434th TCG at Aldermaston. 'Two glider pilots in the squadron, who had been drinking, got into a violent verbal argument which ended up in a tooth and nail fight on the barracks floor. One of them went after his Thompson submachine gun with the intention of killing his opponent. Fortunately he was disarmed by others in the barracks before he could pull the trigger. After the fight was broken up, they still vowed they were going to kill each other. When things finally calmed down and they had been put to bed, everyone passed it off as pre-mission jitters and went to bed.'[17]

During the night ten aircraft of RAF Bomber Command dropped dummies and firing devices west of Utrecht and another ten did so near

Emmerich in an attempt to divert enemy forces from the 'Market' area. The Germans were sufficiently deceived to send troops into the supposed drop areas and as late as D+4 they listed the drops as genuine. However, capture of an Allied field order on the evening of 'D-Day' revealed to the Germans the true location and objectives of 'Market' and thereby destroyed most of the value of the deception.

At about 1800 hours on the 17th General Brereton decided to postpone 'H-Hour' on 'D+1' from 1000 to 1400 hours and to send all his missions over the southern route. The delay was determined by predictions that fog would cover the take-off fields during the early morning and that there would be rain and low clouds over the Channel and the Low Countries until about noon. The change in route was made to avoid flak. If the British and the 101st Division progressed as expected, the southern route would be in friendly; hands as far as Nijmegen. Early on the 18th the weather appeared to be developing as predicted, but by late morning dense masses of low-lying clouds were threatening to make the southern route unusable. Therefore Brereton hastily ordered all missions to fly along the northern route. The arrival time was left at 1400 hours. The effect of these changes was to mass four missions on one route at one time, an achievement made possible by the prior arrangements for three-lane traffic. Serials for the 101st Division would fly in the right lane and head right at the IP to LZ 'W'. Those for the 82nd Division would be in the centre and American aircraft carrying British paratroops to Arnhem would use the left lane and turn left at the IP. Overhead at 2,500 feet would be RAF aircraft towing gliders to the Arnhem area. In all, 1,336 American troop carrier aircraft, 340 RAF troop carriers and 1,205 gliders would be dispatched. Immediately after them 252 B-24s on the bomber resupply mission would fly over the same route to get the benefit of the anti-flak operations set up to protect the troop carriers.

'The next morning' wrote Flight Officer 'Pete' Buckley 'there were marginal weather conditions of low ceilings, rain showers and patches of ground fog, none of which was suited for glider operations. In spite of this the planes and gliders were given the green light to take off. The 101st was in a jam in the Eindhoven-Best area near Zon, trying to hold off German counter attacks and were in desperate need of this resupply mission. As the group approached the Channel, the weather took a turn for the worse, with a solid fog bank ahead of them. Eighty of the C-47s with gliders in tow were given the signal to abort and turned back to England. The rest of the serial did not get the recall message to abort and continued on straight into the fog.' [18]

Chapter 6

'D+1' 18 September - One Way Ticket To War

The next day we did it again. This time my take-off was without incident, but on the climb up to our cruising level I stupidly did a rather tighter turn than usual and suddenly I was being yanked uncomfortably about the sky by my glider, which this time contained a jeep and two trailers, with a few soldiers as well. 'What the hell's going on back there?' I shouted down the intercom. I soon found out when 'Bill' Randall got into the astrodome.

'One of the front bits of rope has got the wrong side of the glider's nose wheel.'

'Can you cope?' I asked the two staff sergeants.

'We've got the controls almost upside down, but we can manage.'

I knew full well that we couldn't fly for four hours like that, but they wouldn't hear of me taking them back.

'We'll carry on like this,' they insisted.

Then I had an idea. 'I'm going to ease the throttles slightly,' I told them 'and then, when the ropes have fallen away from the nose wheel I'll take up the slack.'

'Bill' proceeded to give me a running commentary and after a few minutes of agonizingly careful flying, the rope tautened without breaking and we rejoined the stream.

Again I was impressed by the almost fanatical keenness of these airborne troops. They intended to get into the action at any price. This trip was almost easier than the first and we all marvelled at the lack of opposition as we passed over Arnhem and dropped our gliders on to the now overcrowded target field. Back at Down Ampney

'D+1' 18 SEPTEMBER - ONE WAY TICKET TO WAR

I logged up another six hours of flying. The date was 18 September 1944.

Flight Lieutenant 'Jimmy' Edwards, later famous as a comedic script writer and comedy actor on both radio and television, best known as 'Pa Glum' in *Take It From Here* **and as the headmaster 'Professor' James Edwards in** *Whack-O!*

As dawn broke at Harwell the airfield was covered in thick fog and nothing including four Stirling-Horsa combinations carrying 6080 and 6341 LWUs could move until late morning. Each unit was split into two loads which can be broadly categorized as the receiver and display equipment in one load and the transmitter and aerial in the other load; unit personnel were split between their two gliders. With sufficient visibility by 1200 hours the lift started and first combination airborne was chalk number '5001' with Staff Sergeant John Kennedy as first pilot and Sergeant 'Wag' Watson as co-pilot. The 'tug' was a Stirling on 570 Squadron flown by Flying Officer Spafford RCAF. The formation join up was complicated and Spafford's combination being the first to take off had to fly straight ahead to allow other combinations from Harwell to formate. Stirling LK121 on 570 Squadron piloted by 29-year old Pilot Officer Charles Culling, who was from Birmingham took off at 1208 hours towing Horsa chalk number '5000' with Staff Sergeant 'Lofty' Cummins as pilot and Sergeant McInnes as co-pilot carrying personnel and half the equipment of 6080 LWU. Loaded into 'Chalk 5001' were personnel from 6341 LWU and half the radar equipment. Horsa '5002' piloted by Staff Sergeant 'Teddy' Edwards with Sergeant William 'Fergie' Ferguson as his co-pilot was carrying personnel and equipment of 6080 LWU and was towed by a Stirling on 295 Squadron. The Harwell formation then flew to a main rendezvous at which they joined the main attack force. The main formation comprised three streams of aircraft and gliders on the left of the formation and slightly lower flew combinations of Halifaxes towing Horsas, Halifaxes towing Hamilcars and some Dakotas not towing. To the right there were numerous Dakotas towing Wacos some of them actually towing two Waco gliders. In the centre stream in which the LWUs were flying there were Halifaxes towing Hamilcars and Stirlings towing Horsas; a truly impressive sight.

At Broadwell airfield Lieutenant Colonel 'Tommy' Haddon commanding the 1st Battalion, The Border Regiment had waited to fly out with the Second Lift. Born on 19 February 1913, the son of Major J. T. Haddon of the Cameronians, 'Tommy' was educated at Hamilton Academy and Sandhurst, before being commissioned into the Border Regiment in 1933. With the 2nd Battalion of that Regiment, he served in India and saw active service on the North-West Frontier in 1937. In 1939 he transferred to the 1st Border, which was soon to leave their Aldershot barracks for France as part of the British Expeditionary Force. As a Major, Haddon commanded 'B' Company and spent a cold Christmas on the largely inactive front line, where he found it necessary to keep one eye focused on the enemy and the other on frostbite - his moustache froze on several occasions and became quite uncomfortable as a result. The 1st Border played its part in the desperate rearguard action towards Dunkirk in May 1941, from where they and Haddon were eventually evacuated. In 1941 Haddon left the 1st Border for Staff College and later became Assistant Secretary of the Joint Intelligence Sub-Committee of the War Cabinet. He had been the duty officer on the night when Japanese bombers attacked the US fleet at Pearl Harbor on 7 December. He passed this message on to 10 Downing Street and Churchill promptly got in touch with President Roosevelt and asked. 'What's all this about Japan?' Haddon was quite keen to be relieved from his staff duties at Whitehall and with the help of the Colonel of the Border Regiment, he returned to the now glider-borne 1st Border as Second-in-Command on the 27th January 1943.[1]

At Sicily, like so many others of the 1st Border, Haddon ended up in the Mediterranean. His tug circled several times before turning its back on the flak coming from the mainland and cast off the glider with it having no hope of reaching land. The glider landed hard and the tail and fuselage immediately went under. By the time the emergency doors had been opened, the water was up to the waists of those inside. However, everyone managed to get out with Haddon being the last to depart from his side of the glider. The group recovered on the wings for a short time before swimming ashore. With its job done, the heavily depleted battalion was moved back to North Africa later in July and Haddon was promoted to Lieutenant Colonel and given command of the 1st Border. Sicily was not the first time that the colonel had crashed in the sea and it would not be the last.

Haddon's run of bad luck had continued on 17th September. His glider had only been airborne for moments before the tow rope broke and the pilots were forced to cast off but at least this time they were on dry land.

Haddon and his men returned to Broadwell to await the glider mission on 18 September when they would be towed by a 437 Squadron RCAF crew skippered by Flying Officer George Edgar Henry RCAF from Manitoba operating Dakota KG328, a 575 Squadron aircraft. Henry, his navigator, Flying Officer Henry Joseph Love McKinley, an American from Brooklyn who had joined the RCAF, the wireless operator, Warrant Officer William Fowler and Warrant Officer Albert E. Smith, another navigator, had flown a successful glider tow to Arnhem on the 17th. 'Bert' Smith, born on 30 May 1917 in County Armagh, Northern Ireland had joined the RAF in 1939 and trained as a pilot in Belfast. When he arrived in England he was put down as a navigator, thereafter progressing to become an instructor and then a bomb aimer. When Transport Command established squadrons for the specific purpose of training and deploying airborne troops, Smith was highly recommended for a move to a Dakota squadron as his navigating and aiming skills were much in demand. He got on very well with 'Ed' Henry whom he found to be an easy going Canadian. Henry's crew was one of two stand-by crews brought in at the last moment to tow gliders like Haddon's that had aborted the first lift. Unfortunately, no-one thought to tell them that the southern approach route had been changed to the northern route because it had been affected by a thick raincloud.

The second instalment of paratroops were to drop on DZ 'Y' at Ginkel Heath, an ideal open quadrangle containing well over a mile of ground but about eight miles away from the road bridge. It lay north of the Amsterdam railway about a mile west of LZ 'S'. Gliders would use DZ 'X' as a landing zone and supplies were to be dropped on DZ 'L', an area containing less than a square quarter-mile, located about half a mile east of LZ 'S'. The success of this plan depended on maintaining fairly complete control over a strip of land eight miles long and up to three miles in width extending from DZ 'Y' to the bridge, a very large task for half an airborne division.

As Horsa '5000' in the four LWU combinations piloted by 'Lofty' Cummins and McInnes approached the turning point at Hertogenbosch for the approach to LZ 'X' the combination experienced heavy anti-aircraft fire and Stirling LK121 piloted by Pilot Officer Culling, was hit. Culling advised Cummins that they would have to slow down but shortly thereafter the Stirling reared up and spun into the ground from 3,000 feet killing all on board. Sergeant Vincent Williams was only nineteen and came from Bolton. Corporal John Coleman RCAF aged 26 from Montreal was on the ground staff and had asked if he could go as an observer on the operation. Cummins, showing great presence of mind managed to cut the towline and landed heavily near the village of Hemmen some seven miles from the LZ and the wrong side of the Neder Rijn. It was a quiet area and they were quickly surrounded by Dutch patriots all speaking good English who told them they were in German occupied territory. The radar equipment was destroyed by gunfire. The glider pilots and 6080 LWU personnel then headed on foot for Divisional HQ led by a Dutchman on a bicycle. All but Cummins crossed the Rhine by the Friel-Hevesdorp ferry and reached Oosterbeek. Although it is not clear why Cummins tried to cross the Nijmegen Bridge - the glider landed north of the river Waal - he was shot dead by a sniper in attempting to do so.

Horsa '5001' also experienced heavy ack-ack fire but Staff Sergeant Kennedy was released at the right point and after pulling off to port in a climbing turn made a good approach under machine gun fire and managed to land the glider as briefed running up to the hedge on LZ 'X' where a dangerous situation had developed to the southern end where a strong German force infiltrated between two of the Border Regiment companies defending the LZ and was able to direct machine gun and other fire at landing gliders. Horsa 5002 piloted by 'Teddy' Edwards and Sergeant Ferguson was carrying personnel and equipment of 6080 LWU and was towed by a Stirling on 295 Squadron. The combination reached the cast off point without damage but during the approach to their designated landing spot '5002' was hit and set on fire before it landed. Edwards warned everybody on board to disembark as quickly as possible on landing and 'hit the deck'. The only immediate cover on landing was a field of Brussels sprouts, which the men made good use of. Even so, co-pilot 'Fergie' Ferguson was wounded when a bullet travelled the length of his spine opening the flesh but fortunately not seriously damaging the bone. The glider and its load were completely destroyed by fire.[2]

Horsa '5003' was hit and it appears that its tail was completely shot away from which there was no hope of recovery. The Stirling managed to cut the tow and the glider crashed one kilometre south of the station at Opheusden along the road to Doodeward - all on board were killed. The senior officer on board was Flight Lieutenant Tisshaw with five other ranks. The senior RAF officer on Horsa '5001' decided that it would be impossible to field serviceable radar and so he decided to destroy the equipment on the Horsa which was accomplished by Sten gun fire and explosives. With no chance of becoming operational it was now a case of survival. Personnel from both '5001' and '5002', in the company of some airborne troops, made their way to Oosterbeek. However, after coming under fire en route the party became scattered. Lieutenant Davis, a USAAC controller who had probably been on Horsa '5002' 'acquired' a jeep and after collecting as many LWU personnel as possible made a dash for the Divisional HQ which had been set up at the Hartenstein Hotel. He then set them to work digging in behind the hotel; their timing was good because no sooner had they achieved a reasonable level of protection than the Germans launched a very fierce and intense mortar attack. Radios were the Achilles heels of the operation and the LWUs had lost all of theirs. The army radios did not work and during the mortar attack the US air support team's radio jeep, which was on loan to the Division, was damaged. The Americans sought help from the RAF to repair their radios and LAC Roffer Eden, a 31-year-old wireless mechanic with 6080 LWU, set about trying to salvage something. Shortly thereafter another mortar salvo rained down and Eden had his jugular vein severed. Despite a valiant attempt by Davis to apply first aid, Eden died later. At about the same time an 88mm round burst about 25 yards away and Flight Sergeant Lievense RCAF, the senior radar engineer with 6080 LWU, was hit three times in the back by shrapnel and he died of his wounds on 22 September.

The lift to DZ 'Y' of 2,119 British paratroopers of the 4th Parachute Brigade and with them five tons of supplies including 407 parapacks and door bundles was led by 126 American aircraft. Brigadier General 'Shan' Hackett commanding 4th Parachute Brigade describes the planners: 'The airborne movement was very naive. It was very good on getting airborne troops to battle, but they were innocents when it came to fighting the Germans when we arrived. They used to make a beautiful airborne plan and then added the fighting-the-Germans bit afterwards.' DZ 'Y' was ten miles away from Arnhem, even further than the landings of the First Lift. It would surely have been more prudent to have used LZ 'L', two miles to the east of Wolfheze for 4th Parachute Brigade's drop. Air Vice Marshal Hollinghurst, commander of 38 Group, had decided upon the distant location of the drop zones and despite requests from the 1st Airborne Division, he refused to land troops closer to Arnhem. His reasoning was that the closer his aircraft came to Arnhem, the closer they would come to the large anti-aircraft emplacements (which in the event were not in place) at Deelen airfield.

Fifty-four C-47s in two serials in the 315th Group would carry Lieutenant Colonel Ken Smyth's 10th Parachute Battalion and Battalion Headquarters. Two serials of 36 aircraft in the 314th Group at Saltby would take Lieutenant Colonel George Lea's 11th Battalion of over 900 men that had been billeted at Melton Mowbray.[3] Twenty-six year old Captain Stuart Radcliffe Mawson, regimental medical officer to the 11th Paratroop

Battalion, was assigned to fly in the lead C-47 at Saltby with his colonel. 'The morning of 18 September was windless and the mist still lay very thick in places. It seemed likely in view of this that the take-off would be postponed and I fretted at the prospect of any delay, wanting to come to grips with the thing now as soon as possible.'[4]

C-47 pilot 2nd Lieutenant Eldon Sellers in the 309th Squadron at Spanhoe that had been involved in dropping American paratroopers on the first day, recalled, 'This time we were going to drop British reinforcement troops at Arnhem.' Lieutenant Cecil Dawkins in the 310th Squadron was one of eight pilots taking Brigadier 'Shan' Hackett's Brigade HQ and Defence Platoon. Hackett had a bet about the drop with Dawkins, who as usual wore his coon-skin hat and smoked a large cigar, in which the brigadier promised him a bottle of champagne if his brigade was delivered to the correct place. 'I could tell he was quite calm when the flak started to come up by the lengthening ash on the cigar: his hand was quite steady' said Hackett.

The Second Lift took off at about noon on Monday the 18th and headed for the North Sea. Flying Officer 'Ed' Henry's crew left the stream as KG328 passed over the turning-point at Hatfield. As the other aircraft ahead of them flew north-eastwards Henry turned to the southeast, being forced steadily lower by the thickening cloud on their route. When they reached Belgium they were flying at only 500 feet. Before reaching their zone KG328 was hit by flak in the port side of the cockpit, mortally wounding 'Ed' Henry at the controls. Everyone was carrying a wound of some description. Sergeant 'Bill' Fowler found his lighter in his top pocket was bent in half having been hit by shrapnel. 'Bert' Smith was bleeding from wounds to his chest and the inner side of his right arm. McKinley's map was covered with blood, as his left index finger had been severed and was hanging as if it didn't belong to his hand. His left arm and side had also been hit, but in the excitement pain was not a factor. The crew he said 'didn't even notice the wind blowing through a large hole in the side of the fuselage.'

With no second pilot, the Dakota crew were now in serious trouble. Flying Officer Henry 'Harry' McKinley recalled: 'Here we were, navigator, a map reader and a wireless operator, in a sick plane and none of us had landed one before - and we were lost. We had a problem!'[5]

Having trained as a pilot before becoming a navigator, Warrant Officer 'Bert' Smith struggled to control the badly damaged aircraft. The glider pilots radioed through that their ailerons had been shot away and they would have to cut loose but Smith told them to remain attached until he had brought them back over friendly territory. He did not know until he landed, but most of the tail had been shot away together with the rudders. Although the Dakota was now free of its burden, another problem was discovered when he asked McKinley for a bearing back to base, only to find that he was unable to give one as his navigational equipment had been destroyed. He therefore set the Dakota on a bearing of 270°, reasoning that by heading due west they would reach England sooner or later. The first indication that they had of their position came when they flew over Dunkirk, which was still in German hands at the time and so a good deal of anti-aircraft fire came in their direction. Flying low over the rooftops, Smith evaded this and, with their position now established, corrected their bearing and headed for home. The combination of a damaged craft towing the dead weight of a Horsa made flying conditions most difficult, but Smith managed to get them to the American fighter airfield at Martlesham Heath in Suffolk. It had been 'Bill' Fowler's habit on previous missions to nonchalantly stand in the cockpit doorway, smoking a cigarette, waiting for the order to lower the flaps and undercarriage and, despite the perilous situation they were in on this day, he repeated the same procedure as Smith brought the Dakota in to land. He was, after several hours of wrestling with the damaged aircraft, very tired and had lost a fair quantity of blood; nevertheless he brought the Dakota down safely. It wasn't until he got back to Broadwell and took his trousers off to go to bed that he discovered that he had also been hit in the legs by shrapnel.

'Bert' Smith and McKinley were both awarded the DFC for their actions, but 'Bert', in his modesty, was a little confused by the award as he did not believe that he had done any more than his job had required him to do. Having recovered from his ordeal, he flew to London on the following day to participate in a BBC broadcast. The BBC wanted him to read a script that they had compiled and had not seen before. Smith insisted that there were unacceptable changes made to it. When later he went to the Canadian Club where he was staying, he heard a broadcast by Winston Churchill, followed by his. 'Bert' Smith flew two more sorties to Arnhem, possibly on Wednesday 20th and Thursday 21st September, acting as co-pilot to both the Group Captain and Wing Commander. A short time later, after fourteen months in the Squadron, Smith left 575 on compassionate grounds due to a family tragedy.

Meanwhile, Lieutenant Colonel 'Tommy' Haddon, his Intelligence Officer, Lieutenant Ronald Hope-Jones, their batmen and other Border men were on the ground, 75 miles away from Arnhem and behind enemy lines. However they evaded capture and soon met up with friendly troops of XXX Corps. From here they hitched a lift up the single road to Arnhem, hopeful of being reunited with their comrades. In the final days of 'Market Garden', when the Dorsets were planning to cross the Rhine to assist the Airborne men at Oosterbeek, it was decided that Colonel Haddon and his men would journey across with them. The landing was an utter disaster as the Dorsets landed directly amongst German positions and most were captured. Haddon made his own way towards the Border positions the second he was across the river, but passing through German positions proved to be impossible as daylight arrived and he was captured before he could reach them. So ended his miserable battle. Haddon spent the remainder of the war interned at Oflag XIIB near Hadamar.

Flying in a C-47 in the 50th TCS, 314th Troop Carrier Group from Saltby Major John L. C. Waddy commanding 'B' Company in the 156th Parachute Battalion witnessed a few gliders cast off prematurely to make forced landings in the sea, from where they were quickly attended to by the rescue boats lining the route. Descended from a long line of Army officers it was natural that he joined his family's regiment - the Somerset Light Infantry and was posted in July 1939 to the 2nd Battalion then serving in India. After nearly two years soldiering in the Raj and keen for more adventure, he volunteered for the 151 British Parachute Battalion (later renumbered as 156) which was established in India in 1941. Parachuting was rather rudimentary in India in these early days. Shortly after qualifying he was seriously injured while exiting an aircraft on a parachuting exercise which resulted in him being in a coma for three days. In October 1943 he had received promotion to Major.

Waddy observed that the fighter escort was very effective and following behind were two RAF Typhoons which fired several volleys of rockets at German positions on the ground. He also praised the American aircrews who maintained a tight formation in spite of being subjected to a heavy barrage for half an hour. On the approach to DZ-Y, approximately twelve miles short, he was standing in the open doorway of his C-47, which was towards the front of the formation, when German anti-aircraft fire began to pour up at the planes. They were flying at about 700 feet and were so low that Waddy could see the whites of the gunners' faces as they looked upwards. Then six miles beyond the IP, Waddy, transfixed, saw the lead aircraft in his three-plane 'vic' formation receive a direct hit and explode in a ball of flame. The British major watched it as it went down, passing beneath his aircraft until its port wing hit the ground, causing it to roll over and explode once more.[6]

The C-47,[7] which was piloted by Captain Leonard A. Ottaway, had been carrying eighteen members of 156 Battalion's machine-gun platoon, none of whom survived. Dutch civilians later said that one man was thrown clear, but he died of his injuries in a farmhouse that night. Ottaway, who was born in Kansas in 1917 and had lived in Texas County, Oklahoma, was killed. So too the five other aircrew - 2nd Lieutenant Henry G. Honeysett the 23-year old co-pilot, Captain Herbert Pluemer Jr, navigator of Scotch Plains, New Jersey; Staff Sergeant George A. Collier, crew chief, Staff Sergeant Xon C. Connett the 20-year old radio operator born in Illinois and Sergeant Joseph W. Bobo, radar operator.

Ottaway's C-47 had been the starboard aircraft of a 'vic' of three on take-off at Saltby. However, the leader had been forced to land in England after a badly fitted parachute on one of the supply containers under a wing opened prematurely and the container jettisoned but the parachute then wrapped itself around then tail wheel, with the container hanging below. The pilot landed safely at an airfield in East Anglia where the container was removed and the C-47 took off for Arnhem once more. Ottaway had moved across to fill in the centre position vacated by the leader and it was here that his aircraft was hit in the left wing by small arms causing a large fire, possibly as a result of a ruptured tank. Ottaway was informed of this and immediately set the aircraft into a dive and salvoed the supply bundles from beneath his aircraft. 1st Lieutenant Walter D. Nims reported: 'When I first noticed he was in trouble, his left engine or left gas tank was on fire. Someone notified him by radio and he headed down practically straight ahead and salvoed his bundles. When he left the formation, he was flying at about 1400 feet mean sea level. He headed for the ground as if to make a forced landing. His gear came down and he was apparently ready to land but seemed to be unable to flare out his approach and went right on into the ground, hitting very tail high, buckling the gear and skidded to a stop on its belly. He was indicating about 150 mph. When the plane hit, the gas tank seemed to explode and one wing came half off and the cockpit from the center of the wings forward twisted to one side. The cabin and cockpit were not badly cracked but was on fire when I last saw it. No one parachuted from the plane on the way down.

Three more C-47s in the 314th Troop Carrier Group were shot down in the next few minutes. Captain Warren S. Egbert Jr's C-47 (42-92839) in the 61st Troop Carrier Squadron was hit by flak over the Grebbeberg. When the port engine on caught fire he pulled up alongside his element leader to have the fire checked and then held on until all of the British paratroopers and two of his crew, wireless operator Staff Sergeant J. Yapel and crew chief Technical Sergeant D. Desantis were able to jump. The C-47 crashed on the river bank south west of the rail bridge at Rhenen. Egbert, his co-pilot 2nd Lieutenant Horace M. Jerome and navigator 1st Lieutenant Jacob Feldman were killed. Staff Sergeant J, Yapel was taken prisoner and Technical Sergeant D. Desantis was hidden by the resistance.

Pilot, 2nd Lieutenant George C. Merz in the 61st TCS of Milwaukee, Wisconsin recalled: 'We took off about 1100 hours, crossed the English coast at Aldeburgh and flew across the English Channel to the Dutch Island of Overflakee (no kidding). From there we flew to our Initial Point (IP) at Wageningen before turning toward the drop zone near Ede which is west of Oosterbeek and Arnhem.' At 1400 hours his aircraft was hit by German ground fire and crash-landed in a field between Wageningen and Rhenen. Several in his formation watched Merz go down and since there was fire in the cockpit, none thought that anyone could possibly have survived. Navigator, 2nd Lieutenant Russell C. Stephens and radio operator, Tech Sergeant William Buckley tried to bail out of the small door in front of the left prop and were killed instantly. The crew chief, Corporal Richard Eastman was captured later by the Dutch SS and shot. 'If he hadn't tried to surrender, if he had stayed with the two pilots, he might have gotten to a Dutch doctor' Merz said. 'One of the soldiers from my airplane was never accounted for. I suspect he was the one who came out with his tunic on fire. I pushed him to the ground, rolled him around and patted out the fire. He stood up and I took his helmet off. Even though they had darkened their faces with dark grease paint, his eyebrows and his face were singed. He knew it and he decided he wanted to surrender. He walked across the field while the airplane was burning and the guys were standing around. He walked across the open field with his hands up towards a clump of trees toward one of the German anti-aircraft batteries. A couple of days later one of the Dutch Underground guys reported to me that a British soldier had been captured by the Germans and they had a rope around his neck and his face was burned and they were marching him down the road to their headquarters. Dutch SS guys may have shot him. It was worse to be captured by them than it was to be captured by Germans. My Dutch friends hated their guts. Two of them were involved in the murder of Eastman.'[8]

George Merz and co-pilot, 2nd Lieutenant Ernest 'Woody' Haagensen were hidden by the Dutch underground and eventually joined up with 120 British paratroopers to escape through the German lines in Operation 'Pegasus I'.

Captain Donald A. Broaddus in the 62nd TCS who was leading the fifth element of the second serial, recalled, 'We received flak at the IP and constant fire from there on into the DZ. Approximately three miles out from the DZ on the way in we received a particularly heavy concentration of fire and several ships went down. First Lieutenant Frederick N. Hale Jr. flying C-47A 42-100896 on Broaddus' right wing was hit in the right engine. 'He immediately started bailing out his troopers' recalled Broaddus 'and jettisoned his bundles. He then pulled up beside me and called to me over the radio and asked if his right engine was on fire. His right engine was trailing a huge line of white smoke but his fuselage was between me and the engine and I couldn't tell whether it was blazing or not. His troopers had finished bailing out and he nosed the ship down to gain flying speed and appeared to be trying to make a forced landing. His landing gear was shot out and was dangling underneath the plane. During this entire time we were receiving intense fire from the ground. This action took place at approximately 1,100 feet. Hale disappeared from my sight when he started down as he turned slightly to the left. He did not seem to be hit himself and seemed to have complete control of the plane. Unless he was hit again on the way down he seemed to have a good chance for a crash landing as there were many flat fields in the vicinity suitable for a crash landing.'

'Fred' Hale recalled: 'My aircraft was subjected to severe heavy calibre machine gun fire near the IP. As the gunfire increased I dropped my parabundles. The fuselage was riddled but the aircraft remained under control. In the Wageningen area a 40mm calibre shell hit my right engine, causing it to go afire. Seeing this fire, I ordered the paratroops and my crew to jump from the aircraft.' The troops were a stick in the Support Company, 11th Battalion commanded by Captain Frank King.

Born on 9 March 1919 in Brightwell, Berkshire where his parents, Arthur and Kate King were farmers, Frank King was educated at Wallingford Grammar School and but for the outbreak of the Second World War he would have carried on the family farm. Beginning his Army career in 1940, by October 1943 he had joined the Parachute Regiment. King recalled: 'As we flew in over the DZ, the flak was heavy. The Dakota was leaping around like a bucking bronco at one of those rodeo events in America. I noticed the dispatcher [Tech Sergeant Milfred L. Harrold] leaning against the bulkhead on the other side of the door, his legs slightly buckled, one hand grasping the framework above the door, with his chin on his chest as if he was having a nap. I got angry and pushed him to wake him up. It was then I saw the blood pooling at his feet; he was already dead! Shrapnel had come up through the floor and between his legs and killed him. After I pushed him he simply folded over and fell onto the floor.

'I looked out of the door and immediately noticed the flames coming from the engine. The whole section of wing behind it was on fire and a thick black pall of smoke was flowing through the air behind us like a long tail; then I was drawn to the fact that we were much lower than the rest of the formation; in fact we couldn't have been more than 250 feet off the ground and a parachute needs at least 98 feet to open. I quickly turned and yelled to the CSM to check the cockpit. He opened the door and was literally hit by red flames and more black smoke. The pilot and co-pilot were dead - nobody could live through that inferno. He slammed it shut and looked at me as if to say 'What's next?' There was not time to waste; we had to jump, so I yelled, 'CSM, we're going now!' even though the red light was still on and it went against all our instincts to go.

'I signalled to everyone we were jumping and a moment later I launched myself out the door; hopefully everyone in CHQ would follow in quick succession. I felt my parachute tug at my shoulders; I didn't worry about doing drills as it seemed superfluous - I just dropped my bag and suddenly I was on the ground. I could hear the sharp snapping sounds of the rounds from machine guns as they flew all around me. The air was alive with anti-aircraft and machine-gun fire, but I still stood up for a second or two and watched the aircraft go into a slow spiralling spin and smash into the trees just beyond the DZ. It seemed like an eternity, but obviously it wasn't. The next thing I knew the CSM came rushing up to me and yelled, 'we better bloody move sir before Jerry finds our range!' I got out of my parachute harness, fumbled like a fool opening my bag, grabbed what I could from it and ran for my life. By a miracle we only lost two men in the aircraft. One fell at the door, another one left it too late to exit and a third [25-year old Private John Arthur Barton] was later found on the ground. His parachute probably did not open properly, because his body had his parachute shot to hell on the way down. One was also killed as he ran off the DZ. We were lucky as the majority of the Germans were concentrating on those in the air at that point and basically left us alone. Nevertheless, a few seconds more and none of us would have made it out of the door of the aircraft. And now we had to go to war - and what a war it turned out to be!'[9]

'Fred' Hale in fact had not been killed. He went out through the top. About the time his chute opened he swung once and then he was on the ground. The two dead crewmembers King's CSM saw must have been the 21-year old co-pilot 2nd Lieutenant Thaddeus C. Harvey from Owensmouth, California and radio operator, Staff Sergeant Clarence V. Parsons who were leaving the cockpit when a 40mm shell burst under the companionway and also caused the left engine to fail. Hale recalled, 'This shell killed Harvey and Parsons and started a fire inside the aircraft and also set fire to three paratroops still inside the fuselage. Another shell blew off my aileron controls and rendered my instruments useless. Both engines were dead but I attempted to maintain altitude to allow the three paratroops to jump. The companionway was in flames and the aircraft was enveloped in smoke. Knowing it was impossible to land the aircraft, I jumped out the top escape hatch at an altitude of 150 feet. My parachute opened a second before I hit the ground and I was unhurt in the landing. Small arms fire was directed on me so I hid in a ditch until picked up by the Dutch Underground. I was taken to a farmhouse about one mile from where the aircraft crashed and I had landed by parachute. The Underground also carried to the farmhouse five paratroops from my aircraft. I learned from them that three paratroopers had been seriously wounded and were inside the aircraft at the time of the crash, causing their deaths. Another paratrooper from my aircraft had a leg blown off and died before being taken to hospital. No.16 paratrooper could not see the crew chief because of the smoke but stated that the tail of the aircraft had been riddled and that a large shell had hit the right at the toilet and that the large shell could have killed Milfred Harrold. The Dutch buried seven occupants of my aircraft.' Hale remained in the hands of the Dutch Underground until 23 October at which time he escaped through the German lines, arriving in England on the 25th.

Aubrey L. Ross in the 310th TCS experienced a close call. 'I was leading a flight. There were two planes flying formation with me, one on each wing. As we approached the drop zone, we encountered heavy ground fire. Looking out either side of the plane you could see large black explosions, some seemed just inches from the wings of the airplane. As I began dropping the paratroopers, a shell came through the open door (the rear door was removed for drops) and hit one of the British paratroopers seriously injuring his left arm. The crew chief pulled him aside and all of the others jumped. As normal procedure, just as soon as all troops had cleared the plane, I dove for the deck to make us a more difficult target for the Germans. About this time the crew chief informed me that we had a wounded paratrooper in the back. I sent my co-pilot back to the rear of the airplane to administer first aid. He came back a short time later and, said that he couldn't do anything; the sight of blood made him sick. I was very upset and angry with him. After a few of my favourite curse words, I asked him sarcastically if he thought he could fly the airplane for a short time without getting sick. I gave the controls over telling him what heading and altitude to maintain and I went back to see if

I could aid the injured man. This was the first opportunity I had to practice the first aid training given us in school. The poor guy was in shock, with his left arm hanging by a thin piece of skin almost completely severed at the elbow and blood was squirting out of the blood vessels. With the help of other crew members, I tied a tourniquet around the upper arm to slow the bleeding, administered a shot of Novocain, bandaged to keep the arm together, treated him for shock and then went back to the cockpit and headed for home on the most direct route. I wish I had followed up on the outcome of this trooper's treatment, because it appeared to me that he would lose his arm. Our airplane was only hit by this one shell that entered through the open door.'

In the 43rd TCS the picture was quite different as Lieutenant Bernard Coggins, one of the navigators in the lead plane wrote: 'I don't know what hell will be like, but I think we got a preview. Earlier groups had already dropped and the DZ was a solid ball of fire. At the command to jump, our troops had exited from the plane without any hesitation. My admiration, already at an extremely high level where paratroopers were concerned, went even higher as these brave men dropped into that preview of hell. We immediately pushed the throttles to the firewall, hit the deck and got the hell out of there. The tales about that mission lasted a long, long time.'[10]

Thirteen aircraft in the 34th Troop Carrier Squadron dropped their troops and equipment on the Drop Zone. The fourteenth aircraft flew with another serial and dropped its troops and equipment three-quarters of a mile north of the Drop Zone. Two other aircraft suffered damage and one para-rack would not release. Second Lieutenant Jim Spurrier's aircraft, flying on the right wing of 43rd Squadron Commander, Lieutenant Colonel Peterson, began burning near Herrogenlosch. The crew chief, Corporal Russell Smith, saw the fire inside the front of the aircraft and when he received no response from the pilot's compartment on the intercom, he ordered the troops to jump and he and the radio operator followed, jumping at a very low altitude. They all landed near Opheusden, between the Waal and Rhine rivers. From so low an altitude one paratrooper died and the crew chief and another trooper both broke legs. Spurrier and the co-pilot, 2nd Lieutenant Edward Simons Fulmer then attempted to force-land the burning aircraft but the C-47 hit an electricity pylon, skidded round and was engulfed in flames., Fulmer, born East Syracuse, New York on 16 April 1919, took over the controls. Despite severe burns on his face, neck, back and arms, he managed to land the aircraft in a heroic effort to save the unconscious pilot's life. Fulmer was able to escape through a side window. He was awarded the DSC.[11] Spurrier and Corporal Hollis, radio operator, died of their injuries.

Corporal Smith was hidden by the Dutch underground for several weeks and was later turned over to an American unit.

The last C-47 to go down, piloted by Lieutenant Tommy T. Tucker, of Fairmont, West Virginia and his co-pilot, Lieutenant Dave O. Snowden of Vermont, Illinois, still sixteen miles from the Drop Zone, started burning as a result of enemy ground fire. Flight Sergeant Carter, one of 25 instructors from the Parachute Training School who flew with some of their erstwhile pupils, found himself dispatching Major Pat Anson, commanding 'A' Company in the 10th Battalion, a sergeant major and sixteen men of the 10th Parachute Battalion from the burning Dakota twenty miles or more from the dropping zone. This task he accomplished without loss and himself jumped with the American crew whose pilot, Lieutenant Tucker, remained at the controls to the last possible moment and thus ensured a safe drop. Snowden and crew chief, Tech Sergeant Woodrow W. Durbin of Birmingham, Alabama and radio operator, Staff Sergeant Walter E. Hewett of Wilmington, North Carolina bailed out safely behind the enemy's lines. Tucker then crash-landed his C-47. Carter joined the advanced elements of the leading Corps of the Second Army Corps and was back at his task of instructing four days later.

On the way back, danger spots were carefully avoided and the 314th incurred no further losses though, at least 24 of the returning C-47s had been damaged. The returnees blamed part of their losses on lack of fighter-bomber assistance and claimed they had seen no friendly fighters beyond the IP. In the bad weather, 91 out of 904 gliders taking off failed to arrive or were lost over Holland.

Landmarks and navigational aids combined make it relatively easy for most troop carrier pilots in the mission to locate DZ 'Y'. They make their drop in a shower of tracers between 1406 and about 1420 from heights of 800 to 1,000 feet. The drop is rightly regarded as very successful. All but a couple of parapacks and six paratroops, who are prevented from jumping by wounds or snarled equipment, are dropped. About ninety percent of the drops are, as a British participant put it, 'slap in the right place.' However, one nine-plane flight in the last serial, having become separated from the rest of the formation, dropped its loads a mile or two from the zone. A ten-mile breeze was blowing and the troops came down rather roughly in brush and trees, some on top of the 3rd Dutch SS Police Battalion, which was skirmishing with 1st Airlanding Brigade, causing the Dutch SS to rout. Moreover, substantial numbers of enemy troops are in the drop area. One battalion took eighty prisoners before it reached its rendezvous. Heavy German anti-aircraft fire set fire to the heath.

141

C-47 pilot 2nd Lieutenant Eldon Sellers in the 309th Squadron in the 315th TCG recalled: 'On this mission there wasn't as much flak and the British paratroopers jumped out without problems. We did have a few scary moments when we had dropped the paratroopers. The British didn't use a static line going through the centre of the aisle of the plane like the Americans, so the shroud lines extended from their seats. When they jumped out, part of these shroud lines got caught in our elevator. This made the control wheel shake terribly, which made the plane hard to control. We thought that we had been hit badly by a shell, before the crew chief ran to the cockpit and told us what had happened. Our crew chief asked if he should try to shoot at the lines to dislodge them, but we said that he could easily hit part of the plane. So we decided that I would hold him by his legs, while Roger was doing what he could to rock the plane back and forth and get the lines swaying back and forth. The crew chief leaned outside the plane and cut into the lines to release the heaviest part. We accomplished to do so and freed up the elevator.'

Though flak-damaged, all of the 310th Squadron aircraft including the one carrying 'Shan' Hackett flown by Lieutenant Cecil Dawkins returned safely and he won his bet. 'I could tell he was quite calm when the flak started to come up by the lengthening ash on the cigar: his hand was quite steady' said Hackett.[12] Back at base some pilots in the squadron began talking about 'milk-runs'.

The paratroop mission to DZ 'Y' was followed by 295 Dakota, Stirling and Halifax tugs, (In order to bring in the loads of gliders aborting on the previous day the number dispatched was increased from 270 to 296 tugs but one crashed on take-off because of an engine failure). In the gliders was the second echelon of 1st Airlanding Brigade Group. On 298 and 644 Squadrons at Tarrant Rushden the Halifaxes towed fifteen Hamilcars and sixteen Horsas to LZ 'S' and 'X'. The glider column, supposed to fly at 2,500 feet, ran into 5/10 to 8/10s' cloud as low as 2,000 feet with the result that nine of the gliders broke loose over England and two over the North Sea. Ground fire over Holland was thicker than it had been on the day before, especially in the Hertogenbosch area, where heavy flak was seen bursting and several gliders were hit. The second lift did not arrive until between 1500 and 1600 hours. By now the situation in Arnhem had deteriorated beyond repair. The remainder of the South Staffords and the rest of the divisional troops landed at DZ 'X' (in 194 Horsa and fourteen Hamilcar gliders) towed by Stirling, Halifax and Dakota aircraft and LZ 'S' (in 52 Horsa and one Hamilcar gliders). Only one C-47 was lost, but twenty escorting fighters were shot down holding off ninety Luftwaffe aircraft.

As on the first day the accuracy of the flying was very good. All the pathfinders' beacons and markers were functioning, but again 'Rebecca-Eureka' worked badly. Less than half of those interrogating the 'Eureka' on LZ 'X' received responses. Of 73 glider-tug combinations sent to LZ 'S', 69 reached the landing area and at least 67 put their gliders on or near the zone. Of 223 dispatched to LZ 'X', 203 reported success and photographs showed 189 of their gliders on or close to the zone. The principal flaw in the performance was that most of the glider pilots ignored the 'T's laid out to show wind direction. In spite of this, serious accidents were rare and caused less damage than the German forces just outside the zones. It was estimated that while only 39 of the 533 gliders accounted for in the first two lifts were wrecked at least 47 of the 332 gliders on and around LZ's 'X' and 'Z' were destroyed by mortar fire or burned to prevent their falling into the hands of the enemy.

The mission by 35 Stirlings of 38 Group at Harwell to drop supplies on LZ 'L' at about 1500 ran into trouble because their intended supply drop zone was still in German hands and they copied the British recognition signals. A dozen Stirlings on 570 Squadron were to tow Horsa gliders to Arnhem while eight more carried elements of 1st British Airborne Corps HQ to Nijmegen. Only seven Horsas arrived at Nijmegen as Stirling LK560 piloted by Flight Sergeant N. J. Kirkman had already crashed on takeoff at Harwell due to engine failure. The glider that this aircraft had in tow was airborne at the time of the crash and so it was able to put down safely. The Stirling was wrecked but all aboard survived, though one man was injured.

The Arnhem contingent on 570 Squadron delivered all of their charges without loss, although Acting Squadron Leader James Stewart piloting Stirling LK555 encountered a considerable anti-aircraft fire at the DZ. Having released the Horsa and about to turn away for home, he observed that the gliders that had been released and were on their way down were being fired upon very heavily so he deliberately turned his aircraft across the landing zone to draw the enemy fire and in so doing his aircraft was extensively damaged by flak. His actions and determination undoubtedly helped several of the gliders to achieve a good landing. He was able to bring his damaged aircraft back to Broadwell.

Stirling navigator 'Ted' Wood on 570 Squadron recalled: 'We went in Vics of three until we reached the Dutch coast, where we met two other streams of Vics of three. We were then nine abreast as we went in and it was estimated that there were 2,500 aircraft in the sky at that moment, at 2,000 feet. So what it sounded like on the ground, God alone knows. Amongst that lot were 25 squadrons of fighter escort and any fool who opened up on the ground, you would see the 'Tiffies' go down - and they never missed. They just aimed the aircraft at the target and let the rockets go. That went well and we reached Arnhem and dropped our gliders in the fields outside Arnhem town.'

During the drop at LZ 'L' most of the Stirlings had been hit by AA fire and fourteen aircraft in the formation, including three on 570 Squadron were damaged, one fatally. Flight Lieutenant Dennis Liddle and crew flying LJ913 were thought to have been hit repeatedly by anti-aircraft fire in the area of the DZ and crashed landed at Schaersbergen. Liddle pressed on and dropped his load of supplies on the DZ before the aircraft was seen to crash land to the north-west of Arnhem. All the crew and the two despatchers bailed out and were taken prisoner.

In the region of Stampersyat Stirling AJ594 flown by Pilot Officer D. H. Balmer RCAF, a 25-year old lumberman from Comox, British Columbia was severely hit by flak. Balmer recalled: 'The aircraft immediately caught fire and I gave the order to bail out. Rear gunner, Flight Sergeant J. T. Archer, passenger, Sergeant R. W. Crabb, bomb aimer, Pilot Officer E. G. Blight, flight engineer, Sergeant T. Ireland and navigator, Flying Officer V. C. Keag all bailed out, but as the aircraft was by this time too low for a safe jump I told the remaining members of the crew that I was going to make a crash landing and that they should assume emergency positions.

Second pilot, Flying Officer Geoffrey Adrian Mombrun, at great risk to himself strapped me into my seat, using his arm as a strap, realising that if this was not done I stood a grave risk of being killed on landing. By doing so he thereby jeopardised his own chance of escape. I landed the aircraft in a grass field at Zegge near Boosschenhoofd, badly bruised and shaken but otherwise unhurt. Mombrun and wireless operator, Flight Sergeant R. J. Kempton were in the same state.' (Driver W. H. Bridgeman sustained a dislocated shoulder and was taken prisoner. 31-year old Corporal A. E. Barker who was from Braintree, Essex had a serious head wound and was taken to hospital at Roosendaal where he died). 'The aircraft which was burning was immediately surrounded by Dutch people and Father Pater Raseroms a Catholic priest who spoke English took us to a nearby house where a young girl tended our wounds. From there on my movements were arranged for me.' For nine days the evaders remained in hiding with a downed American Dakota crew[13] and Sergeant Fitzpatrick of the Royal Armoured Corps who had been taken prisoner and had escaped from the Germans at Breda railway station, until

3 October, when they were dispersed to different addresses. Balmer stayed in Breda until the Polish troops entered the town on 31 October.

One returning pilot reported dropping by mistake on LZ 'S', which was about a mile west of 'L'. All but two of the others believed they had made accurate drops, generally from heights of about 500 feet but the 803 panniers and containers dropped were rather widely scattered and many drifted southwest of the zone into enemy territory, probably because the aircraft from which they fell had flown too high. The net weight of supplies dropped was 87 tons and of this only twelve tons were recovered. In contrast, two bulk-loaded Hamilcar gliders yielded fourteen tons of supplies between them.

While the American airborne was having hard fighting on 'D+1', the British had worse. Frost's paratroops at the road bridge were penned in by German guns and armour and suffered severely. The 1st and 3rd Parachute Battalions spent a nightmare day struggling forward down city streets flanked by well chosen and strongly manned German positions. By evening they had gained only a few hundred yards and had been whittled down to about 100 fighting men apiece. To make matters worse, the divisional commander and the commander of 1st Parachute Brigade had been cut off from their men while following the 3rd Battalion in its house-to-house fighting.

Back in the drop and landing areas the glider troops were having a hard fight to hold their perimeter and even had to use the bayonet to throw back attacks in some places. Nevertheless, the commander of the 1st Airlanding Brigade ventured to send half a battalion of the South Staffordshire Regiment down the Heelsum-Arnhem road to reinforce the paratroops. Like their predecessors they reached the western outskirts of Arnhem, rat into strong opposition and could go no farther No more troops could be spared until that day's missions arrived and their arrival had been postponed four hours; a painful delay for the British airborne.

Landmarks and navigational aids combined made it relatively easy for most pilots in the mission to locate DZ 'Y'. They made their drop in a shower of tracers between 1406 and about 1420 from heights of 800 to 1,000 feet. All but a couple of parapacks and six paratroops, who were prevented from jumping by wounds or snarled equipment, were dropped. About ninety percent of the drops were, as a British participant put it, 'slap in the right place.' However, one nine-aircraft flight in the last serial, having become somewhat separated from the rest of the formation, dropped its loads a mile or two from the zone. A ten-mile breeze was blowing and the troops came down rather roughly in brush and trees.

Moreover, substantial numbers of enemy troops were in the drop area. One battalion bagged eighty prisoners before it reached its rendezvous. Despite these minor blemishes and inconveniences, the drop was rightly regarded as very successful.

The paratroop mission to DZ 'Y' was followed by 295 RAF aircraft towing gliders to LZ 'S' and LZ 'X'.[14] In the gliders was the second echelon of 1st Airlanding Brigade Group. The glider column, supposed to fly at 2,500 feet, ran into 5/10ths to 8/10ths cloud as low as 2,000 feet with the result that nine of the gliders broke loose over England and two over the North Sea. Ground fire over Holland was thicker than it had been on the day before, especially in the Hertogenbosch area, where heavy flak was seen bursting and several gliders were hit. Only one of the tugs was shot down, but thirty were damaged. The glider of the destroyed aircraft may have reached the Arnhem area. A total of thirteen gliders were loosed over Holland and one, badly damaged, over friendly Belgium. Some may have snapped their cables, but at least nine of these fourteen releases were caused or necessitated by ground fire.

As on the first day the accuracy of the RAF fliers was very good. All the pathfinders' beacons and markers were functioning, but again 'Rebecca-Eureka' worked badly. Less than half of those interrogating the 'Eureka' on LZ 'X' received responses. Of 73 glider-tug combinations sent to LZ 'S', 69 reached the landing area and at least 67 put their gliders on or near the zone. Of 223 dispatched to LZ 'X', 203 reported success and photographs showed 189 of their gliders on or close to the zone. The principal flaw in the performance was that most of the glider pilots ignored the 'T's laid out to show wind direction. In spite of this, serious accidents were rare and caused less damage than the German forces just outside the zones. It was estimated that while only 39 of the 533 gliders accounted for in the first two lifts were wrecked at least 47 of the 332 gliders on and around LZ's 'X' and 'Z' were destroyed by mortar fire or burned to prevent their falling into the hands of the enemy.

There is an element of mystery surrounding the loss of Dakota KG592 listed as missing on 48 Squadron on 18 September. On 10 September 24-year-old Flying Officer Albert Lavoie RCAF had taken the Dakota off from Down Ampney on a 'dummy' run to Melsbroek to pick-up casualties from a base hospital and return them to England with two nurses accompanying them for this purpose. Lavoie landed at Melsbroek but noticed that he had a flat tail wheel tyre. A tyre replacement was immediately requested. That evening Lavoie; navigator, Flying Officer G. J. McKenzie RCAF; the second pilot 26-year old American Pilot Officer V. L. Pearson RCAF and 25-year old Pilot Officer N. J. Costin the Australian bomb aimer and the nurses went to a concert in Ghent where anyone landing at Melsbroek was billeted. The nurses were billeted at Lille. About 13 September, without a replacement tyre having been received, the two nurses hitched a ride back to England. One of the nurses took her leave in October and found that her parents had received a telegram saying she had been posted 'missing'. As for the Dakota, the replacement tyre arrived before the Operation 'Market Garden' and the Dakota had now disappeared! One of the nurses felt that they took off for England and flying in error over Calais they were shot down into the Channel.[15] Lavoie and his crew were lost without trace and are commemorated at Runneymede.

Dakota KG570 on 512 Squadron at Broadwell piloted by Squadron Leader Trevor Southgate AFC was hit by flak and crashed on fire at Kesteren. Southgate recalled: 'We were detailed to take a Horsa glider from Broadwell to a LZ near Arnhem. The Horsa carried two pilots, a jeep, a 6 pounder anti-tank gun and two army gunners. When a few minutes from the LZ we were hit by flak which set fire to the aircraft below the flight deck floor. This spread rapidly and was soon near the overload tanks within the main cabin. The flight deck escape hatch was jammed, which meant leaving by the rear door after crash landing. Some of these tanks exploded on impact. We all had burns; second pilot Flight Lieutenant A. E. Saunders being the worst, wireless operator Flying Officer J. H. Parry had a broken ankle and me a fractured elbow. Navigator, Flight Lieutenant S. W. Bryant was wounded also. We crawled into a small wood and eventually found by Dutch folks who had been in a church tower and saw us crash. They took charge and moved us away to a house in a small village in the area. We stayed here for about a week looked after by Mr. and Mrs. Tuit who took a great risk and were very brave. Everyone involved were in danger of capture and I cannot speak too highly of their efforts on our behalf. We were finally rescued by an Army unit in a half-track vehicle at night that moved us towards Nijmegen at high speed. Here we separated, Saunders and me to the hospital; none of us ever met again. The war continued and we all went our separate ways. All the crew survived and they were returned on 24 September.'

One returning pilot reported dropping by mistake on LZ 'S', which was about a mile west of 'L'. All but two of the others believed they had made accurate drops, generally from heights of about 500 feet. Actually the 803 panniers and containers dropped were rather widely scattered and many drifted southwest of the zone into enemy territory, probably because the aircraft from which they fell had flown too high. The net weight of supplies dropped was 87 tons and of this only twelve tons were recovered. In contrast, two bulk-loaded Hamilcar gliders yielded fourteen tons of supplies between them.

At the LZ from quite a distance away, Barry Ingham saw a large Hamilcar glider covered in flames trying to land. 'It didn't seem possible that it was still airworthy; there was so much smoke and fire coming from it. Christ! They were still firing at it. I'd never seen a Hamilcar crashing in flames before. It's definitely going into the trees. Long before it got there, it simply splits in half in the sky and rolls over and a Bren gun Carrier drops from inside it and tumbles toward the ground; several bodies follow. Another one, trailing smoke, nosedives and turns on its back about 500 feet above the ground and out the front comes what appears to be a 17-pounder anti-tank gun and a jeep as if someone had pushed it. More bodies fall after it, twisting and turning in the sky before disappearing from my sight. It's a sickening dream I want to switch off, only I can't. And the slaughter goes on as the Germans target the parachutists following the gliders. How anyone could possibly survive the amount of fire coming from the ground is a miracle. Where did all these Germans come from? It's like a shooting gallery and we are all the targets. It's just like grouse shooting on a huge scale, only the targets are human. We could do absolutely nothing to prevent what was happening so the CO ordered the advance and a platoon from 'A' Company moved out first, leading the battalion to its new positions somewhere around Arnhem.'[16]

Twenty-year old Stanley Derbyshire wrote:[17] 'As I stood in the doorway of the Dakota, with a canvas bag containing a large heavy wireless set strapped to my back, an American crewman with a cigar in the corner of his mouth placed a large black jacket on the floor, stood on it, patted me on the back and said, 'Give 'em hell boy...'.

'I replied, 'It's all right for you, you're going back!'

'As the second parachute drop on the DZs took place, the drop zone took on a three-dimensional picture for those on the ground. We had to get out of our parachutes and sort out our equipment, check where our RVs were and at the same time keep an eye out for German fire, flotsam from aircraft that had been hit, falling bodies from burning gliders and equipment that had been jettisoned from them as they split open in the sky. It all came down and could have hit any one of us. On top of this, there were the dead and wounded still in their parachutes. But for me it was the falling bodies that were the worst. One, a lad whose canopy had been shot to ribbons, screamed all the way down before he hit the ground, where he was literally turned into human jelly. He lay there in a broken heap with the remnants of his parachute across him like a shroud. Even though it was risking life and limb to stand upright and present the Germans with a target, I'm almost certain that everyone who saw it wanted to go and see if he was OK, but deep down we knew he wasn't. It seemed like a madman's dream, only I knew it was real and it was a terrible feeling knowing that his young life, along with dozens of others, had been snuffed out before it began. So we tried to forget it and got on with getting off the DZ and not getting shot. How most of us succeeded is a miracle in itself. The smoke from a burning Hamilcar drifting over the DZ gave me the precious cover I needed. As I ran past it, I spotted several bodies, all lying around the burning fuselage, where they'd been shot before they had a chance to fight back. A jeep and trailer full of ammunition had smashed through the side of the fuselage after breaking loose from their moorings; boxes of ammunition lay everywhere, ammunition that we'd desperately need in a few days time. And hanging out of the shattered cockpit window were the two glider pilots.

'I was shot and taken prisoner... As a walking wounded I had to help look after my comrades. One said, 'Stan, I heard the Germans are giving out Bibles, can you get me one?' I thought, how amazing, religion has reached these tough men. And then he said, 'The pages are ideal for cigarette papers!'

'I saw some dreadful things, I had to help a doctor amputate a soldier's leg and then I was asked to bury the leg, whilst fighting off a pack of hungry dogs.'

No time was lost in utilizing the troops delivered in the second lift. As soon as the second half of the South Staffordshires had assembled after landing, they were sent into Arnhem to join the rest of the battalion and at 1515 the divisional operations officer, appearing on DZ 'Y' ordered the 11th Parachute Battalion to follow the South Staffordshires to town. However, the eight miles between DZ 'Y' and Arnhem could not be covered at a bound. Not until late that evening after a march through Wolfhezen and Hartenstein did the paratroops catch up with the Staffordshires near a hospital on the west side of Arnhem. By then the latter had made contact with the remnants of 1 Parachute Battalion and in a conference at about 2000 the commanders of the three units laid plans for an attack toward the road bridge at 0400 next morning.

Kenneth Frere on 296 Squadron recalled: 'Albemarles which took off from Manston towed 42 of the 275 Horsas: of these 257 reached the landing zones. From the astrodome my navigator could see only a part of the glider train which stretched out behind us and ahead of us. Other

38 Group squadrons towed fifteen Hamilcars, fourteen of which made it to Arnhem in spite of much more flak and small arms fire from the German forces along the route.' Flight Lieutenant Dereck John Boyer and his crew on 296 Squadron on Albemarle II 9W-G V1616 had been 'spare' for the operation but when the Albemarle piloted by Flight Lieutenant Lee went u/s at the take-off point, the Horsa glider with chalk number '876' was placed at the end of the stream and taken off by Boyer's crew. The Horsa was loaded with a jeep plus trailer, a 75mm pack howitzer and four troops of the 1st Airlanding Light Regiment, Royal Artillery. The glider pilots were Staff Sergeant Annand and Sergeant Davey, both 'B' Squadron, The Glider Pilot Regiment. On crossing the enemy coast, light flak was encountered and Boyer's tug aircraft badly hit. Among other things, the starboard aileron and aileron trimmer were damaged with resultant loss of control. Boyer told his glider to hang on an even keel while his navigator came back to the second pilot's seat, braced himself sideways and took the strain of holding the control wheel over, while the captain made the smaller corrections necessary to keep on course. In this way Flight Lieutenants Boyer and Croker flew on with their glider to the LZ, where a successful release was made at 1444. In the DZ area, evasive action was taken from light flak. The 296 Squadron Operations Record Book rightly mentions that both Boyer and his navigator pooled their physical resources to bring the aircraft and its crew back to base and make a safe landing.[18]

Flying Office 'Wally' Wallace, an Albemarle pilot on 297 Squadron, flying V1857 and towing a fully loaded Horsa recalled: 'The tow itself was a smooth one and in spite of being in that lengthy stream, my feelings were of being extremely vulnerable in daylight at such a low altitude (2,500 feet) flying so slowly at 120 knots and being incapable of manoeuvre. Like a goldfish in a bowl wondering where the cat was! This is what my previous 136 tows had prepared me for. As a tow, it was just routine until tension manifested itself approaching the DZ. The run to the DZ was good with aircraft seemingly right left and centre. A brief farewell and good luck and the Horsa cast off. The Horsa contained a jeep, trailer, crew and 'ammo' and was flown by Staff Sergeant Woodcock and Staff Sergeant Wilson. I believe they became PoWs. Rated power, nose down and the Albemarle leapt to 280 knots, with the towrope flailing behind. A flailing rope in front of me missed the perspex canopy inches above my head. As soon as it was clear below to drop our rope, I did so and did a steep turn left on course for an uneventful trip home, once the adrenaline stopped pumping. Over the DZ gliders were turning in all directions to lose their height in a clear flight path, by constantly avoiding action. Albemarles and fighters were mixed in a mêlée above them. I did not envy the task of the glider pilots. The 297 operation report complacently records that no enemy fighters were seen. Perhaps it should have said that no enemy fighters were recognized.'

297 Squadron towed twenty-one Horsas to Arnhem, but two did not arrive. One glider become disconnected from its Albemarle five minutes after takeoff and crash landed. The glider pilot remarked that the same thing had happened to him on 'D-Day'. On 19 September, the third wave saw 296 Squadron with one aircraft taking one of the Horsas that failed to arrive on the 18th.

The main body of the 4th Parachute Brigade minus the 11th Battalion moved south of its zone to the Utrecht-Arnhem railway and advanced down the railway with the purpose of taking positions on high ground north of Arnhem as specified in the original plan. However, it halted because of darkness near Wolfhezen, which was at the southeast corner of LZ 'S'. The battalion of glider troops which had held DZ 'Y' during the drop also moved along the railway stopped near the brigade and was attached to it next morning.

The rest of the division abandoned LZ's 'S', 'X' and 'Z' and by nightfall on the 18th had moved into positions further east centred on Hartenstein, which was on the road two miles west of Arnhem and extending to Heveadorp on the Rhine a mile and a half southwest of Hartenstein. Thus the lines held by the main body of First Division roughly resembled an arrowhead with the shaft along the road, the point at Hartenstein and the barbs at Wolfhezen and Heveadorp.

Just before 1500 hours the heavy drone of massed aircraft could be heard approaching from the South West and soon the leading serial of 36 Dakotas came in sight flying at 700 feet, with serials following at one minute intervals - 127 aircraft in all, escorted by RAF Spitfires and Typhoons - to drop 2,300 men of the 4th Parachute Brigade in under ten minutes. For a short time the firing ceased, but as the Dakotas came overhead everything opened up, from the enemy troops in the woods and especially from the trees lining the main road. No.3 Platoon was setting up their beacons to guide in the Second Lift when DZ 'Y' came under attack. Lieutenant Hugh Ashmore and the men of No.3 Platoon were under constant fire at this time but they continued to carry out their work and Ashmore even considered how he might help lessen the fire directed upon the 4th Parachute Brigade when they arrived by using his four 2-inch mortars to lay smoke over where he believed the main enemy opposition to be located.

Through the small rectangular glass windows in the C-47, ominous tell-tale grey and black puffs of smoke could be seen coming from the 88mm anti-aircraft fire near Ginkel Heath six miles outside of Arnhem. At the rear of the aircraft by the door stood a tall American dispatcher, chewing gum and leaning casually on the frame like he'd seen it all before. A loud burst of flak exploded close by, sending pieces of shrapnel into the C-47's metal fuselage prompting a few nervous glances from the less experienced paratroopers as the aircraft shook violently. This was not what the 11th Parachute Battalion, 4th Parachute Brigade had expected. Another anti-aircraft round exploded below the C-47. Several small pieces of shrapnel rip explode through the fuselage floor and disappear out the roof. Daylight was clearly visible through the holes. The dispatcher checked his watch once more, hooked his safety line to the airframe and shouted. The paratroopers stood and attached their parachute static lines to a rod that ran the length of the C-47's fuselage roof. Each man checked the line of the man in front and they sound off down the line. More anti-aircraft air burst shells exploded close by in quick succession rattling the whole airframe. This time small arms fire from Germans on the ground ripped through the fuselage. The two big Pratt & Whitney radial engines were throttled back and the transport lost altitude. The paras were going to jump at just 500 feet. As they waited expectantly they began to shuffle on the spot like commuters waiting to board a train. A red light above the door by the dispatcher's head came on. The red light stayed on. Everyone looked at the unlit green bulb beside it expectantly. There was another explosion close by outside. Things were getting rocky. The dispatcher hurled open the door in readiness and air rushed in. The sound of exploding anti-aircraft fire suddenly got much louder. Explosions and puffs of black smoke rose from the ground. This is a very 'hot' zone. The ground below looked like a patchwork quilt of fields. It was pitted with shell holes and strewn with burning gliders from the previous day's drop throwing up plumes of thick smoke. In the sky all around were C-47s hauling gliders; hundreds of them, shedding their loads. The sky was awash with men and parachutes. Nearby, a large Waco glider detached itself from the C-47 hauling it, the cable dropping away like a streamer. But as the glider's nose pointed down towards the ground it broke up in mid-air spewing out men and equipment like confetti. They had no chance.

Lieutenant John E. Blackwood of No.6 Platoon 'B' Company the 11th Battalion the Parachute Regiment got his green light at 1410. 'I gave the stick a final *Hi-de-hi* and heard their yelp as I jumped. My Sten, magazine-carrier with seven mags, respirator and haversack were in a lashed bundle, attached to my harness by a cord. This was to give me a softer landing as fully-equipped I weighed 2½ hundredweight. But my grip was not secure and the jerk as the 'chute opened wrenched the whole issue from my arms, tore loose the cord and I watched it crash to earth. This was serious, not only the loss of my weapon, but the loss of my 48-hour rations, emergency rations, toilet kit and clean underclothing which the haversack contained. I marked where they fell: made a soft landing and struggled out of harnessing, noticing (a) that my 'chute contained a modicum of bullet holes and (b) that a German machine gun was blasting away thirty yards from me, inside the edge of a wood. However, my one concern was to recover my gear, so I plunged off in the direction of its fall. It was no use. The ground was covered with hundreds of parachutes: hundreds more were coming down; and waves of planes were sweeping in. Nor was the DZ a healthy place in which to linger. The German was ensconced in the woods which bordered the DZ on two sides and was lacing the place with machine-gun and mortar fire. Men were coming down dead in the harness and others were hit before they could extricate themselves. With a curse of regret for the six bars of chocolate I had lost, I gathered some men about me and set off for the RV.'[19]

Sergeant Keith D. 'Tex' Banwell of 4 Platoon, 'A' Company, 10th Parachute Battalion had been standing in the doorway of a C-47, waiting for the order to jump, when his aircraft was repeatedly hit by enemy ground fire. The port engine fell apart in front of him and then the starboard engine was similarly hit and burst into flame. A German machine-gunner fired a volley across the fuselage almost cutting it in two and in the process killed six of the paratroopers inside the C-47. The pilot tried to control the aircraft but it had now descended to 500 feet, so Banwell gave the order to abandon and jumped out, each man behind him struggling over the top of the bodies of their comrades as they followed suit.

Once they had been airborne for a few minutes Lieutenant 'Pat' Glover asked his batman, Private 'Joe' Scott, if he had brought enough feed for 'Myrtle'. Scott explained that he hadn't been able to find any corn but had compensated this with a few handfuls of cornflakes. A War Correspondent, most likely Jack Smyth of Reuters, was in Glover's aircraft and asked him for a crash course of parachuting techniques. The man said he had completed a few practice jumps before but was in need of knowing some of the finer points. Glover was quite surprised but helped him put his parachute on and told him how to make his exit and what he should do when he landed. The formation ran into flak short of Arnhem and a few bursts hit Glover's C-47, the noise of which he described as being similar to someone battering the aircraft with a sledgehammer. Glover was to be the first man to jump from the plane and as the flak grew worse he recalled a few men behind him urging him jump, but naturally the officer preferred to wait for the drop zone to be beneath his feet first. Like everyone else in the 4th Para Brigade, Glover did not expect that the drop would be opposed, but as he was out the door and gliding down he could see that a battle raged beneath his feet and that shots were coming up at them, for a moment he wondered if they had been dropped in the wrong place. As he landed Glover deliberately rolled onto his right shoulder to avoid injury to Myrtle and once he had found 'Joe' Scott he trusted 'Myrtle' to his care as they both headed toward the yellow smoke that marked the rendezvous point. Mortars and shells were exploding everywhere and Ginkel Heath had been set ablaze; fires that some paratroopers fell into. Moving off the zone he ran into a very badly wounded 20-year-old Lieutenant of the 156th Battalion, hit with incendiary rounds in his legs and chest. The man was in a great deal of pain and so Glover administered morphia and left to locate a medic. Other paratroopers came across this man, known only to be a brave and popular officer, but smoke was now coming from his wounds and he pleaded with these men to shoot him. Before they left him, one of the men placed the Lieutenant's cocked revolver in his hand. He was later found dead.

The 4th Parachute Brigade drop was followed by 275 Horsas, fifteen Hamilcars and four Hadrians which had taken off between 1043 hours and 1207 hours bound for LZs 'S' and 'X' and in the case of four of the Horsas, Nijmegen. The loads consisted of more elements of the Air Landing Brigade and, in addition, 2nd Air Landing Anti-tank Battery, elements of 1st and 4th Parachute Brigades and 1st Polish Parachute Brigade. Eighteen Horsas and one Hamilcar failed to arrive because of broken tow ropes, tug engine failure and in two cases having been shot down by flak. Those that did get to the LZs encountered much congestion caused by the previous day's landings on 'S' and considerable damage was caused to gliders and loads as they manoeuvred to find a landing space. They had to contend also with a much heavier concentration of flak and small-arms fire, which caused many casualties.[20]

An air burst ripped the fuselage of the Dakota carrying 31-year-old Major Richard Thomas Henry 'Dickie' Lonsdale DSO the second-in-command of the 11th Parachute Battalion, leaving him with a deep cut in his hand. Two of his men also received leg wounds and were prevented from jumping. The 11th Parachute Battalion was a young unit that had a troubled past but Lonsdale, an athletic and gallant Irishman of strong personality and great courage was soon to leave his mark on this battle. He and his commander, Lieutenant Colonel George Lea, had made great strides in pulling the Battalion into shape. When Lonsdale's C-47 was hit by flak it Lonsdale's injury was serious enough to necessitate his temporary departure from the Battalion after landing to have it attended to. Everyone on Lea's C-47 tried to relax in their seats, but with their eyes glued to a window. 'At first' wrote Stuart Mawson 'Holland seemed to consist of nothing but floods; acres of land were inundated, with here and there a farmstead lying isolated amid a small island of flotsam. There was no sign of life anywhere to be seen, no livestock, no people; no enemy. Every now and then an Allied fighter would slip in and out of view, but for some ten minutes the scene remained quite desolate until my attention was drawn to a field where one of our gliders lay forlornly like a child's broken toy in an empty playground. There was nobody to be seen in the vicinity and I wondered what had happened to its occupants, as we were still some way from the target. I looked at my watch. It was a quarter to two in the afternoon and a quarter of an hour away from the estimated time of the drop.

'That was the last I knew of time, except as something that passed excruciatingly slowly and seemed interminable. Momentarily I had the comfortable illusion of being in a railway carriage, for there came a tap-tapping noise like the man going the length of the train and sounding the wheels, distant at first but steadily approaching until he suddenly seemed to take leave of his senses and start slamming about with his hammer at everything in sight and the comfort abruptly departed. Crawford answered my raised eyebrows. 'Only tracer,' he said disdainfully as a stream of incandescent bullets curved past my window into the sky.'

One aircraft with sixteen parachutists aboard was struck and set alight, but every man was able to leap clear. The American crew stayed and died with their aircraft. A glider, swerving off track, alighted belly-wise on the tops of the trees and remained there, torn, its jeep and anti-tank gun hanging grotesquely in the branches. The heath was aflame in places now, giving an impression of a landing much less successful than in fact it was turning out to be: the wind which fanned the flames carried some parachutists off course into the woods.

'Presently the CO gave the order to stand in file' wrote Stuart Mawson. 'We got up and stood one behind the other, ready in an instant to hurl ourselves through the door like a crowd of passengers pouring out onto a platform. Over the shoulders of Colonel Lea and his batman I could see straight through the door and on to the ground, which now seemed very close indeed. Other Dakotas in the formation lay in easy view, rising and falling rhythmically in the invisible respirations of the afternoon thermal, their markings standing out clearly in the fine afternoon light. Near the door were the unlit red and green signal lights, the former expected to flash on at any moment in preparation for the jump. All at once a cluster of dirty black smoke puffs appeared about fifty yards away, followed a fraction of a second later by a harsh tattoo of explosions which drummed across the sky, a succession of very loud metallic sounds like a nose-to-tail pile-up of vehicles. Soon the whole sky seemed to be sprouting black puffs and reverberating with metallic explosions, the view through the door at one time becoming obscured by dirty splodges, like the windscreen of a car following another through splashing mud and it seemed impossible for any of us to remain unscathed.

'As though in a dream I saw a black puff appear immediately below an adjacent Dakota and one of the supply containers, which was slung like a large bomb from the bottom of the fuselage, become detached at one end, swing awry and fall off. Then another nearby aircraft started to bank slowly out of formation, dragging a wing with dirty yellow flames and black smoke trailing from the engine and with horrible inevitability spiralled slowly earthwards. I could imagine all too clearly the scene inside; imprisoned paratroopers waiting like ourselves for the order to jump, while the pilot fought to keep height and on course. It was already too late; half way to the ground before men appeared, jettisoning themselves with hopelessly slow precision. The first dozen or so parachutes opened; the last few had no time and as the Dakota hit the ground and burst into flames a man was still framed in the doorway.'

Henry Cross in No.1 Platoon, 'A' Company the 11th Parachute Battalion had his eyes on the red light above the door as if they were magnetised to it. Then there was an explosion right outside it. 'Lieutenant [A. A.] Vickers the platoon commander and I could see what was happening below us without straining or craning our necks like the others had to. The drop zone appeared to be on fire, literally. We shouldn't be meeting this kind of resistance. They had told us there were next to no Germans there and those that were, were only second rate: old men and boys, they said. The red light died and suddenly the green appeared. The dispatcher jettisoned the pneumatic trolley that would carry the PIAT and watched the parachute engage. Then he immediately turned bug-eyed to Lieutenant Vickers, shouting at him to 'Go! Go! Go!' The lieutenant moved into the doorway and inexplicably froze with his legs apart, hands either side of the doorframe. Between his legs I could see a C-47 in flames from tip to tail, crashing headlong towards the ground; men jumped from it, many on fire. They were even exiting as it ploughed into the woodland and exploded.

'The dispatcher looked at Vickers angrily. He was holding everyone up. My trolley was now out of sight and I knew that I'd never see it again. The dispatcher shouted at the lieutenant to get out. Finally he hurled himself out through the door. I tried to take a step, but unexpectedly struggled with the huge pack strapped to my leg. Under pressure from the eager men behind me I eventually tumbled awkwardly out through the doorway. My mind was filled with fear as I prayed my parachute would open and I would reach the ground. I felt the tug as the canopy opened and then I was swinging below it, watching the tracer fly by me, feeling that I was the only target in the sky. I suddenly felt my rate of descent increase and looked up to see a huge hole in my canopy; luckily I was only about 100 feet above the ground. I hit the grass so fast I smashed my chin on my knee and felt the blood in my mouth where I had bitten my tongue.

'I rolled onto my back and hit the quick release plate with my hand, turned it and felt the harness fall apart. My Sten gun fell onto the ground and I reached for it. Now I had to get to my kitbag fifteen feet away and all the time spurts of earth exploded around me as some German machine-gunner targeted me. I wanted to curl up into a little ball but I knew it was a waste of time. I had to get off the DZ and I had to take my equipment with me or I'd be defenceless; and all around me men were being killed or wounded, some in the air, some on the ground. How I made it into the trees I don't know. The action between opening my kitbag and scrambling headlong off the DZ was like a Charlie Chaplin slow-motion picture. All I know was I got there and put a magazine on my Sten gun, then just looked in horror at the absolute carnage that was the DZ. It wasn't supposed to be like this.'

After leaving the C-47 carrying Colonel Lea and his paratroopers Stuart Mawson looked down quickly 'because, although after leaving the plane there had been an immediate healing contrast of quiet, I could now again hear the sound of explosions and I looked in horror as the piece of ground on which I was shortly to land erupted all over in tulips of black smoke.'

'Oh, my God,' I found myself shouting out loud, 'they're shelling the DZ.'[21]

His introduction to surgery began on the battlefield. In Arnhem, Stuart and his RAMC section were separated from their battalion and joined the advanced dressing station located in the very heart of the battle. The brigadier commanding the 4th Brigade, Sir John Hackett, was one of the casualties treated at the station.[22] After the remnants of the 1st Airborne Division were evacuated all doctors, orderlies, dentists and padres stayed with the injured and they were captured. Mawson was sent to Stalag Luft IVG in Oschatz, Germany.

During the afternoon of the 18th twenty-three Dakotas on 437 Squadron RCAF braved heavy flak to bring in Horsas on the second lift. The Squadron suffered no losses, although Flying Officer 'Ron' McTeare's aircraft came close to disaster when the glider tow rope of another Dakota became wrapped around his wing but despite the resulting instability of the aircraft he was able to make a safe landing at the American B-17 base at Framlingham in Suffolk. Flying Officer Frank Gee, the second pilot, recalled: 'There was the sound of a very large 'thwack', the same sound as when you hit a car rubber mat against a wall and the whole aircraft shuddered from stem to stern. On looking out of my window I saw that wrapped around the starboard wing was a tow rope dropped by another aircraft. The double ends that affix to the glider blotted out any aileron control and the single shackle that affixes to the tug was trailing out some 300 feet behind.'[23] Despite the resulting instability of the aircraft he was able to make a safe landing at Framlingham. The heavy tug shackle tore up thirty yards of concrete 'as if it were cardboard.'

Seven Horsas and a Hamilcar came down early over England. One of the Horsas, being towed by a 299 Squadron Stirling landed safely at Martlesham Heath. The Stirling pilot, Flight Lieutenant B. H. Berridge, also landed at the Suffolk airfield where he had the glider reattached to the tow line and took off again; but the Stirling was later damaged over Holland and the Horsa had to be cast off. On 17 September, twenty-five Stirlings on 299 Squadron were used to tow Horsa gliders on the First Lift to Arnhem and no losses were suffered. On the 18th, although all 22 Stirlings returned safely to Keevil, many had been damaged by flak.

Over the following days 427 Squadron RCAF played its part in the numerous resupply flights. Anti-aircraft fire was intense, however and on Tuesday 19th September two Dakotas were shot down and another was so badly damaged that it was forced to make a crash landing, having limped back to England.

On Saturday 23rd, eighteen C-47s on 575 Squadron established themselves at a forward base at Evère, in Belgium, greatly reducing the flying time and hopefully enabling them to better support the 1st Airborne Division. Having flown sorties from here on the 23rd and 24th September, seven of the Squadron's aircraft alone marked the last of the resupply flight on Monday 25th. Although the fire from the ground was intense and four of the seven aircraft were damaged, all returned to base except for one which, having been hit a second time near Eindhoven during the return flight, lost its port engine and was forced to put down near Pael, in Belgium, however no one aboard was injured. The Battle of Arnhem had cost the Squadron the lives of five aircrew and four dispatchers.

The first supply mission was flown also by 33 Stirlings of 38 Group. Pilot Officer 'Les' Bellinger on 295 Squadron recalled: 'Information came through that all was not well and 295 Squadron was briefed for a low level daylight drop with arms, ammunition and medical supplies our lads were going to need so desperately. The operation was code named 'Market-Garden' Resupply'. Low level, low speed in daylight was not the most popular way to spend the afternoon, but although there was a greater variety of flak, the losses were not as bad as we expected. Obviously the Germans had one hell of a fight on their hands and possibly didn't expect us. We found our marked zone, unloaded our containers on target, wished our chaps the best of British luck and turned for base. Sadly 'K King' had been damaged and we had to use the spare aircraft.'

Flak was more intense than previously and a 298 Squadron Halifax suffered damage, the navigator being injured, as Alex McCallum recalled: 'Our first flight towing a Horsa glider was uneventful; but our next flight on the 18th when 31 Halifaxes and gliders were airborne in nineteen minutes, fifteen seconds, was a bit different. We towed a Hamilcar glider, which demanded a close watch on our fuel. We had been given emergency landing availability elsewhere if there was a danger. During this flight a shell had exploded beneath the armour-plated seat at 'Mac' McLaren, the navigator's position. If the hole had been any larger he would have lost the use of his parachute. A piece of shrapnel at my feet reminded me how near it was to accompany the smell of explosive. 'Mac' had left school in 1936 to become a peacetime navigator. He had ditched in the sea, was picked up as a shipwrecked mariner, crashed a Wellington through a hangar and was now with our crew at Arnhem. As it turned out, 'Mac's wounds were superficial but still needed attention in the rest bay. In trying to assist I ripped off his trousers at the seams to apply bandages much to his annoyance at the thought of having to buy new trousers.

'Our fuel supply was getting short as we arrived at Tarrant Rushden. I advised our pilot to land without the usual circuit beforehand; it seemed that had been his intention and we landed safely. Apparently not before time, as our outer starboard engine cut out at the end of the runway. That was our 23rd operation.'

Nineteen gliders in all were lost on the 18th before the serials reached the landing zones. The Stirlings meanwhile, were able to drop about 85 per cent of their cargo on LZ 'L'. It was under heavy fire that Lance Sergeant Maddocks

of the South Staffords had to saw off the tail of his glider in order to unload
a Vickers gun. Staff Sergeant Johnny Bowen of the Glider Pilot Regiment
was first pilot of a Horsa glider that carried a load of five gunners, a jeep
and trailer with 75mm gun ammunition. 'We had lost height over the North
Sea' recalls Bowen 'when our Albemarle tug aircraft had engine trouble, but
it recovered and we made the landing area after a two and a half hour flight.
We encountered only light flak on the way. About a mile out and at 1,500 feet
I cast off and glided in towards this LZ. There was some enemy fire as I came
in at ninety knots weaving my way through a large number of other gliders.
Seeing a clear spot near the woods to the West I dived for it and with the use of
my landing flaps I managed to stop in about 150 yards. We had some difficulty
in unloading the glider and it took an hour to get the load clear and drive off to
the Battery RV. Sometime later, with my co-pilot Sergeant Newman, we drove
off with the battery in convoy heading for Oosterbeek. Having carried out our
main task, our next one was to provide local defence for the guns.'[24]

The glider pilots, after having safely brought the troops to the battle,
were now as heavily engaged as their passengers. Those who had flown in
the first lift helped to hold the landing zones and then, when the second lift
had come in, fought side by side with the King's Own Scottish Borderers
and eventually formed part of the defence of Divisional Headquarters,
established at Hartenstein. They were soon heavily engaged and with them
were two Troops of the 4th Parachute Squadron Royal Engineers, one of
whose officers, Captain Harry F. Brown, earned a Military Cross for the
manner in which he led the sappers fighting as infantry. Thus after two and.
a half days of bitter, unceasing strife, the first phase ended.

When he landed on the heath at Arnhem, Sergeant 'Tex' Banwell saw
Pat Mackey charging the German machine-gun position by himself, but
the officer was hit repeatedly and killed, spinning several times before he
fell. Banwell then became the target of machine-gun fire and he had great
difficulty in crawling off the drop zone. The crippled C-47 crashed in the
woodland beyond.

Sergeant 'Bill' Higgs, piloting one of 'D' Squadron's gliders recalled:
'We had started to take a lot of flak. 'You could see all the puffs of smoke
coming across the drop zone. Lots of gliders were hit. The skipper [on the
towing aircraft] said, 'Can you see the DZ?'

'Yes, Skip, I can see it and I'm pulling off.' I had a nice landing in a
ploughed field. I'd landed as close as I could to the trees so we could get
under cover and we all ran out and under these. When we turned round there
was a poor guy hanging out of my glider who'd been hit.

'We went right down to Arnhem, near the music centre there and my captain said, 'Higgs, come on, we'll have a look and see what's going on.' We got as far as the road looking up to the bridge, but we couldn't get any further, they pinned us down with machine-gun fire. The guy up in the cupola of the music room - a Jerry sniper - was shooting at our men there. They got the Vickers machine gun and turned it up and nearly blew the top off the cupola. Anyway, we realised we weren't going to get through there. There was armour coming up and Jerry flame-throwers.'

During the second day of 'Market' the Allies had fallen seriously behind schedule, but success still seemed within their reach. Few of their difficulties could be ascribed to the air side of the venture. The glider mission for the 101st Division had delivered over 95 percent of its loads accurately and safely, an unprecedented achievement. In spite of enemy attacks on the landing zones and despite some pilot errors, the mission for the 82nd Division had been about 85 percent successful. Incomplete data on the paratroop and glider missions to the British that day indicates their score was better than 85 percent. The supply drops had been less satisfactory, but shortages were still not critical. As yet enemy aircraft had not fired a shot at the troop carriers and losses from ground fire continued low.

The British tanks were still at Zon, awaiting the repair of the bridge; the 82nd Division had had to pull out of Nijmegen; and the situation of the British paratroops in Arnhem was known to be serious. However, the big bridges at Arnhem and Nijmegen were still intact and the British airborne and the 82nd Division were preparing to attack toward them next day. Though the British had suffered cruelly, the Polish paratroops due on the 19th would compensate for their losses. If British intelligence was right, the Germans at Arnhem had already committed everything they had and were near the end of their resources. In that case tenacity would win.

None were more tenacious than Sergeant 'Bill' Higgs. 'I looked back at the glider and saw that one of the crew was hanging limp out of it. He'd been hit by the machine gun fire. Without thinking I ran back through the fire and picked him up and carried him to the shelter of the woods. He didn't seem to be seriously wounded. He was lifted on to a Jeep which contained a stretcher and taken away. That was the last I saw of him. An officer reported the incident and I was mentioned in despatches for my action. After a while we moved off from the area where we had landed, passing through Wolfhezen and Oosterbeek until we reached a railway line which we crossed. We were involved in some action here with the Germans, nothing much, just a skirmish. We then took a route along by the river, which was on the Lower Rhine and eventually arrived in Arnhem. From our position on the road we could see Arnhem Bridge about a mile away, when suddenly all hell let loose and we were pinned down. Heavy fire from the Germans had stopped us in our tracks and we began to withdraw.

'We were just fighting and running in the end because we were outnumbered, all our ammunition had gone. We were in a beer garden, I can remember having a bottle of 'Cherry Heering' brandy in my hand and the officer was looking at the map and he said: 'We'll get up there Staff and stay up there and try and hold that until we get news of what's going on.' But as we set off up the brow of the hill they could see us coming and they let us have it from a house up there. The officer said, 'Let's get in' and so we ran towards it. I fired a burst of my Tommy gun and the next thing I knew I was down on the deck. I thought I'd lost my arm because the bullet went through it and into my chest, through my lung and out my back. I was lying on the ground and then I felt the Tommy gun and I thought, 'Oh my God, I haven't lost my arm'. Two guys turned me over on to my back and then dragged me down - I could still hear the bullets hitting the top of the road. They got me under the brow of the hill and into the yard of a house. There was a young Dutch couple in it. They'd got an old velvety armchair and they sat me in this. I could see how frightened this young couple was, so I said, 'Get me out of here, they'll mortar this place, let's get down to the main road, these people are frightened to death.'

Higgs was taken to an old farmer's hut and left there with another twenty wounded men: 'The blood was running out of my mouth. It was filling up my lung, my breath was coming shorter and shorter and I felt I was going to drown in my own blood, so I thought I've got to move, I was panicking. I thought if I don't move I'm going to die. Behind me was a rusty old rail they'd used to tie up the cattle and I got hold of this and I pulled myself over and as I did this I pulled off the patch the Red Cross blokes had put on my back where the bullet had come out. I could feel the hot blood running out of my lung down my back and within five minutes I was breathing again. And then the Germans came.'

Higgs was put into a German ambulance and bumped along the road to hospital. On the ward he asked a medical orderly the name of the hospital: 'The orderly said, 'I'm sorry, I can't tell you that.' 'He wouldn't tell me anything. I thought if I can get through the window, if XXX Corps are coming our way... but of course they never did come our way, did they? That was the tragedy.'[25]

Chapter 7

'D+1' The American Lift

I was towing a CG-4A glider on the second day of the operation. I was flying along in the big formation and about 45 seconds after the glider released - wham!' They were no more than a mile southeast of the release point. The aircraft was hit while in the scheduled right turn, by 20 mm or 40 mm antiaircraft bursts. The fuel lines were severed and gas tanks hit. The right engine quit and while Cox was feathering the prop, the left engine quit. 'We were at about 600' feet at the time and so, I and my crew were desperately busy. I picked a field and down we came. Dodging trees, houses, etc. Just before we landed (wheels up) four foolish cows stood in front of me giving me the most helpless look. All I could do then was to sort of skid a little so they wouldn't come in the cockpit. This would have ended our careers with some immediacy. What a way to go. As you know they are pretty heavy when you hit them going about 90 mph. Anyway we sort of killed them. But, as a result they helped to slow the plane down. We got on the ground OK, bounced over a couple of ditches and through several fences. The radio and crew chief told me later they had been in rougher landings on airfields. Also some Huns were shooting at us as we went down. Guess they were mad as hell because we didn't burn.

Lieutenant Donald W. Cox in the 53rd Squadron in the 61st TCG who the day before had dropped British paratroopers at Arnhem, in a letter home.

On 'D+1' the 82nd around Nijmegen seemed close to disaster. Copies of the operational plan for the American lift had been found on the body of a dead officer by a German patrol in a wrecked glider and were handed to General Student near Nijmegen but when he tried rushing the plans to

General Model the messenger took ten hours to get there. Both Generals suspected that the plans were fakes because they were too detailed, too precise but the Luftwaffe accepted them and at 1000 scrambled every available fighter to intercept the expected glider formations. Soon after daylight two under-strength German battalions began to infiltrate from the Reichswald towards the glider LZs and temporarily captured the LZs around Nijmegen. If the glider formations landed with their three battalions, one parachute and two gliders and a quantity of artillery, there would be a slaughter which would make that on LZ 'W' in Normandy seem insignificant. If the attackers broke through the perimeter into the woods around Groesbeek, it would scarcely be possible to drive them out. Fortunately the German troops involved were a hastily gathered assortment, no match for the paratroops in either quality or quantity and the postponement of the glider missions to 1400 gave sufficient time to counterattack and clear the landing zones, at the cost of just eleven US casualties though the Germans could not be dislodged completely. News of the change in schedule had reached the division at 0840 about the same time as the first reports of the German attacks. Though the landing zones were saved, they were far from safe. The Germans had dug in near enough to both LZ 'T' and LZ 'N' to rake them with small arms fire and bombard them with mortars. Gavin consulted with General Browning over a plan to attack the Nijmegen road bridge that night with a battalion each from 504th and 508th Regiments. Browning at first approved of this plan but then decided that holding the Groesbeek heights south of Nijmegen was more important and Gavin agreed. He issued orders for the defence of the position.

The glider mission dispatched by the 50th and 52nd Wings to the 82nd Division on the 18th was originally to consist of eleven serials with fifty aircraft in the first and forty in each of the rest, but two aircraft had been added to the second and fourth serials, making a total of 454. Like that of the 53rd Wing's mission to the 101st Division, it was divided into two sections with one serial from each of six groups in the lead section and one from each of them except the 439th Group in the rear section. Every aircraft towed a Waco. In the gliders were 1,899 troops - nearly three quarters of who were artillerymen - 206 jeeps, 123 trailers and sixty guns. The great difference between this load and that of the 101st's mission was in the emphasis on artillery. From past experience and in view of its exposed position, the staff of the 82nd rightly judged it would need its guns and had therefore packed into the gliders the 319th, 320th and 456th Field Artillery

Battalions, 'B' Battery of the 80th Anti-tank Battalion and Headquarters Battery of Divisional Artillery.

Orders to use the northern route reached the troop carrier fields at the last minute. When the news arrived at Chilbolton twenty minutes before take-off time, the crews of the 442nd Group were already aboard their aircraft and the group had only enough time to brief the flight leaders on the new plan. The lead serial crews of the 313th Group also had to be called from their aircraft about half an hour before take-off to get the news. Warnings to swing wide at the IP to avoid flak had to be sent by radio. As take-off time approached, fog and low clouds hung over the Grantham area, necessitating a further delay of fifty minutes before starting. The first aircraft took off at 1109 and it was nearly two hours before all tugs and gliders were in the air. A serial which could assemble and set out on course within half an hour of its first take-off was considered to be doing well. The clouds were still low enough to impede assembly and one serial of the 313th Group had to rendezvous over Cottesmore instead of its own base, Folkingham. However, beyond the coast the weather was good, though somewhat hazy and the flying was smooth.

While still over England one glider began to disintegrate in mid-air, a not uncommon trick of the Waco and another was loosed by a hysterical soldier who reached forward and yanked the release handle. Both landed safely. Over the Channel two other gliders, caught in propwash, lurched suddenly and snapped their cables. They ditched and the occupants were quickly rescued. At least one of these ditchings was caused by some of the RAF Stirlings which were supposed to be towing their gliders a thousand feet overhead but had failed to keep their prescribed altitude. There was also some tendency for the serials of the two American glider missions to get in each other's lanes, but except for one aircraft in the 313th Group which fell in with a serial of the 53rd Wing and released its glider on LZ 'W' no mix-up or serious confusion resulted. Three other gliders were released after landfall and before reaching Grave because of accidents or flak damage. Personnel and cargo from two of the three later reached the airborne. Many glider pilots who did complete sorties did so under difficulties. The plexiglas windows of some gliders blew out, letting a 100 mph wind blow through the cockpit. Over twenty percent of the interphones between aircraft and glider failed or worked badly. Several glider pilots reported that the lack of co-pilots greatly increased the strain of the three-hour flight.

Although aircraft losses ran a little higher than those in the parallel mission of the 53rd Wing they were low nevertheless, only ten aircraft in all. One pilot, who had endangered himself by flying slightly off course, was brought down by flak on Schouwen and one other probably went down in that locality. From the coast to the IP, opposition was slight, but flak near Hertogenbosch blew the wing off a C-47 and sent it crashing. The machine guns and light flak of German troops gathering in the Schijndel-Uden area accounted for two more aircraft and two others were shot down within half a minute after releasing gliders over LZ 'T'. Considering how close the Germans were to the zones, it is remarkable that the losses there were not higher. Three additional aircraft were shot down in flames several miles southeast of the release area because of a costly mistake. Their squadron had missed its zone and had flown over strong German forces near Gennep.

Twenty-three troop carrier men on this mission were dead or missing; half a dozen had wounds or injuries; the rest had reported back. The fate of the gliders whose tugs were lost near the coast or over Germany was unknown, but the occupants of the other five reached the Allied lines as did four of their cargoes.

Over ninety percent of the returning aircraft operational and none had to be salvaged. However, about 100 of them had been damaged by ground fire. Since more than half the damage was concentrated in three serials, portions of which had missed their zones and had flown from three to twelve miles beyond them, it can be assumed that if all serials had stayed on course, the repairs resulting from the mission would have been relatively light.

The lead serial in the column was one from the 313th Group, which was flying its first glider mission. As it approached the release area, the formation split down the middle into two columns of pairs far enough apart so that all the glider pilots could make a left turn without causing too much congestion. At 1431 the lead glider cut loose at an altitude of 800 feet and descended in a 360° spiral to the left. The others followed, most of them holding formation in two parallel spirals which fanned out as they approached the ground. On the downwind leg they passed over the panels and smoke, which had been set out by the path-finders about a mile southwest of LZ 'N' because the zone itself was a battlefield. The landing was made directly into a gentle northeast wind.

Most of the 313th's landings were slow and good. Almost every glider incurred some damage in landing on the soft, rough, ground, but only one glider was wrecked and damage to passengers and cargo was slight. Mortar and rifle fire from German positions less than a mile away, supplemented occasionally by a shell from some distant gun, delayed the unloading of the gliders but did little real harm. One glider pilot in the serial was killed by a mortar and two or three of the airborne were wounded.

The experience of the 313th was fairly typical of the mission as a whole. In all, 385 gliders landed within the lines of the 82nd Division. Releases were made consistently at heights of 800 and 1,000 feet. A majority of the gliders came down in orderly fashion. Comparatively few of the glider pilots saw smoke signals and very few sighted panels. Some, seeing the fighting beneath them, chose to come in fast, but most made conservative landings at speeds of 60 to 75 mph. There were cases of gliders being brought to a stop within as little as fifty feet. The arrestor parachutes, which had been installed on about half the gliders, proved very effective brakes and many pilots who used them urged later that they be made standard equipment. Although most of the gliders nosed over or suffered some damage to their landing gear, less than twenty of those in the landing area had been destroyed. Not a single glider pilot is known to have been killed in landing accidents, but two were slain by enemy fire, seven injured and ten wounded during or soon after landing. Thirty-five were missing. Of the airborne only three were killed and 42 wounded or injured during flight or landing, but 117 were missing. Not a single gun was reported to have been damaged in landing, although six of them came down far outside the 82nd Division's area and could not be used by it. Only 29 of the jeeps and seventeen of the trailers were either damaged or missing, so the division was able to employ 85 percent of the vehicles which had been loaded.

Of 212 gliders supposed to land on LZ 'N' about 150 landed within a circle a half-mile in radius centred on the hamlet of Knapheide a mile southwest of the zone. All but a handful of the other gliders in those serials either landed within 1½ miles of Knapheide or stuck to their instructions and landed on LZ 'N'. The 242 intended for LZ 'T' did not fare so well. However, approximately ninety of them did land on the zone and 52 of them west of it but within a mile of the panels and smoke, which had been set out by the pathfinders exactly on its western edge. Another nineteen were well bunched slightly over a mile west of LZ 'T' and nineteen were scattered in German-held territory between one and four miles northeast of the zone.

It seems that, excepting a few individual errors, seriously inaccurate releases were confined to three serials. In the third serial, which was flown by the 316th Group, a flight leader loosed his glider prematurely over LZ 'O' and half the serial followed his example out of obedience and a desire to keep its gliders together. One explanation given was that other gliders had been seen landing on LZ 'O', but indications are that up to that time only one glider had landed there. A dozen glider pilots attest that a panel 'T' was visible near Overasselt and this may well have caused the release. Whether the panels were carelessly left from the day before or set out again by order of someone in the 82nd, which was taking every action it could think of to keep the gliders from landing in the battle area, their effect was harmless, even beneficial, since the landings were made in a safe and suitable area. The other half of the serial reached LZ 'T', but only six released gliders there. Eight kept on going and deposited their gliders between Wyler and Zyfflich northeast of the LZ. This error was costly. From the gliders beyond Wyler the 319th Field Artillery lost five officers and forty men dead or captured and the cargoes of all eight gliders.

To the men in the 316th the second day of Operation 'Husky' and 'D-Day+1' in Normandy were occasions when the losses were worst and 'D+1' in Holland continued the affliction for no less than six C-47s were lost. In the 37th Squadron one aircraft (43-15498) piloted by Lieutenant Jack A. Murrell was unaccounted for and another (42-100502) landed at Biggin Hill having returned from the LZ on one engine. Only Murrell's co-pilot, 2nd Lieutenant Robert G. Lancaster and the radio operator, Pfc William A. Kabaker survived and they were taken into captivity. Crew Chief, Tech Sergeant Edwin G. Tuman as the other crew member who died.

Day 1 had gone smoothly for Lieutenant Julian 'Bud' Rice, the pilot of 'Chalk 10' (43-15212) 'Drastic G-George' and he had dropped the first paratroops without any problems. 'Bud' had been born in Panama where his grandfather had settled and built a brewery. He spent his early childhood there but was sent away to school in New Orleans. Plans to go to Notre Dame were thwarted by the Depression of the 1930s and instead he went back to Panama to work for the Canal Department. People accepted work anywhere they could find it and many American families migrated south in response to jobs offered during the Panama Canal construction.

Day 2 of Market-Garden would not be as straightforward as Day 1 had been for 'Bud' as he recalled: 'Several minutes from the LZ 'we began encountering anti-aircraft flak. As we drew nearer to the Siegfried line the intensity of the aerial barrage became severe. Approaching the LZ at 115 mph I could see soldiers running and firing weapons. Arriving at the LZ I thumb-signalled Sergeant Harold Gondolfe my radio operator, to flash the cut-off signal to our tethered glider. Our airspeed jumped quickly to 130 mph as the loaded CG-4A cut loose. I dropped the right wing and started a 180-degree turn-around and suddenly heard a hail of bullets spray our fuselage. Instead of surprising the Germans, the Germans surprised us.

Their tanks in the woods were not at all abandoned. They were the fully armed 9th and 10th Panzer Divisions who snaked their way during the night into the Arnhem drop zone, waiting to attack us. A large explosion hurled our aircraft violently upward and then down to the right. The left engine stopped dead. The instrument panel gauges for the left engine, the fuel gauge, the oil pressure gauge, all the directional gyro gauges were out. While continuing the turn into the right engine, I became rather busy retrimming the aircraft for emergency single engine procedure. We were halfway through the turn; I was trying to feather the left engine propeller when the right engine began to splutter. With only a few hundred feet of altitude left, I flattened out the turn and prepared to crash land into a wooded area. I saw no alternative and I am certain that a crash into the heavily wooded forest left virtually no chance for survivors. My co-pilot [2nd Lieutenant Clarence E. Powell], who had just joined our outfit and was on his first combat mission was on the microphone reporting that we were hit and preparing to crash.

'Meanwhile, Sergeant Charles Rausa, who was standing in the cockpit between me and the co-pilot methodically assessed the damage. He realised that the fuel pump in the left engine fed both engines during normal operation. With that realization, the right engine began to miss. Without a moment's hesitation, he turned the fuel pump cross feed that activated the right engine pump. There was enough wind-milling of the prop to get the engine fired up again.

'The trees were looming up. Our airspeed had dropped to 110 mph. With the throttle and prop pitch control 'pushed to the firewall' we climbed, hoping that the puffs of black flak bursts would not hit us again. We finally reached the bottom of the cloud ceiling at 3,000 feet where we entered and hid. Instrument flying a C-47 without the aid of gyro instruments was not a good situation. But, we still had the basic needle, ball and airspeed gauges working, so we limped along at slow speed to avoid any excessive stress on the plane, as we were still uncertain as to the extent of the damage.

'As we approached the Channel another pilot from our squadron, 1st Lieutenant Robert F. Scott; pulled up on our wing and asked if we were OK. I asked him to take a close look and give us an assessment of exterior damage. He circled us and reported damage to the leading edge of the wing between the left engine and fuselage. He also said that the left wheel appeared damaged. I told him that we had no instruments left to help us through any serious weather conditions crossing the Channel. He said, 'Grab on to my wing and I'll lead you home' - And he did!' We landed safely at Cottesmore on one good wheel (and a flat tyre), badly shaken but alive; thanks to the very quick thinking of an alert sergeant at a very critical moment in our lives. In those times and in the business we were in, close calls were inevitable and many. Some were too close and things like luck, experience, or quick thinking bring you safely through. In this case the lives of the crew of 'Drastic G-George' were undoubtedly saved by our crew chief, Sergeant Rausa.'

The C-47 (43-15643) captained by 1st Lieutenant Leo L. White was also badly hit in the bottom and right side of the cockpit, after which flames immediately flared up. 'Apparently we had been hit in the gas lines which run through the bottom of the ship' wrote Leo White. 'I ordered the crew to bail out and then tried to set the ship on automatic pilot. After trying to do so several times, I was burned about the face, head and hands and consequently was forced to leave the ship in an uncontrolled state. I left the cockpit and stripped off my flak suit and put on my A-3 type chute and made my way to the rear exit where I bumped into one of my crew. Thinking that he was Staff Sergeant Glick, my radio operator, I told him to jump and then I followed.

'After landing I was joined by the crew chief and radio operator and I asked them about the whereabouts of my co-pilot [2nd Lieutenant Roland V. Dover]. I was then informed that he had been hit and had fallen down in the tail of the ship without a chute on and that he seemed unconscious. Glick told me that he ha d trouble removing his flak suit and when he had succeeded in doing so he had examined Dover to see if he could be of any assistance, but the ship being at such low altitude, he was forced to jump.'

Dover was found dead in the wreckage.

1st Lieutenant John R. Johnson Jr.'s C-47 (43-15638) in the 36th Squadron was set on fire as the co-pilot, 2nd Lieutenant Marion Larrea recalled: 'We were first hit as we entered the LZ area by machine gun fire. Before releasing the glider we were subjected to more ground fire which hit our left auxiliary tank. As soon as our glider cut we started to climb. While climbing there was an explosion in the back of which caused a fire. It is my belief that the gas drained between the floor boards and fuselage, hitting the exhaust causing the explosion and fire. Lieutenant Johnson gave the order to bail out. The crew chief, Pfc Willard R. Friend was the first to go and then the radio operator, Staff Sergeant Carl E. O'Donnell second. I then got Lieutenant Johnson his chute and informed him that the crew had bailed out and that I was leaving. Up to this time no one had been wounded and he had control of the plane although it was burning. I have no idea of altitude when I jumped.

'I landed in a courtyard of a convent where I was hidden by a priest. Later I was taken to another building where I met the radio operator and the head of the 'Underground'. About twenty minutes later they brought the crew chief. They decided to take us, one at a time, to a farmhouse where we could hide out for the night. They gave us civilian clothes to wear. I asked the head of the 'Underground' if he could get me some information about Lieutenant Johnson and was told that he would give me the information the following morning. The next morning this man told me he had reports that one man had jumped from a C-47 further south but it was impossible for them to get to him. He said that it was possible members of the 'Underground' there would get to him and hide him out.

'We left the farmhouse that morning and bicycled into a nearby town. There we waited for a car which took us to Grave. I reported to the Intelligence there and later to the rear Command Post. After spending three days there, we hitchhiked to Brussels where were evacuated to England.'

1st Lieutenant John R. Johnson Jr. was captured at Düsseldorf on 20 September and detained at Dulag Luft West before being sent to a prison camp.

A third crew in the 36th Squadron, captained by 1st Lieutenant Harvey I. Wharton were all taken prisoner after their C-47 was hit by flak and ascended above the formation where all the crew bailed out of their doomed aircraft in along a line about half a mile long about three miles east of Afferdam. The C-47 flew on for about a half mile and then blew up in mid-air.

C-47 43-15641 in the 45th TCS piloted by 1st Lieutenant John S. Melvin was seen to crash after being hit by flak. The navigator, 1st Lieutenant Manuel E. Flores was killed, Melvin was captured but managed to escape and returned to duty. Co-pilot 2nd Lieutenant Edward G. Welsh, radio operator Sergeant Michael J. Malanick and crew chief Tech Sergeant Thomas C. Glaze were taken to the 24th Evacuation Hospital with injuries.[1]

A warning was sent to land on the western edge, away from the tree line, but the second lift arrived under heavy fire. Tug pilots failed to spot hundreds of gliders littering the LZs and General Gavin watched helplessly as 25 tow combinations flew overhead carrying badly needed guns deep into Germany itself. Of 294 gliders that set out, 270 landed by 1530 but this time, warned by Luftwaffe command, the flak was even heavier.

The eighth serial consisting of C-47s in the 61st Group hauling CG-4As to Groesbeek carrying 'B' Battery, 320th Glider Field Artillery, also did badly. The glider of one of its flight leaders cut loose about 45 miles short of the zone as a result of flak damage. The tow pilot turned out of formation, circled to watch the glider land and then went home. The pilot who took the lead went by pilotage alone after passing the IP and got lost. Followed by eight others he curved southward, missed the zone and released his glider inside Germany twelve miles east-southeast of LZ 'T'. Not one man from the gliders in that formation reached the 82nd Division. The lead elements of the other squadron in this serial overshot the zone, with the result that nine of their gliders came down in the Wyler area. Although the Germans attacked this concentration and destroyed the gliders by shelling, most of the troops and glider pilots took cover and held out till nightfall. They then worked their way back to the Groesbeek area. The other 21 gliders in the serial landed on or near the zone. The 320th Field Artillery was forced to defend its landing position until nightfall and then try to make its way ten miles back to American lines, bringing with it 160 airborne troopers, 22 glider pilots, ten jeeps and two field guns.

The following serial may well have been influenced by the errors of its predecessor. It was also handicapped by the fact its 'Gee' sets were jammed and its 'Rebecca's for some reason were not picking up signals from the 'Eureka' on the landing zone. Of 38 gliders in that formation when it reached the Grave-Veghel area, at least 24 and probably thirty made a deviation to the south. However, they recognized their error sooner than those in the eighth serial and made their release between three and five miles south of LZ 'T' in the general vicinity of Gennep. Some ran into close-range fire from anti-aircraft batteries and others into automatic and small arms fire. Three aircraft were brought down and two gliders crashed. Most of the glider pilots protected themselves by slipping or diving to minimum altitude before attempting to land. Gliders landing safely were attacked almost as soon as they hit the ground. Remarkable leadership by some officers of the 320th Field Artillery saved the situation. They gathered together about four separate groups which defended themselves until nightfall and then worked their way north to the American lines. Saved in this way were approximately 160 of the airborne and at least ten jeeps, two guns and 22 glider pilots. Only four glider pilots and nine of the airborne were missing. Of the other gliders in the serial one cut over LZ 'G' after a flak hit, six or seven landed in the vicinity of LZ 'T' and one which had overshot the zone landed in the Wyler area. Its occupants were able to reach friendly territory but had to abandon their cargo.

Allied fighters had to contend with the first strong effort made by the Germans to intercept the Allied airborne mission. This effort was made in accordance with decisions taken by Hitler at a conference on the night of the 17th. The German dictator had decided that since ground reserves were inadequate for a large-scale counter-attack, the Luftwaffe would have to make an all-out effort to tip the scales against 'Market'. The airborne missions on 18 September were protected on the same massive scale as before. Air Defence of Great Britain sent 277 fighters to guard the troop carriers between England and the IP. Of these, sixteen Spitfire squadrons gave escort and area cover, while three squadrons of Spitfires, five of Tempests and three of Mustangs attacked flak positions from Schouwen island to the IP. Six fighters were lost. The Eighth Air Force had 397 fighters make sorties in support of 'Market'. As on 'D-Day', two groups of P-51s flew perimeter patrols on a line curving from Hasselt through Wesel to the Zuider Zee. Between the IP and the zones six P-51 groups flew area cover at and above 2,500 feet, while two P-47 groups and the rocket squadron loaned by the Ninth Air Force attacked flak batteries and other ground targets. The German airmen were met on 'D+1' by the 357th and 359th Fighter Groups. The 359th Group, patrolling the perimeter with 57 aircraft, fought and repelled 35 Focke Wulf 190s about fifteen miles northeast of Arnhem, shooting down three of them and losing two of its own aircraft. The 357th Group, which was supposed to cover the Eindhoven area, was vectored out onto the perimeter about forty miles southeast of Eindhoven to meet an attack. There, at 1505, while troop carrier operations were at their height its 52 aircraft battled about sixty enemy fighters. The pilots claimed 26 of the Germans destroyed at a cost of two of their own aircraft. None of the Germans got through to strike at the troop carrier columns that day. Late in the afternoon of the 18th Lieutenant Colonel Jack Oberhansly leading the 56th Fighter Group succeeded in destroying twelve light flak guns and a 20-30 truck convoy.

Overcast down to 500 feet in some places hampered operations and flak was heavy and accurate. The 56th Fighter Group lost sixteen Thunderbolts shot down and the 78th five. Operations against flak batteries did not go as well as on 'D-Day'. Since it was impossible to know with any accuracy what positions the airborne troops would be holding, the fighters had orders to attack only when fired upon. The Germans quickly learned to hold their fire until the P-47s were almost past, give them a short burst from the rear and cease fire. These tactics made it very difficult to locate hidden batteries or to make sure that a suspected position was hostile. Haze and low clouds further hampered identification and greatly impeded bombing. Out of 95 P-47s three were lost and ten damaged. Only 49 dropped bombs. The pilots claimed 33 flak positions destroyed, four damaged, about 37 silenced and several secondary targets hit. They were sceptical as to their own effectiveness under such baffling conditions particularly in the case of the 'silenced' batteries. However, their purpose was achieved. The troop carriers were able to fly in daylight over more than eighty miles of enemy territory with losses of less than two percent.[2]

Early in the afternoon the Germans attacked with artillery and tank support against the paratroops that were still without artillery. 'Enemy closing in, situation getting desperate,' reads the entry in a 3rd Battalion journal. Bombing and strafing by five P-47s, which arrived in the nick of time, enabled the troops to repel that attack, but bitter and indecisive fighting continued throughout the day in the Best sector, within 1,000 yards west and southwest of LZ 'W'. This situation presented an unexpected hazard to the glider missions landing on LZ 'W' that afternoon.

The 101st Division was to be reinforced on the 18th by a 450 aircraft mission of the 53rd Wing bringing Waco gliders to LZ 'W'. The mission was divided into an 'A' Section and a 'B' Section, each made up of six serials, one from each of the groups at the Wing's disposal. Aboard the gliders were 2,656 troops, 156 jeeps, 111 trailers full of supplies, two bulldozers and no guns. It was assumed that the 101st would be able to get along without artillery, but would need great mobility to cover its long perimeter. The troops carried were principally from the 327th Glider Infantry Regiment (minus the 1st, Battalion), the 326th Airborne Engineer Battalion and the 326th Airborne Medical Company. Among the remainder was a detachment of divisional headquarters including the divisional artillery commander, Brigadier General Anthony C. McAuliffe, who rode in the lead glider of the lead serial. When Flight Officer William Richmond, a glider pilot in the 442nd TCG had found out that he would be one of the pilots on the re-supply mission he had mixed emotions. 'While I wasn't exactly jumping for joy, I wasn't about to go on sick call either' he said.[3]

Take-offs began about 1120 and the serials assembled over the Greenham Common area, took their positions at Hatfield and proceeded 83 miles northeast to Aldeburgh. From there they followed the northern route to the LP below Hertogenbosch and turned south southeast on their final run to LZ 'W'. The weather was good, except for a thick haze, which in places limited visibility to a couple of miles. Despite the favourable weather ten gliders failed to leave England; five of them had structural failures and five broke loose or were prematurely released. Two of the ten crashed. Three Wacos were ditched in the Channel, but alert rescue work saved all aboard them. Another became uncontrollable, was released over Schouwen Island and glided to probable destruction in a heavily fortified area.

174

In general ground fire was unexpectedly slight and inaccurate and no German aircraft were sighted. The first serial suffered worst, two of its aircraft being shot down after their gliders were released and 21 others being damaged, generally after they passed the IP. The other eleven serials in the mission lost only two aircraft between them. One of those was hit about fifteen miles short of the zone, caught fire, released its glider and crashed. The other ditched on the way back but the crew were saved. Casualties among the troop carrier crews totalled only eight dead or missing and about that number wounded or injured. Out of 112 aircraft damaged, 108 were readily repairable. Four, two of which had collided while landing had to be salvaged. A Waco that was hit by flak three miles from the zone disintegrated. Three others were prematurely released over enemy territory and not heard of again. Another three reached the zone but crashed upon it. The remaining 428 gliders landed safely on or near LZ 'W' between 1430 and 1620. The serials arrived at very irregular intervals with two apparently out of sequence. Naturally this led to confusion and interference at the release point and some units reported being forced to release their gliders at altitudes of 1,200 and even 1,500 feet. However, by daylight with plenty of landing room this mix-up produced only minor inconvenience. Captain E. C. Thornton, an airborne observer, called the landings 'splendidly executed'.

Lieutenant William J. McCormick Jr. in the 306th TCS, 442nd TCG was pilot of C-47A 43-15139 on the glider mission to LZ 'W' north of Eindhoven. 'I took off at 1240 hours towing [CG-4A 'Chalk 64B' flown by] Flight Officer Herbert H. Bollum. About 28 miles from the target, at Breda at 1600 we ran into an intense concentration of light flak and my left engine was hit. I couldn't see any signs of smoke or fire at this time because of the position [where the] aircraft was hit, but Bollum told me afterwards that smoke was pouring out of my left engine. I flew on to the LZ and released the glider over the objective at 1615. All this about the time the left engine was running rough. About 22 miles from the Dutch coast on the way back my left engine went out. I feathered the prop, but it immediately unfeathered. By this time the aircraft was filling up with smoke and Staff Sergeant James Powell (radio operator) caught sight of flames under the floor. I instructed co-pilot Flight Officer Logan Atterbury to go the rear of the plane and get the crew ready to jump if the fire became more acute. At the same I cut the mixture on the right engine in order to lose altitude and ditch in the shortest possible time. I could not communicate with the rest of the formation; apparently the radio was hit too.

'I decided to ditch and told the crew to stand by for ditching. The crew remained calm and behaved in a very creditable manner. I nosed the plane down into practically a vertical dive. I looked at the hydraulic pressure gauge and noticed it was indicating 'zero'. I looked out the window and saw the gear was down. The fire must have burned out the hydraulic system. The red warning lights of the heating system were on and both spill valves were open.

'I dived the plane at 220 mph indicated from 4,000 feet indicated altitude, at the same time turning into the wind and started breaking my dive at 1,000 feet. I slowed the plane down to 120 mph and came in and set the plane in a tail low altitude. The last time I looked at the air speed it indicated 80 mph. Shortly after that, with a slight impact the tail hit, immediately followed by a more violent impact when the nose hit the water. The time was 1652 hours.

'From the time the plane filled with smoke, the rest of the crew were in the rear of the plane. The sudden impact of landing tore the dinghy loose from its lashings and threw it forward in a tangled heap. Rather than take valuable time in untangling the dinghy inside the aircraft and because of the possibility of explosion, I instructed the crew to jump and swim clear of the plane. I followed, dragging the dinghy with me. All of us had our life jackets on. In the water, the tide was pinning us down between the trailing edge of the wing and the fuselage. We finally got clear by pulling ourselves alongside the trailing edge of the wing until we were about to the wing tip. The wing was bobbing up and down and we managed to get to the leading edge of the wing by ducking under the bobbing wing.

'Once in the clear and safely away from the plane, we inflated the dinghy and climbed into it. At this time I noticed a large hole on the outboard side of the left engine nacelle. The plane stayed afloat about eighteen minutes. After approximately fifteen minutes in the dinghy, a British air sea rescue launch picked us up and took us to a shore station at Ipswich. There we received a medical examination and were issued new clothes. On behalf of my entire crew, I went to express my thanks and gratitude for the excellent handling accorded us by the Air Sea Rescue Service.'[4]

The focus of the landings was at the extreme west end of the zone and many were made somewhat further west. In such cases the aircraft and gliders came within range of the German troops massed in the vicinity of Best and some of the glider-borne troops were pinned down by rifle and mortar fire as they emerged from their gliders. Assembly on the whole went quickly and well. The men formed in small groups and moved east onto the road where they were sorted out with the aid of a control section established by divisional headquarters. When the returns were in, 2,579 troops had been mustered and 151 jeeps and 109 trailers had been reported on hand and usable. Only 54 of the airborne were dead or missing and 23 were injured. Only five of the jeeps and two of the trailers were lost or damaged.

The bomber resupply mission to the 82nd and 101st Divisions was to arrive twenty minutes after the troop carriers, drop time being set for 1557. It was being flown by 252 B-24s of the 2nd Bombardment Division from bases in Norfolk and Suffolk. Supplies were trucked in on the night of the 17th. The ball turrets and turret fairings were removed to allow the bundles to be released through metal chutes and each aircraft was loaded in bomb racks, waist and bomb bay with about two tons of supplies packed in twenty containers. A trained dropmaster of the 2nd Quartermaster Battalion was assigned to each aircraft to direct the pushing of bundles through the turret well and the rear hatch.

The 20th Wing Liberators, each carrying twelve supply packs stowed in the bomb bays and with trained personnel from the special 9th Troop Carrier Command to supervise the drop, took off early that afternoon. Almost immediately things began to go wrong. Just out of Orfordness, leading elements of the 20th Wing were forced to make a 360 degree turn to port to avoid veering into a C-47 unit. This confused the Groups following and the 448th Bomb Group lost sight of the force completely in the sea haze and continued alone while five 93rd Bomb Group Liberators returned to Hardwick. The remaining Liberators began dropping from 800 to 400 feet but even at this height locating checkpoints over Holland proved very difficult as the coastal area had been completely flooded by the retreating German Army. The previous year, on another low-level mission, to Ploesti, the crews had to pull about 35 inches of manifold pressure to obtain 225 mph. The weight of the Liberators had increased considerably by the time of the Best mission and crews had to apply the same settings just to obtain between 170 and 180 mph.

At the IP the 20th Wing Groups experienced additional difficulties when, because of the failure of the radio beacon, they could not receive recognition signals. But despite this and battle damage, they entered the dropping zone at Groesbeek near Nijmegen in formation.

Two Groups of escorting Thunderbolts failed to nullify the almost constant small-arms fire and seven Liberators were shot down while seventy were damaged. In the 20th Wing the 446th from Bungay and the 448th from Seething each lost three Liberators and had many more damaged. The 14th Wing, meanwhile, with the 491st 'Ringmasters' Bomb Group at its head, was en route for its dropping zone at Best. Leading the 491st and the Wing was the 855th Squadron, which carried food and ammunition for the 101st American Airborne. 'Ted' Parker was the waist gunner in a nine-man

Liberator crew, the other waist gun position being taken by a drop-master. 'The moment we took off' wrote Parker 'the Quartermaster froze with fright and I got no help from him. I placed him on the forward deck and covered him up to keep him warm. He was shaking like a leaf.' They flew on the left of the lead ship *I'll Be Seeing You,* which was flown by Captain Jim Hunter. As the lead plane, one of the group's Operations Officers was required to fly as the co-pilot and several men wanted the position. The final decision was made by the flip of a coin and Captain Anthony Mitchell of Poland, Ohio replaced the co-pilot. Pfc George E. Parrish from Durham, North Carolina was temporarily assigned to the crew as drop master to supervise the dropping of supplies by parachute.

Over the dropping zone small-arms fire inflicted heavy damage. At the target 'Ted' Parker opened the hatch in the floor and had to work quickly because they would be passing the dropping zone fast and at low altitude. 'In my haste my leg became entangled in the parachute straps attached to the ammunition track and I was pulled out of the hole when the last bundle went out. I just managed to cling to the track but my legs were dangling out of the hatch. The Quartermaster ignored my calls for help. Finally the tail gunner, David Slade, heard me and came to my assistance.'

'Ted' Parker's Liberator flew over a small town and received small-arms fire from some Germans who could quite easily be seen in the streets. One bullet, well spent by the time it reached the B-24, hit 'him in the cheek. Within a few minutes the lead plane was hit by flak and a small fire started on the right wing. With only seconds in which to work, Captain Hunter, considered one of the best pilots in the group, picked his spot and started to bring the B-24 in on its belly. At less than 50 feet, however, the right inboard engine burst into flames. The right wing dropped and was too low when the plane hit. The plane then slid on the ground, crashed into a haystack and exploded. It came to rest in a field about three quarters of a mile northeast of a train overpass near the town of Udenhout. They were the unfortunate victims of a 20mm flak gun, which had been mounted by the Germans the day before in the town of Oisterwijk. On 18 September 42 rounds were fired from this gun at the Liberators as they flew overhead on their return to England. The heat from the explosion was so intense that a neighbouring farmhouse caught fire. Because of the low altitude, no one was able to bail out. 'Ted' Parker watched the B-24 go down. 'She took one bounce and struck some haystacks, exploding in a large orange flame. Our altitude was about a hundred feet at the time.' Frank DiPalma the seriously burned tail gunner was the only survivor; he was hidden by some Dutch monks until liberated.

The Liberators took countless hits from the small-arms fire and the 'Ringmasters' lost four B-24s. Five others were forced to land at different bases in the United Kingdom.

When the 44th Bomb Group had released its supplies, it reverted to flying on the deck (having gone in at about 500 feet over the dropping zone). Many B-24s received hits, including the deputy lead ship in the third squadron in the 44th formation piloted by First Lieutenant Pete Henry. It was a brand-new B-24, later named *Henry* after the King Features cartoon character. His leading edge on the left wing was holed by a 0.30 calibre shell which cut the line supplying manifold pressure. It also holed the fuel tank and petrol began leaking into the bomb bays. Henry got his aircraft home but another Liberator in the 44th was forced to ditch in the North Sea. Only three crewmen were seen scrambling from the stricken bomber.

The 14th Wing had had very little trouble with ground fire on the way in and some flights which stayed low and skimmed out on the deck came back untouched. However, most pilots who had dropped on DZ W made a climbing turn to the right, as planned. This tactic posed them like clay pigeons directly over the guns of the Germans at Best. For a minute or two the Germans gave the wing what even the bomber men regarded as a very rough time. Three of their aircraft were shot down, one crash-landed at Brussels and four crash-landed in England fit for nothing but salvage. At least 32 others received some damage. Next day the returned pilots agreed unanimously that the climbing turn was a mistake.

The results were not good. Some 238 tons were dropped but the bundles were badly scattered. On DZ 'W', where 108 of the Liberators were to drop, only about twenty percent of the supplies were recovered. This is less damning than it appears, since the gliders used as checkpoints were at the west end of the zone and a deviation of less than a mile to the west of them would suffice to put the bundles in the hands of the Germans in the Best sector. The failure, however understandable, caused the 101st Division serious shortages of food and other essentials. The 501st Regiment had been given a drop on DZ 'A' by thirteen aircraft. Although the supplies they brought were rather scattered, they were centred 1,000 yards west of the zone. A small-scale German attack in this area had been routed about an hour earlier and the 501st had both time and men to spare for collection details: Under these relatively favourable conditions it was able to retrieve slightly over fifty percent of its bundles.

At the 101st's headquarters in England a carrier pigeon brought a message saying that the 'Screaming Eagles' mission had been about 95 percent successful. On 25 September in a letter to Major General Paul Williams, commanding IX Troop Carrier Command, Brigadier General Jim Gavin, on the ground at Groesbeek said '... All things considered, I would say that the D plus 1 glider landings were very successfully completed.' Five days' earlier Gavin had telephoned Major Ben Kendig the 44th Squadron CO who's C-47 he had flown in on 17 September and told him 'Congratulations and appreciation for a fine job of flying. Hit drop zone right on nose.' Before loading up for the mission Gavin had asked Kendig what he would like for a souvenir. Kendig had said he would like a small silk Nazi flag. Months later Gavin sent the 44th Squadron commander a captured enemy flag at least ten feet wide that had flown over the German HQ in Nijmegen!

On the evening of the 18th General Brereton decreed that all airborne missions next day would take the southern route because of his preference for flight over friendly territory. The outlying areas were to be abandoned to shorten the line of defence. The principal airborne operation, a drop by paratroops of the Polish Brigade, would be directed at DZ 'K', a circular zone three quarters of a mile in diameter on the south side of the Rhine about a mile south of the road bridge. Other troops and materiel of the brigade and of the American 878th Aviation Engineer Battalion would land by glider on DZ/LZ 'L'. If all went well the engineers were to prepare landing strips on which aircraft in subsequent missions could air-land the 52nd Light Division. Supply drops on 'D+2' were to be made at Supply Drop Point (SDP) 'V', a quadrant containing about a quarter-mile of ground at road junction less than a mile west of the outskirts of Arnhem. Brereton further decided that the drops and landings would begin at 1500 hours instead of 1000 after predictions of extensive early morning fog in northern areas and almost unbroken low clouds further south. By afternoon, the fog would be gone and the clouds were expected to lift somewhat. However, bad weather was to make the decision on single-tow a costly one. It would also cause two days of cancellations and frustration for the 1,568 men of the 1st Polish Independent Parachute Brigade Group waiting to take off in 114 C-47s of the 314th and 315th Troop Carrier Groups at Saltby and Spanhoe respectively. John Frost's gallant band of men hanging on by their fingernails at the Arnhem Bridge knew that the Poles would land on a prepared enemy on its southern approaches and General Urquhart reasoned that the drop could end in slaughter for the Poles. He sent a warning signal and requested a new drop zone but the signal was never received. The C-47s would be unable to takeoff anyway because Saltby and Spanhoe as well as many other airfields in England were covered in fog.

Chapter 8

The Third Lift - Tuesday
19 September ('D+2')

On Tuesday 19 September while waiting to hear the result of the action on the 18th, I put in three more hours in the Pied Eyed Piper of Barnes taking a further 5,000lb load of petrol to Belgium. I wasn't able to land at Brussels to unload my petrol, because of the weather, but I got into Lille all right and was back at base before dark. Next day came the news that the forces at Arnhem had met with unexpectedly violent opposition and had been hemmed into a very small area by a German Panzer division. Fresh supplies of ammunition were urgently needed and plans had been made for a mass drop of panniers. There wasn't time to fit Treble Four with the necessary metal rollers, so I took KT500 on the trip. This entailed another five and a half hours in the air and, although the outward journey went off without incident, it was clear as soon as we approached the dropping-zone that things were not going well. The whole landing area was now ringed with German guns, which seemed to be firing continuously at our chaps down there, but the moment we arrived, they were elevated in our direction with scarcely a pause. We were down to about 600 feet, easy targets for the Jerry 88 mm howitzers - but here again luck was on our side, because the Huns chose to fire at the Stirlings which were mixed up with us, because they were twice our size and made much easier shooting.

In the few minutes that I was over the target I saw several Stirlings brought down and they hit the ground with a frightening shower of flames and sparks and smoke. I lost no time in climbing away after we had made our contribution and, although several Daks had been hit, when we got back to Down Ampney and eagerly assembled on the tarmac to talk

it over, we found that nobody in our squadron was missing.
Joubie's eyes were sparkling. At last he had seen some action!
'We've got to put in another effort tomorrow, 'Jim',' he said.
'I need one more, but I can't ask you to go. You've been flying
four days on the trot as it is.

'If Treble Four is ready, you can count me in,' I replied.
I didn't feel in the least bit tired and was quite ready to
volunteer. There were no heroics about it. We would all have
gone anywhere to please the old man.

Flight Lieutenant 'Jimmy' Edwards.

At Nijmegen on the morning of the 19th the 82nd Division eagerly awaited
the coming of the British tanks. Browning had told Gavin on the previous
evening that the Nijmegen Bridge must be taken on the 19th or, at the latest,
very early on the 20th. With tank support this seemed possible. Paradoxically,
although the bridge was the main objective of his division, Gavin could
spare only one battalion to attack it. He had a 25-mile perimeter to defend
and the glider-borne reinforcements scheduled to join him that day failed
to arrive.

Why the Germans had not already blasted the road bridge at Nijmegen
is uncertain. General Gavin, who should know, claims that Dutch guerrilla
fighters kept the Germans from placing charges on the span. The resistance
forces in Nijmegen certainly did a magnificent job of harassing the
garrison, but the Germans did have access to the bridge and could probably
have blown it had they resolved to do so. This lends weight to a post-war
statement by General Student that Model, who believed the bridge could be
held, had prohibited its demolition.

The medium tanks of the Guards moved over secondary roads to the
Maas-Waal Canal and crossed on the bridge at Heumen about 1000. An
hour later a battalion of tanks, a company of British armoured infantry and
the 2nd Battalion of the 505th Regiment headed north to make a renewed
bid for the Nijmegen bridges. They attacked early in the afternoon and
penetrated to the centre of the town without opposition except for some
artillery fire. There they split; one paratroop company and seven tanks
heading for the railway bridge, while the rest struck at the road bridge.
Neither group succeeded. The main body ran into forces ensconced in
revamped Dutch fortifications in a park at the south end of the bridge and
were stopped about 400 yards short of their goal. Repeated assaults lasting
well into the night produced nothing but heavy losses. At the close of its

third day of operations the 82nd Division had 649 casualties in its hospital at Groesbeek and over 150 dead.

Tuesday was a clear day in Holland and the besieged Red Berets of the 1st Airborne Division at Arnhem looked forward to their resupply promised for 10 o'clock but at the 36 and 48 Group bases in England fog in the morning and rain all day delayed the Third airborne lift. But at Down Ampney Alan Hartley a flight mechanic on 271 Squadron, standing by his pilot's Dakota, was not downhearted. Unable to contain his excitement Hartley asked if he could accompany his skipper on the next lift. 'No problem' said 'Len'. 'When you put the pins in, jump aboard'. 'The pins which 'Len' referred to' says Hartley 'were the locking pins on the undercarriage which prevented the undercarriage being raised whilst it was stationary on the ground. My last job when my aircraft took off was to remove the chocks from the wheels, take the pins out with their long red streamers, show them to the pilot who acknowledged the signal and then I would place the pins in the box just inside the open door frame. 'Chiefy' was agreeable for me to go on the lift as there was nothing for us to do whilst our aircraft were away. I was ready to go when 'Len' came over to tell me that another Dakota on our flight had developed a trimming fault and as we needed as many aircraft as possible and as he was a senior pilot, he would be taking FZ626. However, he had had a word with the pilot who was going to take our Dakota and he agreed to take me but when the pilot came to our Dak I recognised him as a peace time officer always in full officer uniform who insisted on being saluted at every meeting. So I backed off and told him that I wasn't allowed to go. I waved 'Len' off little knowing that he would not be returning to base.'

Awaiting favourable weather meant that at Keevil the ten men on guard duty, including John Roberts, a Fleet Air Arm fitter seconded from RNAS Lee-on-Solent, were on continuous duty for four days and five nights without sleep. Not surprisingly, they slept for a full 48 hours after the operation took off. 'Keevil airfield was closed and all fifty Stirlings and 150 Horsa gliders were painted with encircling black and white stripes, an operation that was completed in a single day!...you should have seen the take-off: St. Mary's Church in the village stood like Eros in the middle of Piccadilly Circus as the Stirlings and gliders set off on the historic flight.'[1]

An encouraging feature of 'D+2' was the progress made by the British ground forces. At 0615 their lead tanks rumbled over the bridge at Zon. Half an hour later they rolled into Veghel. By 0830 they had burst across the ten miles of hostile territory north of Veghel and made contact with the 82nd Division at Grave. This was the sort of dash Montgomery had hoped for. However, the contact of both American divisions with Dempsey's army still hung by a thread. Therefore the 101st Division had to retain responsibility for the whole long stretch of road from Veghel to Eindhoven. The 506th Regiment, reinforced by a couple of squadrons of British tanks, held the sector south of Zon. Although the Luftwaffe bombed Eindhoven heavily that night, the regiment was outside the town and had only a handful of casualties. The 501st Regiment continued to have a relatively easy time around Veghel and sent a company on patrol to Dinter four miles northeast of that town. The 502nd sent its second battalion at 0600 to make another assault on the bridge at Best, but once again the attack was beaten back. At 1415 the whole regiment, excepting the 1st Battalion, which was still defending Sint-Oedenrode, was thrown into a coordinated attack on the enemy position. This attack, supported by a squadron of British tanks, smashed through to victory over numerically superior opponents. By 1600 the paratroops had taken the bridge and with it fifteen 88 mm guns and 1,056 prisoners. Over 300 German dead were found on the field.

At Down Ampney, thick mist delayed the take off of the Dakotas of 271 Squadron until late in the day and 21-year old Flight Lieutenant David 'Lummy' Lord DFC and his crew of KG374 could only wait patiently until take off. David and his brother Frank had joined the RAF before the war in a period when breeches and puttees were being abolished and biplanes flew 'tied together' at Hendon Air Displays. First-hand stories were still told of the legendary Lawrence of Arabia, alias Aircraftsman T. E. Shaw and his death on a Brough Superior motorcycle. David Samuel Anthony Lord was born in Cork, Southern Ireland in 1913, the son of Samuel (a Warrant Officer in the Royal Welsh Fusiliers) and Mary Lord. After the First World War the family was posted to British India and Lord attended Lucknow Convent School. On his father's retirement from the Army the family moved to Wrexham and then David was a pupil at St. Mary's College, Aberystwyth from which he matriculated to the University of Wales. On leaving, he studied at the English Ecclesiastical College at Valladolid in Spain to study for the priesthood. Deciding the priesthood was not the career for him he returned to Wrexham after two years to try his hand at writing and was successful in having several stories published. He spent a short time in London as a free-lance journalist before joining the RAF in 1936 as an Uxbridge Cadet. David's proudest moment was being selected for the Cenotaph Squad. After selection for pilot training he soloed within two weeks on a Tiger Moth and by April 1939 had received his 'wings' as a Sergeant pilot. A posting to 31 Squadron at Lahore on the North-West frontier of India followed and he flew Vickers Valentia aircraft in support of the Army and RAF units trying to control the insurgent tribes of Pathans. (It was while on 31 Squadron that he acquired his nickname because 'Lummy' was the strongest expression he ever gave to his feelings). In June 1941 these old biplanes were replaced with Douglas Dakotas and David, now a Warrant Officer, qualified as captain. In October he was part of a detachment of eight Dakota crews in North Africa flying support operations. On one particular sortie he was carrying a mixed load of passengers and stores to an advanced landing ground when he was attacked by three Bf 109s and was forced to make a landing short of his objective. Although slightly wounded in the attack, he gathered his crew and passengers and walked the last ten miles. The next day he was flying again to supply an 8th Army unit.

Returning to India in February Lord was supplying General Orde Wingate's Chindits, a task that called for absolute accuracy in navigation, flying and supply dropping, amongst the jagged hills of the 'Hump' behind enemy lines. His skill and the bravery of the crew were recognised by personal recommendations, mentioned in dispatches and, for David Lord, the award of the Distinguished Flying Cross. He returned to England in January 1944, joining 271 Squadron where he trained with a new crew. The training continued at RAF Down Ampney where it was extended to parachute dropping and glider tugging duties. On the eve of D-Day, 5/6 June David Lord and his crew delivered paratroops near Caen, where, despite flak damage to the Dakota's rudder, elevators and hydraulic system, the crew completed their part in Operation 'Tonga'. During the next few weeks 271 Squadron duties were a continuous round of supply and resupply to the Allied bridgehead with the role changing later to resupply loads outbound and casualty evacuation home bound.

For the supply drop operation on Tuesday the 19th September, 30-year old David Lord's crew consisted of 19-year old Pilot Officer Richard Edward Hastings 'Dickie' Medhurst the second pilot, born at Fulford Vicarage near York, the son of Air Chief Marshal Sir Charles Medhurst CB OBE and the regular wireless operator, 25 year old Flying Officer Alec Forbes Ballantyne, born in Fife. Flying Officer Harry King, a pre-war policeman stood in as navigator. There were four dispatchers from 223 Company, Royal Army Service Corps. The task of 29 year old Corporal

Philip Nixon and Drivers Leonard Harper (also 29), James Ricketts (28) and Arthur Rowbotham (28) was to manhandle the panniers of ammunition down the fuselage to the open door. Two days' earlier when 24 Dakotas of 271 Squadron had set course for Arnhem, Lord was the pilot of one of the Douglas transports. Two of his regular crew were absent that day because Flying Officer D. MacDonnell, his navigator was on leave to be married and Ager's place as 2nd pilot was taken by Dickie Medhurst. They all returned safely and the following day the crew towed a Horsa glider carrying troops of the 1st Airborne to Arnhem. This was successfully released despite the Dakota being peppered by flak.

'After 'D-Day' recalled Flight Lieutenant Alec Blythe on 48 Squadron who flew one of 23 Dakota Mk.IIIs towing 23 Horsas carrying part of the 1st Airborne Division to LZ 'S' on 17 September and again on the 19th, recalled: My squadron transported supplies to Europe and brought casualties back. We were alerted for a number of airborne operations which were cancelled because of the rapid advance of the ground forces. Eventually in September the assault on Arnhem was launched and most of us were to tow gliders. As it was a long way to do this we were fitted with long-range tanks in the fuselage of the Dakotas. There were no fuel gauges with these tanks and we had been briefed that the tanks would get us to the Dutch coast, where we should switch on to main tanks for the remainder of the flight. Somebody had miscalculated, because most of us ran out of fuel about mid-Channel! So there you were, towing a glider with twenty troops on board, suddenly losing power. Fortunately, almost to a man, the pilots immediately switched to the main tanks. We had a hand pump to force the fuel through and those lovely Pratt & Whitney engines immediately sprang to life. One wretched pilot's immediate reaction when his engines spluttered and started to stop was to pull the 'glider release'. I could see this unfortunate glider spiralling down until it landed on the sea. Meanwhile the pilot of the Dakota had restarted his engines and returned home. By some miracle the men in the glider were picked up by an air-sea rescue launch almost before their feet were wet.

'The enormous train of tug aircraft and their gliders was most impressive. You were stimulated by a certain amount of fear, a certain amount of excitement at the very size of the force and of course your adrenalin level was raised when you were attacked by ground fire. Whenever that happened a couple of Mustangs immediately appeared from nowhere and silenced the enemy on the ground. Despite the excellent support of these ground-attacking Mustangs, we had casualties. I watched a Stirling alongside catch fire, which from a small trail of smoke gradually grew until the aircraft was engulfed before crashing into the ground. Nobody got out.

'On the first day the opposition was comparatively slight and the glider landing was successful, despite collisions on the landing zones. A second lift of gliders was flown in the next day, but I was not involved. On the third day we were briefed to resupply 1st Airborne Division. It had been assumed that the Airborne Division would form a perimeter within the environs of Arnhem. In the course of the briefing we were told to drop at a particular DZ. Then as the briefing progressed the DZ was changed. Just before we took off we were told to drop as originally briefed!'[2]

Unbeknown to the crews, on Monday night the Germans had captured SDP (Supply Dropping Point) 'V', 2,000 yards north-west of Arnhem, in the area of Warnsborn. Every anti aircraft gun and even Schmeisser machine guns mounted on orange boxes awaited the arrival of the leading 63 Dakotas and 101 Stirlings flying at 900 feet and in loose formation which were to make the first re-supply missions following the glider landing. The Germans knew the time and place of the drop and they had brought in more flak along the route. There were no RAF flak suppression fighters for the resupply aircraft.

'Arnhem, 19th September, 1630 hours,' runs the war diary of 1 Airborne Division. 'Resupply dropped on prearranged Supply Dropping Point 'V', which was in enemy hands. Yellow smoke, yellow triangles and every conceivable means were used to attract attention of pilots and get them to drop supplies within our lines; this had very limited success.' It had, indeed. The weather was misty, but the arranged dropping point could be seen and the pilots had eyes for nothing else. 'My most poignant memory,' wrote Lieutenant Colonel Packe, of the Royal Army Service Corps, 'will always be the time I spent watching the supply aircraft coming over and dropping their containers on an area not under our control .... They were met by a screen of flak and it was awe-inspiring to see them fly straight into it, straight into a flaming hell. We thought that some would not face it and would jettison their cargoes. In which case we should get them, for they would fall short and therefore in our lines but they all stuck to their course and went on, nor did they hesitate. A Stirling and a Dakota were seen, both on fire, circling round the zone. They were doomed and their pilots knew it, but they might still drop their supplies on the right spot. To do so immediately, however might interfere with those more fortunate than themselves who were timed to arrive a moment or two before them. So they held off, awaiting their turn. It came and they went in, blazing, to release the containers; before they fell 'like two torches from the sky', they had done all in their power to ensure success.'

Had it been possible to form the perimeter outside Arnhem in accordance with the original plan, this zone would have been well within the lines of the defence. But it was not. The high ground near the zone was never captured and both remained in the hands of the enemy. A wireless message explaining this was passed by Division HQ to change the location of the SDP and a new zone nearer to Oosterbeek indicated but the message with this vital alteration was not received in time. The radio frequency used clashed with that of a powerful British station - there seems to have been a blunder in the planning and as early as the middle of the first day heavy interference, amounting to jamming, had been noticed. The lines of a private telephone belonging to a Dutch company, with offices in Arnhem and Nijmegen, were untouched and might have been used. Indeed they were in constant use by the Dutch underground forces, who tried vainly to persuade the British invading forces to take advantage of them. As, however, they ran for the most part under ground occupied by the enemy the Intelligence branches decided that to speak over them was too risky. The Germans had laid out captured markers on the dropping point; the RAF aircrew had been briefed to ignore all other ground signals in case they were made by the enemy.

'Three Royal Army Service Corps dispatchers pushed the panniers along rollers to the side door' recalled Alec Blythe. 'When I went out to my aeroplane the dispatchers were waiting. I said, 'Do you know where we are going?' They replied, 'No, sir'. I told them we were going to Arnhem in Holland, which brought the response, 'That will be nice'. I replied, 'Well, it might be dangerous. We're liable to be fired at, you know.' They just smiled. We used to speak of 'ten-tenths flak', meaning that the sky was just full of exploding shells.'[3]

Finally, at 1300 KG374 and sixteen other Dakotas took off from Down Ampney for the northwest outskirts of Arnhem. At Keevil Stirling crews on 196 Squadron taxied out for take-off. Among them was Australian Flight Lieutenant Henry 'Chuck' Hoysted's crew. Sergeant Mike 'Taff' Stimson was the wireless operator. 'When we were all lined up on the peri track with our engines running, my skipper always liked me to sit down by the back entrance door while we were taxiing. This was so I could lean out and look underneath the wings to tell him if there were any obstructions beneath that he couldn't see from the cockpit because of the nose being so high. I had to make sure that the main wheels stopped on the perimeter track. Right from our very first op dropping supplies to the Resistance, I found that my intercom lead wouldn't reach the plug in the aircraft, so I had it lengthened after the first operation by adding another intercom lead to make it 6-8 feet in length. So, I was sitting there on the taxi track when Jim Metcalfe came running up to us saying his pilot had set an engine on fire and could he come with us. I hurriedly told 'Chuck' about it. 'Get him in,' he said, 'I can always do with another pair of eyes up front. Tell him to come up front and sit in the second dicky's seat.

'Chuck' had been incensed by rumours passed around the station by the 'Poms' about the Aussies hanging back when it came to facing the flak. 'Chuck' was determined that they wouldn't say it about this Aussie. The result was that when we got to Arnhem there were only two people in front of us - the wing commander and the squadron leader. Earlier that day the wing commander had insulted us, calling us pigs and had told us that we would fly at 500 feet, no higher, no lower. Any crew that flew above or below this height and his number was taken, would be out of aircrew. We had also been told to formate in threes as much as we could to increase our firepower. One Stirling was in front of us about 400 yards away, if that. One minute there were three of us, the next minute the middle one had just gone *whoomph* into thousands of bits. We ran the risk of flying through the debris. Luckily the explosion had blown everything out and it was just like flying through a black hole and we emerged the other side virtually untouched, but the fellows on the other side got damaged by bits of the aircraft.

'Just as two more aircraft further in front of us began to drop their supplies and we were about to drop ours, some aircraft from another station that had been miss-briefed came in from our port quarter at right angles, 1,000 feet above us. Wicker baskets containing five cans of petrol each were dropped without parachutes from these aircraft, narrowly missing us. We dropped our supplies and 'Chuck' put the Stirling into a sideslip, nearly taking the top off a church steeple. Above the noise of the engines and although wearing a headset, I could still hear outside our aircraft the sound of *whoomp, whoomp, whoomp, whoomp*. That was the German guns on the deck. I've never forgotten it. 'Jim' Metcalfe, who came to Arnhem with us returned safely. Our navigator [23-year old Flying Officer Frank D. Chalkley RCAF], who went with Warrant Officer Keith Prowd's crew got killed when they all had to bail out with two engines on fire, the third overheating and about to catch fire. They bailed out so high that they were shot to pieces in their harnesses as they floated down. Keith saw four of his crew hanging by their harnesses in the trees all shot up. Flight engineer, Sergeant Dennis

'Lofty' Matthews was seen to come out on a pannier parachute, a smaller 'chute intended for containers. He either fell off or was shot off and killed instantly. His wife was a Canadian nurse who'd travelled to the UK to be with him. She arrived at Steeple Ashton the day he was killed.'[4]

Warrant Officer Prowd RAAF who skippered Stirling EF248 'V-Victor' on 196 Squadron recalled: 'The reason we went on that day was that Pilot Officer 'Cess' Light, who later made quite a name for life saving equipment in the surf business, couldn't go. There was something wrong with his aircraft and the commanding officer asked me if we would go. I needn't have done as we had done our particular duty but the boys agreed and Cess Light's 23-year old navigator, Flying Officer Frank Chalkley RCAF [and 23-year old Air Mechanic 2nd Class Leonard Hooker from HMS *Daedalus*] came with us, plus [Drivers William Chaplin (35) and Frederick Smith (33) of 63rd Airborne Divisional Composite Company, RASC] in the back to push out stuff and the normal crew. Chalkley was a friend of my navigator, 33-year old Flying Officer George Powderhill.

'A very short time before Drop Zone we were hit by flak which set the outer starboard engine on fire, with smoke billowing out from it, making us an easy target. If we had had more time I would have feathered the propeller and used the anti-fire button. Formating on our port wing was another 196 Squadron pilot ('Fred' Powell an Englishman) and we waved to one another just seconds before we were hit by the flak which set us on fire and at the same moment the Dispatchers were pushing the containers out of the side back door. I found out after I was liberated that 'Fred' had reported that no one would get out of 'V-Victor' as it was all smoke and flames and no one could survive. Our height at the time was 1,500 feet and due to the heavy flak we also lost two more engines and a Stirling doesn't fly very far on one engine. I was afraid to increase power to the engines for fear that more petrol would cause an explosion, from which no one would survive, especially at that height. Obviously I instructed the crew to bail out. 'Len' Hooker was apparently behind me near to the navigator and did not have his parachute because it was beyond the main spar where the fire was fiercest and he had asked wireless operator Pilot Officer John Wherry if he could parachute down on his back.

'At about 750 feet I was satisfied everyone had evacuated the 'plane and I put my 'chute on, rushed back to the main spar called out to anyone, no answer so went back to the escape hatch up front and noticed the altimeter was at about 550 feet, I pulled back on the control column, down to the hatch and noticed the ground was so close, uttered a profanity, pulled the ripcord wrapped my arms around the 'chute and jumped; while still falling I heard a very large explosion and thought it was probably 'V-Victor'. I landed in a pine forest; parachute caught in the tree, released myself and stupidly buried my Mae West, but not the parachute. I then knelt down looked up to heaven and said 'What do YOU want me for?' because I really thought I should have been killed. I surveyed the situation and wandered around for quite awhile when to my surprise I was confronted by a squad of German soldiers who lined me up against a tree, I was of the opinion I was to be shot but they searched and then marched me off to Kleine Kweek, where I was informed of another airman in the area and the guard took me over to him; it was 'Mike' Powderhill who had been shot with a spray of machine gun bullets from his head to his thigh.'

Powderhill, after landing in a clearing and discarding his parachute, attempted to run towards some woodland but was hit by small arms fire from German soldiers in a nearby farm. Flying Officer Reginald Gibbs RCAF the 32-year old bomb aimer was shot at on the way down and injured and died of his wounds on 21 September when Germans advancing on the hospital threw grenades. Rear gunner Flight Sergeant Jim Gordon RCAF and Pilot Officer John Wherry were killed by rifle fire during their descent. Driver Chaplin died of his wounds in a German hospital on 11 November. Driver Smith is listed as MIA and has no known grave. AM2 Hooker was the only member of the Royal Navy to be killed during 'Market-Garden'.

'At a holding area in Arnhem I was subjected to severe questioning by a very big blond German who wanted to know if any 'planes were coming over the next day. When I failed to respond he hit me across the face with a small Italian Berita revolver in his hand. Believe me it hurt. He then stole my wristlet watch and signet ring, both given to me by my parents in Australia for my 21st birthday which I had in the UK. I went outside to meet up with John Wherry and Jim Gordon. We were then entrained off to Wiesbaden where I was held for three weeks' interrogation, then sent to Stalag Luft VII twenty kilometres from Krakow in Poland.'[5]

'The re-supply operation was rather different to our first trip' recalled Pilot Officer 'Les' Bellinger. 'Again it was low level, low speed and daylight but this time the Germans were waiting. We were reasonably bunched as we made our approach, but already ahead of us several aircraft were in trouble. One of our flight had received a direct hit in the petrol feed system. All engines had stopped and as a Stirling glides like a brick he was lucky to pull the nose up at the last moment and plough through the soft earth. We thought he had made it, but a wing tip collided with a farm building, the nose crunched round and a fire started.'

As Dakota KG428 on 48 Squadron flown by Pilot Officer Valentine Brock Christie RCAF approached DZ 'V the space around them was full of puffs of smoke the size of footballs; 20mm light flak Christie thought they called it. When it hit the aircraft it sounded like gravel hitting a tin roof. Ahead of him two Dakotas were on fire. Just seconds after giving the signal to the air dispatchers, Drivers H. W. Thompson and R. Olderton, Corporal R. Ballooch and Lance Corporal R. Bradley, one engine failed and seconds later the other engine spluttered and stopped. They had now in Christie's opinion a very heavy glider and with so little height nothing to do but crash land in an opening between trees. At 100 feet altitude a rifle shot from ten o'clock entered the port window and grazed Christie's left shoulder which felt hot like a branding iron' a second or so later and it would have been through his heart. Christie alerted the co-pilot Flight Sergeant Frank Fuller but still kept control of the aircraft. They slid over a single track railway north of Arnhem and the nose of the Dakota only feet away from the trees, twelve inches in diameter. On landing, Christie and Fuller escaped through a split in the starboard side of the cockpit which they squeezed through. There was now no plexiglas left in the windscreen and it was only a few feet to the ground. The normal exit was jammed with radio equipment and part of the supplies that they had been unable to despatch.

The navigator, Warrant Officer Anderson RCAF and wireless operator, Warrant Officer A. R. Fulmore RCAF survived the rough landing but Fulmore had a few cuts from flying cockpit glass. The four dispatchers had all been injured by flak and by the supplies on the roller conveyer and were seen to be bleeding. Corporal Balloch had been wounded in the leg and by a bullet in the left arm and a piece of shell in the left shoulder and Driver Ollerton a broken leg. The navigation maps were buried with their revolvers in the woods as they felt being unarmed if captured would be in their best interests. They spent the 19/20th in the woods and used the contents of their water bottles and lunch packs. On one occasion just as it was getting dark, two German soldiers came walking along the edge of the wood towards their concealed position laughing and talking to each other, when one handed his rifle to the other and walked into the wood stopping only a yard from them. A yard more and he would have stood on them. On the 21st the evaders made contact with a forester named Gerard Bloem who took them into his care and on 2 October they were joined by a GPR pilot and an officer from the Parachute Regiment. On 19 November Anderson and Fulmore were taken prisoner but

Frank Fuller escaped and was liberated on 5 May 1945. With the help of the Dutch resistance Christie was able to evade capture and returned to England.

Stirling losses on the 19th amounted to ten. Twenty-three year old Warrant Officer S. H. Coeshott and his crew were killed when Stirling EF263 on 190 Squadron was hit by flak and crashed and on fire. Flying Officer Reginald Lawton on 190 Squadron, whose Stirling had dropped British Pathfinders on the first day was also returning with supplies for the Airborne with his pilot, 24-year old Squadron Leader John P. Gilliard DFC. '...Over Holland the weather cleared and we were able to map read to the target. The opposition became considerable and we were hit several times. We were at 1,500 feet and there was no cloud or fighter cover. Over the DZ (CV) the flak was intense and we took violent evasive action after we let our supplies go at 1.000 feet. I thought that we were coming through all right, but suddenly, the skipper said over the intercom, 'Prepare to abandon aircraft', followed immediately by 'Abandon aircraft'. I stood up and clipped on my parachute... I passed the skipper at the controls. The aircraft swung sharply upward and I thought that he was giving us some height to jump, but I found out later that the aircraft was out of control... When the escape hatch was open, I sat on the edge and rolled out forwards... I pulled the ripcord and in a second or two the harness gave me a terrific jerk and I was floating down... as I was out of the plane I became conscious of the tremendous noise that was going on: ack-ack shells were bursting all around and there was a full-scale battle going on below the ground rushed up at me... I found myself lying on the ground I was in a sandy clearing in a pinewood.' The aircraft crashed near the Bilderberg Sport Park: Gilliard, who had flown in North Africa and declared that the Arnhem flak to be 'not a patch on Benghazi' was killed. So too, were the 37-year old co-pilot, Flying Officer Norman S. McEwen and the two RASC air dispatchers. Flight Sergeant C. Byrne the flight engineer bailed out but was injured on landing and taken to hospital. Lawton and the bomb aimer, Flying Officer Cullen and Squadron Leader F. N. Royle-Bantoft, who flew as a passenger joined the airborne troops at the Hartenstein and later escaped.

On 295 Squadron Stirling LJ652 flown by Flight Lieutenant, Acting Squadron Leader Clifford Hodges Potter DFC was hit many times on the run in but was able to drop his supplies, although, his homeward journey was made on three engines. When he could not maintain height sufficiently to reach base he force landed at an emergency landing strip at RAF Woodbridge, he had carried out twenty operations and a total of 216 flying hours previously with Bomber Command. Stirling LK170 flown by 22-year old Flight Sergeant 'Ray' Hall was hit returning from the resupply mission and crashed in German held territory near the house of Mr. F. B. van Rie in the Commune of Aardenburg. There were no survivors. The Stirling of Flying Officer 'Ron' Sloan on 295 Squadron had been keeping company with Flight Sergeant Hall's Stirling, with Hall flying on Sloan's port wing. They must have been just north of the prescribed route, just a little too close to the German front line. 'Ron' Sloan describes what happened: 'Suddenly - flak! Out of the corner of my eye I saw Flight Sergeant Hall's aircraft suddenly dip a wing. His starboard wing came up almost vertical and for a split second he looked for the world like a fighter aircraft doing a 'peel-off. There was an urgent call from our rear turret - 'He's hit!' 'Watch him,' I ordered. 'See if any bail out.' Another urgent call from our rear gunner gave us the information that it had gone straight in and exploded. No one jumped.'[6] One of the crews on a Stirling, badly hit but still able to fly, looked back at the dropping zone he had just left. 'I could see black puffs round the aircraft behind us,' he noted in his diary. 'It must have been a terrible spot to be in and we were glad to get out of it. I wondered what sort of battle the airborne men were having and knew it must be tough; but they had guts and plenty of them. We all wanted to do everything we could to help them.'

570 Squadron delivered a single Horsa to Arnhem whilst seventeen other aircraft brought in supplies, each carrying twenty-four containers and four packages. Flak over the route was severe, especially over the drop zone, and although all supplies were dropped it was felt to be an unsatisfactory outing as the accuracy of the drop was doubtful. Furthermore, three Stirlings were shot down and most of the remainder had sustained some form of damage, though only two of any great note, one of which was on fire when it landed at Harwell. Acting Squadron Leader Arthur Hudson crash landed Stirling LJ944 at Ghent after flak badly damaged one of the port engines. All the crew and the two despatchers returned safely the following day. Stirling EH897 skippered by Pilot Officer F. R. J. Mortimore was hit by flak and crash-landed at Schaarsbergen. All eight men were taken prisoner. 570 Squadron lost nine of its Stirlings during September, with twenty-two dead and sixteen PoWs and was forced to 'pause and lick its wounds'. 38 Group in total had lost 43 Stirlings and about a third of its strength during Operation 'Market'.

Seven Stirlings on 299 Squadron towed Horsas while a further seventeen took part in a resupply flight. Twenty-year old Sergeant Walter T. Simpson was air gunner on LJ868/R piloted by Flight Lieutenant Geoff C. Liggins who took off from Keevil at 1245 carrying twenty-four containers and panniers. 'Wally' recalled: 'Tuesday 19th September found me and my crew on our way across South East England on our way to Arnhem to re-supply the 1st Airborne dropped during Sunday and Monday. Having been briefed to fly at some given height and in 'V' formation of three aircraft, this had to be given up during flight as a bad job due to poor visibility, so we climbed above it and reached blue sky and sunshine. All was quiet crossing the coast, not even a shot fired in anger. That was until we crossed over into enemy held territory. Then all hell let loose; big stuff, little stuff; everything including the kitchen sink. The war virtually stopped on the ground and all guns were pointed skywards. You could hear it hitting the aircraft and could smell the cordite fumes of the exploding shells.

'The pilot was trying to take evasive action but as we had now regained our 'V' formation, we could only move to the right and back again. The closer we moved to our target the more we were hit. One shell burst somewhere near my turret as shrapnel passed through the top of my turret and the blast forced me over onto my right shoulder. I regained my position and blasted away at anything that moved. We were now getting closer to our dropping zone and I could hear the bomb aimer giving instructions to the pilot. Sergeant Runsdale the WOp came down the fuselage and gave Corporal Prior and Driver Braid the two dispatchers a hand and gave them the signal to drop the baskets which would be pushed out through the well in the fuselage floor. Bomb doors opened, we were nearly there and still in one piece.

'Flight Sergeant Ken Crowther the bomb aimer was still giving the pilot instructions and then I heard 'hold it!' and away went our supply load beneath my turret. With bomb doors closing and heading for home, a turn to port and bingo, we had it; the swine's set our port wing on fire. As I rotated my turret to see if I could see anything, the pilot told us to take up our crash positions. He was going to put her down. I acknowledged that I was leaving my turret to take up my crash position. I indicated to the WOp and the two RASC dispatchers from 253 Airborne RASC that we were going to crash and by movement of my hands suggested that they got down. I took up my position, knees up, hands behind my head, elbows forward and waited. Waited for what? Would it be the end for some of us, or all of us? We couldn't and wouldn't know until it was all over. If we survived we were going to be very, very lucky indeed. We waited, engines throttled back, a change of note, a bump, engines picked up and then by the time I came to, it was all over, so I thought.'

The aircraft, which had broken in half and was on fire, had landed in the river behind the church at Oosterbeek. The two air dispatchers, Corporal Prior and Driver Braid along with Walter were unhurt. Runsdale and the flight engineer Sergeant D. G. Gaskin were hurt and unable to get out of the aircraft so Walter went back to get them out. He then realised that Crowther was also missing so he went back in and got him out. The pilot and navigator Flight Sergeant Humphrey, were rescued by Prior and Braid. Liggins was in great pain and given morphine by Braid.

'There's a fire' continues 'Wally' Simpson. 'Someone screamed from up front. I found that my legs were trapped underneath the WOp's body. I moved, he shouted out with pain, he had sustained a back injury. I couldn't open the fuselage door. I assisted him to the rear escape hatch only to find it missing and my parachute gone with it. We got ourselves out and took up a sheltered position near the aircraft. The water of the Rhine was almost lapping the aircraft's tail. Our sheltered spot was a breakwater bank which shielded us from the blazing aircraft and the German snipers. Only then did I realise that Gaskin and Crowther were still in the aircraft and were trapped due to their injuries. I re-entered the bomber and brought out the flight engineer who had a broken leg. I then returned for the bomb aimer. The snipers were still having a go at us. I reached him and brought him to safety. His injuries included both arms broken and a partly severed foot. Some thirty seconds later the aircraft blew up and burnt itself out.

'By now the local Dutch people had arrived to help us, they had come from the village of Driel. After attending the wounded as best they could, it was decided to take them into the village. Anything that could be used for a stretcher was used. I recall a ladder being used. I was told by one of the Dutch ladies who could speak English that they would come back for me and my two dispatchers when it got dark, but due to a misunderstanding we missed each other.'

At 2000 hours Dutch civilians arrived, with them, a lady doctor and two nursing sisters, the wounded were taken to a barn for immediate first aid treatment, here they stayed until the 20th. The whole time they were under sniper and 88mm cannon shellfire being aimed at the stricken aircraft while the injured men were carried on makeshift stretchers made out of ladders and an open cart to the vicarage in the village of Driel where they were tended by a Mr. Hendrick, a first aid man and Cora and Reat Baltussen. Hendrick had a special pass issued by the Germans which enabled him to carry out his duties and so he could tell the Germans that the wounded were too ill to move, although in fact much of the dressings were 'Window

Dressing', about sixty to seventy evacuated civilians were also there, the Germans were looking for them in the village. For the next three days Prior, Braid and Simpson were hidden in a drainage tunnel let into the riverbank. The food they had was from Walter's air box and twenty-four hour pack from the aircraft's dingy, it contained Horlicks' tablets, sweets and chocolate, but they had no water and going down to the river would mean exposing their position to the German patrols in the area. But as it happened it was not a German patrol they heard but a friendly one. A farmer came and brought someone who could speak English but all he could say was that the British were expected on the 23rd. He came from Driel and said that the people there were nervous. It was not unexpected as five had been shot a few days ago for helping evaders. The British arrived on the 21st but owing to a lack of transport they had to stay there until the 24th. On the 21st a Polish patrol got into the village and a fought with the Germans with the result being the Polish had to retire leaving behind a Polish doctor to treat Liggins and the other injured crew men. He had to amputate part of Crowther's foot due to gangrene setting into his heel; he had also broken both arms, a fractured skull and shrapnel wounds.[7]

'So with my crew gone to receive medical attention' continues 'Wally' Simpson 'I was left with my two dispatchers. It was decided that we should leave the crash site and move away from the direction where the snipers were firing from. We had not moved many yards when a single shot whined through the air in our direction. In no time at all we were flat on our bellies not daring to move. By now it was getting dusk so we crawled forward until we reached the next breakwater. We made a quick dash, up and over and stayed put. We now found that we had cover from three sides so we were fairly safe from surprise (we hoped). During the hours of darkness a patrol passed within thirty feet of where we were lying. We froze not knowing if they were friend or foe. (Only four years later did I find out that they were friends and they were out looking for us). It was a cold, damp, long night. Would daylight ever come? A river meadow was not the best of places to spend a night under the stars. We went into hiding for three days and managed to survive on my 24-hour ration pack.

'On Friday 22 September we were able to join up with a patrol of the Polish Parachute Brigade and were taken to their Headquarters in Driel. We were there for approximately 36 hours in which time we had been shelled and nearly killed. During the short stay in Driel I was able to see the five members of my crew. The staff at the Medical Centre did not know if the bomb aimer was going to pull through as his leg had been amputated because gangrene had set in. Pull through he did and was returned to Wharton Military Hospital, (Wiltshire) three weeks later where further amputations took place. The rest of my crew returned to the UK to receive further medical attention. All survived their ordeal but did not return to the Squadron. I returned to duties with 299 Squadron.'[8]

Hilary Upward, a WAAF at Keevil thought it would be a break from her work in Operations to fly on one of the re-supply trips and permission was obtained to go with Flight Lieutenant Rees' crew on 299 Squadron on the 19th. 'Our Stirling, X9-B, assembled as lead of a three-plane vic and set off line astern behind two other vics. Approaching the drop zone we reduced altitude to the required 800 feet. The Germans let fly with everything they had and while I couldn't hear anything over the din of our Stirling's engines, there were lots of little black puffs sailing past the cockpit windows. Looking down I saw a Stirling on the ground aflame from end to end. Sitting in the navigator's seat the thought came to my mind that it had been foolish to make this flight which I expected any moment, to be my last. We were briefed to make a climbing turn to port as soon as we had dropped our panniers. All at once I heard over the intercom, 'Panniers gone' and Rees exclaimed 'Bugger me!' The sky ahead was criss-crossed with tracer and exploding shells. Rees immediately pushed the control column forward and dived the aircraft. Looking back as we sped low over the Dutch countryside I saw that several other aircraft had followed our move, diving to tree-top height to escape the flak. After what seemed an age Rees started to climb and it was a relief to find we had come through the hail of fire without a hit on our aircraft. Rees told us that three of the six aircraft ahead, including the CO's, had been shot down. In total the two Keevil squadrons lost fifteen Stirlings during the Arnhem operations with many damaged and several returning with wounded aircrew.'[9]

'The approach to the dropping area' says Flight Lieutenant Y. R. W. Lovegrove, co-pilot on EF319, the Stirling piloted by the 28-year old CO of 299 Squadron; Wing Commander Peter Brian Newsom Davis 'was rather a disconcerting spectacle. Flak was simply being pumped up; heavy flak, light flak, machine-gun fire and rifle fire'. Having watched a Stirling go down in flames, they reached the dropping zone where they were at once hit in the bomb-bay by a shell. 'As we were carrying petrol, the aircraft was immediately aflame. Glancing down from the co-pilot's seat I saw my navigation table on fire and I remember with a curious detachment noticing that the Very cartridges were giving a firework display of their own.' Davis called calmly on the intercom: 'Don't panic chaps,' followed swiftly by the order to 'Abandon aircraft' an instruction that he himself ignored.[10] The flames were roaring up through the aperture through which the rear gunner had to jump. Lovegrove bailed out successfully, but the Wing Commander who had inspired his crews with a spirit of resolution equal to his own was killed. Davis, who came from Harpenden, was getting married in a few weeks time and the crew had all been invited to the wedding. The 25-year old navigator, Flight Lieutenant Freddie Mason, 31-year old Squadron Leader Cecil Aubrey Gerald Wingfield, a scientist from Boscombe Down who had some secret equipment to test during the flight and one of the air dispatchers, 29-year old Driver Richard E. Ashton of 63 Company RASC were all killed. Thirty-five year old Colonel Kenneth Darling commanding 1st Parachute Battalion, who was recovering from wounds suffered on the first day and still had his right arm encased in plaster was originally allotted a place on Davis' Stirling but at the last moment his place was taken by Wingfield and Darling, smallish in stature but tough and resolute, had gone to Arnhem on another aircraft. From his vantage point in another Stirling below, Darling saw Davis' Stirling go down. Darling's aircraft was hit and limped home on three engines.[11]

On 299 also Pilot Officer C. A. R. Bayne RAAF at the controls of Stirling EF267 attempted a crash landing south of the Rhine at Leur, near Wiehen. Despite initial signs of success the aircraft suddenly somersaulted and burst into flames, although despite a few serious injuries, no one was killed. Bayne and his crew were taken prisoner. These were the Squadron's first losses of Operation 'Market Garden'.

'The second Operation 'Market' re-supply was rather different to the first' recalled Pilot Officer 'Les' Bellinger on 295 Squadron. 'Again it was low level, low speed and daylight but this time the Germans were waiting. We were reasonably bunched as we made our approach, but already ahead of us several aircraft were in trouble. One of our flight had received a direct hit in the petrol feed system. All engines had stopped and as a Stirling glides like a brick he was lucky to pull the nose up at the last moment and plough through the soft earth. We thought he had made it, but a wing tip collided with a farm building, the nose crunched round and a fire started.

'We found our target marker, made our run and dropped our containers. As we climbed away, we were hit by several chunks of flak. One piece came through the bomb bay doors through the bomb carrier sections and hit the armour plating under my seat, where it shattered and ricocheted up front into the bomb aimer's space and behind me around the navigator's cabin.

Scottie, the navigator, leaped up yelling and later we found a piece of very hot metal had landed on the back of his hand raising a decent sized blister. 'O-Orange' like 'K-King', a very tough customer, had shuddered, slowed, but now seemed unperturbed. A quick intercom check confirmed plenty of holes, but no one wounded and no serious damage. The engines were turning, controls were working; all was well.

'Another of our chaps on the port side had a starboard engine on fire, but just ahead Flying Officer Simmonds ('Simmo' to his pals) was in real trouble. The port inner engine was on fire but seriously. We formated on his port side climbing with him as he desperately gained height for his crew to bail out. This was an engine oil fire and we had been warned you had approximately two minutes, once it had taken hold, before the main wing spar burnt through and separated from the fuselage. He had gained enough height and as he levelled out and trimmed the aircraft, spinning the gyros for 'George' the automatic pilot to take over; his crew was already jumping clear and floating safely away. We were counting heads and it was just 'Simmo' to go. We saw him drop down from the pilot's seat and mentally followed him through the navigator's cabin, past the wireless operator's nook, over the main wing spar and down the long fuselage.

'Come on 'Simmo', hurry up, there isn't much more time'. Suddenly he was at the rear door and falling clear.

'Good old 'Simmo'; pull your cord old lad'. But 'Simmo' turning slowly over and over, was getting smaller and smaller and abruptly for him there was no more time at all. Just after 'Simmo' left the Stirling, there was a small explosion, the port wing broke away and the fuselage, with the two starboard engines still turning, curved away in a downward spiral to join 'Simmo'. The two partners in war were side by side on Dutch soil.

'We carried on climbing and set course for home. Eventually, just ahead we spotted the Stirling with the engine fire problem. The paint on the cowlings and wing was charred but the fire was out, the prop was feathered and he was happy on three engines. We weren't in a hurry; he might have problems over the sea, so we reduced speed, tucked in alongside and escorted him home. We watched him land and then made our own circuit for approach but all was not well. We had a problem. Remembering the nudges we had received, I planned to make a longer down-wind leg than usual, to test in easy stages the full flap movement. I took this precaution because in the crew room we had news of a Stirling on returning from a trip had flipped upside down on the final approach.

'Talking between ourselves, we decided the most likely explanation was that only one side of the flaps had operated, the other side having been damaged by flak. Flaps are very large metal panels, part of the main wing structure but designed to swing down and form an air brake to slow you down more quickly after landing. Full flap is only selected at the last stage of the approach and certainly if anything went wrong there would be no time for any correction! Taking an aim view or having thirty tons of Stirling sitting on our chests and feeling that it certainly reduced our chances of drawing the OAP we completed our flap check. All was well. We set the flaps to 12° down, this position gives maximum lift with no extra drag and selected under carriage down. Red warning lights, replaced by green; good show, this meant the undercarriage was locked in position for landing. That was a relief, I expected trouble. However, glancing out of the port window at the 'drome below I looked across at the port tyre and something wasn't right. Yes we had a problem.

'On the intercom I called on Flight Sergeant 'Les' Gardner, bomb aimer and Flight Sergeant John Pritchard engineer, to have a good hard look at the starboard tyre and then come over and look at the port. The starboard tyre seemed fine, like the port tyre it was turning gently in the slipstream and it looked normal. 'Les' and John came over and with Flight Lieutenant 'Scottie' McBain, navigator, joining us, four pairs of saucer-sized eyes peered intently at the offending tyre. Hmm the flak had definitely nudged it, but was it flat? It still looked round. Well, do we land with the wheels up? Even using the grass between the runways the ground was so hard the very least damage would be props and engine and heavy bruising underneath the fuselage and what if when they lifted 'O-Orange' the tyre was found to have a decent pressure! It would take some living down. Leg pulling was a favourite past time and went on forever. Let's call the control tower and get advice. Hmm, fly past, low level and low speed they will check the tyre using binoculars and report back. We were climbing back to circuit height as they reported 'Sorry old boy, there are a few holes here and there in the fuselage but the tyre looks in good shape, you must make up your own mind. Either way, we will have the crash wagon and the ambulance watching your approach in case things go wrong!'

'What could go wrong? Well this question had been churning through my mind since the glance from the window. Bearing in mind the tyres were almost six feet tall with a very fat girth, a flat one on touch-down would certainly wrap itself around the undercarriage leg and act as a very effective brake. The enormous dragging load generated would snap the leg off, the wing with its heavy motors would drop, hit the ground and break away and certainly because of the side pressure, the other side would follow suit. O Lord what a mess. Well we can't cruise around all day, so crash positions chaps, check the fire extinguishers and axes; we're going for a normal landing. Say a prayer and keep your fingers crossed.

'Luckily it was a perfect flying day. Crystal clear visibility and a steady breeze down the long runway. We made a power approach to have positive control over the landing speed, 95 knots and have the aircraft in almost the three-point position on touch-down. We came over the boundary fence, plenty of power holding 'O-Orange' just above the stalling speed, full flap to reduce our speed smoothly after touch-down and port wing slightly high. The starboard wheel gently kissed the tarmac, the tail wheel settled and I gradually reduced the power. The port wing settled lower and lower and lower and we started on ever increasing swing to port. I yelled to 'Les' to cut the engines, we weren't going anywhere and it reduced the risk of fire and warned the crew to hold tight and wait for the crunch. But that day luck was very much on our side, there was air in the tyre and although it was moving out fairly quickly and the tyre was dragging and pulling us round, the tyre was keeping a reasonable shape and turning!! We were covering ground and the speed was coming down quickly but smoothly.

'Suddenly a rumbling and vibrations started and we knew that we were on the hub. There was a terrific groaning from tortured metal as the undercarriage and wing spar took the enormous strain, but everything held together, the noise subsided, the huge cloud of dust settled and 'O-Orange' was in one piece. We gave him our heartfelt thanks. Flying control was bleating over the intercom that we were too close to the main runway, could we taxi away!! There were WAAFs in the tower and to spare their blushes I didn't answer. The crash wagon and ambulance came alongside and took very little persuasion to drop us outside the de-briefing room. We dropped in to answer the usual questions and more important, collect a very welcome mug of hot, strong, sweet tea. One way and another it had been quite a day.

'The pilot of the Stirling that had lost power on all engines and hit the farm building came back to the Mess on crutches to say hello. He told us that when the wing hit the building the nose crunched around against a high wall and the dashboard was pushed back trapping his right leg just below the knee. The fire started, but although he wriggled and pulled, he was trapped. Then the pain became so severe he fainted. He regained consciousness in a German army field hospital. A German doctor had almost certainly saved his life by immediate, superb surgery on his leg. Actually, his life had been saved twice that day, because the Dutch farmer and his son, watching events from the shelter of the barn had witnessed the whole incident. Without hesitating and ignoring the fire they had grabbed axes, climbed on to the wing of the Stirling, chopped away the canopy and pulled him out of the cockpit. His right leg, now completely severed below the knee was left in the aircraft. Using the farm tractor and trailer they had taken him to the German field hospital not far away. The German doctor apparently, gave preference for attention not to nationality, but severity of the injury and he gave our lad immediate attention. When he was fit enough to travel, he was repatriated home. Before he left us, he cheerfully mentioned that he was being fitted for a new leg later that week!'

Maurice Perdrizet (later General Maurice T. Perdrizet) led 345 (Free French) Squadron's Spitfires at Deanland, near Lewes in Sussex when seventeen Spitfire squadrons were detailed to escort a wave of DC-3s and gliders to Arnhem. Only 345 (FAF) Squadron partially accomplished the operation, with visibility 100 yards and ceiling: 10/10ths cloud at 200 feet.)

'The Arnhem adventure is in its third day and seems to be running into difficulty .... The wing has been able to put up one or two shows a day up till now, but the morning has been very damp and misty and it is still barely possible to see the control tower, a hundred yards away, through the fog... At around 1500 hours, the telephone rings. The duty officer picks up the receiver and almost at once puts it down. 'Briefing!' he shouts...

'The paratroops are clearly now in a desperate situation and must, at all costs, be resupplied. The DC-3s and gliders are about to take off and our three squadrons, forming the escort, are to follow at short intervals...

'As we take off and head northeast towards Manston in tight formation, the ceiling is down to 300 feet and visibility, in the heavy rain, is steadily deteriorating. Crossing the coast and heading out across the North Sea, we plunge into fog, but the twelve aircraft tuck in tight keeping solid formation...

The leader of the squadron ahead of us announces that he is turning back; almost at once the controller asks me about my intentions. 'We'll have a try,' I say. Immediately there is a shout over the R/T: 'Lagos! Look out ahead.' There is just time to pull up sharply and pass over the top of the DC-3s and gliders which have also turned for home.

'We cross the coast at Ostend and set course across Belgium. But now the controller calls again. 'We're still trying,' I reply. Soon it is obvious that there will be no improvement in the conditions and there is plainly no point in going on. We turn slowly and smoothly, keeping the squadron together and start heading back towards Manston...

'Suddenly, just ahead, there are chimneys and factories and houses, hundreds of houses ... and now the flak and clouds of tracer, firing at point-blank range from all sides. It's Dunkirk! We have come out four miles too far west. As all twelve aircraft dive towards the sea, the port's 88mm guns keep up their barrage and shells throw up spouts of water around our wing tips. We have not seen this before - heavy ack-ack firing very accurately on a dead flat trajectory... These last few seconds have seemed like an eternity.

'We head for base and now I call the leaders of the three sections; every one of them is still there...As the twelve Spitfires skim the treetops and weave a way along railway lines and rivers, only the Lord knows how we have contrived to make it safely home... But we had, at least, had a try...'[12]

'Arnhem, 19th September, 1630 hours,' runs the war diary of the 1st Airborne Division. 'Re-supply dropped on pre-arranged SDP 'V' which was in enemy's hands. Yellow smoke, yellow triangles and livery conceivable means, were used to attract attention of pilots and get them to drop supplies within our lines; this had very limited success.' The weather was misty, but the arranged dropping point could be seen and the pilots had eyes for nothing else...' My most poignant memory,' wrote Lieutenant Colonel Michael St. John Packe, in charge of the Royal Army Service Corps elements in Oosterbeek, 'will always be the time I spent watching the supply aircraft coming over and dropping their containers on an area not under our control...They were met by a screen of flak and it was awe-inspiring to see them fly straight into it, straight into a flaming hell. We thought that some would not face it and would jettison their cargoes, in which case we should get them, for they would fall short and therefore in our lines; but they all stuck to their course and went on, nor did they hesitate.'

A Stirling and a Dakota were seen, both on fire, circling round the zone. They were doomed and their pilots knew it, but they might still drop their supplies on the right spot. They held off, awaiting their turn. It came and they went in, blazing, to release the containers; before they fell 'like two torches from the sky,' they had done all in their power to ensure success. 'Such cold-blooded courage is the extreme of heroism' said the official account of the British Airborne Division. 'It was prompted, not merely by a strong sense of duty, but also by a feeling of comradeship with those fighting a doughty and perilous battle in the woods beneath which 'looked so quiet and clean,' but were full of strife and carnage.'

Four Dakotas, including two that were shot down on the approach, one crashing almost on the DZ, were shot down also and three aircraft had to force-land in Belgium. At Down Ampney Alan Hartley waited anxiously for the return of 'Len' Wilson. Equally, there was no word from KG374 and David Lord's crew. 'Unsuspecting, our Squadron flew in and were met with a tremendous curtain of exploding shells and tracer bullets' recalls Alan Hartley. 'Many Dakotas were shot out of the sky and 'Len' Wilson in his FZ626 as he pulled away from the DZ over Arnhem was hit by flak. Badly damaged he tried to crash his Dakota on the gun site in an attempt to wipe out the gun to make sure it did not shoot down any other following Daks. As he aimed his stricken plane, three parachutes - 'Les' Gaydon, the navigator and two air dispatchers [Driver V. Dillworth who was wounded and Driver W. Jenkins], the RASC soldiers who were responsible for the Army supplies we were carrying were seen to leave. 'Len' must have died for at the last minute of this drama he must have slumped over the controls and the aircraft suddenly swung to port, slicing the top of a tall tree, hitting a house in Bakenbergseweg and crashing into the back garden of the Roell family's house.'

The explosion of the aircraft and the fuel in the panniers caused huge disarray amongst the gun crews who were witnessed running from their positions in a state of panic.

Besides Wilson, Flight Sergeant Herbert Osborne the 23-year old second pilot; Flight Sergeant Reginald French the 24-year old wireless operator and the third dispatcher, 28-year old Lance Corporal James Grace also died. Alexander 'Lex' Roell and his brother Eric buried all of them in the garden. They were later re-buried in the Airborne Cemetery at Oosterbeek. 'The fourth dispatcher, 35-year old Driver Richard Newth was taken to the Diogenes command bunker near Deelen airfield where he died of his wounds on the 23rd.[13]

'Jimmy' Edwards managed to avoid the flak in KG444 *The Pied Eyes Piper of Barnes* and cleared the Arnhem area on his way back to base. He told his wireless operator, 'Bill' Randall, to get the sandwiches and coffee flask then suddenly there was a tremendous noise and the aircraft shook violently. Jim thought that they had been hit by flak but looking out of his window he saw the ugly snout and yellow spinners of an FW 190, who proceeded to rake them again. The engines suddenly went into fine pitch - Jim gave the order to bail out, which second pilot Alan Clarke and navigator Harry Sorensen promptly obeyed. Flight Sergeant Clarke was one of a large bunch of new pilots who had recently arrived in case replacements were needed. He had been trained in Rhodesia and after returning to England had just spent a whole year in a hotel in Harrogate waiting for a posting. I found him sitting on the grass with his mates and laughingly threw him a small pamphlet which we all had to carry, entitled 'Useful phrases in the event of being shot down behind enemy lines.'

'Read this, Nobby,' I said, 'You never know!' Three days later he was using it.'

Then Jim collected his parachute, put the automatic pilot in and raced down the aircraft to bail out through the open door. But lying near the door were the four air dispatchers and Jim yelled 'Why haven't you jumped.' 'Can't, sir' came the reply, 'all wounded in the legs'. So throwing his chute down, Jim went back to the cockpit but he couldn't see through the windscreen which was now covered in black soot and oil. So he knocked out the escape exit in the roof and by standing in the seat with his head in the slip stream he brought the aircraft down into a small wood where the small saplings broke his speed without breaking the aircraft up. As he landed the nose dug in and catapulted Jim out of the top hatch and on to the ground where he was joined by 'Bill' Randall who had also stayed on board. Jim said that they felt very vulnerable lying there in the yellow Mae Wests but as the Focke Wulf came in for the kill, he ran out of ammunition for only three rounds were fired. Jim had many burns to his face and ears, his ears shrivelled like cockleshells (the reason he wore his hair long to hide them) and for his brave action Jim received the DFC.

On board David Lord's Dakota Harry King navigated by 'Dead Reckoning' and 'Gee' and shortly before 1500 hours the Dakota began his decent into the swirling haze. At 1,500 feet they broke out of cloud and were immediately targeted by intense flak. The Dakota was hit in the starboard engine which promptly burst into flames. The crew's chances of extinguishing the fire would have been greatly improved had Lord shut down the engine and feathered the propeller but instead he kept the engine running to complete the first run. By now the starboard engine was burning furiously. Lord went down to 900 feet where he was singled out for the concentrated fire of all the AA guns. On reaching the dropping zone he kept the Dakota on a straight and level course while supplies were dropped. At the end of the run, he was told that two containers remained. Although he must have known that the collapse of the starboard wing would not be long delayed Lord circled, rejoined the stream of aircraft and made a second run to drop the remaining supplies. These manoeuvres took eight minutes in all, the Dakota being continuously under heavy AA fire. His task completed, Lord ordered his crew to abandon the aircraft, making no attempt himself to leave the Dakota, which was down to 500 feet. Harry King later recounted that he had been ordered to go to the open door of the Dakota and assist the dispatchers to don their parachutes and get out. When the wing collapsed he was blown out of the aircraft. Surviving the descent he then took part in the perimeter defences at Arnhem. Later captured, he survived the war. The Dakota crashed in flames near Reijers Camp on LZ 'S'.

Sixteen aircraft on 48 Squadron participated in 'Market III', flying through intense flak with no fighter escort. Many aircraft were hit and two, (KG401 and KG428), failed to return. Dakota III KG401 on 48 Squadron had just dropped its supplies from 700 feet when it was met with intense anti-aircraft fire. The tail unit, rudder, port aileron and engine, the starboard auxiliary fuel tank and all the gyro instruments were either damaged or put out of action and one of the Army dispatchers was mortally wounded. Flying Officer L. R. Pattee RCAF and his co-pilot, Flying Officer A. C. Kent flew the crippled aircraft back to the British lines, through three more areas of enemy flak, where they sustained further serious damage, including a five foot hole in the starboard wing which caught fire and complete electrical and communications failure. Once over the British lines, Pattee gave the crew and the two dispatchers the opportunity to bail out, but they refused and the pilots then made a successful belly-landing in a field near Kessel. No sooner had they all quit the Dakota, than it was engulfed by flames. One of the dispatchers, 38-year old Driver H. Davis died soon after the landing. Lance Corporal Wilbys Whittaker RASC survived but he was suffering from shock and he developed a bad stammer. Even so, he immediately volunteered to go on further operational sorties although he was not permitted to do so. He was awarded the DFM on 28 October. The survivors were taken to Brussels and the crew returned to Down Ampney. Over the following four days the Squadron lost another six Dakotas on re-supply missions to Arnhem. Pattee was awarded DFC.

Twenty-three year old Flight Lieutenant Charles R. Slack on 575 Squadron was flying Dakota KG88 when his aircraft was hit by flak and crashed. All four crew and the four dispatchers were killed. Driver Robert Hodgkinson (33) from Preston managed to bail out but he was shot and killed by a German soldier when he came down near one of the gun batteries. Driver W. D. Cross (33) was also killed after bailing out. KG368 on 512 Squadron flown by Flight Lieutenant William Pearson was badly damaged by flak over the DZ including parts of the control surfaces. Having made one run Pearson made a second one through even heavier flak to ensure the remaining panniers were dropped. On returning to base he had no hydraulic pressure and subsequent inspection of the aircraft it revealed the aircraft was riddled with bullet holes, it was his twenty-seventh operation and 130 flying hours. For his actions he was awarded an immediate Distinguished Flying Cross.

Flight Lieutenant Alec Blythe on 48 Squadron recalled: 'As you approached Arnhem you got the impression that there wasn't wing-span room between flak bursts, not to mention the small-arms fire! To my right a Dakota, I think flown by Flight Lieutenant Lord, caught fire. One of the dispatchers was desperately trying to get out but he couldn't get through the door. Unknown to us the DZ was in the hands of the Germans. Whatever our troops may have done to attract our attention we probably wouldn't have seen. And, after the briefing change, we would have ignored any ground signals as decoys. Having dropped our load, we banked and weaved as violently as possible to avoid fire from the ground and headed home. When we got back to base my three dispatchers were full of the joys and said, 'Well, sir, we thoroughly enjoyed all that weaving and turning on the way back!' Ignorance is bliss.[14]

General Urquhart was among the soldiers on the ground that saw Lord's aircraft and his desperate attempt to drop his cargo. 'We were spellbound and speechless and I daresay there is not a survivor of Arnhem who will ever forget, or want to forget, the courage we were privileged to witness in those terrible eight minutes. We saw the machine crashing in flames as one of its wings collapsed and this incident was talked about long afterwards by men who had grown accustomed to bravery.' Major Geoffrey Powell was 'awestruck'. 'I couldn't take my eyes off the craft. Suddenly it wasn't a plane anymore, just a big orange ball of fire.' When Lord's aircraft crashed, Powell said to someone by his side: 'That bugger got a VC.' It was not until sometime after the operation that Urquhart learned the name of the Dakota pilot. 'We did not know that Lord had ordered his crew to abandon while making no effort to leave himself.' David Lord and all his crew, including the dispatchers, lie buried together at Oosterbeek. Flying Officer Harry King, navigator was flung out while assisting other members of the crew to put on their parachutes. Surviving the descent he then took part in the perimeter defences at Arnhem. On 13 November 1945 Flight Lieutenant David Samuel Anthony Lord DFC was awarded a posthumous Victoria Cross.[15]

As for the Halifax squadrons, 298 Squadron was towing ten Horsas as the five Hamilcars that were to have been used were stood down, while 644 Squadron was left to tow a lone Hamilcar, in company with ten Horsas. The combinations took off from Tarrant Rushden in eleven minutes. 644 Squadron escaped flak damage but lost two of its gliders over the

Channel, only one of them reaching the coast. The Hamilcar flown by Captain Bernard Holt Halsall MC crash-landed in a farmer's field at Andover after casting off its tow when an engine on the tug aircraft caught fire. Only one of the tugs was shot down, but thirty were damaged. The glider of the destroyed aircraft may have reached the Arnhem area. A total of thirteen gliders were loosed over Holland and one, badly damaged, over friendly Belgium. Some may have snapped their cables, but at least nine of these fourteen releases were caused or necessitated by ground fire.[16] Alex McCallum on 298 Squadron, who flew his 24th operation on the 19th, knew where to draw the line. 'Immediately I completed my ops tour I became engaged to Cynthia - I was afraid of US troops who were looking for British wives to take back to the States. Having completed eighteen months and 27 operational flights, I was temporarily grounded and missed the Rhine crossing 'Varsity,' but I was still present when the crews returned. Some spoke of icing problems, but the death toll was tremendous. Those on parachutes were already dead on landing.'

As the Halifax was generally unsuited to the despatching of supply containers, 298 and 644 Squadrons played no further part in 'Market-Garden' after the 19th, 644 and 298 each having flown a total of 46 sorties, delivering fifteen Hamilcar gliders and thirty Horsas without loss throughout 'Market-Garden'.

On the 19th weather conditions over the Channel had deteriorated slightly and although they began to improve over the Continent, a persistent haze made visibility poor. By now the enemy defences had improved greatly and German fighters appeared in strength. Because of a misunderstanding, there was no fighter escort for the glider force and some of the 298 Squadron crews later reported seeing several gliders shot down; but fortunately, there were no losses amongst its own charges. Despite damage to two of the Halifaxes, all of the gliders were released over the correct dropping zone. 644 Squadron encountered very stiff resistance during the final run-in and several Halifaxes were damaged by flak and three gliders failed to reach the dropping zone, two through broken tow ropes. The third combination had reached the Group Rendezvous point but a flak-hit near the tail caused the Horsa to dive towards the ground. The tug pilot, Pilot Officer McConville dived the Halifax with the glider in an attempt to hold its nose up but the tow rope snapped under the strain and the Horsa went straight into the ground. Elsewhere in the area, Captain Bernard Halsall was not having much luck but was determined to get to the battle so he crash-landed the glider near Ghent, close to a small Belgian village. Initially hostile, the locals soon realised that Halsall and his troops were part of the invasion forces; they sheltered the soldiers before they drove the lorry and anti-tank gun to Nijmegen.[17]

Flight Lieutenant Alec Blythe on 48 Squadron says: 'The resupply continued for a further six days and losses were severe but I never ceased to be amazed at the damage the Dakota could sustain and continue to fly. One came back with a hole in the fuselage large enough to push a chair through. Many flew all the way back on one engine. Others with lesser damage were repaired by the ever-willing and untiring ground crews to be ready for the next day.

'Arnhem was a disaster. We could have flown the 1st Airborne Division there in one day. It would have meant some of us flying two sorties in the day. In Burma we flew as many as three sorties a day. Had we delivered the division more quickly they would have had a better chance to form a firm perimeter and secure the bridge. Our resupply would then have been successful instead of so much gallantry being wasted in sending supplies down to the Germans.'[18]

Alan Hartley concluded: 'The greatest disappointment of this gallant sacrifice by our aircrews who flew these suicidal missions for four days on the trot, was that less than 20% of the drop were received by the paras on the ground for there was no radio communication to tell our pilots that the DZs had been captured. At Down Ampney we all felt very depressed by this severe setback to our Airborne operations and were appalled by the state of our battered aircraft staggering back from Arnhem with huge holes in the wings and fuselage and engines smoking through over-boosting. On the neighbouring airfield of Fairford, their Stirlings were also streaming back and one day we were horrified to see a Stirling coming in against the circuit firing red Very flares indicating a request for priority to land because of casualties on board and this Stirling crashed head on with another Stirling on the circuit. Locked together in a lethal embrace, they plummeted to earth leaving a long thick black column of smoke hanging in the sky. We, the ground crew, felt very sorry for our aircrew that carried out this re-supply mission knowing that although many of them were flying to their deaths, the supplies had to be taken to the beleaguered paras who needed them so badly. I have always maintained that this was the most courageous flying of the war. Broad daylight, no fighter escort, no guns to defend themselves at 500 feet and 120 mph into an inferno of anti aircraft gunfire was absolutely suicidal. Nevertheless, work continued with our Transport duties, flying in all weathers with urgently needed supplies and the return of casualties.'[19]

THE THIRD LIFT - TUESDAY 19 SEPTEMBER ('D+2')

At dawn on the 19th a last attempt was made to break through to the bridge. The Staffordshires advanced down the Heelsum-Arnhem road, followed by the 11th Parachute Battalion, while the remnants of the 1st and 3rd Parachute Battalions moved along the riverbank, which was only a couple of hundred yards to the right of the road. They battled onward for about half a mile to a point called The Monastery, where after exhausting their supply of antitank ammunition, they were overrun by tanks. They fell back, engaged enemy forces flanking them on the slopes of Den Brink and were again terribly mauled by mortar fire and tanks, followed up by infantry. Barely 400 survivors of the four battalions were able to withdraw to Oosterbeek, a mile further west, where they had the support of divisional artillery.

At 0500 that morning 4th Parachute Brigade had attacked from the Wolfhezen area in an effort to take high ground at Koepei, just beyond which lay Drop Point 'V'. The attack stalled more than half a mile west of Koepei, leaving the drop point in enemy hands. By mid-afternoon it was all too clear that the brigade could get no further, so it was ordered to fall back on Wolfhezen and thence south to the main divisional position around Hartenstein. Thus it happened that the gliders which were to land on LZ 'L', a mile east of Wolfhezen, came down at 1600 in the front lines of a force attempting to disengage under heavy pressure.

Perhaps even worse than these reverses was the fact that the 114 C-47s in the 314th and 315th Troop Carrier Groups which were to carry the Polish Parachute Brigade to DZ 'K' south of the Arnhem bridge were grounded by the impenetrable overcast in their area. Also postponed were glider missions by eighty American and ten RAF aircraft to land the 878th (US) Aviation Engineer Battalion on LZ's 'X' and 'L'. Their gliders stood ready; the weather at their bases was favourable; but the land on which to build an airstrip outside Arnhem had not been won and, indeed, never was won; so the engineers waited and their aircraft stood idle.

The RAF was able to send out a resupply mission and a small glider mission from then-bases in southern England, but those, too, were jinxed. They dispatched 35 Horsas carrying Polish headquarters and artillerymen to LZ 'L' and also eight to LZ 'X' and one to LZ 'S' with cargoes returned from previous missions. Of these gliders, five broke loose over England, two over the sea and five more over Belgium and Holland. The pilots reported seeing considerable flak, especially near the zones and had no fighter support at all. One glider was shot loose and another was so damaged it had to be released. None of the rug aircraft were lost, but nine of them were damaged. The pathfinders had all their equipment including 'Eureka' working nicely on LZ 'L' and 28 pilots reported releasing gliders there. However, the Horsas had to land in the middle of a battle. Some were bit by shells and others had to be abandoned with their cargoes. A majority of the Polish troops were able to report for duty, but losses were heavy.

Only two or three of the gliders bound for LZ's 'S' and 'X' reached the Arnhem area and they probably fell into enemy hands, since little, if any, of those zones was held by the British.

As for the resupply mission, every effort had been made to deflect it from Drop Point 'V' to a safe point south of Hartenstein, but in vain. A message sent on the 18th was not received. The airborne set up a 'Eureka' in a tower at the new point, but that could be used only intermittently for fear of exhausting the battery. Although about half of the pilots interrogating it reported success, it seems to have done them singularly little good. This may have been partly due to the set being turned on late and partly to the tendency of the blips on a 'Rebecca' screen to merge when it was within about two miles of its 'Eureka'. The old drop point was less than a mile and a half northeast of the new one. Smoke, panels and Very lights were also used, but because of trees surrounding the new DP an aerial observer would have had to be almost directly overhead to see them. Almost none of the pilots on the mission did pass close enough to the spot to sight the visual aids.

The upshot of these failures in communication was that the resupply mission headed for its original DP, crossed the enemy lines at about 1,000 feet through intense flak and dropped most of its supplies in the Koepei area. Out of 100 Stirlings of 38 Group and 63 Dakotas of 46 Group, thirteen were destroyed and 97 damaged. The heroic persistence of the pilots only ensured that their loads would go to the Germans. Out of 388 tons of supplies dropped, only 21 tons, less than six percent, was recovered. Most of this was probably from five aircraft which dropped their loads by mistake near Wolfhezen and from an extra couple of Stirlings which had been sent to drop on DZ 'L' and appear to have done so.

By nightfall on 19 September the main body of the British airborne, terribly short of ammunition, food and water, held an area of less than two square miles between Oosterbeek and Hartenstein on the east and Heveadorp and Bilderberg on the west. The glider battalion which had been with 4th Parachute Brigade entered the perimeter that night. The brigade itself was still near Wolfhezen and in danger of being cut off. General Urquhart, seeing no hope of rescuing his battalion at the Arnhem Bridge, decided to have the Polish paratroops dropped on the south bank of the river opposite his positions at Heveadorp, since the ferry there might yet be used to affect a crossing. Messages requesting this change, use of the Hartenstein drop point for supply drops and selection of LZ 'Z' for further glider landings were sent and reached Eastcote. It seems doubtful whether the division actually held LZ 'Z' at the end of the 19th, but the enemy in that sector had been inactive enough to make occupation of the zone seem feasible. The power of German attacks on the north and east made it certain the other zones could not be used. To the British troops at Arnhem 19 September was a day of disaster. Their attacks failed and by nightfall it was evident that the initiative had passed to the enemy. Had the Poles arrived at 1000 on the morning of the 19th as planned, they might conceivably have saved the bridge or at least rescued what was left of the 2nd Parachute Battalion. It was not until that afternoon that German tanks were able to close in on Frost's men and begin systematic destruction of their positions dominating the north end of the span and up to that time the Germans appear to have had few troops and no tanks on the south bank of the river. When the Poles did come two days later, bridge and battalion were lost beyond redemption.

Chapter 9

'Bloody Tuesday' 'D+2'
19 September - The American Lift

The plans were to marshal a total of 96 planes of the 440th, with each to tow a CG-4A glider. This total was the full capacity of our outfit. Every plane capable of flying was to be committed to this mission, including my plane, Roger The Dodger. I could only hope that she would again be able to dodge all that flak and gunfire. We worked throughout the night to get the planes in then proper position in the line-up. One responsibility of the crew chief was to taxi the plane into the proper position, so that took most of the night's rest from me. It was quite a chore to line up that many planes with the glider ropes attached to its glider, which was lined up outboard of the line of powered aircraft.

Charles Everett Bullard, crew chief, C-47
Roger The Dodger **in the 440th TCG.**

Early on the morning of the 19th, Flight Officer George E. 'Pete' Buckley in the 74th Troop Carrier Squadron, 434th Troop Carrier Group reported to the flight line at Aldermaston to check over his CG-4A, which was loaded and ready to go. 'Our objective was Landing Zone 'W' between Zon and Sint-Oedenrode, on the main road of this airborne corridor leading to the Rhine. Due to a shortage of glider pilots, one of the three 101st glidermen in my glider, Lieutenant Tony Linz, was to sit in the right seat as my co-pilot because of some previous time he had in Piper Cubs. The two other men in the glider were Pfc's 'Fred' Miller and Hubert Warren. All were from the 321st Glider Field Artillery Battalion. Tony did not show too much enthusiasm for the job and I was only able to give him about ten minutes instruction on the basics of flying the big bird. I'm certain that his main concern was the possibility that I would get hit and he would have to take over and get us down in one piece. I must admit I gave this a great deal of thought throughout the flight. On the first day of operations, 17 September, the 434th Group with ninety C-47s of the 71st, 72nd, 73rd and 74th squadrons carried men of the 501st Parachute Infantry Regiment of the 101st Airborne Division. They jumped into three areas of Drop Zone 'A' between Eerd and Vechel. Subsequent flights by the 434th, on the 18th and 19th to LZ 'W' would be glider tows carrying glidermen, medics, ammunition, supplies, artillery and other support units of the 101st.'[1]

The 101st Division had decided it wanted artillery in the third lift, so the five serials originally tasked to drop supplies to it were transformed into glider serials to bring in guns and gunners. Instead of 191 Wacos the division would receive 382 and to this were added three more carrying the loads of gliders which had aborted earlier. In addition, the low attrition rate in the previous missions made it possible to increase the number of gliders going to the 82nd Division from 209 to 219, the resupply aircraft for that division from 142 to 167 and the aircraft carrying Polish paratroops to Arnhem from 108 to 114. The RAF would send to Arnhem a parachute resupply mission of 163 aircraft and a glider mission of 52 aircraft, including seven added to bring in replacements for gliders which had aborted on previous missions.

Weather conditions proved to be much worse than had been predicted. Throughout the day haze and stratus blanketed the Grantham area and great masses of low cloud persisted over the Channel and the Low Countries. Lowering clouds over the bases of the 50th and 52nd Wings forced them to postpone the glider mission which had been prepared to deliver the 325th Glider Infantry Regiment and some other troops to the 82nd Division at 1000 on the 19th. A few aircraft and gliders got off the ground but were recalled almost immediately. Along most of the troop carrier route haze limited visibility to about half a mile. The only area on the route with even relatively good weather was that around Arnhem.

The resupply mission of 167 aircraft, which was to drop 265 tons of supplies to the 82nd, did somewhat better, because it staged from the bases of the 53rd Wing in southern England and two serials had been sent to those bases on the day before. One serial of 25 aircraft flown by the 439th Group ran into heavy cloud off the Belgian coast and broke up. One of its aircraft followed the gliders going to LZ 'W' and dropped its bundles near there. Another got far enough to be damaged by anti-aircraft fire. The rest apparently turned back before reaching the Continent. The other serial, 35 aircraft of the 61st Group, began taking off from Aldermaston at 1250. They flew across the Channel through dense haze under a 200-foot ceiling.

Over Holland the weather improved greatly, but flak was thick and no friendly fighters were sighted north of Gheel. Two aircraft were shot down, one west of Veghel and another shortly after making its drop. Fifteen were damaged and five men were missing, including a quartermaster bundle-dropper who fell out the door of his aircraft.

The glider mission flown on 'D+2' by the 53rd Wing and 442nd Group for the 101st Division took off between about 1130 and 1320 in ten serials containing 385 aircraft-glider combinations. The weather over the assembly area around Greenham Common was barely passable with visibility poor and clouds closing in at about 1,200 feet. Beyond Hatfield, conditions deteriorated rapidly and before reaching the coast the serials ran into deep, dense clouds in which visibility was zero. Glider pilots unable to see their tugs had to guide their craft by the tilt of the tow rope and by telephone conversation with the aircraft crew. At most points over the Channel it was possible to get under the clouds by going down to about 200 feet but even then visibility was generally half a mile or less.

'Take-off was uneventful' continues Flight Officer 'Pete' Buckley 'and the 434th Group, after forming up with hundreds of other gliders and tow planes from other troop carrier groups, headed for the continent. Little did we know that this day would turn out to be 'Bloody Tuesday'. Shortly after we crossed the English coast and a quarter of the way across the Channel, the entire formation flew straight into a heavy fog bank. If there's one thing in this world that really upsets a glider pilot and I'm sure the tow pilots as well, it's flying into a dense fog in tight formation with over 700 planes and gliders. You have no way of knowing who's going to go where, when, or how and the possibility of a midair collision or accidental release is enough to make your hair stand on end. I could only see about three feet of the tow rope and had to fly blind for what seemed like an eternity. Fortunately I had the glider in perfect trim, so it practically flew by itself. Even so, I had no way of knowing what the tow plane would do. If he made a sudden change in any direction we'd be in big trouble. Fortunately for us he did not. When we emerged on the other side of the fog bank there was not another plane or glider in sight in any direction. It was the biggest vanishing act I have ever seen.'

Lavish air support had again been planned, but, because of the widespread bad weather, very few of the support missions could be flown. Escort and cover duties between England and the southern IP near Gheel had been assigned to fifteen Spitfire squadrons of ADGB, but only one of those squadrons carried out its mission as planned and only 68 of the Spits made sorties. The rest had to turn back. Of seven groups of P-51s which the Eighth Air Force was to furnish for perimeter patrols and area cover,[2] five groups were able to reach the battle area and make a total of about 180 sorties. Two of these groups had to battle German fighters which were seeking to penetrate the perimeter. At 1445 near Wesel the 364th Group sighted and engaged more than thirty enemy aircraft. It reported the destruction of five of them and the loss of one of its own. The 357th Fighter Group, which had 54 aircraft on patrol in the Arnhem area, had four such clashes. It encountered 25 Messerschmitts at 1610 hours, about thirty Focke Wulfs at 1620, between twenty and thirty assorted fighters at 1705 and fifteen Messerschmitts at 1720. The group claimed to have shot down eighteen of the enemy and lost five of its aircraft. Except for the fight near Wesel these air battles were fought after the troop carrier serials had left the combat area, but they undoubtedly saved the airborne troops some punishment. If the Germans had struck earlier, their chances of getting at the troop carriers would have been better, since because of the weather two P-51 groups on area patrol were late in getting into position.

The Eighth Air Force had also agreed to send two P-47 groups and the rocket squadron for anti-flak work south of Hertogenbosch, but they were unable to make any sorties. Flak neutralization beyond Hertogenbosch for missions to Nijmegen and Arnhem was a responsibility of Ninth Air Force units based in northern France. These dispatched 171 aircraft, but few of the aircraft reached the front and none of them went into action. The principal reason for their failure was the impossibility of attacking ground positions through low clouds and thick haze. Thus weather had prevented any effective operations against anti-aircraft positions.

'We had been briefed before take-off that things were not going too well in the landing areas' continues 'Pete' Buckley 'and the men and supplies we carried must get through. Our tow pilot Captain 'Bill' Miller, being well aware of this, continued on towards the continent as if nothing had gone wrong. I had no intercom on this trip, but I knew what his intentions: to press on. What most glider pilots say in a case like this is: 'where he goes, I go.' As long as the rope stays hooked, you have no choice.

'After crossing the coasts we took a heading into Belgium which would take us to the Holland border and into enemy territory beyond. Captain Miller started to circle at this time, waiting to see if any other 434th planes would show up so we could go in together. He did not realize it, but his 360 degree turn kept getting tighter and tighter and it was all I could do to hold the proper position on tow behind him. By then we had been in the air for over three hours and my hands and arms were tightening up and beginning to cramp and fall asleep. I shouted over to Lieutenant Linz that I thought the tow ship was lost and did he want to cut loose here and make our way to the landing zone by land? I'm not sure he understood what I said, even though he shook his head in the negative, so we hung on. I don't think he knew how tired I was.

'Miller, in the tow ship, at this moment received a go ahead by radio from our CO, Colonel Strean, to proceed to the landing zone by ourselves and we took off on a beeline for the Holland border, I hoped. As soon as I realized that this was the last leg of our flight, I began to wonder what kind of reception the Germans would have for one lone C-47 with a glider in tow at 600 feet. Even a duck hunter could hit us at this altitude! In about fifteen minutes we received an answer.'[3]

Many gliders towed by the 53rd Wing broke loose, cut loose or were brought back; the whole last serial was called bad after it was well out over the Channel. Of these gliders, eighty landed more or less smoothly in England and two in the last serial collided over their base, killing their pilots and six troops. Another seventeen gliders had to be ditched in the Channel, but were located by rescue launches in time to save all personnel. During the flight over friendly Belgium 31 more gliders broke loose or were released, al presumably as a result of the weather. Three of them crashed, killing five men, injuring four and putting two jeeps out of action. The rest landed well and all the troops and materiel aboard they reached the 101st within a week.

'Our course brought us into the landing zone between the town of Best on our left and Eindhoven on our right; continues Pete' Buckley, 'which was less than one minute away from our objective on the outskirts of Zon. At Best, off to our left, a battle was still raging between the Germans and our own paratroopers for control of a key railroad bridge near the town. Eindhoven was still not fully secured and some fighting was still going on in the streets between the 506th Parachute infantry and the Germans. As we flew past Best at roughly 600 feet a mobile flak wagon, which I could see on my left out of the corner of my eye, opened up on our tow plane. I watched, fascinated, as shells went up through the left wing and into the left side of the fuselage and exited out the top right side where the radio compartment is located. Small bits of aluminium from the plane and spent pieces of flak flew back and peppered the front of our glider. Just when I thought the enemy fire would move back along the tow rope and knock hell out of our glider, it stopped. We really lucked out on that one. Throughout the whole time we were under fire, our tow ship never wavered, changed course, or took evasive action. I found out later from Captain Miller that my tow plane, on the way back from the LZ after I had cut loose, was hit so bad by flak in the rear fuselage and tail section, that he had great difficulty maintaining control. The tail surfaces were shredded, vibrating and shaking so bad that he contemplated landing somewhere in France or Belgium. Because the engines were functioning properly and he was still able to hold his altitude, he made the decision to try for England. They struggled across the channel in their plane which could very well be called 'Old Shaky' at this stage of the game. They landed at the first English airfield in sight to check the plane out before continuing on to our home base at Aldermaston. What they saw when they climbed out of the plane scared the hell out of them. The tail section was riddled, in tatters and looked like it was ready to fall off. Miller after talking it over with the crew decided to continue on to their base. That beautiful old bird had brought them this far and they had enough confidence in her to know she could get them home safely. They made it.

'In a matter of seconds the landing zone appeared directly in front of us, strewn with hundreds of parachutes and gliders. Some were in one piece, others had crashed badly and their cargo was scattered around the wreckage. The wreckage of two C-47s that had been shot down moments before were still burning in the craters they made when they crashed in the centre of the LZ. I cut loose and made an approach well into the centre of the area, just in case the Germans were in the dense woods around the edge waiting for us. I found out after we landed that indeed they were there, but some of the 506th paratroopers held their attention while we landed.'

Contrary to expectations, the route instead of passing over the new salient ran just west of it and with visibility so low, the airmen probably blundered over some strong points they would normally have avoided. In spite of clouds and mist German gunners sent up intense and accurate light flak from Rethy, Moll and Best. Small-arms fire probably aided by the fact that the mission had to fly low, also took its toll. The troops on LZ 'W' could see the formations approaching over the battlefield between Best and the zone and could certainly have saved some losses by recommencing a detour if a ground-air radio had been provided. As it was seventeen aircraft, seven percent of those making sorties, were destroyed and five others had to be salvaged after landing at friendly bases. Almost all had received the fatal damage before reaching the LZ. Among the crews 31 men were dead or missing. Approximately 170 of the returning aircraft had been damaged, but this ratio, seventy percent of those exposed, is offset by the fact that in most cases the damage was slight.

'After we touched down' continues 'Pete' Buckley 'we came to an abrupt stop in the soft dirt of a potato field, which partially buried the nose of the glider. The first thing I did when I got out was to bend down and run my fingers through the dirt; it was so nice to be down in one piece. After about fifteen minutes of digging, we managed to get the front section of the glider opened up and the jeep and equipment unloaded. Not knowing exactly where we were located, Lieutenant Linz and Miller and Warren took off in the general direction of Best where the firing seemed to be the heaviest. I took off on foot across the landing zone to find the road to Eindhoven. On the way I stopped at the 326th medical tent which was set up on the edge of the LZ. Inside, a surgical team of airborne medics that had flown in by glider were performing operations on the wounded and victims of glider crashes. Some of the medics there were the same ones that we, the 434th, had flown into Normandy on 'D-Day'.

'I stuck my head in to see if any glider pilots were being treated there. Some had been and some of the crew members of the C-47s that had been terribly burned on the faces, head and hands before they had bailed out were still there. Within sight of the hospital tent you could see what was left of their planes still burning on the LZ and in the wreckage were what was left of the crew members that were unable to get out in time. All the time that these medics and surgeons were working on casualties, the Germans outside the perimeter were shelling the LZ at random. These courageous medics of the 326th never batted an eye; they just kept right on working.

'Before the morning was over, seventeen of the gliders were forced to ditch in dense fog over the Channel, five others crashed over land because of bad weather, dozens of others were cut loose or broke loose over Belgium and seventeen C-47s were shot down by enemy flak fire over Holland. Of the 385 gliders that had left England carrying members of the 101st Airborne Division, only 209 made it to the LZ in Holland.'[4]

About half of the pilots whose aircraft were shot down managed to release their gliders on or close to LZ 'W'. Among the bravest and the luckiest were 24-year old 1st Lieutenant Jesse M. Harrison in the 435th Group and his co-pilot. On 17 September at the controls of the *Urgin' Virgin* Harrison had flown a stick of 101st paratroopers to DZ 'C' near Son. Four months before, on 'D-Day' 6 June, Harrison and the *Urgin' Virgin* had carried 'G' Company, 501st Regiment to Normandy and returned with 67 holes in the aircraft. On 18 September Harrison's crew and the *Urgin' Virgin* towed a glider to

Holland without incident but on the 19th the doors of the *Virgin* would not close due to stress from glider towing and Harrison used another C-47 to tow another glider to Holland. Hit by machine gun tracers a few miles short of the LZ, the fuselage caught fire and the C-47 began losing altitude and Harrison's crew bailed out. Despite the smoke and flames, he noticed that the glider pilot he was towing still hadn't released from the tow rope. 'If he has the guts to hang in there, I'll stay at my controls', Harrison decided. They flew on, still losing altitude, but reached the designated release point, above the Landing Zone. Releasing too soon would have landed the glider and its occupants in German territory, most likely resulting in their death or capture. After the glider was released, Harrison left the controls and went to the radio operator's table to find a bail out chute. In the smoke he managed to snap on the right side, but was unable to fasten the left side. He made his way back to the cabin and finished securing the parachute. Glancing at the altimeter, he saw that the C-47 was down to 300 feet and still descending. Now he had to move briskly toward the tail, through a solid wall of flame to reach the exit door. He made his exit, pulled the ripcord handle and heard his plane go in. A second or two later, he hit the ground. Badly burned on the face and hands, Jesse Harrison's war was over. He would spend many months in seven different hospitals, receiving skin grafts to his face, in a slow, painful recovery period.

The C-47 was destroyed, but Harrison received the Silver Star for staying at the controls of his burning plane, to deliver the glider to the LZ. After Jesse was WIA, his radio operator and flight engineer continued to fly in the *Urgin' Virgin*. At one point, the flight engineer was forced to paint the word 'Censored' over the word *Virgin* on the nose art. With a new pilot and co-pilot, the *Urgin' Virgin* went on a resupply mission over France, lost bearings in the fog and crashed into the side of a mountain, killing all aboard. (The usual crew chief was not aboard as he had swapped places with another that needed flight time to get his flight pay.)

Many gliders were shot loose, broke loose or were prematurely released as a result of enemy action. One squadron in the next-to-last serial released fifteen gliders by mistake nearly ten miles west of the zone. Since the ceiling in the release area was about 600 feet and visibility less than a mile, the wonder is not that they went wrong, but that so many went right. In all sixteen gliders landed safely in enemy territory, their occupants and most of their cargoes eventually reaching the 101st Division. Another 26 Wacos were unaccounted for, almost certainly because they had come down in hostile territory and all aboard them had been killed or captured.

Of 213 gliders reaching the drop zone one was shot down, two or three crashed and 209 made good landings with very little damage, a remarkable performance under the circumstances even if some allowance be made for the smooth and spacious character of the landing zone. Landings began at 1437 and ended about 1600.

The mission had carried 2,310 troops, of whom 1,341 reached their destination in safety, eleven were dead, eleven were injured and 157 were missing. The remainder had been returned to England or landed safely somewhere short of the zone. Out of 136 jeeps loaded into the gliders 79 arrived at the zone in good condition, as did 49 out of 77 trailers and forty out of 68 guns. By far the most depleted unit was the 907th Field Artillery Battalion, which had been carried by the last two serials and one flight of the serial preceding. Of its 89 gliders 57 had been returned to England, four had ditched and about seventeen were missing or down in enemy territory. Only 24 men of the battalion and none of its twelve 105 mm howitzers were landed in the vicinity of LZ 'W'. The other units carried were the 81st Airborne Antitank Battalion, the 321st Glider Field Artillery Battalion and portions of the 327th Glider Infantry Regiment, the 377th Parachute Field Artillery Battalion and divisional artillery headquarters. These came in at between 55 and 95 percent of strength. The antitank battalion had on hand only fourteen of the 24 guns with which it had started, but the 377th Field Artillery had all twelve of its 75 mm howitzers in position and ready to fire by 1710, an hour and forty minutes after it landed.

The guns which did arrive proved their worth almost immediately. About 1700 a German force with tanks and self-propelled guns struck at Zon from the east and got to within a few hundred yards of the Zon Bridge, which the 502nd Regiment had left lightly defended while it concentrated on winning its battle at Best and guarding its landing zone. Since by that time the landings were over and victory had been won at Best, the 502nd had ample resources to counter the threat. Antitank guns of the 81st Battalion knocked out two German tanks and the rest retreated. Had this thrust come a couple of hours earlier, it might have achieved the destruction of the bridge, a most serious possibility.

Later on the night of the 19th, still on his own, 'Pete' Buckley crawled into a foxhole on the side of the road near the Wilhelmina Canal at Zon, just outside the drop done. 'The nights are the worst part of these landings behind enemy lines. It's dark and, being alone as I was, every sound, no matter how slight, is magnified threefold. Your skin crawls at any little noise and your imagination runs absolutely wild; you're your own worst enemy. All night long, occasional artillery shells kept dropping into the area. Parachute flares went off every few minutes turning night into day and trigger happy soldiers around the area, probably just as nervous and jumpy as I was, kept shooting at sounds and shadows. This was a good time to hole up and not be walking around. To top all this off, German planes flew over Eindhoven, which was only a short distance away, dropped flares and bombed the hell out of the town. The sound and concussion from this made the ground shake and any kind of sleep was impossible. The thing that bothered me most was the fact I didn't know what was going on. At this stage of the game you start to pray a lot and promise God that, if he gets you out of this one, you'll lead a better life.

'When the sun finally came up, I heard voices close by and, not knowing exactly who it was, I peeked slowly over the edge of the foxhole with my Thompson at the ready. There, directly in front of me, staring back at me from another foxhole ten feet away, were two British soldiers who had spent the entire night there also. We all breathed a sigh of relief and they brewed up tea and shared their biscuits and jam with me. Both were from a British reconnaissance team that got separated during the night.

'Shortly after this I started out on foot again down the road towards Eindhoven. Near Zon, alongside a large wind mill, a British tank had just been hit in the turret by an '88' and one of the crewmen was hanging out with his head blown off.

'A little further on, in an open field was a large group of German prisoners guarded by 101st men and a few glider pilots. One tough sergeant of the 101st, who spoke German, was shaking them down for concealed weapons and asking them a lot of questions about what unit they were from, etc. Occasionally he would come up against a really arrogant German who would not cooperate in any way. His favourite tactic then was to plant the muzzle of his Thompson firmly under the guy's chin and push up hard while glaring straight into his eyes. From then on there was usually a sincere and humble spirit of cooperation from that particular individual and from the others that had been watching. I was tempted to stay around to see if he really would blow someone's head off that might have called his bluff.

'About three hundred feet south of the temporary Zon Bridge - the original had been blown up by the Germans - two British lorries in a convoy carrying ammunition were coming towards me going north when they took direct hits from German tanks, backed up by infantry. These Germans were attempting a counterattack and trying to cut the road. When the ammunition on the trucks started to explode, I jumped into a ditch by the side of the road in front of a small white farmhouse. From the open front door a woman beckoned to me. Thinking that she needed help, I crawled over and went into the house and there on the table in the kitchen were cookies and hot coffee. She and her husband pointed to a chair, so I sat down with them and for a few precious moments we forgot there was a war on. Mind you, the tanks were still shelling the road outside. The counterattack was still in progress and the ammunition in the trucks was still exploding.

'While I was enjoying this respite, two P-47s came over. One peeled off and strafed the attacking enemy infantry column and tanks east of the road. The other followed it down and dropped two five hundred pound bombs in the same area The shelling and mortaring stopped and the truck convoy continued north up the road. I thanked my two Dutch friends and went back out on the road to hitch a ride. A Scottish motorcycle dispatch rider picked me up and we started south again. There were two speeds he used on this trip: full speed and dead stop, nothing in between - and it scared the hell out of me. I had both arms wrapped around his waist, with my head lying against his back and my eyes closed tightly. I didn't dare look.

'We were held up on two more occasions by German attempts to cut the road by shelling it. The British, who were this far up the road, nipped it in the bud each time by calling in air strikes. The airborne men that I had left behind are a fantastic bunch of guys when the chips are down. They are highly professional, deadly and dedicated to their job. I'm glad they're on our side. Before I left Eindhoven one of them conned me out of my Thompson, which was all right with me. They had more need of it.

'When we reached a small Belgium town just over the Dutch border, the Scotsman dropped me off and I proceeded on foot toward Brussels where our C-47s were supposed to pick up returning glider pilots. Later in the afternoon, dog tired and almost out on my feet, I stopped at a tavern on the main street of another small Belgium town to spend the night. Much to my surprise, it turned out to be the headquarters for the local resistance movement. Inside were about twenty partisans, heavily armed with weapons they had captured from the enemy and looking as tough as any human beings could look. In addition they had a German prisoner with them who looked like he had been run over by a truck. I guess they had been taking turns beating him. He was in sad shape, with blackened eyes, his head had swelled up like a balloon and I think his nose was broken, I actually felt a little sorry for him. After I showed up he stayed very close to me like a puppy dog looking for protection. They were impressed with the fact that I was a glider pilot returning from Holland and also an American to boot.

They fed me well and put me up for the night. Their leader was a bleached blonde woman who looked to be in her mid-thirties and had probably suffered at the hands of the Germans. She was by now one tough cookie out for revenge.

'The next morning after breakfast, I told her that I had to leave and that I would take the prisoner with me. As much as I hated Germans, I still had sympathy for the poor bastard and wanted to get him away from these people. The answer was a firm no and that is when the atmosphere turned very chilly. Nothing I said could change her mind. With great difficulty and in broken English, she told me that the filthy Germans were going to pay for what they had done to her family and to her country. After hearing her story I can well imagine what they had in store for their prisoner after I left. Being greatly outnumbered, a little bit scared and not wishing to create an international incident, I let the matter drop.

'Just before I started to leave she asked me for my .45 pistol and I thought to myself, 'oh-oh, this is it! What do I do now?' Maybe they wanted me as a prisoner also, which really didn't make sense since we were on the same side, I hoped. Stalling for time so I could figure out what to do, I pointed to a mint condition P-38 she was carrying and, using sign language, indicated I would give her mine for hers. She slowly drew the pistol from its holster with no expression on her face and I thought, 'here it comes, the showdown.' She handed it to me and with a sigh of relief I handed my .45 over to her and got a big smile in return. After much hand shaking, back slapping, hugging and cheek kissing from all of them and a glass of awful wine, I continued on to Brussels. I carried the P-38 with me until the following march when it was stolen by a DP (displaced person) who got into our tent area at Mourmelon while we were away flying.

'Before the day was out, I got to Brussels absolutely pooped and fell sound asleep in a sand pile at the edge of the airport. Fifty or sixty other glider pilots who had arrived earlier from the LZs were also waiting around for a ride back across the channel. We eventually hopped on some C-47s that arrived later in the day and were back in England by nightfall. I landed at an RAF base at Northolt and they let my home base group (the 434th) at Aldermaston know I was there. Much to my surprise they sent a C-47 down to pick me up and I felt like a real big shot. When the plane landed back at Aldermaston and I stepped off the plane alone, I was given a very warm welcome and wined and dined at the squadron mess hall (74th squadron).

'Getting back to the landing in the drop zone, Lieutenant Linz and Pfc's Miller and Warren took off in a jeep to find the rest of the 200 men in their unit, the 321st Glider Field Artillery Battalion. Within the hour they linked up and their guns were set up and were firing support missions for the paratroopers and glidermen. The first round they fired hit the church steeple which was being used by their own forward observer. Possibly they did this to make sure he was awake and alert. Fortunately no one was hurt. In the next few days Linz's unit worked its way north to Vechel and was involved with many fire missions in support of our airborne troops who were fighting off repeated attempts by the Germans to cut the road and retake the drop and landing zones. At times their own unit (the 321st) was cut off several times and came under heavy mortar, shelling and machine gun attacks from the enemy. Their unit remained in combat over 49 days before being withdrawn and finally was relocated to Camp Mourmelon le Grand, located ten miles from Rheims, France. By then my own group, the 434th, had moved from England to France and occupied the airfield at Mourmelon le Grande with our old friends, the 101st.

'When the eighty tow planes and gliders which had aborted arrived back at their home base, the ceiling had lifted from tree top to about 600 feet. The planes and gliders came over the field in echelons of four and began to cut loose. Two of the gliders, while still in the air, turned directly into each other, collided head on and crashed on the field in a twisted ball of burning wreckage. Crash crews and medics dashed out and pulled the pilots and glidermen from what was left of the gliders, but it was too late, the two pilots and six passengers were dead. The pilots, one from each glider, were identified as the combatants of the night before who had vowed to kill each other. Their wish had been fulfilled, but unfortunately they took six innocent men with them. Fate had indeed dealt a cruel hand. Though it was a twist of fate and probably accidental, no one will really ever know.

'So ended my second glider mission on the continent. I was a few years older, much smarter I hoped and thank God, still in one piece.

'After two days off, the glider pilots went back to work again, pinch hitting as C-47 co-pilots in order to give the power jockeys, who had been flying night and day round the clock, a much needed rest. From 'D-Day', to this point in time, until the Ardennes breakthrough on 17 December 1944 ('The Battle of the Bulge'), all troop carrier groups were flying seven days a week carrying food, ammo and supplies to the front. The big item we supplied was gasoline to Patton's Third Army tanks which were going hell for leather way out in advance of the infantry. The C-47s were often times landing in small grass fields still under enemy fire and, on the return trip, brought out wounded to rear echelon hospitals. In between all this activity we still flew glider training flights and ferried newly assembled gliders to various TC groups to replace gliders lost in Holland. Most of us hoped and prayed that the war would end before the big wheels planned another mission, but it was not to be.

'Some empty bunks and a few names missing from the roster after each mission have a very sobering effect on you. You feel older than you are. Can you survive another landing behind enemy lines? Well, you try not to think about it.'

The series of resupply missions on 'D+2' and thereafter were to play an important and tragic part in 'Market'. Whether fair weather on the 19th would have brought success to 'Market' is far from certain. The arrival of the 325th Glider Infantry Regiment at 1000 hours as planned might have enabled the 82nd Division to take the Nijmegen Bridge that day. Had the Polish Parachute Brigade dropped at the south end of the Arnhem Bridge they might have been able to secure it and join forces with Frost's battalion before the latter had been crippled by losses. Even so, they might not have been able to hold the north end of the bridge against German tanks and artillery for the time which it would probably have taken the British ground forces to get there from Nijmegen. What is certain is that after the 19th the Allied chances of getting a bridgehead across the Rhine were very, very small.

Chapter 10

Wednesday 20 September - The Fourth Lift

Although the outward journey went off without incident, it was clear as soon as we approached the dropping-zone that things were not going well. The whole landing area was now ringed with German guns, which seemed to be firing continuously at our chaps down there, but the moment we arrived, they were elevated in our direction with scarcely a pause. We were down to about 600 feet, easy targets for the Jerry 88 mm howitzers - but here again luck was on our side, because the Huns chose to fire at the Stirlings which were mixed up with us, because they were twice our size and made much easier shooting. In the few minutes that I was over the target I saw several Stirlings brought down and they hit the ground with a frightening shower of flames and sparks and smoke.

'Jimmy' Edwards' flight in KT500 on 271 Squadron entailed another five and a-half-hours in the air on the 20th.

On 19 September 'Jimmy' Edwards had set off in the *Pie-eyed Piper* to Belgium with a 5,000lb load of petrol but was unable to land at Brussels because of the weather. He got into Lille and was back at Down Ampney before dark. 'Next day' he wrote 'came the news that the forces at Arnhem had met with unexpectedly violent opposition and had been hemmed into a very small area by a German Panzer division. Fresh supplies of ammunition were urgently needed and plans had been made for a mass drop of panniers. There wasn't time to fit Treble Four with the necessary metal rollers so I took KT500 on the trip.'

During the late afternoon of the 19 September, news of the situation at Arnhem was received at the Command Post, Eastcote. It was then known that supply dropping would be required for several more days and DZ 'V' a new supply-dropping zone was therefore chosen. The location of DZ, consisting of small fields about 1 mile south, was south east of the landing zone 'L', a road junction 200 yards west of the Hartenstein. The message of the 19th also stated that LZ 'Z' was still being held and so it was arranged for a supply drop to take place in new supply dropping point. However, in the eighteen hours elapsing since the message had been sent to England concerning the taking of DZ 'Z', it had been re-taken by the Germans.

38 Group despatched 101 Stirlings. From Fairford came thirty-four Stirlings on 620 Squadron, seventeen on 295 and sixteen on 570 Squadron at Harwell led by 32-year old Group Captain Wilfred 'Bill' Surplice DSO DFC, the station commander. From Keevil came thirty-three Stirlings on 196 and 299 Squadrons. Added to this was one crew from 1665 Conversion Unit at Tilstock. Thirty-two Dakotas at Down Ampney were detailed to drop 512 panniers containing badly needed food. In all, 46 Group despatched 163 Dakotas.

Early on the 20th British troops of 32 Brigade and the Coldstream Guards relieved units of the 504th which were holding the bridges at Grave and Heumen and the regiment assembled in woods east of the Honinghutie Bridge. It had seen little fighting since 'D-Day' and was in good shape. At 1400 the battalion of the 505th engaged the German defenders in the strong points south of the bridge and at 1500, exactly on schedule, the first boats, carrying the 3rd Battalion of the 504th, pushed out into the river. The 1st battalion was to follow with the 2nd standing in reserve.

At that point the stream was about 1,000 feet across and the enemy held the opposite shore in strength. Artillery, mortars and RAF fighter-bombers had hammered their positions and smoke had been used to obscure the crossing. Nevertheless, their fire was effective. Many men were hit before the boats left the bank and only eleven of the 26 boats in the first wave got back to make a second trip. Not much more than a battalion of paratroops got across, but their peerless fighting qualities enabled them to sweep through the German defenders. By 1600 they had a beachhead 1,000 yards deep. By 1700 they had taken the north end of the railway bridge. By 1830 they had the road bridge itself under fire. At that moment five British tanks broke through onto the south end of the bridge. Two were hit, but the others, raking the span from end to end, abruptly terminated the battle. Nijmegen Bridge had been taken and none too soon. German tanks heading south had begun crossing the Arnhem Bridge three hours earlier.

At Arnhem, where the day was one of defeat in all sectors for the British airborne, the Germans had won access to the bridge during the afternoon after point blank fire from tanks and artillery had reduced Frost's positions to a flaming shambles. The two battalions of 4 Parachute Brigade isolated near Wolfhezen had to run a terrible gauntlet to get back to the division and only about 130 of their men reached the Hartenstein perimeter. Into that perimeter the Germans, seeing they had their foe at bay, directed all the artillery and mortar fire they could muster until mortar shells were pouring down at a rate of fifty a minute. At intervals German infantry, supported by tanks, would close in for the kill. Their attacks did not break the lines of 1st Airborne, but bit by bit they bent them inward. The only good news for the division was a message received that night that the Nijmegen Bridge had been captured intact.

As revised on the evening of the 19th, plans for troop carrier operations on 'D+3' called for all missions to take the southern route and for four of them to arrive simultaneously at their zones at 1500 hours. Again the timing was dictated by predictions of extensive fog throughout the forenoon. The original southern route was modified to permit the missions to fly up the British salient and pass close to Eindhoven with missions to the Arnhem and Nijmegen sectors using Schijndel as their IP. At the last minute Eindhoven was made IP for all airborne missions that day, Schijndel being regarded as too hot a spot.

In an effort to make up for lost time 1,047 aircraft and 405 gliders were to be dispatched, with all the gliders and 317 resupply craft going down the centre lane to DZ/LZ 'O' for the 82nd Division. A 51-aircraft paratroop and resupply mission for the 101st would follow the right lane to DZ 'W' and 114 aircraft of the postponed Polish paratroop mission to Arnhem would use the left lane. Overhead would fly 160 RAF aircraft with supplies for 1st Airborne Division. As a result of its struggle for LZ's 'N' and 'T' on the 18th, the 82nd Division had decided to use DZ 'O' as both drop and landing zone for the time being, so its pathfinders set out their aids on that zone.

Escort as far as Schijndel was to be furnished by three Spitfire and three Mustang Squadrons of Air Defence, Great Britain, making a total of sixty-five aircraft, with forty-six P-51s of the US 8th Air Force being despatched. The first two waves of the four was adequately covered by a fighter escort but the last two were not because the majority of the US 9th fighters were grounded owing to the weather. The Eighth Air Force was to fly its usual perimeter patrols between Maastricht, Wesel, Apeldoorn and Zwolle, supply area cover beyond the IP and attack flak positions between the IP and Nijmegen. The Ninth Air Force was to neutralize flak batteries between the IP and Arnhem, but it does not seem to have gotten a clear statement of its assignment until 1430 on the 20th.

Once again unfavourable weather grievously curtailed the troop carrier operations. On the morning of the 20th the weathermen decided that the overcast would lift later than they had thought, so arrival time for the missions was set back from 1500 to 1700 hours. Then in view of the urgent need of the British at Arnhem it was decided to split the RAF resupply mission and send 67 of its aircraft to drop at 1345. Arrival time for the other missions was moved to 1720. Although at take-off time ceilings over eastern England were between 1,000 and 2,000 feet and visibility was only one or two miles, the first wave of 67 Stirlings departed for Arnhem. Area cover was provided by 46 P-51s of Eighth Air Force, while ADGB furnished a total of 65 aircraft from three Spitfire and three Mustang squadrons for escort and anti-flak operations. Visibility in the Arnhem area was poor, making an already difficult operation even more difficult. One Spitfire and one Mustang were lost.

The later missions were given escort and cover to the IP by seventeen squadrons of Spitfires, of which one squadron ran into bad weather over the Channel and turned back. The rest made 173 sorties but saw no action and had no losses. The Eighth Air Force had five P-51 groups on area cover beyond the IP and six flying the perimeter. These flew 430 uneventful sorties, losing only one aircraft and that by accident. Because the Ninth Air Force was unable to contribute its quota of fighters, the Eighth had to handle all flak suppression beyond the IP. It sent four groups of P-47s and the rocket squadron to do the job. They flew 179 sorties, but, hampered by bad visibility and by lack of briefing in the case of those substituting for Ninth Air Force units, they were able to claim only two gun positions destroyed and two others damaged. They had no losses and not very much damage.[1]

The second wave of RAF supply aircraft to Arnhem numbered 97 aircraft. Since available British sources lump this drop and the earlier one together, they must be treated as one. Out of 100 Stirlings and 64 Dakotas dispatched only two Stirlings aborted. Flak was reported as very heavy, especially in the target area. It brought down nine aircraft and damaged 62. Of the remainder, thirty Stirlings were scheduled to make their drop on DZ 'Z' and their pilots reported doing so. That zone was entirely held by the Germans and all that was dropped on or near it probably fell into their hands. At the Hartenstein drop point a 'Eureka' and visual aids had been set out despite the incessant bombardment and 122 pilots reported dropping supplies there. Although only thirteen of them picked up the 'Eureka' and 32 sighted visual aids (Very lights being much the most effective, probably because they rose above tree-top level), results were decidedly better than on the day before.

Edmund 'Teddy' Townshend of the *Daily Telegraph* flew to Arnhem in Stirling EF260 'R for Roger' on 190 Squadron piloted by 22-year old Flying Officer John D. LeBouvier. Born on 28 May 1912 at Bourneville, Birmingham, as a child Townshend often saw George Cadbury, the chocolate magnate, walking home. After matriculating at Kings Norton secondary school 'Teddy' started work with a chartered accountancy firm but soon found a job, at ten shillings a week, with a local weekly newspaper. He progressed to the *Birmingham Mail* and then the *Daily Mail* in London before joining the *Telegraph* in 1944. As the invasion of Normandy was about to begin he was attached to the Merchant Navy and given blue battledress, with a war correspondent's shoulder tabs and a big 'MN' on the chest, 'I don't envy you, old man,' said the news editor. On the morning of 'D-Day' Townshend was in a troopship in the Strait of Dover, watching a ship astern take a direct hit which cost twenty lives. When he looked from the bridge at a clock tower on land to check the time for his dispatch, he saw a shell from a British battleship neatly remove it. Later, in another ship, which was loaded with 800 tons of high explosive ammunition, the chief officer observed: 'One enemy shell into this lot and you won't know where to look for your typewriter.'

'R for Roger' had just dropped its supplies to troops on the ground amid heavy flak and 'Teddy' Townshend was watching from Flying Officer 'Tom' Oliver's co-pilot's seat. Oliver, who was 30 years of age, had been a policeman in the City of London before the war. Townshend saw the coloured parachutes floating down like autumn leaves when he heard over the intercom: 'Weave, skipper, weave... Keep weaving.'

'Engineer officer,' called the pilot, 'come forward and take a look at the port outer motor on fire.'

'What port outer motor on fire?' asked the engineer officer.

'Bail out,' came the order and, after clipping on his parachute, Townshend found himself being bundled to the open hatch in the nose.

'Gripping the parachute release handle to make sure I had it, I leapt into space too eager to escape from the blazing plane to feel fear at the drop,' he wrote in his front page story. 'For minutes like hours, dreading attack by machine-gunners below, I swayed slowly to earth. Breathlessly I watched the Stirling roar away in flames, losing height. With relief I saw other parachutes opening in its wake.'

On landing in a ploughed field south of the Rhine, Townshend was immediately met by members of the Dutch underground who gave him food and drink and buried his parachute and Mae West. They were disappointed that he carried nothing more dangerous than a pencil and notebook, but escorted him along dykes and behind hedges to meet up with nine fliers, including four of the crew and one of the dispatchers on 'R for Roger' (Flight Sergeants' D. Martin and G. Kershaw and the other dispatcher, Driver H. S. Hill having been taken prisoner), whom they made lie down in a beech wood in silence for fear of enemy patrols.

At dawn the underground returned with hot milk and sandwiches. German ack-ack fire whistled through the tops of the trees as another supply flight passed overhead in the afternoon and the group ended the day crouching in a tunnel as the artillery of both sides exchanged shells. A farmer's family invited all of them into their house, where 'Tom' Oliver sat down at the harmonium to play the Dutch national anthem and a picture of Queen Wilhelmina was pinned on the wall. A dozen more fleeing airmen appeared - one had landed in the river and swum 100 yards to the Dutch side as the Germans fired at the floating body of his co-pilot; others had watched the enemy retreating without shoes. Setting out at dusk with a map, compass and hard rations they found the roads too dangerous and the dykes too wide and deep to cross. They encountered their first Allied patrol the next morning. John LeBouvier was returned to the Squadron on 25 September and he was awarded the DFC.

'Teddy' Townshend meanwhile, hitched a lift to Brussels to phone over his story. When he submitted his expenses back in London they included 'replacement of splinter-proof spectacles swept away by an involuntary parachute exit' and 'rewards to Dutch underground workers for protection from enemy search parties'. The news editor paid up with a wry grin.[2]

In total 190 Squadron lost three Stirlings to add to the two they had lost the day before. Stirling LJ829 flown by 26-year old Flying Officer Roderick James Matheson RCAF of Edmonton, Alberta was shot down and crashed at Doorwerth with the loss of all nine men aboard. His Commonwealth crew: Pilot Officer Reginald Austin Davis the 27-year old second pilot from Leichhardt, New South Wales and Pilot Officer Keith Willett the 29-year old navigator-bomb aimer of Gympie, Queensland, were Australians. Warrant Officer1s' Thomas William Allen the 21-year old WOp/AG and David Lorne Brouse the 23-year old air gunner from Iroquois, Ontario were, like their skipper, Canadians. The other two members of the crew - Sergeants Edward Francis Keen (21) of Stoneleigh, Surrey and Stanley James Cooke (27) of

Macclesfield, Cheshire the two flight engineers, were RAF aircrew. Lance Corporal 'Fred' Rexstrew (30) and Driver 'Joe' Leech (22) of the RASC came from Mitcham in Surrey and Wigan in Lancashire respectively. All are buried in the Arnhem Oosterbeek War Cemetery, which contains the graves of 1,754 Allied troops, most of whom were killed during Market Garden. Matheson left a grieving widow, Mary Irene. Leila Annie Marie Willett, Neillie Cooke and Gladys Rextrew were also widowed as a result of this action.

Stirling LJ831 skippered by Flight Lieutenant Douglas R. Robertson RCAF was hit by flak at the DZ and suffered damaged elevator tabs. It went into a steep dive which the pilots pulled out with the help of the bomb aimer, Flight Lieutenant Norman Rosedale RCAF. Robertson flew away from the danger area and gave the crew the chance to bail out but his wireless operator, Flight Sergeant George E. Thompson, had been wounded and could not jump, so the whole crew stayed with the damaged aircraft. Thompson remained at his post and continued to keep watch, transmit messages and make entries in his log until Robertson was able to make a successful belly landing at Ghent airfield.[3]

Of the seventeen Stirlings dispatched by 196 Squadron, one was forced to ditch en-route to Arnhem, without casualties and a further five were shot down. Ten men died but most had escaped the crashes unscathed. LJ840 piloted by Flight Sergeant J. P. Averill successfully dropped their four panniers and all except six of their 24 containers before the Stirling was badly hit and set on fire over the DZ. The crew and the two dispatchers bailed out successfully. Next day Pilot Officer Reginald Ernest Marshall's crew arrived back, having crash landed Stirling LJ947 at Aalst north of Brussels after being hit by flak. Marshall and one of his crew were wounded. There were no other injuries.[4] Flight Lieutenant A. E. W. Laband and three members of Pilot Officer Ellis' crew also arrived back having successfully crash landed LJ945 North of Brussels. The pilot was injured and aircraft badly damaged. LJ851 piloted by Warrant Officer Oliver was shot down landing just south of Eindhoven before reaching the DZ. The two dispatchers were taken prisoner but the crew arrived home by Anson from Brussels. Pilot Officer C. W. King force landed EF318 at RAF Woodbridge after making his way home after successfully dropping his supplies at the DZ. LK556 piloted by Flying Officer John W. McOmbie was shot down before reaching the drop zone and crashed in the Valsburg/Elst area. Before crashing the crew had jettisoned their containers and panniers but the two dispatchers, 39-year old Robert Frank Pragnell and 38-year old Corporal A. W. J. Pescodd were killed. The 22-year old air gunner, Sergeant D. Clough was found dead in a field and the two dispatchers were killed in the attack. The five survivors, who possessed a total of three pistols between them, were soon surrounded by Dutch peasants who told them that there were Germans all around and that they should go north with a view to crossing the river and joining up with the airborne troops at Arnhem. The pilot was dressed as a Dutchman in a cap, clogs and overalls over his uniform, furiously pedalling a child's bicycle. They started to stroll across an open field; but sniper-fire drove them to take shelter in a ditch before they were taken to a tactical headquarters. On the 23rd a farmer told them that British troops were in Valburg so they walked back and reported to the HQ and from there, they hitch-hiked to Brussels arriving on the 25th. Sixteen Stirlings in all had been dispatched by 299 Squadron and only eleven would be fit to fly on Thursday's effort.

Flight Lieutenant Roy Scott, a pilot on 295 Squadron recalled: 'We continued en-route to Arnhem at about 3,000 feet. The flak was quite heavy and I can recall feeling through the seat of my pants, the air pressure from the bursts of flak which damaged the undercarriage area. As we approached the container dropping zone at Oosterbeek near Arnhem, I let down until we were at the height for container dropping - 600 feet - and reduced speed to about 140 mph. On the run in an aircraft flying ahead and just above us dropped his containers and they very nearly hit us. Whew! …

'My concentration was now on flying at the correct height and speed and following the bomb aimer's instructions - left a bit - steady - steady - right a bit, etc. This seemed to go on for a long time and must have seemed like ages for the rest of the crew who at this point could just sit and watch. It couldn't have been too pleasant for the two dispatchers in the body of the aircraft either, whose job it was to push out the four packages through the hatch which was now open, as were the bomb doors ready for the release of 24 containers. Then we were over the dropping zone; the bomb aimer pressed the release button and the containers were away and we felt a little lift as each one dropped. We were hit several times by flak.

'Out of the cockpit window I could see a Stirling close to the ground with the engines on both sides on fire … The pilot belly landed and the whole thing seemed to explode in flames, a sad and moving sight.'

Flying Officer Bassarab, the Intelligence Officer on 299 Squadron, the navigator on Stirling EF323 wrote: 'We flew in that narrow corridor past Eindhoven, which had proved so successful the previous day, but were ever mindful of flak. It wasn't until we reached the DZ, still in the same relative locality, that we encountered opposition and here there was plenty. With airspeed of 140 mph and height of 1,000 feet we lumbered in to drop our containers. As the last container dropped away and we passed the clearing and over the wooded section that surrounded the area, all hell seemed to break loose. Metal tearing through metal, angry black puffs completely encompassed us and no immediate escape in view. We were thoroughly boxed and the German gunners were letting us have the works.

'The chatter of machine-gun fire from the rear gunner could be heard through all the racket but his targets were well screened by trees and I doubt if his fire availed any satisfaction … As we looked back the area seemed full of flak and aircraft; it was a terrible spot to be in and we were glad to be out of it.'

Warrant Officer Bernard Harvey on 299 Squadron recalled: 'We were briefed to drop on orange candles but we found orange candles all over the place. So we just pitched the stuff where we thought best as long as it was on the far side of the Rhine. That was the best we could do.' Warrant Officer Arthur Batten on a 190 Squadron Stirling recalled: 'Things had changed dramatically and recognition from an aircraft was practically impossible. You could see men waving and sheets being laid out but you had lost them in smoke or woods by the time you came round again to drop.' Warrant Officer 'Joe' Corless, in a 299 Squadron Stirling, describes typical difficulties: 'We got a very hot reception with all kinds of rubbish coming up at us. The Skipper was taking violent evasive action. We managed to drop the containers, but one of the hampers jammed in the hatch and the wireless operator and flight engineer were jumping up and down on it in an effort to free it when we were hit in both elevators, rear turret and fuselage, with both rear gunner and flight engineer being wounded, fortunately not too seriously. Combined with the evasive action, we were by now in a very unhealthy nose-up attitude, with both the pilot and me doing our utmost to raise the air speed, which was fast approaching stalling speed. We managed to achieve this, got rid of the hamper and limped home feeling that it had been our lucky day.[5]

Flying Officer Dennis Henden Hardwick piloting Stirling LK118 on 299 Squadron had taken part in twelve bombing operations before joining the Squadron and up to the time of Arnhem had completed a further twenty-one. Flying in loose pairs in company with other Stirlings on 299 Squadron, they had to fly at 2,500 feet and then lose height to 1,000 feet over the drop zone at 140mph. Over the DZ the Stirling came under severe enemy flak. The crew was unable to drop their twenty-four containers and four panniers because the bomb aimer, Pilot Officer Karl B. Ketcheson RCAF was not sure that they would fall in the correct place. On the second run Ketcheson reported the containers gone when the aircraft was hit in several places. Ketcheson was killed instantly, hit by the only bullet to enter the Stirling. LK118 went into a sudden dive owing to the elevator trimmer control cable being severed by flak. Hits had also been made on the tailplane and the escape hatch. The flight engineer, Flight Sergeant White, although wounded, went to the rear of the aircraft and discovered the break in the trim cable but he was unable to rejoin the cable so he cut one of the pannier straps and tied the loose ends of the control wire to the side of the aircraft. By pulling on these he was able to operate the trimmer tabs and to assist the pilot in controlling the aircraft. Hardwick was able to recover control at less than 200 feet and land safely. 'It was a great surprise when we got out of the aircraft to discover the troops in the area were German and obviously much in control' he said.

It was not until 1440 hours that the first of seventeen Stirlings on 620 Squadron at Fairford took off along the southern route to Holland to resupply beleaguered British paratroopers on the ground at Oosterbeek that were being slowly encircled by German panzer tanks. Two of the Stirlings were destined not to return. LK127 flown by 29- year old Flying Officer Athol Richard 'Bluey' Scanlon RAAF was hit by flak and crashed at Vorstenbosch. 'Bluey', his 31-year old wireless operator/air gunner Warrant Officer Edward Joseph McGilvray RAAF and Flight Sergeant Raymond Joseph Lamont BA RCAF, who has no known grave and is commemorated on the Runneymede memorial and the two dispatchers, were killed. Twenty-two-year old Sergeant John William Marshall drowned in the Rhine after bailing out. Two others on the crew, Flying Officer Eric B. Dane and Flight Sergeant W. J. Murray who were wounded, were taken into captivity.

Twenty-one year old Pilot Officer Maurice McHugh RAAF had taken Stirling LK548 off with a crew of seven including two British army dispatchers from Fairford at 1445. Three days earlier he and his crew of five on LJ946 had towed a Horsa glider loaded with twelve soldiers, a jeep and trailer carrying mortars and ammunition to the drop zone. Born in St. Kilda, a suburb of Melbourne on 9 July 1923, McHugh was one of four children. He and his crew had returned safely to Fairford at 1530 hours. Over the succeeding days McHugh's crew dropped supplies to allied troops on the ground near Arnhem. On 20 September the Australian was again towing a Horsa loaded with twelve soldiers, a jeep and trailer carrying mortars and ammunition to the drop zone near Arnhem. LK548 was hit by fire from flak barges on the Rhine and the aircraft was almost capsized by the discharge of rocket salvos. Incendiary bullets ripped into the aircraft hitting the trailing edge of the starboard wing, with flames licking over the edge of the wing. The starboard wing caught fire and continued to blaze for several seconds but seemed to peter out. The flight engineer, Sergeant David P. Ivens and the 19-year old rear gunner, Sergeant T. Vickers, kept an eye on it until the fire had blown itself out. Ivens wrote: 'As we approached Arnhem from the southerly direction the flak appeared much heavier than the previous day. Incendiary bullets tore into the trailing edge of the starboard edge and set it alight and from my position in the astrodome I could see the flames. Minutes later I was momentarily blinded by dust as a cannon shell pierced the wooden frame of the astrodome within an inch of my nose. I was shocked that my position was straddled by cannon fire which made very neat holes about eighteen inches apart in the floor of the compartment. Air bomber Flight Sergeant 'Nick' Gascoyne wrote: 'Maurice McHugh made his turn with the calm assurance of a veteran. We were hit in numerous places during the bombing run but he kept a straight course and did his utmost to drop the supplies in the correct area and was successful.' Intense ack-ack was encountered at a height of about 1,500 feet as the 21-year old wireless operator, Flight Sergeant Eric Arthur Bradshaw and the two air dispatchers, Lance Corporal John Waring of 398 (Airborne) Division Company and Driver Ernest Victor Heckford, only 19, pushed the container baskets out through the despatch hatch.

Ivens, still watching from the astrodome, said: 'After dropping the supplies, the captain put the aircraft into a climb, turning back at the same time. Then a hole suddenly appeared on the surface of the starboard wing where an 88mm shell had passed through one of the main petrol tanks immediately forward of the aileron but fortunately without exploding. The high octane fuel gushed out like a fountain of white spray, which in seconds became a roaring jet of flame as the wing and inside the fuselage was ablaze. In no time at all the main spar was a roaring fire.' Ivens used the aircraft fire extinguisher which had no effect so he clipped on his parachute and made his way forward. 'I advised McHugh as to the condition of the aircraft. By now the whole starboard wing and the centre section were alight and the captain was struggling hard to maintain height which was impossible.' And the Stirling had dropped to about 800-1,000 feet. McHugh gave the abandon order. Ivens put on a chute, took off his helmet and helped 'Jock' Hume remove his helmet. Hurrying down the steps leading to the nose, Hume, followed closely by David Ivens reached the esc ape hatch in the floor that 'Nick' Gascoyne had opened immediately after donning his chute.

Hume said 'I was the first to leave the aircraft, which was then approximately at 1,000 feet, followed closely by the engineer and air-bomber. The pilot refused his parachute when it was offered to him. Ivens went out head first and was knocked unconscious by the opening of the chute and did not see the aircraft crash. He landed about three miles North of Uden, came too and was helped to his feet by farm workers. 'Jock' Hume says: 'The Dutch people who saw us bail out confirmed the fact that only three chutes were seen to leave the aircraft. We couldn't examine the wreck because the area in which it was situated was held by the enemy.'

'Nick' Gascoyne had followed Hume and Evans as soon as the exit was clear and was the last member to leave. 'On leaving the aircraft I was hit on the head and lost consciousness for several seconds before pulling my ripcord. Consequently I didn't witness what became of the aircraft after my hasty exit.

'On recovering my senses after bailing out I pulled my ripcord and sailed gently down to earth from approximately 800 feet' says 'Jock' Hume. 'I saw the aircraft spin down to earth out of control in blaze of flames and hit the ground at an angle of forty-five degrees. [LK548 crashed at Vorstenbosch]. I saw only two other chutes in the sky. The remainder of the crew were still in it, so I can only surmise that they perished - they certainly did not bail out. I discovered that I had landed about six miles NNE of the village of Udon where I finally contacted David Ivens and 'Nick' Gascoyne.'

Ivens had spent some time in identifying himself for the benefit of the Dutch resistance. At Uden he found 'Jock' Hume and 'Nick' Gasgoyne being treated for minor cuts by nuns of a nursing order. They were the only ones to survive the shoot down. McHugh was one of only thirteen Australian aircrew killed at Arnhem. Bradshaw, Vickers and the two dispatchers also died on the aircraft. As German troops searched for the evaders the local Dutch Resistance hid the injured airmen in a local church. Ivens, Hume and Gascoyne were flown to Northolt and finally to Fairford via Eindhoven and Brussels. At Fairford they found a new crew had taken over their billet and were given overnight accommodation in the station sick quarters. The injuries Ivens sustained when parachuting out of LK548 was the end of his war service in the RAF The next day the three men were visited by the 620 Squadron Commander, Wing Commander D. H. Lee DFC, who was to crash-land at Ussen near Oss on 23 September.[6]

By the time Stirling LJ618 on 295 Squadron approached the dropping zone the aircraft had suffered considerable damage and was full of blackish, acrid smoke and cordite fumes. The 21-year old skipper, Pilot Officer

Neil Banks Couper was a New Zealander, as was the navigator Sergeant 'Jack' Corcoran. The bomb aimer, Flying Officer E. T. W. Harris and flight engineer 'Johnny' Johnston were English. The rear gunner, Sergeant Desmond 'Paddy' Bowers came from Dublin. Two British dispatchers would jettison large cane baskets through the floor hatch. The WOp/AG, Flight Sergeant Ken Nolan was the only Australian crew member. He recalled: 'As we approached Arnhem we ran into intense and accurate 88mm cannon fire from gun emplacements, vehicles and flak barges on the rivers. It sounded like being inside a tin shed and being bombarded with small stones and gravel. Large holes were appearing in the side of the aircraft. We released the containers in the bomb bays by parachute and the dispatchers pushed the large basket of supplies out to the troops below. We were at about 500 feet and received several direct hits which set the aircraft on fire. Couper gave the order to bail out but there was no reply from the rear gunner and the dispatchers, so I went down the fuselage to convey the order. The dispatchers had pulled their plugs out of the intercom as they moved around, so I shouted at them, clipped on their parachutes and opened the rear door for them. When I reached the rear gunner I could see that his turret had been hit, his intercom cut and his leg jammed. I managed to turn the turret until the doors faced outwards and undid his flying boot. He left his boot behind as he bailed out backwards. I then headed back to the pilot. By now the engines and fuel tanks were on fire and the cabin full of thick smoke. When I reached Neil Couper he was standing up at the controls and beating his chest, indicating that he did not have his parachute. I searched for it desperately, eventually locating it under the navigator's table. I clipped on his 'chute, then mine and he gave me the thumbs up. With my arms raised, I dropped my legs through the front hatch to bail out. Then, almost immediately, the aircraft exploded. There was an awesome noise and searing heat and then silence. I must have been stunned because I have no recollection of pulling the ripcord, although my hand was on it when I jumped.'

Helped by the Dutch underground, Ken Nolan, 'Paddy' Bowers, Jack' Corcoran and 'Johnny' Johnson successfully evaded capture. Flying Officer Harris was taken prisoner. Neil Banks Couper RNZAF is buried at Druten (Puiflijk) Roman Catholic Churchyard in Holland.[7]

In all, no less than fourteen Stirlings (and four Dakotas) were lost on 20 September. In 46 Group 48 and 271 Squadrons each lost one and 437 RCAF lost two Dakotas. The Canadian Squadron, which had begun to form at Blakehill Farm on 4 September, was led by Wing Commander

John Alexander Sproule, a veteran of Normandy paratroop operations. He had remained the only pilot on strength until 15 September when enough aircrew arrived to form a single flight. On 17 September 437 Squadron went to war, making thirteen successful sorties towing Horsa gliders to Arnhem. On 18 September six successful sorties towing Horsa gliders were flown. On 19 and 20 September 22 Dakota aircraft on 437 RCAF Squadron were engaged in freighting operations from Britain to airfields in Belgium.

Flight Lieutenant Peter W. Smith and Ian Robinson on 48 Squadron had taken off at 1415 and flew the first Dakota over the DZ. About seventy Daks from various squadrons were due to follow. Smith and Robinson had flown patrols on Hudsons on 59 Squadron and then in the Far East before converting to Dakotas training with the Ghurkhas dropping supplies and parachutists and then dropping supplies to General Wingate's Chindits. Unlike their operations in Burma, where they operated alone and had circled the small DZ several times to deliver the load, they now had to drop in one pass. Each pannier had a parachute attached connected to a rail on the roof of the aircraft by a static line, a hook on the static line moved along the rail as the panniers moved back, when pushed out, the line opened the parachute. Over the DZ at 800 feet, they could see puffs of flak which meant the enemy was ready for them. As soon as the DZ was identified, Robinson went back to assist at the open door. When the green light came on, the panniers were pushed out by the RASC air dispatchers who moved them towards Robinson and Warrant Officer 'Jimmy' Golton. When the red light came on they knew they had passed the area of the drop. The aircraft was now weaving to avoid the enemy gunfire and Ian Robinson went back to the front of the aircraft. Peter Smith reported that a Stirling flying close by had suffered a direct hit and had burst into flames. As Smith approached the North Sea a Dakota ahead (KG423 flown by Flying Officer Martin R. S. Mackay) was seen with a large panel of its fuselage hanging down below the aircraft. MacKay had come under fire on his run up over the drop zone at a 1,000 feet and the starboard engine was hit. As the whole of the load could not be despatched during the first run-up, a second run up was made, in spite of a failing engine. When the aircraft was down to 300 feet he, having feathered the starboard propeller, set off for home and, gradually gaining height, brought his aircraft home, Smith landed at 1952 hours and MacKay carried out a masterly single engine landing at 2016 hours in the dark. Smith's Dak only had superficial damage but one of the bursts must have been close as it had blown away the radio aerial.

Several Dakotas on 512 Squadron commanded by Wing Commander Basil Coventry were badly damaged. Flight Lieutenant Matthews, flying KG418, was hit by flak and crash landed and 24-year old Pilot Officer William Perry DFM flying KG324 was hit by flak after dropping his panniers, crashing near a brick factory by the Den Bosch-Nijmegen road at Schayk. Flying Officer Alexander Campbell piloting KG314 made two runs over the DZ before dropping his supplies. He had one engine hit, his aileron controls rendered inoperative and made a crash landing at Brussels in poor weather conditions. He was later awarded the DFC. Flight Lieutenant James Atkin on 575 Squadron was flying KG327, when his aircraft was hit by flak and one engine put out of commission, in spite of this he carried on and completed the supply drop. He flew the damaged aircraft back to the UK and carried out a successful force landing, for this and later the Rhine Crossing, he was awarded the DFC.

The intelligence report for 38 Group stated that there were eighty-seven successful drops, with 2,063 containers, 325 panniers, three packages, two kitbags and one sack being dropped. Out of 386 tons of supplies dropped, about 300 tons was intended for the Hartenstein drop point and 41 tons or about fourteen percent of this was reported as collected. Considering that recovery was possible only within an area of about one square mile and that in the turmoil of battle much that was recovered was never reported, the precision of the drop was greater than the statistics indicate. Assuredly, the rations which were recovered were worth their weight in gold to the airborne, most of who had had almost nothing to eat for 24 hours or more.

'Jimmy' Edwards' on 271 Squadron had lost no time in climbing away after the crew of KT500 had made their contribution. 'Although several Daks had been hit, when we got back to 'DA' and eagerly assembled on the tarmac to talk it over, we found that nobody in our squadron was missing. 'Jouby's eyes were sparkling. At last he had seen some action! 'We've got to put in another effort tomorrow Jim' he said. 'I need one more but I can't ask you to go. You've been flying four days on the trot as it is.

'If Treble Four is ready, you can count me in,' I replied. I didn't feel in the least bit tired and was quite ready to volunteer. There were no heroics about it. We would all have gone anywhere to please 'the old man'.'

The Polish paratroop mission was again postponed because of fog, which persisted until late in the day in the Grantham area. The aircraft were loaded and warmed up, ready to go if there was the slightest break in the overcast, but the opportunity never came. Finally, five minutes before take-off time the mission was delayed another 24 hours.

The big glider mission marshalled for the Division was also grounded by the fog in Grantham area. Fortunately the resupply mission to that division had been delegated to the 53rd Wing and its bases in the south were completely clear. Beginning about 1430 the wing put 310 aircraft in the air with the 434th, 435th and 438th Groups contributing one serial each; the 436th and 437th Groups two apiece.[8] They carried a cargo of 441 tons, of which the greater part was ammunition.

One aircraft had to turn back with pararack trouble. The others flew over the southern route close to Eindhoven, past Best and then up the road to DZ 'O'. Fighter cover was good and in spite of the lack of anti-flak activity, ground fire was conspicuous by its absence. Some serials could report that not a shot was fired at them. Not an aircraft was lost and only six were damaged. This experience, so different from that of the RAF mission that day, can be attributed to the fact that the Americans were over friendly territory almost the way to their drop zone.

The lead serial reached DZ 'O' at 1648 and the others followed at extremely irregular intervals, some arriving almost simultaneously, others much as twenty minutes apart, with the last one turning up at 1749. In addition, most of the serials were loose or broken, probably because of bad weather en route. However, since the pilots and navigators in the 53rd Wing had become familiar with the southern route as far as Best and the way from there up the main road to the Grave Bridge was unmistakable, none of the stragglers lost their way. Although one squadron claimed it got no response, the 'Eureka' was probably functioning effectively. The panels and smoke on the zone were clearly visible. One pilot dropped his bundles prematurely near Hertogenbosch and another straggled off and followed a British formation to Arnhem. However, 32 aircraft reached the vicinity of DZ 'O' at 1530. Remembering their stinging reception on the previous day, the troop carriers made a fast, high drop. Authorized to go in at 1,000 feet, they let go their bundles at speeds up to 135 mph from as high as 2,500 feet. As might be expected, the drop was disorganized and spasmodic with each serial or separate element using its own tactics. Some released the bundles as low as 400 feet, others as high as 1,800 feet. Although there was the usual difficulty getting bundles out the door in time and fourteen parapacks stuck, over 99 percent of the cargo was delivered. Its concentration, however, was most unsatisfactory. The bundles landed in a pattern about two miles wide and six miles long centred considerably northwest of the zone. The 82nd Division called the amount recovered negligible and official estimates put it at only twenty percent of the quantity dropped. The 82nd Division reported recovering sixty percent of these supplies with Dutch assistance and according to some estimates eighty percent was ultimately recovered, but the hunt was long and difficult. It was sheer good luck that most of the supplies landed in friendly territory. The value of the mission was very great nevertheless. The supply dumps of the 82nd were running low and it had not yet received any supplies by road. Indeed, the first truck convoys for the division had just reached the Meuse-Escaut Canal; some of those first trucks had been loaded with shells of the wrong calibre; and others by some strange oversight were empty. The failure of this mission was a real blow to the 82nd Division, since it was becoming critically short of both food and ammunition.

The 101st Division, being in firm contact with the Allied ground forces, had much less need of supply by air. However, 35 aircraft of the 442nd and 439th Groups took off from Greenham Common with seventeen tons of supplies for that division. They flew unharmed over the new southern route to DZ 'W' and dropped their loads at 1748. Again the drop was inaccurate and only about thirty percent of the bundles were reported as recovered.[9]

A miniature paratroop mission was also flown to DZ 'W' by twelve C-47s of the 442nd Group carrying 'B' Battery of the 377th Parachute Field Artillery. The aircraft had to fly to Ramsbury to take on their load, 125 artillerymen and six 75 mm howitzers. Somewhat late in arriving, the aircraft were not loaded until about 1500 and in the turmoil the pilots were not informed of the changes made in the southern route. They therefore took the 'D-Day' route west of the salient and ran into intense light flak and small-arms fire which damaged five of the aircraft, one severely. The mission did not reach the zone until 1831 by which time the sun was setting and the haze was growing thick. In the face of these difficulties the pilots made an accurate and very compact drop from perfect formation. An hour after its jump the battery had assembled 119 men and almost all its equipment, including five howitzers, ready for action. The other howitzer was ready by morning.

On 20 September the fortunes of the airborne divisions varied greatly. The 101st continued to have a fairly easy time. Its only important action was the repulse of an attack by the 107th Panzer Brigade[10] from Nunen toward the Zon Bridge at 0630. This came near enough to interrupt traffic before being driven back. A battalion of the 506th Regiment riding British tanks, tried to intercept the Germans' retreat, but they got away with little loss. In the Veghel area, the 1st Battalion of the 501st Regiment occupied Dinter and pushed on to Heeswijk, five miles northeast of Veghel. The German losses of about forty killed and 418 captured in this operation and the fact that almost all the captives were from improvised units composed of air force personnel led the 501st momentarily to the rash conclusion that it had destroyed the enemy forces in its vicinity.

For the 82nd Division 20 September was a strenuous day on which, while undertaking the capture of the Nijmegen bridge, it had also to beat back the first major counterattack against the Allied corridor. The attack was made by the 6th Parachute Division. After pushing the 508th Regiment out of advanced positions near Wyler during the morning one regiment supported by armour attacked it at Beek about noon, while at Mook on the southern side of the perimeter another regiment with strong artillery support drove against the lines of the 505th Regiment. In bitter fighting, which raged far into the night, the Germans penetrated as much as 1,000 yards in both sectors but failed in their purpose, which was to pinch off the whole east end of the area held by the 82nd Division and seize the Groesbeek ridge. The situation that night was so critical that 185 glider pilots were hurried to the front near Mook to reinforce the 505th Regiment.

While holding off a German division on its right, the 82nd jabbed ferociously to its left. On the night of the 19th Browning, Gavin and Lieutenant General B. G. Horrocks of XXX Corps had worked out a plan to take the Nijmegen Bridge from the rear by sending the 504th Regiment across the Waal in assault boats about a mile downstream from the town. At the same time a new frontal attack by the 2nd Battalion of the 505th and tanks of the Grenadier Guards would hit the south end of the bridge.

At the close of 'D+3', the Allied commanders believed success was still within their reach, provided that the ground forces could strike north from the captured Nijmegen bridge and reach the British airborne troops at Arnhem next day. So far as they knew the Arnhem Bridge was still in British hands. Defence of the salient against German counterattacks was obviously a prerequisite to a sustained advance toward Arnhem, but no serious threat to the salient was in sight. Troop carrier delivery of the Polish Parachute Brigade and the 325th Glider Infantry was expected to offset British losses at Arnhem and provide the weary 82nd Division with fresh infantry for either defence or offence.

The plans laid on the 20th for airborne operations on D+4 called for over 840 transport aircraft to be sent to Holland in four waves, really separate missions, to reduce the flak hazard, with the first arriving at 1315 and the last, not until 1615. The boldest venture on 21 September would finally be attempted by 114 aircraft of the 52nd Troop Carrier Wing, flying in 52 year old Major General Stanisław Franciszek Sosabowski's 1,568 strong 1st Polish Independent Paratroop Brigade, who had been kicking their heels in Britain waiting for good weather since the first day of 'Market-Garden'. On 17 September the first ten gliders carrying the Brigade had landed with minimal opposition. On 18 September the other 35 gliders landed but their arrival was met with strong opposition and only three out of ten six-pounder anti-tank guns remained operational. The Brigade's anti-tank battery had gone into Arnhem on the third day of the battle on 19 September, supporting the British paratroopers at Oosterbeek. This left Sosabowski without any anti-tank capability. The light artillery battery was left behind in England due to a shortage of gliders. Due to bad weather in England the Brigade's parachute lift had not taken place, much to the annoyance of Major General Sosabowski, who had previously expressed his reservations about the operation to his superiors.

On Thursday 21 September a message for Major General Sosabowski, who had previously expressed his reservations about the operation to his superiors, arrived from General Urquhart with revised orders. The main elements of the Polish Brigade, initially, were to land south of the Arnhem Bridge, cross it and establish defensive positions on the outskirts of the town but bad weather had been working against the 314th and 315th Troop Carrier Groups in the 52nd Troop Carrier Wing and the Polish Brigade, whom they were to have dropped on 19 September. On this and the following day, flying was again impossible due to the weather. The remainder of the Brigade consisting mainly of the anti-tank battery was to land on the northern side of the Rhine together with the 1st British Airborne Division, in 45 Horsa gliders eventually making rendezvous when the town was taken. The Polish survivors had joined the 1st British Airborne Division either as replacement gunners or as infantry. Now, the Brigade was to land at Driel, a small village south of the Rhine, cross using the Driel-Heveadorp ferry and join the by now hard pressed 1st British Airborne Division on the northern bank. Accurate information about the situation at Arnhem was scarce, but it was obvious that something had gone badly wrong. The ferry operator had seen the German capture of Westerbouwing and so had scuttled the ferry to deny them its use.

The weather on the Thursday was almost identical with that of the preceding day. Layer upon layer of clouds from 150 feet above the ground to heights of 9,000 feet pressed down on its bases. Low stratus persisted between 600 and 1,200 feet and haze restricted visibility to as little as a mile in some areas. Conditions were much better outside England and over

Holland there was only 4/10ths to 7/10ths cloud at about 3,000 feet. These conditions were outweighed by the desperate need of 1st Airborne Division for immediate assistance, which only the Poles could provide. As one flier wrote, 'The weather was impossible. No one believed until actual take-off that the mission would actually run. But run it did.'

All told the American troop carriers were to send a total of 806 aircraft on 21 September. In the centre lane would fly 419 Troop Carrier aircraft with gliders for the 82nd Division, 82 towing gliders to the 101st Division and a parachute resupply mission of 191 aircraft for the 101st Division. The glider and resupply serials for the 101st Division were sandwiched in between the first four and the last four serials going to the 82nd, probably to give the latter division time to clear its landing zone before the second batch of gliders arrived. The 114 troop carrier aircraft carrying Polish paratroops would fly in the left lane to Holland - weather permitting.

Two days of cancellations and frustration when attempts by the 1,568 men of the 1st Polish Independent Parachute Brigade to jump into battle for the first time to try and relieve the beleaguered 1st Airborne Division had caused a period of frustration. The stress of boarding the aircraft in anticipation of a combat drop, then de-boarding due to the weather, was immense. The constant delays in getting the Poles into action had serious consequences. Kazimerz Szmid, born on a farm in Eastern Poland near the town of Nieswiez and accepted into the 5th Kresowa (Borderland) Division in March 1942, recalled: 'This was not to be a rosy experience. Our officers briefed us and prepared us, however the night before I didn't sleep at all. At 0500 we were woken for breakfast, hardly anyone ate. We gathered our equipment, collected our parachutes, boarded lorries and made our way to the airfields. Nobody spoke. At the airfields the weather was poor, fog, we couldn't take off, so we sat around all day hoping that it would clear. The flights were cancelled and we returned to barracks which were not expecting us. Nobody again slept or ate due to the tension. The next day the same poor weather conditions. However our glider element had taken off the previous day from another location. Waiting, waiting, nothing we could do about it, we were so keyed up. Orders to board; travel to the edge of the runway, engines shut off, disembark. I took all of my 500-cigarette allowance and managed to smoke it all whist waiting. In the evening the same order came through, drop postponed and we stood down. The tension got to one of my comrades, who put his gun to his head and before anyone could stop him, pulled the trigger and blew his head off. Back to barracks, another poor night and return to the airfield the next day.'

Chapter 11

Thursday 21 September ('D+4')

On the 21st it was impossible to leave the Hartenstein Hotel area, due to the fact that the enemy made a very determined attempt to break into the perimeter. What with this and the recommencement of the heavy mortaring and shelling it was a wonder any of us lived through it, but we did. Defending the perimeter, in addition to the Para and the South Staffs, there were elements of REs, RAs, Royal Signals, Glider Pilots, Pathfinders, RASC who fought as hard and viciously as the rest. It was a case of their life or yours and although airborne troops do not require to have their back to the wall in order to fight, this was literally a case of give an inch and we were all done.

The RAF supply planes and their dispatchers were giants among brave men; whenever they came over with supplies (which unfortunately usually fell to the enemy) all the fury of the enemy was directed against them, but steadfastly they flew straight and level through the most fearful 'flak' - the dispatchers at the doors, chucking out the containers, even when repeatedly hit and set on fire, flying on, blazing torches in the sky, until they eventually crashed in flames. What devotion to duty and so sorrowful to watch. There wasn't a man on the ground that wasn't moved by this display of courage and, in the main, with no benefit to us.

Sergeant Gordon 'Jock' Walker, born in Glasgow in 1916, Army Film & Photographic Unit, 1st Airborne Division, who, having planned for a two-day operation, he had long since run out of cine film.

Though the weather over Holland was clear on 21 September visibility at the 52nd Troop Carrier Wings bases in the Grantham area was close to zero.

Thick fog was general over England during the morning and the appalling weather in the Grantham area made it impossible to dispatch the gliders marshalled for the 82nd Division but the fog lifted in the south and the first resupply wave began taking off. Although conditions at the bases of the 53rd Wing in southern England were better, they were bad enough to ground the gliders intended for the 101st Division also, particularly since the 101st was in no great need of reinforcement. The parachute resupply mission set up for the 101st was sent, but it is reduced to two small serials. Another serial with emergency supplies was arranged for the 82nd Division. The 438th and 437th Troop Carrier Groups dispatched fifteen C-47s each carrying about sixteen tons of rations to LZ 'W for the 101st. During the early part of their flight they had to contend with haze, which limited visibility to as little as half a mile and with 7/10ths cloud between the altitudes of 500 and about 6,000 feet. Three pilots straggled, lost their way and returned because of the weather and three others turned back because of mechanical difficulties. The remainder, twelve in each serial, flew unopposed over the southern route and dropped their loads over DZ 'W at 1631 and 1640. Although as a result of the weather the drop was not well concentrated, it was fairly accurate and about 31 percent of the rations were recovered. All aircraft returned undamaged, having probably been over friendly territory all the way. Another 33 C-47s with about fifteen tons of rations were dispatched by the 438th Troop Carrier Group to DZ 'O' for the 82nd Division. Two of them aborted on account of the weather. The rest reached the drop zone at 1700 after a difficult but uneventful trip and made a somewhat scattered drop from a height of 1,500 feet.

Protection of the first three waves of 117 RAF resupply aircraft to drop near Hartenstein about 200 yards east of the DZ used on 'D+3' was to be handled by six Spitfire squadrons of ADGB. The last wave of the RAF resupply sorties and the long American column were to be guarded from the Belgian coast to Eindhoven by fifteen squadrons of fighters from ADGB. Between Eindhoven and their destination: protection would be by fifteen fighter groups of Eighth Air Force.

As before, the long haul by the RAF C-47s and Stirlings from base to Holland was trouble-free but despite the entry in the ORB (Operations Record Book) for 271 Squadron which stated that the operation was a great success, in fact very few of the ninety-eight gliders landed undamaged on the correct LZs and twenty-seven glider pilots were killed. On arriving over the DZ, Major Pierre Simond 'Joubie' Joubert on 271 Squadron, which dropped 192 containers of ammunition and food, saw the other eleven

Dakotas ahead of him dropping their panniers from 2,000 to 3,000 feet. Joubert had flown in the 1914-1918 war and wore World War I ribbons. After service in the First World War in South, West and East Africa, he transferred to the Royal Flying Corps and gained his wings in the last few months of the war. After the war he flew mail and other civilian flying roles but was still on the reserve with the South African Air Force. In June 1940 he was re-commissioned into the South African Air Force but owing to his age (he was born in South Africa in 1896 and was 48 years of age) he had been farmed out to Transport Command and for the first years of the war he was assigned to ferry duties. Joubert again met up with the RAF and was based at RAF Uxbridge as a ferry pilot. He then trained on Wellington bombers but it was not a bomber squadron he was posted to but a Transport Command Squadron 271, part of 46 Group, as a flight commander on the 29 February 1944. His crew was the same for the whole of 1944; Flight Lieutenant Ralph Fellows, Flight Lieutenant David Grant and Flight Sergeant David Butterworth. With his crew he followed an intense few months of training, consisting of towing gliders, dropping paratroopers, supplies and on odd occasion leaflet dropping over France. In September 1944 he was awarded the Air Force Cross.[1]

Because of this rather high height for supply dropping, it meant many aircraft were having to take evasive action and Joubert saw one pannier hit the main plane of one of the aircraft, one of the air dispatchers came up to him and said that fighters were attacking a Dakota to the rear of them, at the time they at 6,000 feet and flying into scattered cloud. Below he saw another Dakota attacked and burst into flames. Putting his Dakota into a dive, Joubert waited for the fighters to attack, Flight Sergeant Butterworth in the astrodome giving him the positions of the fighters and warning him to prepare to take evasive action. Somehow Joubert's aircraft was not hit and he reached a solid bank of cloud where he remained. It was well after he had passed south of Nijmegen before he saw the first allied fighter support. From then on the operation was without incident. In all he saw three Dakotas going down in flames.

Twenty-three year old Pilot Officer Frank Wilson Cuer flying Dakota KG340 *The Saint!* had only arrived at the aircraft ten minutes before takeoff having replaced the crew who had been assigned. Warrant Officer C. A. Anderson, the 23-year old navigator explained to Corporal E. A. Slade in charge of the despatch team the route, Margate, Ostend, Antwerp, Nijmegen and then Arnhem and then he told them there was ten minutes to go and to stand by ready to drop on the DZ. Ten minutes later, at 1600 hours Cuer

82nd HQ Company in the 44th Troop Carrier Squadron, 316th Troop Carrier Group at Cottesmore on 17 September. Note the door has been removed as was the procedure for airdrop missions.

Flying *Miss Yank*, a 96th Troop Carrier Squadron C-47 (42-100965), Lieutenant Colonel Frank X. Krebs, commander of the 440th Group and his crew were shot down over Holland during the operation. Except for the navigator, who was captured by the Germans, the entire crew escaped detection for six weeks before making their way back to American lines. Krebs's aircraft and one other C-47 were the only American transport losses during the initial phase of the operation. Other aircraft and gliders were lost in resupply efforts over the next few days.

315th Troop Carrier Group en route to Arnhem over Geel, Belguim.

Civilians in the town of Geel in Belgium watch as the C-47s of the 315th Troop Carrier Group pass overhead en route to Holland.

C-47 42-100874 in the 306th Squadron, 442nd Troop Carrier Group at Chilbolton was en route back from having dropped paratroopers of the 3rd Battalion, 506th PIR, 101st Airborne Division over Son near Eindhoven on 17 September when it was hit by flak and crashed in an open field in friendly territory, North-East of Geel. It hit the only obstacle in the otherwise clear field: an abandoned 45 ton Jagdpanther of 1. Kompanie of the schwere Panzer-Jäger Abteilung 559. Flight Officer John K. Barber, co-pilot and Staff Sergeant Jessie H. Beal, crew chief, bailed out before it was too low for a safe jump. 1st Lieutenants Thomas H. Mills, pilot; Olin H. Jennings, navigator and Staff Sergeant Rollin R. Bailey, radio operator survived the crash.

C-47 on fire.

Above: C-47 tugs and Waco gliders en route to Eindhoven.

Left: Lieutenant Colonel 'Tommy' Haddon commanding the 1st Battalion, The Border Regiment.

Above left: Captain Stuart Radcliffe Mawson, regimental medical officer to the 11th Paratroop Battalion.

Above right: Twenty-year old Flying Officer Geoffrey Adrian Mombrun a Stirling second pilot on 570 Squadron. He flew a Stirling on Operation 'Varsity'. On 22 April 1945, flying a SOE operation to Denmark, his Stirling IV (LJ645) was badly hit by flak over the Jutland coastline and he crash landed in a field north of Aarhus. Three of his crew were killed. He and the two remaining crew managed to get out of the aircraft before it exploded in flames. They were taken prisoner by the Germans within a few hours of the crash. Badly burned, 'Geoff' Mombrun lost his fight for life in a German hospital on 26 April.

Lieutenant Julian 'Bud' Rice, pilot of 'Chalk 10' (43-15212) 'Drastic G-George' in the 316th Troop Carrier Group at Cottesmore.

B-24 Liberator *I'll Be Seeing You* piloted by Captains' James K. Hunter and Anthony Mitchell in the 491st 'Ringmasters' Bomb Group, which was shot down by 20mm flak on 18 September during the re-supply mission to LZ N Knapheide-Klein ('Little America') near Groesbeek. The Liberator then slid on the ground at Tilburg, crashed into a haystack and exploded. The seriously burned tail gunner was the only survivor on the ten-man crew.

B-24 Liberators in the 44th 'Flying Eightballs' Bomb Group flying at very low level drop their supplies to the ground troops in Holland on 18 September.

B-24 Liberators over the drop zone near Son on 18 September.

Hamilcar pilot Captain Bernard Holt Halsall MC.

Dakota III KG401 on 48 Squadron piloted by Flying Officers' L. R. Pattee RCAF and A. C. Kent, which was hit by intense anti-aircraft fire which damaged the tail unit, rudder, port aileron and engine and the starboard auxiliary fuel tank and all the gyro instruments were put out of action. One of the Army dispatchers was mortally wounded. The two pilots flew the crippled aircraft back to the British lines, where the pilots made a successful belly-landing in a field near Kessel. No sooner had they all evacuated the Dakota, than it was engulfed by flames.

Stirling EF2675 nicknamed *The Saint* (visible below the cockpit) was being flown by Flying Officer D. Hardwick of the RAF Keevil-based 299 Squadron when it was shot down on 19 September.

Wing Commander John Alexander Sproule commanding 437 RCAF Squadron.

Left: Flying Officer Errol Q. Semple of Quebec City on 233 Squadron who on 21 September evaded two FW 190 fighters by diving into cloud.

Below: Wing Commander Graeme Elliott Harrison DFC, the 29-year old CO of 190 Squadron.

Stirling IV LK171 flown by the RAF Harwell station commander, Group Captain 'Bill' Surplice. Because LK171 was placed at the personal disposal of Surplice it did not carry the regular squadron code of either of the Rivenhall squadrons, instead bearing his personal initials, WE-S. These it bore until the day it crashed in bad weather on a supply drop to Norwegian resistance forces on 2/3 November. Surplice ordered his crew to bail out after the Stirling iced up and became difficult to handle. All of the crew managed to escape from the doomed aircraft before it crashed into a mountain near Rjukan at Skarfjell, killing Surplice. (K. A. Merrick)

Three men of the Army Film and Photographic Unit at Pinewood Studios (where they had received their photographic training) after returning from Arnhem. Left to right: Sergeants' Dennis Smith and Gordon 'Jock' Walker a veteran of Dunkirk and North Africa, who flew to Arnhem in a glider and C. M. 'Mike' Lewis who had served with the Airborne Forces since its inception in 1941 jumped into battle. The photograph was taken by Lieutenant Barker.

1st Polish Brigade troopers getting ready to fly to Holland, probably on Tuesday 19 September.

Polish paratroopers en route to Holland.

Polish paratroopers dropping near Grave on 23 September.

Charles Edward 'Chuck' Skidmore Jr., a CG-4A pilot in the 91st Squadron, 439th Troop Carrier Group, a veteran of 'D-Day' and 'Market-Garden', the last combat mission he flew. The strain of combat had taken a toll on his nervous system. He began to have flashbacks of his close calls in France and Holland. On one occasion German soldiers passed within a few feet of him as he lay in an apple orchard on a pile of canvas bags used to drop supplies from the air by B-17s. Another time he watched the reflection of war from a glassed-in porch of a Dutch home and become so entranced that he did not notice the bullets coming his way until the glass shattered. He had bad dreams about the incident later.

C-47s in the 71st Troop Carrier Squadron, 434th Troop Carrier Group on a daytime
Supply Mission in Northern France in 1944.

Dutch civilians and paratroopers in the 101st Airborne study local maps after the drops.

de Havilland Mosquito MM345 in the 25th Bombardment Group at RAF Watton. Bad weather made regular air reconnaissance over the Arnhem Bridge impossible, so on 22nd September three Mosquitoes in the 25th Bomb Group were dispatched on 'Bluestocking' missions. MM345 was delivered by 4 May 1944 and was damaged on 8 September at Watton in a landing accident whilst being piloted by 1st Lieutenant Robert C. Grimes. It was Struck Off Charge on 25 July 1945.

Turf and Sport Special in the 61st Troop Carrier Squadron, 314th Troop Carrier Group on a supply drop. The fuselage shows signs of flak damage.

British troopers unloading C-47 43-15509 on 26 September 1933. It was delivered to the USAAF in April 1944 and served in the 37th Troop Carrier Squadron, 316th Troop Carrier Group at Cottesmore for a year. In 1944 it dropped troops over Normandy in June, Holland in September and Germany in March 1945. It was used as a commercial airliner after the war. This aircraft is now on display at the IWM, Duxford.

dropped his panniers on the DZ and was turning away when the Dakota was hit by a 20mm flak in the fuselage and port engine and the petrol tanks burst into flames. This cut off the RAF aircrew from the dispatchers and smoke and flames were rushing through towards them so Flight Sergeant Jim Bayley RAAF closed the cabin door and opened the overhead escape hatch, were dropped on the DZ. Then the port engines and body were hit by 20mm shells and the petrol and tanks burst into flames. They were at 700 feet at the time and everything seemed to happen at once, the communication door in the Dakota jammed so Slade ordered his team to bail out, three made it; Robinson was wounded but made it back via the Dutch underground. As soon as Corporal Slade's chute opened he followed the direction of the stricken plane and saw it crash near a school or church wall in a small village about three quarters of a mile north of the Rhine.

Warrant Officer Anderson and Pilot Officer Cuer were killed in the aircraft. Cuer left a widow, Margaret, of Knighton, Lancashire. Out went Bayley and Flight Sergeant 'Bert' Tipping the wireless operator, followed by Corporal Slade saw a stream of tracer bullets come through the floor and the Dakota burst into flames. He clipped on his chute and bailed out. As he came down he saw the aircraft break in half and crash on the outskirts of a village in a mass of flames. On landing he broke his ankle and was taken prisoner but was repatriated on the 23 April 1945. Driver Heywood was also taken prisoner. Another member of the despatch team, Driver Robinson, evaded capture and got back to the UK. Another dispatcher, 34-year old Driver George High was killed.

Flight Lieutenant C. W. Mott piloting Dakota KG516, having despatched his panniers, was hit in the tail by tracer fire which did not interfere with his flight, but at a position between Uden and Nijmegen he was attacked by two FW 190s. The first came from above astern and the rudder and elevator controls were shot away, both engines were dead, as he began to descend he was again attacked by an enemy fighter and raked from beam to astern, the last burst setting the cockpit panel on fire. The order to bail out was given and the navigator, Flying Officer R. J. Wells was first out, followed by the three dispatchers, the co-pilot, Flight Lieutenant E. J. Packer, a fourth dispatcher, the wireless operator, Pilot Officer T. Kennedy and then Mott whose chute partially opened before he was able to get out of the escape door and was slightly damaged on the tail plane. They landed two miles west of Uden and the aircraft crashed two miles southwest of Uden, where two men of the Royal Corps Signals picked up Mott and one of the dispatchers. Then Wells and Kennedy were contacted, they then proceeded to Uden and discovered that Flight Lieutenant Packer had been taken to Veghel by a Dutch policemen. Mott and Kennedy went to examine the wrecked aircraft and found it to be total write off. They then went back to Uden and then on to Veghel where they found Flight Lieutenant Packer. On the 22nd they hitchhiked to Brussels, reached there at 1900 and found the three missing dispatchers waiting for them. They were then flown back to Down Ampney on the 23rd.

'Jimmy' Edwards dropped his panniers right alongside the temporary Brigade Headquarters and made a circuit at 6,000 feet before turning for home. With an understandable sense of self-satisfaction he put in 'George', the Auto-pilot and ordered up a coffee. Then, to his horror, he glimpsed a Focke-Wulf 190 closing fast with guns blazing. Evasive action proved useless and the order to bail out was given. Realising that three of his four RASC dispatchers were wounded (sic)[2] Edwards heroically stayed at the controls and brought 'Treble Four' in for a crash-landing near Oploo. The landing was far from smooth as Edwards recalled: 'I looked along the port wing and had a glimpse of it being smashed against a number of small trees and then the aircraft hit the ground. With the impact I was thrown half way out of the hatch and was enveloped by a sheet of flame. I hung on because I feared being thrown completely out of the path of the aircraft which was still sliding along the ground. Suddenly the nose dipped down and the tail came up almost vertical and as it fell back again I was flung out backwards on to the top of the aircraft whence I fell to the ground in front of the starboard engine. I picked myself up and ran away from the machine which was now a mass of flames.'

Flight Sergeants' A. W. Clarke the second pilot and H. Sorenson the navigator were taken prisoner. 'Jimmy' and his wireless operator, Flight Sergeant 'Bill' Randall, who were both wounded and Corporal Deridisi, the fourth dispatcher, evaded. Edwards was suffering from burns but felt fit enough to travel. After burying his Mae West and checking everyone's escape kits, he set a southerly course in the hope of meeting up with the advancing Allied Forces. After a short while they came upon a Dutch civilian who offered him and Randall assistance. Due to the language problem Edwards nearly resorted to 'letting him have it' from his revolver, but good luck prevailed and their differences were sorted out. After various adventures Edwards, Randall and Deridisi were offered a trip on the back of some cart horses but seeing the anxiety on Edwards' face a two-wheel horse buggy was found and ultimately they entered Grave aboard a large continental car and went straight to No. 186 Field Hospital. By now Deridisi was finding it difficult to walk due to his ankle and thigh wounds he was found to have, so he was left at the hospital. 'Jimmy' and 'Bill' Randall were taken by ambulance to No. 163 Field Ambulance Staging Post, Oldenrode and after examination sent in another ambulance to Bourg-Leopold where they were given further treatment. They were, again by ambulance, taken to No. 86 British General Hospital at Diest where 'Jimmy' became a stretcher case and was kept in hospital. Randall was taken by ambulance to Sint Pierre Hospital and No. 55 MF Hospital, Brussels and put to bed; here he stayed until the 24 September when he was flown home to Down Ampney by air from Brussels, Evère.

At the first Field Hospital the bandages on 'Jimmy's face were taken off to relieve the pressure and replace it with the proper dressing and a bag of lint with holes which had been cut for his nose and eyes. He was given an injection of penicillin, a sedative and on his battledress, labels saying what treatment he had been given. 'Bill' Randall's ankle was strapped and then they were taken to the General Hospital where 'Jimmy's burns were found to be worse than thought. After a few days 'Jimmy' was taken to Brussels and a special burns ward, where he stayed until the 27th when he was flown back to Down Ampney. For eight days he had been reported missing and on his return he learned that 'Lummie' Lord had been killed on the same day.[3]

Twenty-five year old Captain Colin Herbert Campbell saaf of Claremont, Cape Town flying Dakota KG346 on 48 Squadron, having been damaged by flak attempting to crash land, came down at Dingle Flats, three miles southeast of Bradwell Bay. Five bodies were recovered from the sea, only one was identified as Flying Officer John P. Mudge the 32-year old navigator, the condition of the others made burial at sea necessary. Flying Officer John Garvey the 21-year old second pilot and Flight Sergeant John Anderson (28) and Flying Officer Mudge are all buried in Brookwood Military Cemetery. One of the two dispatchers, 32-year old Driver G. P. Sleet, has no known grave.

Flight Sergeant S. H. Webster at the controls of FZ620 on 48 Squadron saw two Dakotas ahead of him hit and crash as he approached the DZ with a load of panniers at 1,000 feet. He carried on and after dropping them all he was hit by flak aft of the cabin; he did a sharp turn to the left, opened the throttles and started to climb. The port wing was then hit and a large hole torn near the trailing edge and small holes appeared in both wings, he now found it impossible to straighten the aircraft out and the cabin began to fill with smoke and flames began to appear aft of the cabin. Seeing the situation was hopeless he gave the order to bail out, opened up the engines to their maximum boost and trimmed back, he left his seat, unzipped his flak suit, grabbed his chute and made his way to the rear of the aircraft. By this time the flames were licking up the side of the aircraft and it was full of smoke, when he got to the rear door four had already gone and the others including himself soon followed. After jumping he got caught in the slipstream and commenced to turn over and over in somersaults, he then pulled what he thought was the ripcord but after falling some distance he realised he had pulled the cloth handle instead of the ripcord. When he did pull the actual rip cord the chute opened instantly, he experienced a terrific jerk, although he was the last to leave, he was, because of his free falling, the first to land. He dropped into the Rhine near the northern bank and after discarding his chute and inflating his Mae West he began to swim for the southern bank where several civilians were waving and shouting to him. Despite the strong current he was able to reach the bank and was pulled out by a youth who it turned out belonged to the Dutch Underground movement, he then saw Corporal C. Conquest, one of his air dispatchers and they were both taken to a house and given a change of clothing, hot drinks and sandwiches. Webster, Conquest, Lance Corporal Hammon and Drivers R. C. Jones and Fiskin evaded successfully and were eventually flown back to Down Ampney.

KG579 on 48 Squadron flown by 22-year old Warrant Officer David A. Webb RCAF and 26-year old co-pilot Flight Sergeant Denis H. R. Plear was hit by cannon fire after dropping his supplies. At first the cannon fire was thought to be flak and evasion action was taken but then a FW 190 was seen flying past the starboard side and Pilot Officer F. C. Clarke got into the astrodome to give Webb evasive instructions and saw no less than fifteen FW 190s on the port quarter. Coming into attack on the starboard quarter there was another ten FW 190s starting to peel off to attack. It has to be said that by the actions of the pilot and the instructions from Clarke only four hits were made but which resulted in a fire breaking out underneath the centre section of the wings, another hit was made and the astrodome shot away. At the time Clarke had ducked down to indicate to the pilot to go into a steep dive, a two second burst by another fighter resulted in a fire in the starboard engine and the aircraft into an even steeper dive. The air dispatchers and the wireless operator bailed out on the instructions of Clarke who yelled at Webb that the aircraft was on fire, upon which the pilot waved back as if to say 'thanks for telling me'. Clarke, who had been wounded in the legs made his way to the rear door pulling himself along by means of the fuselage ribs owing to the steep angle of the dive, he was able to get far enough out of the door and the slipstream did the rest. As he was making his way to the door more hits were received on the Dakota by the fighters.

On the way down by parachute, six FW 190s remained and strafed them, killing, it is believed, David Webb and Denis Plear. Clarke was able to avoid this by swinging violently in his chute and evading the fighter's fire. One fighter passed within two feet of him and he could see the pilot laughing, it also caused his chute to collapse but it opened again at about 500 feet from the ground. After he had landed safely the fighters came in and as he rolled away he saw cannon hits about five to six yards away, he then saw a girl waving at him from a farmhouse 200 yards away. She took him to another farmhouse where he met up with an air dispatcher who was also slightly wounded and first aid was given, again by Dutch Red Cross workers, who dressed their wounds. They then heard that four other parachutists had landed, he was taken to one spot where two dispatchers were found. One, Lance Corporal James Pilson of 223 Airborne RASC, was seriously wounded and subsequently died and the other was wounded no less than nine times. After fifteen minutes the fourth air dispatcher, also wounded in the legs, arrived.

Clarke got some Dutchmen to intercept transport and a British ambulance arrived and took the wounded survivors to Grave. Here was the body of Warrant Officer Gordon Birlison the 24-year old wireless operator who was riddled from head to foot with bullets, he had come down in a tree and as he hid there it would appear the fighters had strafed him. It was in the village of Zeeland they had come down and were taken from Grave to Eindhoven where they spent the night at St. Francis hospital just outside the town. On the 22nd they hitchhiked to the Escant Canal where they were picked up by a RAF Regiment officer in two jeeps, who drove them to XXX Corps. From there they were taken in two staff cars to Brussels and Pilot Officer Clarke was brought back to the UK by Flight Lieutenant Alford on 48 Squadron. Clarke reported that two of the FW 190s were shot down by a Spitfire.

Dakota KG417 on 48 Squadron skippered by 21- year old Flying Officer Jack Gordon Wills RCAF was hit from above by supplies dropped by another aircraft. The wing dropped off and the C-47 crashed in Volkel north of Driel. Wills, Flight Sergeant D. S. Black the 22-year old second pilot, Flying Officer James William Erickson RCAF (23) of Banff, Alberta and Pilot Officer D. G. Hardy (24) were killed, as were the four dispatchers, including the only officer air dispatcher, 27-year old Lieutenant Herbert Edwards of 223 Airborne Company. He left a widow, Lily Edwards in Barnsley. Squadron Leader P. O. M. Duff-Mitchell AFC on 48 Squadron crash landed at B56 Brussels in KG350, having had his oil and fuel pipes severed.

One re-supply serial involved eighteen Dakotas on 233 Squadron and ten on 437 Squadron RCAF carrying 488 panniers loaded with ammunition, food and medical supplies. The aircraft took off between 1310-1315 hours, led by Wing Commander William Coles DFC AFC (later Sir William Coles KCB KBE DSO DFC* AFC) the commanding officer of 233 Squadron. Three aircraft on 437 Squadron took off slightly later than the rest, between 1335-1337 hours. Dakota KG559 flown by Wing Commander Coles was hit over the DZ in both wings and elevator, making the aircraft very difficult to control. Despite this he made a second run over the DZ to drop the remainder of his panniers and was again hit a number of times, he flew the aircraft back to Brussels where his aircraft was declared a write off. Unfortunately one of his air dispatchers, 29-year old Lance Corporal Ronald N. Clements of 800 Airborne Company was pulled out of the aircraft without a parachute as the containers were being released near Ravnestyne, Wireless operator Flying Officer E. J. Sharpe was wounded in the right thigh.

On 233 Squadron also twenty-one year old Flying Officer Charles Douglas Hamilton RAAF flying KG566 was shot down by fighters and he and his crew were killed. Warrant Officer F. R. Russell flying KG586 crash landed at Bennekom and he and his crew were taken prisoner. Dakota KG399 piloted by 20-year old Flying Officer Michael Ades and his second pilot, 20-year old Flight Sergeant George Kenneth Dorville was loaded with oil and mortar bombs in sixteen panniers and had four soldiers aboard to put the load out when they reached the DZ.

'Everything went OK until we reached the DZ at 1606' recalled navigator, 23-year old Flying Officer Frederick Stephen William Dyer RAAF from South Australia. 'We had to run through a lot of light flak. I think we were hit, but not seriously and we began the return trip. About ten minutes after leaving Arnhem, at 5,000 feet, we received several hits from an Oerlikon gun on the ground, being hit in the port wing and in the fuselage, one shot came through the floor just in front of Mike's feet and out through the top of the cabin. Several minutes later, the army men drew attention to flames coming through the floor and after telling Mike, I tried to put them out with the fire extinguisher, but they had a firm hold by that time and I had to abandon the extinguisher. Mike decided to try to reach the British lines before crash landing and when we were down to 2,000 feet he told me to get the Army chaps into crash-landing positions. Before going aft to do so, I clipped my parachute pack onto my harness.

THURSDAY 21 SEPTEMBER ('D+4')

'I went back to the aft door where 'Jack' [Flight Sergeant John Hickey AFM, the wireless operator, who was from Lancaster] was standing reassuring the Army men and told them we were going to crash-land. They said it was too late and pointed over my shoulder. I turned and saw that in the last few seconds the forward part of the fuselage had been enveloped in flame and smoke. 'Jack' and I decided the time had come to abandon aircraft and told the Army men to Jump with us. I went out and 'Jack' followed, but the others failed to do so. [Years later I discovered that the Army men did jump and became PoWs]. The pilots were trapped by the flames and died of burns near the crash [KG399 came down near a gunpowder factory at Arendonk, near Brabant].

'By the time we jumped, we were only at about 800 feet and so it only took us about twenty seconds to reach the ground. Just as we left the aircraft, it was engaged by heavy machine-gun fire from a position about half a mile away from us and when the aircraft drew out of range, they fired a few bursts at us, but did not hit either of us. We hit the ground at 1640 about fifty yards apart, in a small clearing in a large forest, both landing unhurt. We hid our parachutes and Mae Wests in a ditch and ran off in a westerly direction in order to get away from our landing position as quickly as possible. We heard rifle shots from the direction of the machine gun and heard a couple of hits in the trees near us, but after about an hour things quietened down and we hid in some thick undergrowth to work out a plan. We decided that we must first contact a friendly farmer [as briefed] and moved through the woods until we came to a large barn. We found that it was part of a farm of about 400 acres, surrounded by woods and seemed quite secluded, which was what we wanted. Several people were digging potatoes at the southern end and as twilight gathered they walked northwards and would have passed about a hundred yards away. As they came near, we showed ourselves and when we saw that we had been observed, walked towards them. They were Dutch people and one of them spoke a very little English, so we were able to gather that we were in Holland and about thirty miles from the British front line. They took us to the barn and after about fifteen minutes we went across to the house, which was in the northwest of the clearing. The whole family held a conference and finally motioned us into the house and gave us a meal of bacon and eggs. After this, we were returned to the barn for the night and hid in the straw. As I had been working in my shirt-sleeves, my jacket was left in the aircraft, so the eldest daughter gave me a pair of old overalls and a red woollen scarf. We spent a very chilly night, but slept fairly well as we had had a busy day.

'During the next day, a man, who spoke English, came to see us and told us we must remain in hiding, as there were many Germans around, about 200 Supply Personnel being stationed the village of Hooge Mierde, five kilometres away. We stayed in the barn most of the next twelve days and were fed by the family, whose name, we found, was Valckx. The family consisted of eleven children from about 12 to 25. Three days were fine enough and safe enough for -us to sit in the woods, about 100 yards from the house and were thus able to have a change of surroundings, as well as the slight exercise gained in the brisk walks to and from the barn, as the barn was too full to make exercise practical. One night we decided to stay in the woods, as there was brisk fighting in the woods to the south and the barn promised good cover and observation positions if the fighting came north. However, it died out next day and after drying ourselves in the kitchen, (it rained all night), we returned to the barn.

'After the first three nights, when it became obvious that the Allied Armies lightning advance from Normandy must have been stopped, we hollowed out a deep shelter in the straw and it enabled us to lie about four feet below the surface; besides giving us a feeling of greater safety, it was much warmer at night. We descended into our pit at dark and came up in the mornings when the farmers gave us the 'all clear'. The fine pieces of straw working beneath our clothing, irritated us constantly, the stiff straws were forever poking our faces, ears and noses. From an opening in one end of the barn we could see the Church steeple of Hooge Mierde and beyond it the steeple of Laage Mierde and we spent most of our time gazing at them. We slept a lot during the first few days, but we soon weren't tired enough to sleep in the daytime and just lay in the straw looking out at the two steeples. The food was nourishing, mainly hot potatoes and milk for dinner and cheese and half-cured ham sandwiches for breakfast and tea.

'The number of Germans in the vicinity varied; at one time there were 1,000 in the village, with mechanised forces and artillery dispersed in the woods and at other times there were only a few dozen.

'Night and day the air was almost unceasingly humming with aircraft engines (all Allied). We saw several big Fortress and Liberator forces go over and heard quite a few night bomber forces. We also saw a lot of medium bomber forces and occasionally a roving band of Spitfires passed overhead. We saw two Spitfires diving and cannon-firing near Hooge Mierde. During our last four days in the barn we heard artillery firing and shells bursting to the east, north and south, the nearest was about a mile away. One night we heard an explosion which shook the barn; we subsequently found out that it was the blowing of a vital bridge by the Germans. On 1 October a Squadron of Spitfires strafed the artillery positions south of us for 20 minutes. On 3 October we decided to try and walk through to the British lines and borrowed overalls, scarf, can and overcoat for disguise. Jerard, our main guardian and the English-speaking man from the village, started out to guide us, but we had only got as far as the village, when we saw an armoured car patrol from the Welsh Division. After returning our disguise, we rode back with them to Reusal, eight kilometres to the east, where heavy fighting had been in progress for the last four days. We were stupefied when we heard that Arnhem was evacuated. From there we went in a jeep to Divisional Headquarters, where we had tea and I got an issue of Jacket and greatcoat. The Divisional Provost Marshal sent us to Diest in his personal car and next day we went by truck to Brussels. We spent two days there and were then flown to Croydon.

'Since the above was written, I have heard from our Dutch friends that our aircraft crashed about two miles from Hooge Mierde. The two pilots were found by the Belgians, who tried to give them first aid and a drink, but 'it was not permitted', apparently the Germans also found them. The British Liberation Army found their bodies by the aircraft on 25 September and a padre buried them nearby. Since then they have been - moved to a British War Cemetery. No mention was made of the four Amy chaps, so it appears that they also bailed out.'[4]

Dyer landed at Hoogemiede, near Brabant and hid his flying kit in a drain, a farmer nearby took him and Hickey, who had also landed nearby, to his farm. They were hidden in a barn and nearby woods. The farmer, H. Valckx and his family brought them hot food and drinks three times a day. On 2 October the British overran the area and they were helped by 'B' Squadron, of 53 Reconnaissance Regiment, to Brussels. All four army dispatchers - Lance Corporals A. North and R. Scott and Drivers J. Warner and George Woodcock of 799 Airborne Company were taken prisoner. Driver Woodcock died on the 27 February 1945 as a prisoner at Stalag XIIa.

Two of the three Dakotas on 437 Squadron that had taken off slightly later than the rest were 'tail end Charlie's' flying in the rear of the resupply force and amongst the nine Dakotas that did not return. KG489 flown by 21-year old Flying Officer John Spencer Blair RCAF was hit by machine-gun and cannon fire from Focke-Wulf 190 fighters and crashed at Eerschot. None of the crew and the air dispatchers had any chance to bail out and the aircraft was seen going down and disintegrating before hitting the ground. All aboard were buried near the crash site. One of the dead could not be identified and 21-year old Flying Officer Charles Herbert Cressman RCAF was buried at Uden War Cemetery as an 'Unknown British Airman.'[5]

Dakota KG376 piloted by Flying Officer Gerald Puruis Hagerman RCAF was also hit on the first run over the DZ. The crash of these two Dakotas was witnessed by George Koskimaki, the radio operator for the 101st Airborne Division's Commanding Officer, General Maxwell D. Taylor, whose headquarters had just moved from Eindhoven to Henkenshage Castle, south of Sint-Oedenrode. According to Koskimaki, 'Two German fighter planes appeared from the clouds and quickly shot them down almost directly overhead.' Though none of those on board Blair's Dakota survived, three of the four dispatchers on KG376 survived. The one exception was 29-year old Lance Corporal James Adamson who was wounded and not all the panniers were dropped but a second run was made successfully. As the Dakota climbed away above the cloud, six or seven FW 190s in line astern came in from the port beam. Hagerman made for the clouds but the first enemy fighter was able to get an attack in, breaking off at 100 yards. The 36-year old wireless operator, Flight Sergeant John C. H. Hackett and the 28-year old navigator, Flying Officer Michael Stanley Reece Mahon RCAF of Barbados, British West Indies were attending to Adamson at the time and the navigator and dispatcher were killed by cannon fire. The port engine caught fire and the windscreen was smashed and the intercom rendered u/s. Warrant Officer J. P. DeChamplain RCAF the second pilot warned the remainder of the crew to put on the chutes, when minutes later a fire broke out in the fuselage and the second pilot went back to order them to abandon the aircraft. Hagerman left through the emergency escape hatch, the wireless operator who had a slight leg wound and the dispatchers, some of whom were wounded, landed four miles south-east of Veghel. The Dutch people provided a horse and trap to Veghel where the injured dispatchers were admitted to hospital. United States Airborne troops were contacted and the uninjured helped to Brussels. Gerald Hagerman was later awarded the DFC.

In all three Dakotas on 437 Squadron were shot down with eight aircrew killed and two taken prisoner. (Eight Royal Army Service Corps (RASC) dispatchers aboard the lost aircraft also died). After dropping supplies 24-year-old Squadron Leader Robert Wilfred Alexander DFC RCAF flying Dakota KG387 climbed to 7,000 feet above the haze that persisted in the area of the DZ. Flying Officer John Rechenau RCAF who was in the astrodome, was told by the pilot to go to the rear to see if there had been any damage, he reported back that there was no damage. He then went back to his radio seat to record what he had done, then they were hit and Alexander was wounded with his head and arm bleeding badly, he slumped over the controls and did not move again. The starboard controls were shot away and the engine ran away at a very high pitch. Then came a second hit, this time Flying Officer William McLintock the 22-year old navigator and the second pilot were hit and wounded and Flight Sergeant Andrew McHugh, on hearing the metal striking, stood up, but as he did a bullet lodged in his back and he fell face downwards in the aisle. Then there came a succession of about seven bursts and the aircraft was on fire from stem to stern. Rechenau then went over to McHugh to see how badly he was hit. McHugh stood up and gave the order to bail out. In the meantime McLintock had taken over the controls and given the order to bail out, they put on their chutes and made their way to the back of the aircraft where the three air dispatchers were lying on the floor of the aircraft in pools of blood with no sign of movement from them. The fourth air dispatcher, Lance Corporal Jones, was putting on his chute. By this time the tail of the aircraft was a mass of flames, John Rechenau bailed out and McHugh pushed the air dispatcher out. The Dakota did a half circle to the left and disappeared behind a clump of trees in a dive, all that could be seen after that was a great big puff of black smoke from where the aircraft disappeared, this was at Vetchel, 22 miles south of Hertogenbosch. John Rechenau made his way to an American hospital, where the Americans told him there was nothing left of his aircraft and it was a waste of time going back to it, also they were expecting a German attack that night. He had seen McHugh being taken into the operating theatre having landed in the Wilhelmina Canal and got out by the Americans, the same Americans who had manned the anti-aircraft battery, which had opened up on the German fighters. He received the DFM in December 1944.

Alexander and McLintock are remembered on the Runneymede Memorial, only Lance Corporal Jones of the four dispatchers survived, the other three died and are buried in the Bergen-Op-Zoom Cemetery. He had been taken on a wheelbarrow to 'Zonehove' Children's Sanatorium at Son, being used as a hospital, by the 101st US Airborne Division. This was the same hospital that McHugh had been seen by John Rechenau. From here McHugh was taken to a dressing station at 'Kindengarten' and then to the RAF Hospital in Brussels. He had two bullets in his back and burns to his face. Jones had suffered multiple wounds to the left shoulder, left forearm and right leg.

One 437 Squadron pilot who escaped from Luftwaffe attention on the 21st was Flying Officer Errol Q. Semple of Quebec City. He had flown Dakotas on 233 Squadron on the night of 5/6 June 1944. On 21 September he evaded two FW 190 fighters by diving into cloud. Dakota KG389 piloted by Flying Officer G. P. Chambers was written off following battle damage and a crash landing at Brussels. Pilot Officer R. A. Kenny crash landed Dakota FZ656 at Turnhout in Belgium after being hit by flak getting their panniers out. One dispatcher was hit in the leg and wounded but the rest of the crew suffered no lasting injuries and all were returned to England in due course.

The Dakota flown by Squadron Leader Richard Cleaver DSO DFC on 575 Squadron was hit at the DZ and badly damaged with the main plane catching fire. Despite this he carried on and returned to Broadwell. While on 644 Squadron he was shot down on 6 April 1944 by flak from a Luftwaffe airfield at Cognac but was able to evade capture and get back to the UK.

Two aircraft on 271 Squadron were employed on shuttling wounded back to Down Ampney and on the outward journey taking stretchers and blood. Flight Lieutenant Beddow piloting FZ615 reached the DZ easily and all panniers were dropped in the target area, but when turning his starboard engine and tailplane was shot up by flak. He attempted to feather the engine but it seized and the Dakota was flown on one engine at 1,500 feet. Between Schundel and Veghel FZ615 was again hit by flak and the fuselage damaged, but Beddow landed safely at B56 Brussels Evère. All the crew arrived back at base on the 22nd.

On 196 Squadron at Keevil seventeen aircrew were killed on the day's dropping mission. Ten Stirling crews were detailed and of these six were successful and three aircraft failed to return. It being Yom Kippur, Mark Azouz, who had been awarded the DFC and promoted to Pilot Officer, could have taken leave on the 21st but he refused as men at Arnhem were waiting for supplies. Azouz and crew by now had made four supply flights to Arnhem: on the 17th, from Wethersfield on the 18th, on the 19th, when they dropped 24 containers and four panniers but sustained 27 holes from light and heavy flak at the TRV and LZ; and on the 20th. On the 21st in LJ810, they left Keevil at noon with a similar load for Arnhem. Arriving twenty minutes late owing to engine trouble, after dropping his supplies, Azouz's Stirling was hit by flak over the DZ, but he got away and took the transport up to 4,000 feet. 'The natives were hostile' wrote 'Bert' Turner the flight engineer 'and they threw everything at us but we got through badly damaged. As we flew out of the target area, Mark asked the navigator 'Ginger' Greenwell for a course to Brussels. Before we could do anything else we were attacked by three to five FW 190s. Flight Sergeant Peter Bode the 21-year old rear gunner shot one down'

THURSDAY 21 SEPTEMBER ('D+4')

At 1415 the fighters set the Stirling's tail and both wings on fire and the aircraft was going down when Mark Azouz gave the order to abandon. Everyone answered except for 'Pete' Bode who was dead. Spitfires and Thunderbolts then appeared and covered their descent. Flight Sergeant Leo Hartman, air bomber, having bailed out, landed by a farm near Wijchen and sprained his ankle. Some farmers who had seen him bail out of his aircraft took him in and a member of the underground arrived and took away his parachute and Mae West.

'When we landed; says 'Bert' Turner 'we were taken to Dutch farmhouse where we were treated like royalty. There were now only six of us, we had somehow lost Mark.' 'Ginger' Greenwell, John McQuiggan, 'Bert' Turner and their two army dispatchers, Lance Corporal Day and 43-year old Driver A. E. Norton, evaded. All arrived in the UK on the 27th. Greenwell was recommended and awarded the DFM.[6] Lance Corporal Day, a member of 63 Airborne RASC, was awarded the Military Medal.

Stirling LJ843 on 196 Squadron piloted by 23-year old Flight Sergeant C. R. J. Green was shot down by flak and crashed at Wageningen with no survivors on the crew. The two dispatchers were killed also. Stirling LJ928 flown by 23-year old Flight Sergeant Ronald E. G. Waltrich was shot down by an enemy fighter and crashed north of Heveadorp at Johanniterweg in Doorwerth, west of Oosterbeek. All four RAF crewmembers and one of the dispatchers were killed. Only Driver W. H. Brook of 63 Airborne RASC survived and he was taken prisoner. Pilot Officer 'Chuck' Hoysted's crew was forced to abort the mission when the rear gunner collapsed before the Stirling crossed the English coast.

On 295 Squadron Stirling LJ115 flown by Pilot Officer Denis M. Peel was hit by flak. 'When we opened the bomb doors,' Peel later explained, 'we were about 700-800 feet and as slow as possible. We then realised we were being shot at and our starboard inner engine was on fire. I was told the fuselage was on fire and the dispatchers had jumped out to avoid the flames.' Peel belly-landed the Stirling at Dennenkamp. All of the flight crew survived and were taken prisoner but the two RASC dispatchers; Drivers W. G. Thompson and J. F. Johnston were killed after bailing out at too low a height for their parachutes to open.[7]

Eleven of 620 Squadron's aircraft took part in Thursday's resupply effort and in spite of an extreme level of anti-aircraft fire coupled with interception by enemy fighters, the Fairford Squadrons managed to deliver 240 canisters and 34 supply panniers. Two aircraft were lost in the attempt. LJ830 skippered by Flying Officer H. M. 'Nipper' McLeod was damaged by flak and fighters and he had to make an emergency landing near Schweilzerhohe. Flying Officer 'Jack' Thomas the Canadian air gunner was killed when he was thrown out during one of the fighter attacks. McLeod and Flight Sergeant H. Bale were taken into captivity but Flying Officers' R. Newton and C. C. King and Sergeant T. Haig evaded. Both dispatchers were killed. Pilot Officer John C. L. Carey flying LJ946 was forced to crash land near Benneken west of Arnhem after being hit by flak. All the crew survived. Carey hid in a boat at Wolfswaard, Wageningen and for two days received food and clothing from the Dutch. On the 22nd he was joined by three other RAF personnel and they were hidden in a tent in the undergrowth until the 23rd. They were about to cross the river in a boat when a German recce patrol arrived and they had to dash for cover. After an hour their Dutch friends produced bicycles and they split into two parties and rode into Wageningen. Later, they crossed the river without incident and after making contact with the 43rd Recce Regiment, on 24 September they were taken to Brussels. 620 Squadron's final sorties were carried out that day, with just five aircraft carrying supplies to the beleaguered 1st Airborne Division. However the situation on the ground was now so confused that only one of these was able to locate the dropping point. From the 17th to the 24th September, 620 Squadron had flown a total of 104 sorties to the Arnhem area, at a cost of five aircraft lost, eight aircrew and seven RASC dispatchers killed and seven men taken prisoner. A further fifteen men had bailed out over Arnhem, but these were successfully evacuated to the Allied lines when the 1st Airborne Division withdrew across the Rhine.

190 Squadron had only ten flyable Stirlings for the re-supply operation. Seven of them were shot down and the lives of twenty-four aircrew and six dispatchers were lost. Wing Commander Graeme Elliott Harrison DFC US Silver Star the CO and a 29-year old veteran who had joined the RAF in 1939, was at the controls of 'N-Nan' (LJ082). Harrison reached the DZ and his dispatchers managed to get their supplies away before 'Nan' was shot down by flak in the Hartenstein Hotel area and crashed near Zethen, 15 kilometres southwest of Arnhem. Harrison, who was born on 21 July 1915 at Townsend, Waterford, Ontario, his crew and the two dispatchers, were killed. Harrison left a widow. Aline Cynthia Stevens whom he had married in Trincomalee, Ceylon in March 1940 and two young daughters. The second pilot, Warrant Officer Thomas Barry Brierley was a 21-year old New Zealander from Wellington. Flight Sergeant Robert Percy, the 25-year old flight engineer was from Ballymena, County Antrim. Pilot Officer Comte Jacques Fernand Gabriel de Cordoue RCAF, the 29-year old

air gunner, was born on 13 June 1915 in Montreal, the son of a Marquis and Marquise. Flight Lieutenant Norman Edward Skinner, the 32-year old WOp/AG was born in Scarborough in 1933 and had married Marjorie Emily Daisy Adams there in 1933. They had two children. The navigators, Flying Officer Neil MacKay (35) had been born in 1909 at Thurso in Caithness-shire and Warrant Officer Donald Meldrum Mathewson a 36-year old New Zealander, had been born in 1908 in Kokomga, Otago. The two dispatchers, Lance Corporal Leslie H. Caldecott, a 22-year old from Cornwall and Driver Harold Gregory a 28-year old Lancastrian, both left bereaved wives.[8]

Stirling LJ943 on 190 Squadron flown by 23-year old Pilot Officer Robert Blair Herger RCAF which was towing Horsa 'Chalk Number 1007' flown by Staff Sergeant Newton and Sergeant Douglas Smithson was drawn into the slipstream of a Dakota. The Horsa rose as Herger put his nose down to avoid the Dakota and the tow-rope snapped. The Horsa landed safely near the village of Oude-Tonge with its cargo of a jeep and 6-pounder anti-tank gun and three troops of the 1st.Airlanding Anti-Tank Battery Royal Artillery. The Stirling crashed near Zetten killing all nine members of the crew. Stirling LJ916 piloted by Flying Officer J. S. Hay crash-landed near Tilburg after it was hit by flak and then finished off by two German fighters. Hay tried to set the plane alight but was captured before he managed to do so. The Stirling flown by Pilot Officer N. W. Sutherland RNZAF was hit by flak and machine gun fire on the run up and severely damaged but the pilot was able to fly the aircraft back and land successfully. Twenty-three-year old New Zealand Flying Officer Brian Arthur Bebarfald RNZAF from Wanganui, Wellington flying Stirling LJ881 successfully dropped his supplies before the aircraft was hit by flak and then attacked by an enemy fighter. As the Stirling began to disintegrate in the air Bebarfald gave the order to bail out but, in spite of his efforts at the controls, there was only time for two of his crew to escape before the machine went down. Flight Lieutenant Leslie Munro the Canadian wireless operator from Vancouver landed two miles east of Zetten. On landing he sprained his ankle and was soon surrounded by Dutch people who gave him civilian clothes and took him to Zetten and hid him in a house until dark. From there he was moved to the village of Hemen. While he was there the rear gunner, Warrant Officer G. Morris RAAF turned up. Both men stayed until 24 September when a member of the underground movement picked them up in a car and took them to an advanced British unit. Driver Hughes, one of the dispatchers, also evaded successfully but 28-year old Driver G. E. Jones died of his wounds.

26-year old Flight Lieutenant Alexander 'Sandy' Anderson from Dundee in Scotland and his twenty-year old co-pilot, Flight Sergeant George Felix Conry-Candler RNZAF flying Stirling LJ833 found that there was no fighter escort and none waiting for them over the DZ. LJ933 was hit by flak over the DZ and then approached by enemy fighters. One engine was hit and stopped quickly, followed by the wing catching fire. The order was given to bail out, but before they were able to do so they were down to 500 feet. Anderson decided to crash land, but right in the flight path was the village of Batenburg. If he crashed on the village most of the houses and farm with thatched roofs would have caught fire, somehow Anderson managed to clear the village and crashed in the middle of the River Maas. The fuselage broke off and the aircraft began to sink, but thanks to the help of the villagers three of the crew were saved. The remainder, including the gallant Anderson and Conry-Candler and 33-year old Flying Officer Alexander Dalgetty Adamson, twenty year old Flight Sergeant Arthur George Oliver Bellamy and 21-year old Flight Sergeant William George Tolley went down with the aircraft and were washed ashore days later. Flight Sergeant George E. Orange the bomb aimer and Sergeant Alfred J. Smith after ditching were able to swim ashore and were met by Dutchmen on the shore. Thirty year old Driver Albert Edward Abbott drowned in the Maas. The other dispatcher, Driver L. E. Bloomfield, who was badly wounded but had managed to swim ashore with them, was looked after by a local doctor who said he would be okay, but sadly it was learned later that he had died. Orange and Smith were given a boat and rowed across the river, on the other side they made contact with forward patrols of the 2nd Army; they were then sent to Brussels on the 22nd and flown to Croydon overnight on the 22 /23 September.

Stirling LJ823 piloted by Flying Officer A. C. Farren was shot down by three fighters after being hit by flak. Four of the crew, including Farren, who was thrown through the windscreen when the aircraft crashed near Haren and injured his back, were wounded. Twenty-two year old Warrant Officer Leslie John Billen drowned and Flight Sergeants William Louis Pretsell. Cairns (22) and 23-year old William Henry Skewes were killed when they jumped too low for their parachutes to open fully. Flight Sergeant Frederic Ross, wounded after jumping, was sheltered in Holland until liberated at Oss. The two dispatchers evaded also. Flight Sergeant F. M. T. Stone, the second pilot and Flight Sergeant A. J. H. Brown, who were both wounded were taken to hospital and later incarcerated in PoW camps.

Flying Officer Frank E. Pascoe RAAF piloting Stirling 'F for Fox' (LK498) arrived at the DZ and found about twenty Me 109s and FW 190s attacking each aircraft as they came in to drop their supplies; also the sky was patchy and dark with flak bursts; smoking aircraft could be seen falling headlong out of the sky. Pascoe reduced height to tree-top level to make the expected enemy fighter attacks less easy for them. At this height the aircraft was also a large, albeit fleeting target for enemy machine gunners and the rattle of bullets hitting the aircraft sounded like heavy hail against a window pane … Miraculously, no member of the crew was hit, although the aircraft was holed in a number of places … The DZ was found and the supplies were dropped, save some which failed to leave the aircraft, due no doubt to the release mechanism being damaged. At the DZ there were few signs of our own troops and it seemed possible, in the heat of battle, their supplies were dropped into enemy hands.

As the Stirling turned away, a false reading on the repeater compass due, no doubt, to the gyro unit being damaged, caused Pascoe to turn too far and the bomber banked round and back into the inferno. The fire abated momentarily, but soon burst back into life. It was obvious that the aircraft was doomed, but it was too low for the crew to make their escape by parachute. And there would not be sufficient power from the two port engines to gain height quickly, if at all. Frank Pascoe coolly announced over the intercom that he would put the aircraft down and ordered the crew to their crash positions as they reached a point south of Grave. The aircraft skimmed along very low, lopped off a few trees, lightly struck a farm building or two and then belly-landed in a large cultivated field, carving out a deep furrow, which might be expected from thirty tons of metal hurtling along at 100mph.

On coming to rest the Stirling seemed full of chocking, blinding dust, but Sergeant 'Taff' Hughes the flight engineer who was on his fourth sortie to Arnhem found his way through it to the rear door, which, surprisingly, he was able to open quite easily. He made a quick getaway in the knowledge that the aircraft was still burning; there remained a lot of fuel in the tanks and perhaps some of the hung up containers in the bomb bay were packed with ammunition. Pascoe was quickly joined in a nearby ditch by the wireless operator and the rear gunner. A few shouts brought over the navigator and the bomb aimer and after a few moments Pascoe calmly emerged from the far side of the burning aircraft. On hearing their shouts, he joined the other crew members in the ditch. All except one of the dispatchers, Driver T. C. Fitzhugh, who was wounded, survived unhurt. When Pascoe went to get an ambulance for him the Dutch stripped the aircraft. Fitzhugh was taken away to an advance field hospital nearby and the remaining crewmembers made their way back to safety.

Flying Officer Cyril 'Larry' Siegert RNZAF flying 'T-Tommy' (LJ876) was able to drop his 24 containers and four panniers but as he turned away he was attacked by two FW 190s, one of which damaged the aircraft. Four further attacks followed but rear gunner Flight Sergeant Jack Welton, who was on his twentieth operation, gave a running commentary to the pilot which enabled him to take evasive action. Welton fired at one of the fighter's which was seen to dive steeply towards the ground with smoke pouring from it. Siegert managed to shake off the rest by a violent high-speed dive and was able to get his seriously damaged aircraft back to base. Siegert was awarded the DFC on 24 September. Flight Sergeant Welton was awarded the DFM.

570 Squadron dispatched eleven Stirlings to Arnhem without loss. Leading Air Fitter Frank Corbett, a member of the Royal Navy's Fleet Air Arm, was a part of one of several maintenance crews who were seconded to the RAF and were involved in airborne operations from Normandy onwards. On 21 September, his only air operation of the war, he went to Arnhem on a supply dropping mission in a Stirling piloted by Warrant Officer Parker RCAF as a supernumerary to aid the dispatcher in the rear fuselage. 'Before entering the Navy my early youth was taken up in building Hawker Hurricanes and Short Stirlings at the Austin Motor Works Shadow Factory at Longbridge, Birmingham from whence I came so I had an idea of the Stirling's robustness. They were built like a 'Brick Outhouse'. Their rate of climb and their speed were slow and their ceiling was low, but I knew that it could take a tremendous hammering; an admirable aeroplane for this job. I occupied the right hand seat in the cockpit and on the way over, kept thinking of our self-sealing fuel tanks each time we ran into light flak (remember, this was my first AIR operation). When near the area, the dispatcher was sufficiently organised for me to stay in the co-pilot's seat. From the air it was unforgettable. The 88mm on the ground seemed to be as thick as fleas on a dog's back. It was possible at our height to see Germans with lighter weapons aiming at us. Oh for a front gun turret then in the Stirling. The aircraft took a beating on the way in and out without getting a direct hit from anything big. One large piece of shrapnel came in through the nose, shaved the bomb aimer's helmet, came up between the captain and myself and crashed into the armour plating at the end of the navigator's table. Under such conditions, a low flying large aircraft was a sitting duck and it wasn't easy to locate a shifting drop zone on the ground, although everyone who could was looking. We did our very best and made the drop. To have attempted to go round a second time without a guaranteed result would have been suicide. But that scarred Stirling and a good driver brought us back.'[9]

In all, Stirling navigator, 'Ted' Wood on 570 Squadron flew four supply flights over Arnhem. He recalled: 'On the 19th we went with resupply - the usual twenty containers and two panniers. We dropped them on the same place that we had dropped the gliders the day before - it seemed alright again. We got a bit of flak, mainly after we'd dropped the supplies, because we were flying at 500 feet with bomb doors open and flap down throttle back at 140 mph. The fourth day we went and we led forty aircraft over France, this time, not over the North Sea. Over the battle zone you had to fly above 3,500 feet, because of your own troops and we met cloud. We stayed above the cloud and got higher up at the rendezvous for the start of the run-in, at about 6,500 feet above 10/10 cloud. We'd got to get down to 500 feet and make fairly quick decisions. I said to the old man that we'd better go underneath it - Holland is pretty flat and there are no large lumps sticking up - so we waggled our wings at the rest of the forty and stuck our nose down. We broke cloud at about 1,000 feet and I said to the old man that I didn't like flying at 1,000 under that lot - you were a sitting duck. I suggested we got down on the deck. The Dutch maps were very good, with every duck-pond and tree marked, so we went down to nought feet for this run-in. We climbed up to 500 feet as we crossed the Rhine. We were obviously the first in and when we arrived at the new dropping zone, it turned out to be a field the size of a football pitch, completely surrounded by woods. I could see all this, lying in the nose, ready to drop the containers. Now, because the blokes the day before had had some casualties over the dropping zone, we had agreed it would be suicide to pull up after you had dropped, because you had no speed and you were offering the whole of this damn great aircraft to a gunner. So we arranged that, as soon as the last container was away, we were going to go down. We'd slam open all four motors and go down on the treetops - you'd offer no target then.

'I was having a good look round as we were dropping the containers and I could see our blokes in one corner of this dropping zone, burning smoke flares for us. I could see a couple of jeeps with a red cross on them - but it was obvious by the flashes, that Jerry had got the other three sides. It was like someone kicking the side of the aircraft in with hob-nailed boots, they were so close. The old man was a lunatic pilot at the best of times - he was doing rate-four turns over the treetops in this damn great thing and I could have picked leaves.

'We were due to go again on the Friday, with a brand new aircraft because one of the flight commanders had borrowed our aircraft and pranged it. We were literally waiting to go when they cancelled it and said they were going to pull out what was left. Totting it up, we started the week with 34 aircraft and crews on the squadron and it had twelve new aircraft delivered. By Friday we hadn't twelve fit to fly.'

Flight Lieutenant 'Reg' Turner DFC had served on 120 Squadron in 1942-43 and on 15 February 1942 had made three attacks on surfaced U-boats, one of which, U-225, was credited as 'sunk' after he dropped six depth charges. Now on 299 Squadron, he had flown Stirling LJ971 to Arnhem on the 17th but he had to abort shortly after takeoff with outer engine problems. After casting his glider off over the airfield he had then landed safely and the glider was taken by another crew. His flight on the 21st was his third to Arnhem, this time at the controls of LK545 'T-Tommy' carrying twenty-four containers to be dropped near the Hartenstein Hotel. 'Our journey had been quiet until we crossed the Rhine over the DZ,' recalled Turner, 'when heavy, light and medium flak concentration opened up, followed by enemy fighters who were waiting outside the DZ area to catch who dodged to get in. We had no fighter cover, so enemy aircraft were able to attack in numbers, until air cover arrived later and the enemy dispersed. While over the DZ we were hit by flak and the tail caught fire, forcing Flying Officer Sutton DFM the rear gunner who was wounded to bail out, after attempts had been made to get him out. I continued course, but the fire got out of control, so I chose a position in or near our territory and crash landed. No-one was hurt and the secret equipment was destroyed.'

Over the DZ the two air dispatchers, Corporal Clemont Burton Sproston and Driver Brackman of 253 Airborne Divisional Composite Company RASC, 49 Air Despatch Group were given orders to despatch the load. Although the aircraft was well ablaze and the rear gunner's ammunition was exploding inside the fuselage, Sproston continued to despatch the load, which consisted of high explosives, at the right moment. It was entirely due to his coolness and courage in despatching this extremely dangerous load, that Turner was able to crash land it without loss of life.

Flight Sergeant Price, the navigator, Flight Sergeant Sedgwick the bomb aimer and Flying Officer Sutton were captured. Turner and Warrant Officer Bernard H. Harvey the flight engineer and the two dispatchers, helped by Dutch civilians and the Resistance evaded capture but en route to XXX Corps' headquarters that night they became embroiled in a ground battle as the party they were travelling with in convoy chanced upon by four Tiger tanks, which immediately engaged their vehicles. A number of British trucks were knocked out, but a small party from the group took up a position in a nearby house. Corporal Sproston took charge of a forward observation post and directed fire from a Bofors gun which succeeded in fending off the attack. For his actions this day Sproston was awarded a well-deserved Military Medal. Turner was awarded the Military Cross.[10]

'Our Squadrons were badly mauled this day,' wrote a New Zealand Dakota captain. 'As we sighted Arnhem some four engined Stirlings were just finishing their supply drop. All hell seemed to have been let loose. The sky was black with flak bursts over the army lads. As we approached, two Stirlings blew up with a terrific flash and the picture looked far from rosy. We were at 3,500 feet and had to get down to 1,200 feet before releasing the panniers at 110 mph. There seemed to be hundreds of gun flashes from the ground. To complicate things, the three aircraft in front were dropping higher than I was so that panniers dangling from parachutes were filling the air all around, a grave menace if a wing should foul them. Somehow we jockeyed across. As soon as the word was passed that the supplies were gone, I turned the wick up to full power and climbed faster than a lift taking evasive action all the time till the thumps, twangs and bursting shells were far behind.

'Like everyone else, I suppose, I made a hasty check of engine instruments. They seemed OK and I turned to watch the following aircraft go through. The CO had turned and run back across the dropping zone to rid the aircraft of a few baskets not dropped on the first run. As he crossed the river, I could see a pannier trailing from behind his tail. I turned to go and inspect when it suddenly broke away and fell to the ground but no parachute appeared. There was a dispatcher, RASC private, clinging to it as it went. His harness had been caught up and he had been dragged from the aircraft without his parachute pack. These RASC men did a grand job. Most of them had only had an hour or two in the air before being called upon for these supply operations.

'Our troubles were not yet over. A few minutes after leaving Arnhem dozens of Hun fighters appeared up to twenty at one time attacking a Dakota. Soon some Spitfires appeared and began to mix it but Dakota after Dakota was going down - my No. 2 in formation had not been able to keep station with me and was one of the first victims. When the air fighting started, I made myself scarce among fluffy cloud which half filled the sky at 6,000 feet. The transports struggled to out manoeuvre the fighters. One survived six attacks without any return fire before he crash-landed in flames. It was so hot inside that the pilot opened the hatch above his head, stood up in the cockpit and landed it leaning out the top.'

A total of 23 Stirlings and Dakotas (20% of the force) were unaccounted for; a further seven were damaged by fighters and 31 by flak which was more intense than ever along the route and in the target area. Only 7.4 per cent of the total number of tons of food and ammunition (including the wrong shells for the 75mm guns) dropped was collected by the beleaguered 1st Airborne Division at Oosterbeek (for, after the evening of the fifth day, that was what the airborne troops were). Just 41 out of 300 tons got through. 'It was bloody awful looking up', a soldier in the 3rd Battalion thought 'and seeing all that stuff dropping down. I thought to myself maybe there's a bottle of beer in that lot. God, I was thirsty!' Men risked their lives, crawling out into the open. Snipers were active, persistent and ubiquitous and all the roads were blocked by trunks and branches of trees, bricks and masonry strewn over their surface. Sometimes their brave attempts were for nothing. 'Bloody few rations there', Lieutenant Colonel Michael St. John Packe, in charge of the RASC elements in Oosterbeek, complained bitterly to Lieutenant Colonel Henry Preston, Brigadier Hicks' principal administrative officer, when he discovered that some that had got through was 'damn useless stuff' and that all the things the Division really needed had 'gone down the drain'. 'Do you know what these are full of?' he added, kicking viciously at some panniers against which Preston was leaning, 'Berets! Red, bloody berets! And that one, that's full of stationery!' And now when the men of the Division desperately needed food and ammunition and water - above all water - they got soap.

Sapper Arthur Ayers could not believe how the Dakotas and Stirlings stuck to their course as the black puffs of ack-ack shells exploded all around them. 'One aircraft, its starboard engine on fire, circled once before discharging its cargo of supplies. Then, as it started to gain altitude, the fire spread to the wing and it immediately lost height before spiralling into a wood. I wondered how many of those brave men would get safely back home to England.'[11]

Bob Leeder, a glider pilot, remembered the supply flights: 'It was a high point of each day. The planes were very low, 500 to 1,000 feet and sometimes lower and the flak bursts were thus very close to us and therefore very loud. Some of the planes were already hit when they came into sight, showing signs of smoke or even flames. Some came round twice. Once I saw a Dakota come round three times. When he came round the last time, the lower side of the fuselage was on fire, the fire spreading out to the wings with a lot of black smoke and the RASC man visible in the doorway still pushing out the panniers. There seemed to be absolute silence on that last run. The flak had stopped and we all came out of our trenches and stood gaping at this. One of my friends told me after the war that he had felt tears in his eyes and his companion was sobbing also.'[12]

Corporal Don Collins of the Royal Signals remembers what was probably the same Dakota: 'The whole of its under-part was ablaze. It passed by, flying in a steady line as though on a training run but gradually losing height. Framed in the open door was the dispatcher calmly pushing out the panniers of supplies. He must have known the plane was on fire, as the flames were enormous. It was an awesome and very moving sight. I felt a lump in my throat and was cursing the Germans and yet, at the same time, the courage of the pilot and the dispatcher made me feel proud to be British.'[13]

Ritter Fassbinder was a radio operator in General Bittrich's HQ and recalled: 'We had the English signal codes, their attack plan and English radio sets, so it was quite easy to find out what frequency they were transmitting on. Once we heard that the General issued instructions that we were to order certain supplies and food to be dropped onto the captured landing zones we had under our complete control. Our men were also told to stand on the edge of the drop zones and whatever smoke bombs the British used, they were to throw the same colour to confuse the pilots and it worked perfectly. We knew they would send resupply aircraft and although we would shoot many of them down, enough supplies would land for us to use. Some of our labour battalions, who were basically non-combatants and who'd been thrown in on the first day, were still fighting with old French weapons and soon we had enough brand new British ones with plenty of ammunition, care of the British aircraft. It seemed ironic that we would fight them with their own weapons, but we did. And the food - the luxuries, real coffee, chocolate and tins of meat we had never seen since the beginning of the war, as well as unheard of medical supplies and real cigarettes by the box load. If I remember rightly, they were called 'Woodbine' and 'Craven A'; I nearly choked to death when I first inhaled one. And best of all, there was nothing the English could do about it.'[14]

Henry Preston continued to watch the aircraft until only two Dakotas remained in sight. 'And from somewhere in both of them a slow flame started to curl, gradually enveloping each fuselage. Flying lower and lower they continued to drop their panniers whose parachutes showed for a moment, red and blue and yellow against the dark green of the trees. I could not get rid of the impression, which was strengthened by my being unable to hear their engines that this was no living scene I was watching but something out of a silent film. Soon they disappeared and for a short time there was a strange silence. Then the 88s, freed from the task of dealing with the aircraft, turned once again to us. The rain started again and the crowd in front of the hotel broke up. I exchanged a few words with Michael Packe, just setting out on his forlorn task of trying to locate the few panniers that had fallen within the perimeter. Then, carrying a useless Very pistol and an incongruously gay yellow handkerchief, I walked slowly back to the hotel, feeling more futile than I had done since the operation began.'

All of the 64 Stirlings dispatched by 38 Group in the first three RAF resupply waves reached Holland and 61 are believed to have accomplished their mission. However, the weather kept all but nineteen of their Spitfire escorts from leaving England and they did not catch up with the mission until after it had reached the Arnhem area. Although the 56th Fighter Group of Eighth Air Force sent 34 P-47s as area cover, they also arrived late.

This inadequate fighter protection gave the Luftwaffe its first good chance to attack an Allied airborne mission and it made the most of the occasion. One squadron of Focke-Wulfs swooping down out of the clouds shot down seven out of a sequence of ten Stirlings within a few moments. The Spitfires do not appear to have engaged the enemy. Some of their pilots sighted German aircraft but mistook them for P-51s on area cover until it was too late to catch them. Near Lochem about 1505 the 56th Group did intercept 22 or more German fighters (mostly Focke-Wulfs with square wingtips somewhat resembling P-51s) on their way back to Germany from the Arnhem area. The group claimed to have destroyed fifteen of them at a cost of two missing and one salvaged. Thus, although the raiders had done their mischief, they paid high for the opportunity.

Escort for the main troop carrier effort that day was also much curtailed because of weather. Five out of fifteen RAF fighter squadrons failed to leave England because of the overcast and the 118 ADGB fighters which did make sorties sighted only a few German aircraft, which made off as fast as they could. As for Eighth Air Force, it cancelled the missions of thirteen of its fifteen supporting groups. Thirty-six P-47s of the 353rd Fighter Group patrolled the Eindhoven-Arnhem area faithfully from 1610 to 1650. At 1630 about five miles southwest of Nijmegen it came upon approximately thirty German fighters of II and III./JG 26, some attacking C-47s while others acted as top cover. After a sharp clash in which the enemy displayed considerable skill the 353rd Group drove them off, claiming three FW 190s destroyed and one 'probable' and one damaged for the loss of one Thunderbolt. The 56th Fighter Group claimed fifteen fighters shot down and one damaged for the loss of one Thunderbolt.

The 53 Dakotas of 46 Group which flew the last wave of the RAF resupply lift suffered almost as severely as the Stirlings preceding them. They lost ten aircraft to flak and fighters. In all, out of 117 aircraft dispatched by 38 Group and 46 Group on the 21st, no fewer than sixteen Stirlings and fourteen Dakotas were lost and 38 were damaged, a disturbingly high proportion. Two other 'Daks' made emergency landings in Belgium.

Once again 1st Airborne Division had a 'Eureka' beacon functioning, at least some of the time, on the roof of its headquarters, but only a couple of navigators are known to have signalled it and neither got responses. The lack of use may be attributed to the pilots' growing familiarity with the route and to the relatively good flying conditions over Holland. Again panels, Very lights, smoke and an Aldis lamp were used to mark the drop point and once again the Very lights were by far the most effective with thirty pilots sighting them as compared to fourteen seeing panels and one seeing smoke. Although 91 crews reported successful drops and some others probably reached the drop point, the intense fire of the German forces surrounding 1st Airborne effectively disrupted the drop. Out of 271 tons of supplies parachuted, only about eleven tons or four percent was officially recovered. It is, however, likely that the starving and desperate troops picked up some food and ammunition which they did not declare or turn in.

Chapter 12

Thursday 21 September ('D+4')
The Polish Lift

We had trained hard in Scotland and were as good as any unit in the 1st Airborne Division. All we needed was to prove our worth and fight the Germans.

19-year old Antoni Szulakowski, a signalman (Lacznosciowiec) in the Anti-tank Airlanding Battery in the 4th Company, 2nd Battalion.

On Tuesday C-47 pilots like 2nd Lieutenant Eldon Sellers in the 309th Squadron at Spanhoe had been ready to drop the 1st Independent Polish Brigade south of the bridge at Arnhem. However the weather was too bad to take off, so the mission was called off for that day. All the men went back to the camp. Sellers found that the Polish were very eager to go and had a very difficult time dealing with the postponing of the mission and had heard about the Polish paratrooper that killed himself when he heard that the mission was called off for that day. 'On Wednesday it was the same story as the day before' wrote Sellers. 'We were once again all set and ready for takeoff but the weather remained bad. Thursday we were finally able to take off.' Antoni Szulakowski, born in the village of Sienkiewicze, close to the Soviet border, on 5 December 1924, summed up the feeling among the proud Poles. He was not afraid to die, as he simply had nothing to lose, nothing to go home to and no family. The Nazis had taken everything from Poland and he was proud to be fighting for his country - come what may.

The 314th Troop Carrier Group's two serials (A-86 with 27 aircraft and A-87 with 33 aircraft) had taken off from Saltby in single file between 1405 and 1413. The new tactics appeared to work, with just eleven aborts and three aborts respectively. But things had not gone smoothly at all. Weather conditions were so poor that the C-47s at first struggled to gain altitude and it become clear to those on the ground that, by the time the aircraft returned from the drop, landing conditions would be dangerous. Over the

276

first part of its route the mission remained close to 10,000 feet, but near the Belgian coast the clouds thinned and broke, enabling the 314th and 315th TCG formations to descend to the 1,500-foot level. One straggler, hit by flak near the mouth of the Scheldt, had to drop its troops near Ghent and limp home on one engine. The rest swung up the west side of the salient to the drop zone, a large area of open, ditched land northeast of the town of Driel on the south side of the Rhine opposite Heveadorp. No pathfinders had been sent to mark the zone, but the leaders found their way to it by good visual navigation, checked occasionally by 'Gee', which was functioning well and without much jamming.

At 1545 hours while crossing the Channel a flight leader in the 314th Group repeatedly received a message on the flight control frequency which he was unable to decode because the crews had been issued with the wrong codes and so it was left to the judgement of individual crews as to whether or not they were indeed being asked to abort. As a result of this confusion, forty-one aircraft, turned around but, due to the poor conditions, most put down at the first airfield they could find; one aircraft became so lost that it landed in Ireland. Eldon Sellers was one of the pilots who had to return early. 'We were supposed to join other planes and fall into the usual formation after takeoff, but we went into some thick clouds. It was almost like overcast. Our flight instruments started acting erratically. We were very lucky to get out of the weather without crashing and there was nothing else left to do then find the nearest airbase and land our plane.[1] I later heard that the other planes that had succeeded in delivering their paratroopers had had a hard time. That was the only mission in which guys that I knew were killed.'

The 1,003 Poles in the 73 aircraft in the 309th and 310th Squadrons in the 315th Group that had flown on arrived over their dropping zone south of the river just east of Driel between 1708 and 1715. The 359th Fighter Group from Eighth Air Force which was to escort the Polish paratroop mission managed to get twenty picked pilots into the air, but conditions were so bad that they had to be recalled beyond Eindhoven just before the troop carriers arrived. Luckily, no hostile fighters had spotted the C-47 serials but there was some ground fire along the way and much light flak and small arms fire near the drop zone. Several aircraft were hit and at least one very hard hit during the approach, but all managed to make their drops. The C-47 serials passed over the zone in sunshine and on target at altitudes between 700 and 850 feet. On the run-in, the 314th TCG could see the 315th Troop Carrier Group crossing the DZ from left to right. Their C-47s seemed to be taking a beating.

'So many were the guns and so incessant their firing that the little town reminded one flier of 'a pinball machine gone mad.' Aubrey Ross in the 310th Squadron confirmed as much: 'The drop zone was reached at 1700 hours and we encountered considerable flak and a number of airplanes were hit, but, in spite of the flak, all planes dropped their loads of Polish troopers. The heavily burdened Polish troops took longer to clear the airplanes than was estimated.' Normally, eighteen paratroopers could exit a C-47 in about eighteen seconds. The Polish troopers of this drop were encumbered with a heavy equipment bag that had to be pushed out the door ahead of each trooper resulting in an exit time of up to 45 seconds. Because normal procedure during the drop was to reduce power on the left engine in order to reduce the propwash on the troopers exiting the aircraft, the aircraft lost considerable altitude and closed the range of the German gunners.

'This prevented the formation from turning as soon as planned' continues Aubrey Ross 'and as a result, when we did complete our turn, we were over the town of Elst and severe flak. As usual, we dived to get as close to the ground as possible to avoid the German flak. Five airplanes were shot down and several others landed at nearby air strips because of severe damage. A friend and fellow pilot of mine from the 310th, Lieutenant Kenneth Wakley was shot down in plane 612. Lieutenant Bruce Borth, co-pilot, Lieutenant M. C. Beerman, navigator, Tech Sergeant Magnus, crew chief and Staff Sergeant Carl Javorsky, radio operator, were killed as well as Lieutenant Wakely. Approaching the DZ, another 310th pilot and friend, Lieutenant Cecil Dawkins, was wounded in the face and head when his plane took two flak bursts. With one of the fuel tanks in port wing burning and flames sweeping down the left side of the fuselage, Lieutenant Dawkins moved his plane out of formation, dropped his troops and then ordered his crew to bail out. Lieutenant Cleon 'Moose' Worley, one of my roommates, was flying co-pilot on this mission with Dawkins. At the last minute the regular co-pilot became ill, so 'Moose' volunteered to go in his place. 'Moose' was an old timer having come up with the group of us from Italy and had been a first pilot and flight leader for some time, so it was most unusual for him to be a co-pilot. 'Moose' along with Lieutenant J. R. Wilson, navigator, Staff Sergeant W. O. White, crew chief and Staff Sergeant J. Ludwig landed safely and made their escape with the assistance of the Dutch civilians. None of these crew members ever saw Lieutenant Dawkins leave the stricken aircraft and everybody assumed that he had died when the airplane crashed.'[2]

As the Poles jumped into battle for the first time the mood of the paratroopers was serious, but they were happy that the waiting was over and that finally, they were to meet the Germans in combat. Kazimerz Szmid recalled: 'It wasn't until we were on the aircraft that we were informed that our drop-zone had been changed and we were to land at the village of Driel. As we approached the target we flew through heavy barrages of flak, which threw our aircraft about. Green light, jump and immediately into a hail of bullets by Germans on the ground who had been forewarned of our approach. I landed luckily unhurt, but the rest of the 1st Battalion to which I belonged had been recalled back to England, which we didn't know about until later. In the fluid situation we were assigned to the 3rd Battalion.'[3]

Antoni Szulakowski went into action when Dakota 'Chalk 99' dropped its stick of paratroopers just after 1700 over Driel on the southern side of the Lower Rhine (DZ 'K'). 'When it came to the parachute drop, it happened too quickly for me to really grasp what was going on. The dispatcher pointed at the red light and we were all ready to go. The green light came on and our lieutenant was out the door followed by our sergeant and we quickly followed them. Even with all the weight we carried we couldn't get out fast enough as we had been waiting for so long to get to grips with the enemy. In spite of the noise of the aircraft and the Nazi guns I was aware of how loud and how fast my heart was beating. My parachute opened and I prayed I would not get killed in the air as I desperately wanted to kill some Nazis first. The wind pressed hard against my face until my chute opened. As I looked down, past my legs and kitbag (attached to my ankle) I could see the tracer bullets coming upwards and flak exploding in the air, which alerted me to the fact that we had been dropped onto the Nazi positions. Not far away from me I saw someone's parachute collapse as the tracer ripped through it - what a way to die, having done all this training and now not to come to grips with the Nazis. My thoughts went from 'Please, chute open' to 'Please, let me land safely', to 'Please, let me find cover'. Some of my colleagues prayed during their descent, but my head was just full of what needed to be done and his priority was to find a supply canister with a British 68P radio set. (This set was carried as a heavy back-pack and only used for short-range communication up to ten miles).'[4]

The aircraft took evasive action from the fire coming up at them and in so doing hurled the Polish paratroopers about the cabin and delayed their jump. As the Poles descended they were fired at by German troops on the ground, resulting in five men killed and twenty-five wounded. Despite this, the drop had been successful, if a little untidy and the Brigade faced no serious opposition in the immediate area.

The 21st of September would be a day long-remembered by the 310th Squadron, which had lost five C-47s and eleven men dead or missing and at least ten wounded or injured but all of the paratroopers aboard were able to jump before they crashed. Those in the 310th who could were instructed to return to Spanhoe but because of damage, darkness and thickening fog only two of the Squadron's C-47s returned to the base: Lieutenant Sutton made his drop and came back; Lieutenant Berman became separated from the formation due to weather, flew alone and ended up over the Ruhr, with intense fire coming up at him before he turned back. Some pilots landing at Bradwell had to have the aid of a FIDO fog dispersal unit. Lieutenant Colonel Hamby's ship had 150 holes in it but despite the damage he somehow got it down at Brussels safely. As Hamby had started a left turn to escape the DZ, his aircraft took three hits from 20mm fire; the first round hitting the left engine stopping it from hitting him, the second round impacting the fuselage and the third round exploding inside the cargo compartment wrecking his rudder controls and seriously wounding Sergeant Combetty his crew chief who was retrieving the static lines and wounding Sergeant Harrod, his radio operator also. Hamby, who had his rudder controls shot away, was hit in the chest by shell fragments. He felt certain that the flak vest he was wearing saved his life. Hamby's crew were joined at Brussels by other aircraft, having fired a red flare as they approached to signify wounded on board. The first aircraft landed at 1350 hours as the long train of 'Skytrains' circled overhead waiting their turn. At one time there were more than 100 C-47s on the field, all being co-ordinated by one C-47 on the ground. At 1650 hours, the last of the C-47s took off from the bases in Belgium, many loaded with wounded and glider personnel who had been stranded since the initial assaults. It was the most dangerous re-supply mission ever undertaken by air to the front battle lines. German fire had damaged 33 aircraft, fourteen of them so severely that they had to be turned over to service groups for repair. The night of the 21st was a wretched one for those of the men who had to stay at Spanhoe: with no word from so many planes, with the story of Lieutenant Sutton about the extreme difficulty of the operation and the intense enemy reaction and the report of planes going down in flames, that was not a pleasant evening. The next day, however, some good news came through. Colonel Hamby returned in another plane and several others also returned. Four planes were still unreported, however, on the 22nd. All of the aircraft which returned had much flak damage and many holes.

'Lieutenant 'Moose' Worley, Lieutenant Wilson, Sergeants, White and Ludwig, were back at Spanhoe in just a few days after they bailed out', recalled Aubrey Ross. 'They had been walking along a canal when they met a Dutch farmer carrying a machine gun walking behind a German Soldier who had surrendered. The Dutch farmer handed the weapon to 'Moose' and wanted him to take charge of the prisoner. They were all taken to a member of the underground who made arrangements for them to be escorted to British-American lines. Soon after they were flown back to England to join their unit. They were debriefed and sent home to the states in a matter of a few days, because it was a policy to transfer people who had been shot down and escaped through the underground to another theatre. This was done to protect members of the underground because if an escapee fell into the enemy hands, they might be made to tell what he knew about the underground. Another 310th plane piloted by Lieutenant Jacob Boon was struck by enemy fire after the Polish jumped and later crashed in the drop area. The co-pilot, crew chief and radio operator were all wounded but Lieutenant Boon was able to crash land and get all of them out before the plane exploded. For this heroic act he was awarded the Silver Star. Lieutenant O. J. Smith, 310th Squadron, had his crew chief, Corporal Doan and radio operator Sergeant James wounded and bleeding profusely, so he sat down at Eindhoven to get immediate medical attention for them. This aircraft had a damaged rudder control and a total of 600 holes were counted. Captain F. K. Stephenson's plane was riddled by flak and was burning as he skilfully crashed landed in a wooded area. Stephenson, along with his 309th crew of Lieutenant Garber, Lieutenant Arnold, Tech Sergeant Berotti and Staff Sergeant Maxwell, escaped serious injury.'

Another 309th C-47, piloted by 1st Lieutenants' Cecil W. Biggs of Teague, Texas and William L. Pearce of San Antonio and crewed by 2nd Lieutenant Thomas R. Yenner, navigator, of Kingston, Pa; Tech Sergeant Russell W. Abendschoen, crew chief, of York, Pa and Staff Sergeant George G. Herbst, radio operator, of Brooklyn, New York burst into flames when hit by flak and exploded as it crashed into the ground near Elst. All were killed. The Germans opened the dykes in the region where the plane crashed and flooded the area before any remains could be recovered. Born in Freestone, Texas on 13 June 1917, Biggs had a wife, Mary Nan and an 18 month-old son 'Bill'. An engineering student at Texas Tech University when he enlisted in the USAAC in 1941, being an only son he had to receive his parent's permission to enlist in the military. His nickname was 'Ace.' He was very smart. He never opened a book to study, but he always managed to make straight A's.[5]

Aubrey Ross adds: 'A 43rd Squadron C-47, piloted by Lieutenant Cook received several hits while returning along the Brussels corridor. He lost all hydraulic pressure and most of his fuel, so he made an emergency landing at one of the Brussels airports. He narrowly missed crashing into several parked airplanes and finally came to rest against a hangar. The entire crew escaped uninjured.

'I was lucky again, no serious hits to my airplane. There were a lot of empty beds in the quarters at Spanhoe that night. We would wait a while hoping for some good news before we packed and stored their personnel belongings. This was a very sad thing that we had to do from time to time. Worse were the letters that the chaplain and squadron commander had to write to the families. There were only three of us in the room now, my good friends Terry Colwell, Jason Rawls and myself.'

For his action in leading the serial into the drop, Lieutenant Colonel Henry G. Hamby was presented the Polish Cross of Valour by the Polish Government in Exile. Faced with miserable weather conditions at the altitudes considered best for paradrops he had led his serial after takeoff up to 10,000 feet and then went over to Holland for the drop, letting down over France and finally getting into the DZ [Nijmegen] and making a successful drop. The troop carriers had delivered 132 jeeps, 73 jeep quarter ton trailers, 31 motorcycles, 3,374 gallons of gasoline, 38,700 lbs of ammunition and 60,730 lbs of rations. In all, 657,995 lbs of combat equipment and 882 fighting men were unloaded on a field 1,000 by 1,400 yards.

In Holland meanwhile, to the great dismay of Major General Sosabowski almost one third of the Brigade's strength was missing. The five hundred Polish paratroopers that had returned to England would endure a further delay of 48 hours before, at last, they were dropped near Grave, deep into the 82nd Airborne Division's area, on 23 September; the drop zones closer to the Rhine being considered too hazardous at this time. Of the Polish paratroopers who set off on the mission on the 21st only 998 men and 69 tons of supplies from the 100 tons that had been loaded were dropped in the vicinity of the prescribed zone. About 750 Polish paratroops, three-quarters those who had been dropped, were able to assemble that evening. Statistically speaking the mission was only about fifty percent effective but although Arnhem Bridge could not be taken, the 1st Polish Independent Parachute Brigade did manage to send some of their number across the river to reinforce the British paratroopers trapped in Oosterbeek and secure a corridor for their eventual evacuation. In terms of difficulties and hazards overcome the drop on the 21st was a brilliant performance. Major General Sosabowski wrote 'I cannot praise too much the perfect dropping, which in difficult weather condition; and in spite of strong enemy anti-aircraft fire over the DZ was equal to the best dropping during any exercise this Brigade Group has ever had.'

Chapter 13

'D+6' Saturday 23 September

We went to our Nissen huts where a fire was burning; blankets and sheets had been made up into comfortable looking beds. There were only two of us alone in a hut that held twenty-six beds. It was too much. Without a word, we dumped our kit and rifle on the bed and left.

British glider pilot 'Andy' Andrews.

Bad weather made regular air reconnaissance over the Arnhem Bridge impossible, so on Friday, 22nd September three Mosquitoes in the 25th Bomb Group at RAF Watton were dispatched on 'Bluestocking' missions. Lieutenant Robert P. 'Paddy' Walker's navigator, Roy C. Conyers, recalled: 'We were to dip as low as possible to try to establish by visual observation who controlled the bridge, the Germans or the British. 1 thought that this regularity was crazy and mentioned it to Edwin R. Cerrutti, 654th navigator. His only comment was that the German Command wouldn't believe that we were that stupid.' As they flew over the north end of the bridge just below the fog, at less than 500 feet, 'Paddy' Walker and Roy Conyers could see Germans running for their anti-aircraft guns. The bridge was in German hands. 'Ground fire from both ends of the bridge began almost immediately' Walker remembers. 'This continued as we flew over and past the other end, on towards the coast. Tracer fire could be seen coming up around us and the plane was hit by 20mm or .50 calibre rounds that disintegrated the left wing drop tank. I immediately punched off both tanks. The right engine was soon in flames. I feathered the propeller and shut off fuel to that engine. The fire went out, but the engine was inoperative. I was flying as low and as fast as possible to get out of range and made for the coast but soon ran into anti-aircraft fire from the coastal batteries. We were trying to get out of range of their guns while staying near sea level. I remember the water spouts from rounds hitting the sea around us. However, we were not hit. After we got out of range of the shore batteries I climbed up into the weather, still on one engine, to gain enough altitude to make an emergency Mayday radio call, to get a 'steer' to the nearest base where the weather was suitable to land. All England was socked in. There was no way to reach Manston, our emergency base near Dover. We steered to Bournemouth. My Mayday call was answered by the sweetest girl's British accent - 'Tommy' Settle, a beautiful blonde WAAF at Tangmere. During the days that it took to repair the plane she and I became better acquainted.' Upon returning from this flight Roy Conyers learned that his brother-in-law, Willard Hesketh was killed during 'Market-Garden'. Hesketh was flying a C-47 pulling a glider loaded with paratroopers in the 101st Airborne when hit by German anti-aircraft fire.[1]

The follow-on drop scheduled for the Polish Brigade on the 22nd was grounded again due to bad weather. After waiting until midday, Airborne Army cancelled all its missions. Fog had been widespread over England and the Low Countries throughout the morning and was replaced in the afternoon by stratus with ceilings about 1,000 feet and in places as low as 300 feet. In the course of the afternoon rain spreading over England from the west lowered the ceiling to between 500 and 1,000 feet and reduced visibility to between 1,000 and 2,000 yards. Although 38 Group stated in its report that resupply missions could have been flown, the advancing disturbance could have made the return to base very hazardous and this risk may have been the decisive consideration. The Eighth Air Force did dispatch two groups of P-47s to patrol the Arnhem area. They flew 77 uneventful sorties and returned safely.

The renewed activity of the Allied air forces was a bright feature of 'D+6' on Saturday 23 September when the second Polish drop was launched. A resupply drop to 1st Airborne would be made at 1400 by 123 Stirlings and Dakotas of 38 and 46 Groups, flying at 2,500 feet. After reconnaissance by weather aircraft on the morning of the 23rd, all arrival times were postponed two hours to give the weather on the continent more time to clear after the cold front passed.

In England Saturday was fair, the clouds high and broken and only a few patches of light rain marred the prospect. Fog and overcast lingered over the Low Countries during the morning but were swept away early in the afternoon by a cold front, which left behind it clearing skies and brisk westerly winds. At 1421 hours Colonel 'Fred' Gray led his P-47s off from Duxford to Holland to carry out flak suppression in the RAF resupply drop-zone although unbeknown to the Allied Commander the British troops had withdrawn some time previously. Circling Arnhem, the Thunderbolts approached from the south and turned 90° west to Kasteel where they were enveloped by 20-40mm light flak from along nearby hedgerows and woods north of the town. Colonel Gray took a squadron and temporarily silenced these guns while enemy guns in a church south of the woods were put out of action by other P-47s. Just west of Heteren, 2nd Lieutenant Dunstan D. Hartley, Gray's wingman, received a direct hit and he went straight into the ground. Another formation of C-47s approached the drop zone from the south at extremely low altitude to drop their supplies. Three were shot down by some of the guns, which were soon silenced again by the Thunderbolts. The enemy flak emplacements were very well hidden and the Germans held their fire until the P-47s had passed and were banking away. It was only when they began firing again that the Thunderbolt pilots knew where they were and could attack them again. More and more C-47s and Stirlings appeared at very low level and in areas which had been flak suppressed they were able to drop their supplies without drawing fire but in an area where there was no flak suppression, four Stirlings were shot down in flames. Thirteen of the Thunderbolts returned to Duxford showing signs of battle damage.

At 1600 the RAF mounted its usual gallant attempts by the re-supply crews to get supplies into the perimeter as the flak took a further heavy toll. The 73 Stirlings and fifty Dakotas dispatched to bring supplies to 1st Airborne had a most difficult mission. The area still held by British troops had shrunk to 1,000 yards in diameter and was ringed with enemy guns. The drop point was even harder to locate than before. The Eureka was not working because the batteries were dead and the Germans had captured the pathfinders' reserve stock. Parties attempting to use visual signals were harassed by snipers, by mortars and twice by strafing. Moreover; the Germans seem to have used bogus signals to mislead the pilots. Very lights were seen by 22 crews and other signals by thirteen, but only a handful dropped their loads within the British lines. Even well-placed bundles were hard to retrieve, since much of the terrain still held by the British was under observed fire and hardly any vehicles were left for supply details to use. No doubt some were recovered by individuals and small units and used on the spot without any accounting. Even if we assume arbitrarily that four times as much was picked up as was ever reported, the amount reaching the troops was still less than 10 percent of what was sent. There was no alternative. Landing gliders in such a situation was out of the question.

Two aircraft aborted. Six were shot down, all apparently in or near the drop area and 63 were damaged. Had not the 78th Fighter Group been on hand to keep down the fire the toll would have been much larger.

Air Vice-Marshal Hollinghurst, who was controlling these operations from Eastcote, had naturally been concerned about the high cost to his squadrons. Earlier in the week, the extent of the losses and the uncertainty about the usefulness of the dropping points had prompted Air Commodore L. Darvall, commanding 46 Group, to inspect at first hand the tactical situation as it affected re-supply. The upshot of this visit was that one of the supply squadrons was moved from England to an airfield near Brussels on this Saturday.[2] On this Saturday afternoon only a minute proportion of the panniers came our way and the food contents were taken to the wounded.

'Rations as such', Major H. S. Cousens wrote afterwards, 'were non-existent and men were living on potatoes and any other food they could find.' They looked at each other with red-rimmed, bloodshot eyes asking 'what the hell had happened to the 2nd bloody Army and what the devil the RAF thought they were at'. No one blamed the transport crews whose bravery was evident to all. 'The cold-blooded pluck of the pilots was quite incredible', a soldier who watched them thought. They came on, in their lumbering four-engine machines, at 1,500 feet, searching for our position. The ack-ack was such as I have only heard during the worst raids on London but concentrated on one small area. The German gunners were firing at point-blank range and the supply planes were more or less sitting targets...It made you feel terribly small, frightened and insignificant... One could do nothing but stare awe-inspired at the inferno above...The Americans were included in our boundless admiration, for they came along in their unarmed, slow, twin-engined Dakotas as regularly as clock-work... Hardly any of their supplies reached us.' Less than one-seventh of the total tonnage dropped during the operation was collected by the Division and the sight of the Stirlings and Dakotas flying unhesitatingly into the German barrage where sometimes, although hit and on fire, they continued to circle above the German lines while the Royal Army Service Corps dispatchers threw out the supplies before the aircraft crashed into the earth, was so moving that for many of those who witnessed it no more poignant memory of Arnhem remains.

Glider pilot, Louis Hagen, a Jew born in Germany, recalled: 'That afternoon, another fleet of supply planes came over to drop urgently needed ammo and food. The cold-blooded pluck and heroism of the pilots was quite incredible. They came in in their lumbering four-engined machines at 1,500 feet, searching for our position. The ack-ack was such as I have only heard during the worst raids on London, but concentrated on one small area. The German gunners were firing at point blank range and the supply planes were more or less sitting targets. The rattle of machine guns from the scores of planes, the heavy ack-ack batteries all round us, the sky filled with flashes and puffs of exploding shells, burning planes diving towards the ground and hundreds and hundreds of red, white, yellow and blue supply parachutes dropping all in this very small area, looked more like an overcrowded and crazy illustration to a child's book. This was war on such a concentrated scale that it made you feel terribly small, frightened and insignificant: something like an ant menaced by a steam roller. All activity on the ground seemed to be suspended and forgotten on both sides. One could do nothing but stare awe-inspired at the inferno above. How those pilots could have gone into it with their eyes open is beyond my imagination. Later on, when I got back to the 'drome, I heard something of what they had felt. And I was told of their tremendous losses.

'When we saw the supply planes coming in over our position, we knew nothing of the hell they had been through already; many of them had failed to get this far. They had first had to deal with great packs of Focke Wulfs and in one of the trips; they crossed into Holland without any fighter support as the weather did not permit it. When they met the Focke Wulfs, they had very little chance to defend themselves. The Americans were included in our boundless admiration, for they came along in their unarmed, slow, twin-engined Dakotas as regularly as clock-work. The greatest tragedy of all, I think, is that hardly any of these supplies reached us. It makes the heroism of the crews of the planes even more incredible when one realises that they must have known that there was very little chance of their sacrifice being of any use to us.'[3]

Despite mounting casualties and an almost impossible task, the supply aircraft continued their gallant if fruitless efforts. Altogether eight supply lifts were flown in circumstances which became worse and worse. 190 Squadron could only muster seven Stirlings on the 23rd and they dropped 168 containers and twenty-eight panniers before all returned safely.[4] 233 Squadron were able to muster seventeen Dakotas. On 271 Squadron Dakotas managed to drop 122 panniers and thirty-four boxes of medical supplies. Flight Lieutenant Alastair Mackie DFC on 233 Squadron at Blakehill Farm flying Dakota KG433 described the DZ as having 'a weirdly festive air, with puffs of sand coloured smoke and coloured Very pistol rounds everywhere.' With the air thick with shells he saw aircraft being destroyed. 'Paddy', one of his air dispatchers had trouble getting the panniers away because of the evasive action his pilot was taking and it took three runs before all the panniers were away. Mackie, who on 'D-Day' 5/6

June 1944 had made three runs over the DZ due to the paratroopers being delayed and the following day had re-supplied troops on the beachhead, in all flying eighty-seven operations, was awarded a bar to his DFC.

Warrant Officer Knivett Garton Cranefield, always known as 'Ken' piloting FZ692 *Kwicherbichen* was hit by bullets in the knee and thigh and there was a hole in the starboard wing of his aircraft two feet in diameter removing part of the aileron, making the Dakota difficult to control. Born in Ealing in May 1922 he enlisted in the RAF in February 1941 and trained as a pilot in the USA. After completing his training on Vickers Wellingtons in the UK, he ferried one of the twin-engine bombers to North Africa, being intercepted en route by three long-range Luftwaffe fighters, which fortunately he managed to evade. On his return to Britain he converted to the Dakota and joined 233 Squadron at Blakehill Farm and flew on the Normandy invasion on 5/6 June and in the period following the 'D-Day' landings made numerous flights transporting military supplies and men into the Advanced Landing Grounds hastily constructed in France. On 17 September Cranefield was the captain of one of 22 Dakotas on 233 Squadron that towed Horsa gliders to Arnhem when all but one of the gliders arrived safely on LZ 'S'. Despite his severe injuries on 23 September he carried on to the DZ where intense flak was experienced on the run in. Ken later recalled that it 'sounded like peanuts raking the length of the fuselage'. Then his wireless operator shouted over the intercom: 'Skipper', the starboard wing is on fire'. It was then that he was wounded again. Despite this he was able to drop his panniers before handing over to his second pilot, Flight Sergeant Barry Stapleford RNZAF, who flew the aircraft back. Cranefield's leg was bleeding badly and was tended by a crew member who used a length of microphone flex as a tourniquet to stem the blood loss. The cockpit being full of burning cordite Ken managed to stay awake, as Stapleford, who had not completed his training on Dakotas, made a superb landing at Blakehill Farm. On 4 October Cranefield was awarded an immediate DFC, the citation stating that he 'proved himself to be a courageous and resolute captain, setting a very fine example'. Ken remained in hospital for many weeks; his wounds so serious that he was unable to return to flying duties. In fact he received treatment for the next ten years. Whilst in hospital he met an RAF nursing sister, Marjorie, who he married in 1945.[5]

Flying Officer Samuel Finlay RCAF of Toronto on 48 Squadron piloting Dakota KG404 dropped his panniers from 800 feet, although there was a considerable amount of gun fire over the DZ he was untouched, but as he turned he saw the first fighters coming from the north of Eindhoven.

His dispatchers had already told him they had seen two Dakotas shot down. Flight Sergeant Roy L. T. Gray went into the astrodome and saw no less than six fighters 5,000 yards behind the Dakota. On hearing this Finlay dived into the cloud and Pilot Officer Rice, the wireless operator, took over in the astrodome. He saw three Dakotas, each with an engine on fire and about eight fighters milling around for the kill. Two broke away to attack KG404 which was then 4,000 to 5,000 yards ahead and 2,000 feet below them. One flew off but the second came into the attack from the port quarter and began to close in. Finlay was now taking instruction from Rice and taking evasive action to avoid the fighter's fire with hits registered on the lower starboard side of the fuselage. The auxiliary tank caught fire as a result and the starboard wing and whole of the fuselage aft of the cockpit was on fire. The starboard motor was put out of action and the port motor showing signs that it was about to stop. Finlay gave the order to the air dispatchers of 223 Company to bail out but because the fire was too much for them they had already bailed out. They were picked up by the 7th British Field Dressing Station. One of them, Corporal Matthews, had been wounded in the fighter attack. Driver Backler of 223 Airborne Company tried to get to the door to jump but could not get the door open because the aircraft rubber dinghy was burning in the doorway, so he did the only thing open to him by rolling out on the roller runway which was used to roll the supplies out of a Dakota. He then went out head first and fell several hundred feet before pulling the rip cord, after making a good landing he was surrounded by Belgium's who seemed pleased to see him. The crew then went to their crash positions, Flight Sergeant Gray behind the bulkhead at the rear of the navigator's department and Pilot Officer Rice braced himself against the armour plating to the rear of the pilot's seat, Finlay and the second pilot, Pilot Officer W. J. Walsh stayed in their seats. At 1,000 feet with smoke in the cabin and their vision obscured for some seconds, the aircraft was set to crash land in a field near Helmond but within 500 yards of the touchdown and just as the vision in the cabin cleared, a fair sized tree was seen ahead where they were going to land. They hit the tall tree and the nose of the aircraft caved in, the windscreen shattered and one large branch pierced the cockpit forcing Finlay's rudder pedals back to his seat spraining both his ankles very badly.

The Dakota came to rest in a turnip field with most of the aircraft on fire and they escaped through the upper emergency hatch and the rear door, no knowing that the air dispatchers had already gone. Walsh went back in to call them but the intense heat drove him back out. They were picked up by the 58 Light Anti-Aircraft Regiment of the 11th Armoured Division and given first aid for their injuries and then were handed over to the 7th Field Dressing Station where they met up with Corporal Matthews and the other three air dispatchers. He was treated as an air evacuation casualty and the others transported to B56 where they were flown back to Down Ampney by Senior Lieutenant Wheatley-Smith on 48 Squadron. On 18 December Samuel Finlay was awarded the DFC.

Dakota KG370 on 48 Squadron flown by 26 year-old Pilot Officer Walter Pring known as 'Ralph' was last seen with the whole underside on fire and a dispatcher still pushing out the panniers after being hit by light flak. One of the dispatchers, Lance Corporal F. W. R. Simpson, was wounded and died later of his wounds. Drivers Ben Hastings and Alexander Dunford were taken prisoner. When Durnford bailed out his parachute caught fire and instinctively he put his hands up to protect his face receiving severe burns to both. Hastings was being machine-gunned as he left the aircraft and although he got down safely he was so badly wounded he could not move. Pring was hit by bullets as he tried to crash land the aircraft. Although in great pain he made a perfect landing at Rosande Polder between the River Rhine and Bencdendorpsweg near to a railway bridge before he died. In so doing he saved the lives of some of those aboard the aircraft. Flight Sergeant Derek Gleave jumped out at the front of the aircraft and hit the ground hard.

He later recalled: 'There were flames in the cockpit and I was burnt on the hands and face. The pilot was absolutely marvellous. He saw this field and said, 'I'm going to land there.' He must have been burned as well. I was struggling to open the escape hatch, which was right above me. I got it open all right but that caused a further rush of fire through the cockpit area, although we were nearly on the ground by then. That's where it becomes very vague in my mind, but Ralph must have made a very smooth landing.

'I was the first out and the wireless operator and the second pilot followed me. As far as I know, the pilot never got out; he may have been wounded by the flak. The three of us moved away from the aircraft because it was burning fiercely, but some Germans opened fire on us. All three of us were hit. Springsteele, the wireless operator, was killed at once; I was hit by two bullets in the abdomen and Colman was hit several times. He told me to wave something white, but I only had a blue RAF handkerchief.

'Some German medics eventually came up. The other Germans were still firing at someone and the medics got annoyed with them and shouted at them to stop. Colman and I were taken by ambulance to St Elizabeth Hospital. Colman was still quite coherent, despite all his bullet wounds. A German surgeon operated on me and removed the bullets and I was put in the basement with the airborne casualties. There were some terrible cases there - men shouting that they wanted to die, etc. - it was terrible. I asked about Colman, but Father Egan, a Catholic padre, told me that he was dead. There was a brigadier in the next bed to me later, without his rank badges; the medics were hoping to get him away to prevent a high-ranking officer becoming a prisoner.'[6]

Gleave then heard Pilot Officer 'Jim' Springsteele RCAF and nineteen year old Pilot Officer Henry Coleman RCAF shouting to him to get away from the aircraft, so he got up and ran taking cover so as not to be hit. Then SS troops started sniping killing Springsteele instantly and badly wounding Henry Coleman. With two bullets in his stomach Coleman was taken to hospital but died on the operating table on 24 September. Derek Gleave was taken prisoner. Driver W. T. Crossley was still in the aircraft when it crashed and was killed by a sniper.

On 48 Squadron Warrant Officer S. McLaughlin piloting Dakota KG321 dropped thirteen panniers and medical supplies to DZ 'V before flak hit the nacelle of the port engine. When the navigator went back to examine the damage he found oil gushing out. The oil pressure gauge registered zero so McLaughlin decided to make for the nearest aerodrome, which was Eindhoven. He made a tight circuit at 500 feet and had intended a crash-landing but at the last moment, when 25 feet from touchdown, he decided to lower the undercarriage and although it was not fully extended he made a safe landing. McLaughlin, Pilot Officer L. T. Bentley the second pilot, Flying Officer E. S. Clark and Pilot Officer S. Melidones spent the night in the officer's mess at Eindhoven and the next morning joined a convoy going to Brussels, from there they and the four air dispatchers of 253 Company were flown to Down Ampney.

Dakota KG391 on 48 Squadron flown by Warrant Officer F. F. Felton was hit by flak in the tail just after dropping panniers on the DZ. There was a blinding flash, the fuselage became full of smoke and the aircraft went out of control. Felton had no rudder control or elevator trim in one direction, the aircraft climbed quickly but after Felton reduced the boost he exerted considerable pressure on the stick and the aircraft assumed a more or less level flying altitude at about 110 mph. The dispatchers were moved forward as far as possible to help to keep the nose up. Felton decided to make for B56. Despite light and heavy flak on route, the wireless operator contacted flying control and when at 500 feet was given permission to crash-land. On impact with the ground the port propeller sliced into the fuselage and the starboard prop cut a hole in the starboard wing.

Flying Officer Martin MacKay, whose Dakota had been hit on the 20th was hit again on the 23rd when the fuselage was severely damaged whilst over the DZ. One dispatcher was wounded and was unable get his entire load away on the first run so MacKay went around again organising his crew to help with the despatching. He was awarded the DFC.

Two Dakotas and eight Stirlings were lost on 23 September. 'On D+6 we guessed that things were desperate' reported the rear gunner of a Stirling, 'for we had been given a new dropping zone very much smaller in size and ringed by the enemy. All was plain sailing until we reached the Neder Rijn where we encountered very heavy fire. The Stirling bounced about all over the place... We decided we should drop immediately, then turn to port and go down low. This we did, descending to 300 feet and I could see everything very clearly. There were men shooting at us with rifles and light machine-guns and Bofors on lorries. I fired one long burst into a lorry in which I could see German soldiers; their heads tilted back looking at us. At that moment my turret jammed and I got a bullet through the shoulder'. The Stirling was riddled but could still fly and it landed safely at Harwell, two of its engines seizing as it touched down.[7]

The Stirling flown by Squadron Leader Richard 'Dickie' Bunker DFC*, a flight commander on 620 Squadron in the second stream was hit by flak which knocked out one engine. When the leading aircraft was forced to land and realising the danger of the stream splitting up, Bunker took over the lead and led the stream into the dropping zone despite the damage to his own aircraft. He was awarded the DSO. He had joined the RAF in 1938 and joined 83 Squadron at RAF Scampton in 1939 at the same time as Wing Commander Guy Gibson vc who led the famous Dam Buster raid in May 1943. 'Dickie' Bunker later joined 9 Squadron flying Lancasters as a flight commander and was awarded a second bar to his DFC. In June 1944 he joined 620 Squadron and in October 1944 became the commanding officer of 190 Squadron. In April 1945 he had gone to Brussels to take petrol for the advancing army, he brought back prisoners of war to RAF Odiham then took off to return to RAF Great Dunmow with a flat rear tyre. When he got off the ground the tail unit caught fire and the rear turret fell away from the aircraft. It was only as a result of the bravery and skill of 'Dickie' Bunker that they did not crash on to the village of Windlesham. He turned the stricken Stirling away from the village and crashed in a field 400 yards away. Everyone on board was killed.

On 22 September a new crew skippered by Flying Officer Clinton M. Beck had reported to 570 Squadron. They included four members of the RCAF.

On Saturday they were thrown into the cauldron, flying their first and last operation of the war when four of the fourteen Stirlings on the Squadron were lost. Fatalities were suffered on three of the four Stirlings shot down; in total; fifteen aircrew and four RASC dispatchers were killed, with only three crew and two dispatchers escaping from these aircraft. Beck's Stirling (LJ991) was hit by flak over the drop zone and set on fire but he managed to reach friendly territory. One crewman and an RASC dispatcher bailed out safely before low altitude ruled out further escapes. Beck pulled up sharply to avoid hitting a Dutch farm and then crashed heavily at Heteren. The impact threw him clear and he survived with shrapnel wounds in one leg and two fractures in the other. Five others - three of them RCAF - died in the wreckage. LJ996 flown by Pilot Officer F. B. S. Murphy was hit by flak and was crash landed at Ghent. All six crew and the two dispatchers were later returned to base.

Twenty-one year old Flying Officer William Kirkham flying LJ883 was hit by flak at 500 feet and set on fire. It crashed at Planken Wambuis, west of Arnhem. He and all his crew, save for the rear gunner Flight Sergeant G. Wood, who came from Hull and one of the air dispatchers, Driver S. Badham of 253 Company, who had two broken ribs, were killed. Wood and Badham joined a party of paratroopers who were in hiding and on the third day they were approached by two men from the Dutch resistance who took them to Ede, from where their journey was arranged for them. Flying Officer David Campbell flying LK117, was hit by flak during the run over the DZ. Corporal William Hutchins, one of his air dispatchers, was wounded in both legs and his back, despite this he carried on despatching large panniers over the DZ. Hutchins was awarded the DFM. Lastly, LJ622 flown by Flying Officer G. J. H. Burkby, badly damaged by flak, had to be force landed at Manston. 570 Squadron now received eight new aircraft to replace their losses, which were so high that crews from 295 Squadron and 1665 HCU had to be posted in to fill vacancies. However, 570 Squadron played no further part in 'Market Garden', which had cost them eleven aircraft and the lives of twenty-three aircrew and four dispatchers. Sixteen men who had bailed out were taken prisoner, though a further eighteen men shot down returned to the Allied lines when the 1st Airborne Division withdrew on 25/26 September.

On 196 Squadron EF298 skippered by 22-two year old Flying Officer William 'Bill' Baker RCAF had dropped their supplies and were on their way home when they were hit by flak and crashed at Panoramhoeve. Baker had owned his own aircraft in the States and he had volunteered for the Royal

Canadian Air Force as a way of 'seeing the action.' He and his crew were killed. Sergeant Richard B. Bond the 24-year old flight engineer whose navigator brother 'Stan' had been killed on a Stirling on 620 Squadron on 27 August 1943 left a wife and baby daughter.[8]

On 437 Squadron RCAF Dakota KG305 flown by 28-year old Flying Officer William Richard Paget RCAF was shot down by flak and crashed at Eerschot southwest of Driel. There were no survivors. Three Dakotas on 233 Squadron took 54 Spitfire drop tanks to B56 (Brussels/Evère) as part of the sixth lift. On the 23rd two Dakotas took petrol tanks to B56 as part of the seventh lift. This was to be the last re-supply attempt from the UK. On the 23rd casualties were fifty-eight per cent, with eight Stirlings failing to return and no less than sixty-three aircraft damaged by flak. Had the 78th Fighter Group not been on hand the casualties would have been greater.

Meanwhile, another American paradrop in Holland went ahead when 41 C-47s in the 315th Troop Carrier Group at Spanhoe led by Lieutenant Colonel Peterson, 43rd Squadron commander dropped 560 Polish troops and 28 tons of supplies and equipment in 219 parapacks over LZ 'O' near Grave, southwest of Nijmegen at 1643 and experienced very little ground fire. All planes returned without damage without loss, or casualties. This 'milk run' stands in singular contrast to the experience of the glider serials which had flown to that zone just ahead of it. Whether this was because it flew the left hand lane 1½ miles west of the gliders or for some other reason is nowhere explained. All aircraft, reporting strong fighter protection returned safely from this operation. Six-hour passes were now authorized. Another piece of good news that cheered the 310th Squadron was that Cecil Dawkins was a PoW in Germany. After Dawkins gave the order for the crew to bail out and as he was attempting to leave his seat, there was an explosion under the cockpit floor. Slightly wounded in the face and head during the mission, he had bailed out at 300 feet, landing in water and was rescued. When he regained consciousness, he was aware of being on the back of a German tank rolling down a blacktop road. At the first aid station where his wounds were being attended, a German nurse who spoke English told him that a German tank crew pulled him from the river after his plane exploded and they saw him thrown into the water with no parachute. He was interrogated for several days and then sent to Stalag Luft I on the Baltic. After two weeks in the camp, Dawkins and two others attempted to escape, one was caught by guard dogs, one was shot and killed and only Dawkins was successful. He made contact with advancing Russians, where he stayed until a British unit was encountered during the last days of the war.

He was later awarded the DSC by his country and the Order of the Bronze Lion by the Queen of the Netherlands. Then came the report that Lieutenant Jacob Boon and his crew and Lieutenant Richard Bohannan and Sergeants Couch and Chambers were also safe and Boon returned after having been thoroughly taken care of by the underground in Holland, after his plane was shot down. He had been behind the German lines for two days and had the usual help that is always a tribute to the bravery of the patriots of those countries so long occupied by the Germans. Boon was sent to London the next day to give a full report of his evasion. Couch and Chambers were still in the hospital in Aldermaston.

Bad weather on 24 September once again halted all troop carrier missions from England. In the morning, rain lashed England and the Continent. Overcast hung unbroken at 300 to 800 feet and winds of 25 to 30 mph swept across the airfields. Conditions improved somewhat over southern England in the afternoon, but not enough to warrant a mission. As a result of the losses suffered on D+4 Air Commodore L. Darvall commanding 46 Group had moved one of his squadrons to Brussels on the 23rd, so that it could be escorted throughout its missions by fighters of 83 Group. This squadron dispatched 21 Dakotas escorted by 36 Spitfires on a supply mission to the Hartenstein pocket. The weather was so unfavourable that only four got there and only two of them dropped more or less at random without sighting any signals. They must have been over enemy territory for 1st Airborne was unaware that any drop had been made. The other seventeen aircraft gave up at Nijmegen, fifteen of them dropping their supplies to the 82nd Division and two air-landing them at a newly discovered airstrip near Grave. All returned safely, but four C-47s had been damaged by flak. On 25 September the squadron of 46 Group at Brussels sent seven Dakotas with medical supplies and food over the southern route to a drop point at Heveadorp. One was shot down and three damaged by flak. At least six C-47s dropped their loads and four did so within sight of 1st Airborne, but the troops were so pinned down that they could not recover a single bundle. The resupply missions were protected by sixty Spitfires and 36 Mustangs of ADGB. These encountered about fifty enemy fighters near Arnhem and about forty near Hengelo and claimed four destroyed at a cost of two Mustangs. Anti-aircraft fire against the British missions was probably reduced by seven Typhoons, 54 Mitchells and 24 Bostons of 2nd TAF which were operating against enemy guns in the Arnhem area, primarily to ease the pressure on the airborne.

The 78th Fighter Group flew no missions on the 25th because of the weather. Next day Major Leonard Marshall, the new 84th Squadron CO vice Ben Mayo, who having finished his tour returned to the States, led the Group on their final Arnhem support mission. The P-47s patrolling the area at 2,500 feet for almost an hour but the only activity they saw was a few bursts of flak at Arnhem and Hertogenbosch and some C-47s landing and taking off from a strip in the area. The 237 sorties the Group flew in support of the operations at Arnhem and Nijmegen earned the Duxford outfit its first AAF Distinguished Unit Citation. Altogether, the Group claimed thirteen aerial victories, 47 ground victories and eighty locomotives during twenty momentous missions in September for eighteen P-47s lost. Losses were high mainly because of the strafing missions on 10 September and six flak-suppression and air support missions the Group flew during Operation 'Market-Garden', 17-26 September.

Direct air support during the nine decisive days of 'Market' was decidedly inadequate except in a handful of cases. On 18 September 97 Spitfires and Mustangs were sent to help the 82nd Division beat off the German attacks out of the Reichswald and on 22 September 119 aircraft were sent to the assistance of the 101st Division, probably in response to a specific request from the division which 2nd TAF had accepted. The first direct support at Arnhem came on 24 September when 22 Typhoons attacked German positions around 1st Airborne and on the 25th when seven Typhoons and 74 Mitchells and Bostons did likewise, all too very good effect but much too late to win. Some armed reconnaissance was also flown but to comparatively little avail, since the Germans simply silenced their guns until the aircraft were past and waited until the coast was clear before sending in their own aircraft in repeated hit-and-run attacks, principally against 1st Airborne and the 82nd Division. All in all, it must be said that ground support in 'Market' was a difficult task badly handled and that the support provided was too little and too late.

On 29 September 209 C-47s in the 52nd Troop Carrier Wing, commanded by Brigadier General Harold L. Clark flew a mission to re-supply the Polish and British paratroopers with reinforcements, equipment and food in the corridor near Arnhem. It had been nine days since the initial airborne assault of the operation. The Polish Brigade had lost 25% of its fighting strength, amounting to 590 casualties. General Clark's plan called for landings at three German airbases in Holland two miles north of the town of Grave and eight miles southwest of Nijmegen. The bases were still in enemy hands and their securing by the Allies was not certain. At 1115 hours, the first of the C-47s, took off for one of the airfields, to be escorted by 9th Air Force and RAF fighters. On the approach, the fighters attacked flak guns hidden in haystacks and some flew ahead to form a protective ring around their grass field two miles west of Grave. With obstacles around the field removed, there were 4,200 feet of usable landing area. The 315th sent 72 planes led by Lieutenant Colonel Howard B. Lyon to transport an anti-aircraft battery and units of a Forward Delivery Airfield Group. In addition to men, the cargo consisted of jeeps, trailers, antiaircraft guns, ammunition, rations, gasoline and motorcycles. 'We took off from Spanhoe at 1130 hours' recalled Aubrey Ross 'and were escorted by Mustangs and Spitfires all of the time we were over the continent. No enemy planes got through to strike the congested landing area. We were told that several German fighters tried to intercept us but were shot down by our escort. After landing, the transports were unloaded and sent off as rapidly as possible to make way for succeeding serials to land. Two hundred and nine C-47s landed at Grave between 1350 and 1740 hours and brought in 657,995 lbs of combat equipment plus 882 men. Occasional ground fire was encountered on approaches and return routes, but no 315th airplanes failed to return from this airborne landing mission. As soon as an airplane landed, all crew members regardless of rank jumped in to assist with the unloading for nobody wanted to be on the ground any longer than necessary.'

When all is said, it is neither the monumental size nor the operational intricacies of 'Market' which linger longest in the memory. It is the heroism of the men who flew burning, disintegrating aircraft over their zones as coolly as if on review and gave their lives to get the last trooper out, the last bundle dropped. It is the stubborn courage of the airborne troops who would not surrender though an army came against them. In the sense that both troop carrier crews and airborne troops did all that men could do, there was, as General Gavin said, no failure in 'Market'.

'Market-Garden' has been described in an official report as 'by far the biggest and most ambitious airborne operation ever carried out by any nation or nations.' Of over 10,200 British airborne troops landed in the Arnhem area, 1,440 were killed or died of their wounds. 3,000 were wounded and taken prisoner. Of 47 officers and 545 other ranks of the Royal Army Medical Corps that took off for Holland, many were made prisoner in the very early stages of the battle but continued working throughout. At the end, before dispersal to Germany, 25 officers and 400 other ranks were accountable as being in German hands together with over 2,000 British wounded. Chaplains also remained behind with the wounded and about 2,500 uninjured troops also became PoWs. There were also 225 prisoners from the 4th Battalion, the Dorsetshire Regiment. About 450 Dutch civilians were killed. The operation also cost 160 RAF and Dominions aircrew, 27 USAAF aircrew and 79 Royal Army Service Corps dispatchers were killed and 127 taken prisoner. A total of 55 Albemarle, Stirling, Halifax and Dakota aircraft from Nos. 38 and 46 Groups failed to return and a further 320 damaged by flak and seven by fighters while 105 Allied fighter aircraft were lost.

The weather, which had played so important a part in the defeat of the British airborne, saved them in the end from annihilation. On the night of the 25th in rain and howling wind the division stealthily made its way to the river, leaving its wounded to man the defences. The Germans, apparently unaware of what was going on, made no effort to intervene. Before morning 1,741 men of 1st Airborne, 422 glider pilots, 160 Polish troops and 75 of the Dorsets had swum or been ferried across the Rhine. About 110 hid or escaped and crossed the river later, thanks to heroic efforts by the Dutch. The rest had to be written off as lost.

Thus ended in failure the greatest airborne venture of the war. Although General Montgomery asserted that it had been ninety percent successful, his statement was merely a consoling figure of speech. All objectives save Arnhem had been won, but without Arnhem the rest were as nothing. In return for so much courage and sacrifice, the Allies had won a fifty-mile salient - leading nowhere.

A few months previously Flight Lieutenant A. A. Williams had joined SHAEF Joint Field Censorship Group and censors were needed to accompany the Public Relations party, which included BBC and the press reporters. He was the only member of the RAF to be dropped with the ground forces. 'What the hell are you sticking your neck out in this lot for?' said an old squadron leader friend in the mess at the airfield of our embarkation. The full significance of his remark failed then to register, but within a few hours I was to know what he meant. Four years as an intelligence officer on Fighter Command stations was scarcely a fitting preparation for an airborne operation and for the 'Hell of Arnhem' at that. But, looking back and packed with excitement as every minute of those momentous ten days and nights were, I now know that I would not have missed one minute of it all. It seems now that, for me, all the wars in history were packed into those brief ten days.

'The enemy was undoubtedly taken by surprise; the weather was favourable. The German General Staff, however, recovered rapidly within a short time of the initial landings as to extemporize a formidable reply. Apparently resigning himself to conceding to the advancing British 2nd Army the two bridges at Eindhoven and Nijmegen, the enemy concentrated all his available and formidable forces, with powerful reinforcements from Northern Holland and Germany itself, in his savage and desperate endeavour to annihilate the small force that alone stood in his way to the consolidation of his positions in defence of one of the most formidable natural barriers in Europe.

'By holding Arnhem as they did, the 1st Airborne Division achieved a great part of their object by preventing its use by the Germans as a short route to reinforce their troops defending the vital bridge farther south, at Nijmegen. General Eisenhower has stated that the results achieved by the division were of incalculable value. The enemy reinforcements which the 'Red Devils' fought and held at Arnhem were the best troops he had available. The utmost savagery with which he fought - formidable 88s, self-propelled guns, six-inch mortars, numerous tanks, flame-throwers, machine guns and snipers, all concentrated upon a position that had shrunk to a bare thousand yards square - was sufficient proof of his intention to hold Arnhem at all costs. It is said that between 12,000 and 15,000 Germans were killed. At least 25 tanks and many SP guns were destroyed by a force whose armaments, glider-borne as they were, were severely limited not only in numbers, but also in size.

'As a RAF officer with little experience of military operations or of the Army in general, let me say at once that those soldiers were magnificent. No words of mine can describe with anything approaching adequacy the calm confidence and debonair bearing of the officers, the sheer determination and eagerness of their men, to smash tanks and to kill as many Germans as possible. As the days went by, when the position became more and more critical and the already small perimeter of operations was being gradually reduced under great pressure; when ammunition dwindled and food and water became non-existent, the stark determination of these supermen increased. So often has the word 'heroes' been heard during this grim war that it is in danger of growing trite. But these airborne soldiers were magnificent indeed. As the story of their heroic battle against every sort of odds has been unfolded, it is fitting that the whole world, not excluding even Germany, has paid tribute to the epic character of the 1st Airborne Division's stand at Arnhem.

'The scenes at the airfield of our embarkation were unforgettable. Hundreds of Horsa gliders, numbered and spick and span, awaited the split-second timing of attachment to the giant Stirlings and the take-off. One had the impression of a huge race-course paddock - hundreds of thoroughbreds being saddled and cantering up the 'straight' - in this case the wide runway - to the starting-post. Everyone was in holiday mood, but for sheer efficiency and accuracy of 'timing' it approached perfection. At last our turn came. 'All aboard!' said the sergeant pilot, with a wide grin. Jeep and trailer, packed with vital radio apparatus and other gear, had been previously loaded and securely clamped down. The last cigarette, the last 'Good luck everybody!' and my first glider flight had begun. People would be going to church now, I thought. The huge air armada, with the tremendous roar of its engines, must have been somewhat disturbing for the good citizens of Southern England. But to us, off on a great adventure, it was indeed thrilling. 'You may stand at the back of the cockpit,' the pilot told us. How peaceful and beautiful the English countryside looked that Sunday morning!

'Trouble began early; in fact, before we even crossed the Dutch coast. Flak! A noise like a thousand woodpeckers pecking at the bottom of our glider. Big holes torn in the wings. Not until we actually landed did we know that our Signals staff sergeant had been hit in three places. Not a word did he say about it for the rest of the journey. At last our pilot turned and pointed downwards. There, between patches of beautiful woods, in a stubble clearing sat dozens and dozens of gliders. Most had made perfect landings; a few had come to grief; wings torn off through colliding with trees; some had side-slipped in. How can we possibly get down among that lot? I thought. But - by a miracle it seemed to my uninitiated eye - our grinning pilot found a lane and made a wizard landing. For a moment we all looked at each other and then - action!

'We had landed right in the middle of a major war. Fierce fighting was going on in the woods all around. Bullets whistled over our heads as we set about unloading. It was then we discovered that the staff sergeant was badly wounded. A hasty field dressing was all we could do. Jeep and trailer unloaded, we piled in, the wounded man made as comfortable as possible. Then followed a nightmare ride through the woods, through a din of bullets and the rat-tat-tat of machine guns. We had our rendezvous, but our first objective was the casualty station. This proved lucky for us, really, for we actually took what was perhaps the only 'safe' lane through those woods.

'Eventually we hit a road leading to the main Arnhem highway. Pleasant Dutch farms came into view. Outside of one a group of Dutch people, obviously beside themselves with delight at our coming, greeted us with the traditional 'V' sign. There were the old and the quite young - we saw few of military age. Very friendly and in typically Dutch style, long wide trousers and peak caps. We gave them chocolate from our smock pockets. How delighted they all were!

'Oosterbeek is a pretty village of artistically designed villas. That is - it was! In the centre stood a large house, obviously a country sports club in peacetime, with a really charming wooded part, of stately beech trees and laurel bushes, adjoining. This was to be divisional headquarters; our home for nine days of sheer hell. A target of major importance to the ever-closing-in enemy, he gave us all he had to give, a simply terrific pounding - shells, mortars, machine guns and snipers in the adjoining woods - for the whole nine days and nights.

'Dig or die!' is an old Army slogan. How we dug! I myself dug four slit trenches; two caved in through shell-blast; one was pinched by two Bren gun lads (with a strong Midlands accent) because of its clear line of fire; while the fourth received a direct hit by a mortar bomb just before we left. At the time we were being 'briefed' for the final effort - that nightmare mile and a half creep through enemy-held woods to the river and ultimate safety.

'Nine days and nights of murderous concentrated fire, of never-ceasing shelling and mortaring of a space no larger than a square quarter-mile, had left nothing but destruction. Tall stately beeches reduced to mere stumps. Jeeps, trailers, mess-tins, everything riddled by shrapnel. Yet men lived through that hell - thanks to slit trenches - and a few saved themselves.

'Vivid impressions of those days will remain. The frequent 'stand-to's' to resist enemy infiltrations into our positions from the woods adjoining our little patch; the constant screech of shells and bullets from snipers perched in trees; the sleek brown pony we found grazing, peacefully enough, on our arrival. Some risked their lives to move him to fresh pastures. 'He's a Hun horse all right,' said our major. 'I took him some water and he kicked the bucket over.' On the third day he was badly wounded by shrapnel; we had to shoot him. The amazing collection of animals that strayed in from the woods. A stately stag with his retinue of does. 'Venison, by gad!' said an officer, but we had no chance of that, unfortunately. Cows and heifers and finally and incongruously enough, a pig.

'On Sunday evening, a week after our arrival, I looked out of my trench to see a truly amazing sight. I literally rubbed my eyes and looked again. A little old lady, dressed in black silk or satin, adorned with white lace, was walking slowly and with dignity into our clearing. She was obviously dazed or shell-shocked but she walked on. The snipers had apparently let her through. She was eighty; we were told and lived in the house by the well. There was, of course, nothing we could do; she was led back again by a big and somewhat embarrassed sergeant-major. One could picture her on happier Sunday evenings, dressing just as carefully for her visit to the village church. Her house was damaged by shell-fire later. I wonder what became of her.

'More and more memories! The magnificent lads of the Glider Pilot Regiment, now fighting as infantry. A few would form up. 'We are going to get back the hospital from Jerry,' they told me. 'There's a tank giving our boys hell in the woods over there.' 'Jerry's got a flame-thrower nearby - we're going to get it.' Sometimes they came back, some of them. The German prisoners, a nondescript lot of about 230 SS troops arrogant and sullen; boys of nineteen and twenty and men of over forty, eager to do odd jobs in return for tea and biscuits. The German equivalent to a WAAF who had returned from leave and had walked into our lines. Fat, dowdy and coarse-looking, she was said to be secretary to the local Gestapo. She cried bitterly the first night, but later, being reassured by considerate treatment, regained her composure. Together with other women suspected of collaborating with the Nazis, she was given comfortable enough quarters in a tennis pavilion and trenches were dug for them.

'On the third day the Germans cut off our water supply. This meant a hazardous journey to the well. Jerry soon realized this and the snipers indulged in their favourite sport. Yet there was no lack of volunteers to fetch water. On the fifth day our rations gave out, yet one did not want to eat. It did not seem much of a hardship, to go three days on tea and a biscuit or two. Carefully and exactly our War Office Public Relations Officer doled out what was left. Cigarettes were plentiful at first, then seven, then five and finally two a day to each of us.

'Rumours were abundant and varied. The 2nd Army is on its way! It is just over the river! No! The Guards Armoured Division has been involved in fierce fighting only five miles to the south; this latter unfortunately true. The resentment at the rosy 'picture' given on the BBC news. At last came good news; the Poles had dropped by parachute south of the river. Several hundred came over during the night. Their losses were grievous; it is stated that two-thirds were killed. A battalion of infantry were crossing at dusk! Actually some companies of the Dorsets crossed for the purpose of forming a bridgehead. Volunteers all, it is understood. Without this invaluable aid even 'the few' could not have got away. *Who's Afear'd*? is the Dorsets' motto. How well they lived up to it! Their losses were heavy in that gallant act of self-sacrifice.

'Many stories have been told of the indomitable 1st Airborne Division. Many will never be told. The sergeant who waited in a lane in the woods for an approaching tank. At the crucial moment his PIAT refused to fire. Immediately the tank was surrounded by men whose only weapons were hand grenades. But they got the tank. The German psychological warfare weapon: 'You are surrounded and have no chance,' they bawled. 'Think of your families and homes!' The answer was a howl of derision from the 'Red Devils' and a burst of Bren and Sten gun fire. Jerry hastily withdrew. 'Hold your fire, Tommy!' he would yell. 'We are friends.' 'Tommy' held his fire until the enemy was within a few yards. The slaughter went on. No words can picture it in its grim and bloody detail.

'A flame-thrower gave some trouble before it was disposed of. At last it came up to a position where an officer stood up with his 'walkie-talkie,' calling for artillery support to wipe it out. The Germans spotted him and from a few yards gave him a squirt. He rushed up the road, flaming from head to foot, but his men got to him, put out the flames and got him to the MDS, where they were told he would recover. A six-pounder gun crew eventually got the flame-thrower first shot and then gave it another five for luck. The boys went mad with joy.

'Memories! The padre who braved everything to comfort the wounded regardless of danger finally decided to remain with his boys, in company with the medical staff. How those doctors worked right up to that final and magnificent decision! A major of Carstairs (Border Regiment), who was wounded in all limbs on the second day, but fought on to the end. He would say, 'This position will be held!' His men replied, 'That's OK sir!' and 'OK' it was. Of Major General Urquhart, who when the situation was at its worst went out defiantly to stick his 'Airborne' flag on the lawn of his HQ; by now a sad wreck. Of the glider pilots who would shout to Jerry, 'Come on and fight!' and sang *Lili Marlene* when they refused. Of the two South Staffs men who 'annexed' my trench. Putting their Bren pat on the parapet of sand and shouting 'Come on, Jerry, blaze away, let's get this over, we want a drink in Arnhem!'

'The unforgettable sight of our re-supply bombers. Never have Stirlings, Halifaxes and Dakotas looked so beautiful. Wave after wave came in to drop their vital supplies of ammunition and food. How we danced and waved everything on which we could get our hands to show them where to drop! What guts those boys had - it was not their fault that most of the parachutes with their precious canisters fell in enemy-held territory, for by this time our perimeter had shrunk to a mere 1,200 yards by 900 yards. The flak that the Germans had brought up was intense; at a few hundred feet the bombers were just 'sitting birds' for the light stuff. Yet a number of aircraft made two or more 'runs up' in order to drop accurately. From a number of blazing aircraft the crews continued to unload when conceivably they might have bailed out themselves. 'What guts!' said a major next to me. The RAF did their damnedest to help us in the face of that intense flak. No one could have tried harder.

'Not the least of our troubles was the regular three or four times a day visit from the Luftwaffe. Thirty or forty Me 109s at a time circled our little patch. They did not always attack, but when they did it was from almost tree-top height and most unpleasant. How heartened we were when our own air support arrived, to shoot-up the Hun positions! How those Typhoons, with their rockets and cannon, must have frightened Jerry! How we hoped they had spotted those 88s and SP guns that were giving us hell day and night! But if they did so the enemy brought up more. The last four days were just a repetition of intense mortaring and shelling.

'And so on until the end. On the evening of the ninth day orders came to us to break out from our citadel - what was left of that once beautiful wood - and make our way across the Rhine. Sick and lightly wounded left their beds to take their chance with escape parties. Wherever possible these were given priority. Following the 'briefing our party moves off at ten-four' we were told. 'Anyone wounded on the way will be carried to the river.'

'It's going to be a tight finish,' said one glider pilot to me.

'The silent, eerie journey through the woods, each holding the tail of the man in front. The rat-tat-tat of machine guns and the shells screaming over our heads. Every minute packed with intense drama. Would we make it? The river at last. 'Get down flat!' Star shells lighting up everything; how we cursed them! Occasional mortaring. Two hours wait in drenching rain for the boats. At last came our turn - no! There's more wounded! Those Canadian Royal Engineers who worked all night until dawn to get us across the Rhine. Arnhem burning in the distance. 'Across at last; wading up to our waists for the last ten yards. But we were across - and alive! At dawn a number of the little band still left on the north bank were mown down by German guns. The evacuation was called 'Operation Berlin.'

'The rest of the story is now history.'[9]

At Fairford in Gloucestershire Corporal Ruth Mary Parker's task was to type the letters informing the next of kin that their son or husband was missing, believed killed on active service - a very sad task but one which had to be done. 'The atmosphere was very sombre' she recalled 'because many of us had known those who never returned. One happy memory I have was that about two to three weeks after the end of the operation some of the pilots of the gliders and some of the paratroopers turned up on the station. They had been hiding in Holland, some in drainpipes, some in farm out-buildings. All had been helped by the courageous Dutch people and the Dutch Resistance, who had risked their lives to shelter and feed these soldiers and airmen. Those who returned were a dishevelled lot but we were so delighted to see them again. They all wore a piece of orange material in the buttonholes of their battledress, as a symbol of their wonderful Dutch friends.'

Out of a total of 10,005 men landed, an estimated 1,130 British and Polish troops perished in the battle of Arnhem and 6,200 were taken prisoner. Up to 25 September the 101st Division had 315 dead, 547 missing and 1,248 wounded; the 82nd Division had 215 dead, 427 missing and 790 wounded in that period. Over the whole of Operation 'Market', 4,050 aircraft (1,336 Dakotas, fifty Albemarles and 340 Stirlings) were involved. Most of these aircraft towed the 1,205 Hadrian and Horsa gliders and were confronted by an unknown number of Luftwaffe aircraft. At one time, twenty 109s were strafing the dropping zone and altogether 29 Bf 109s were shot down. 867 Typhoons, Tempests, Spitfires etc joined the party. 6,674 troops were dropped by parachute and glider. 681 jeeps and trailers, sixty field guns with 'ammo' and two bulldozers were dropped by glider. The RAF lost 294 aircrew. A total of 52% of the force was lost or damaged. In the Arnhem area of operations alone, 79 transport aircraft were lost - 68 of 38 and 46 Groups RAF and eleven of 52nd Troop Carrier Wing USAF; with the loss of 160 RAF, RCAF, RAAF and RNZAF aircrew killed and eighty taken prisoner and 27 USAAF aircrew killed and three captured. In addition 79 Army air dispatchers of the Royal Army Service Corps were killed and 44 taken prisoner.110 fighter aircraft of the USAAF and RAF (including Dominion Air Forces) were lost during Operation 'Market-Garden'.

C-47 pilot Aubrey Ross in the 315th Troop Carrier Group wrote: 'Approximately 3,500 men from the American 82nd and 101st Divisions were listed as killed, wounded, or missing. All objectives but the bridge at Arnhem had been achieved, but without that key bridge over the Rhine, the operation had failed. All troops, both Airborne and Troop Carrier had done all they could do, but in the end, it was not enough. Who was to blame for this failed mission was anybody's guess. I suspect that there was enough blame to go around and then some. The flying, the fighting, the dying was mostly done by the very young, 18- to 25-year old men who just obeyed orders from their superiors without question. Wars must be fought by the young who are immature, naive and adventuresome.'

'They were the bravest of men and we were proud to support them' wrote 'Bud' Rice. 'Many of us crashed and burned alongside them, but we considered it an honour to help them train, deliver them safely, supply them in Africa, Sicily, Normandy, Bastogne, Holland and Germany. It was an honour to evacuate their wounded back to England. The enemy was clear and the enemy was evil. Duty called and having the support of every American back home is what kept us strong.

'May God bless all who served, especially those who remained behind. The brave souls we lost will always be the real heroes of WWII. We will never forget you and history will always honour your sacrifice.'

Notes

1. From 'Neptune' to 'Market'

1. On the 12th SHAEF did promise to divert to his service enough American trucks and aircraft to bring 1,000 tons a day to Brussels for 'Garden'. Satisfied that this met his minimum requirements, Montgomery then set 17 September as 'D-Day' for 'Market-Garden'.
2. *A Drop Too Many* by Lieutenant Colonel John Frost.
3. Quoted in *A Bridge To Far* by Cornelius Ryan. Hamish Hamilton 1974).
4. The British used parachute clusters to drop whole jeeps and artillery pieces from the bomb bays of Halifaxes. However, even with them the dropping of heavy equipment was still in the experimental stage. Not until after the war, when they received the Fairchild C-82 'Packet' with its big cargo door in the rear, were the American troop carriers able to make such drops.
5. Rear echelons of both the wing and its groups were still functioning at Exeter, Upottery and Merryfield.
6. The equipment and briefing of the glider pilots was unsuitable for a mission such as 'Market'. They were given no compasses; about half of them got no maps of their destination; and the others received only a single map on a scale of 1:100,000. Most seem to have had a rather indistinct blow-up of a high-altitude photograph of the landing area. The briefings were more concerned with the landing fields than with the surrounding terrain and said little of how and where the airborne units intended to deploy.

2. 'D-1'

1. On 18 September five Mosquito weather scouts were dispatched to Holland. 1st Lieutenant Robert Tunnel and his 19-year old navigator-cameraman, Staff Sergeant John G. Cunney failed to return. They appeared over the German airfield at Planlunne far from their objective and were caught in a searchlight, which blinded the pilot. Tunnell took evasive action, hit an oak tree and crashed on a hillside near Lignin on the Dutch-German border. The Mosquito exploded, killing both crewmembers. They are interred in the American War Cemetery at Neuville en Condroz, Belgium.

3. 'Market' Sunday 17 September 'D-Day' - The British Lift

1. *'First In - The Parachute Pathfinder Company'* by Ron Kent (Batsford 1979).
2. *The History of the Glider Pilot Regiment* by Claude Smith (Leo Cooper 1992).
3. Quoted in *'D-Day To Berlin'* by Andrew Williams (Hodder & Stoughton, 2004).
4. 23 Dakotas towed 23 Horsas carrying part of the 1st. Airborne Division to LZ 'S'. Clouds were low but appeared to be breaking up for take-off, which took 18 minutes. Three Dakotas experienced cutting repeatedly, losing considerable height. One of these had to release his glider at 800 feet over the Channel. Another was still trying to re-start his engines when the glider cast off, both these glider crews were picked up very quickly by Air Sea Rescue craft. The third got as far as the Dutch coast when his engines and R/T failed, so he released his glider, which landed safely on the Island of Schouwen. A fourth lost his glider in thick cloud over England, which landed safely five miles west of Abingdon aerodrome. The remaining Dakotas arrived safely over the LZ on time; the Horsas casting off in rapid succession. All aircraft returned safely, having encountered no enemy air opposition and very little flak. Total load carried to the L.Z. was 292 troops; 2 cars (5 cwts); 17 Jeeps; 22 trailers (10 cwts); 2 hand carts; 18 heavy and 2 folding motor bicycles; 22 bicycles and one 6 pounder gun. On the second lift 26 Dakotas and Horsas took off from Base in fairly good weather to LZ 'S'. The aircraft made good time to the LZ,, releasing all gliders as briefed, except one, which sustained a severed tow rope, landing safely 5 miles ENE of Hertogenbosch, approximately 10 miles away. A certain amount of light flak was experienced east of Hertogenbosch and around the TRV. The weather was fairly hazy over the Continent with 7/10ths Stratus over Eastern England and the sea. No enemy aircraft were sighted and all aircraft returned safely to Base. *The Pegasus Archive.*
5. *Six of the Best; the spirited 'war memoirs of ex-Flight Lieutenant Edwards. J. 123886 DFC* (Robson Books 1984).
6. The 61st TCS flew 71 C-47 missions carrying 1,166 British troops on the first lift without loss. The group later flew 158 missions for the US airborne divisions with the loss of four aircraft. The 314th TCG flew 198 C-47 and six C-53 missions carrying 2,330 British and 604 Polish troops on 17, 18 and 21 September, losing four aircraft with fifteen men killed, one PoW and four men returning safely. The group also flew 29 missions for a US division without loss. The 315th Troop Carrier Group flew 149 C-47 missions carrying 902 British and 964 Polish troops on 18, 20 and 21 September, losing seven aircraft, with twelve men killed, two prisoners and nineteen returning safely. The group also flew 162 missions for US divisions with the loss of one aircraft.

7. Fifteen chaplains were present at Arnhem. On 17 September nine took off by glider and six parachuted in. Pare received a Mention in Dispatches at Arnhem.

8. 'Eureka' worked in conjunction with the 'Rebecca' navigational aid. The 'Rebecca', an airborne sender-receiver indicated on its scope the direction and approximate range of the 'Eureka', a responsor beacon.

9. See *The Gliders; An Action packed Story of the Wooden Chariots of World War II* by Alan Lloyd (Leo Cooper 1982).

10. Egan, seriously wounded, was subsequently taken prisoner at Arnhem Bridge and finally ended up in a PoW hospital at Obermaasfeldt in Germany in bed next to his CO, John Frost.

11. '*First In - The Parachute Pathfinder Company*' by Ron Kent (Batsford 1979).

12. *Handley Page Halifax: From Hell to Victory and Beyond* by K. A. Merrick (Chevron Publishing Ltd 2009).

13. The U-boat was finished off by a Royal Navy sloop on 28 May after Stark and a US Navy Catalina had damaged the vessel.

14. Quoted in *Arnhem 1944: The Airborne Battle* by Martin Middlebrook (Viking 1994 and Pen & Sword 2009).

15. *Battle Flight to Arnhem, RAF Flying Review*, October 1962.

16. *Battle Flight to Arnhem, RAF Flying Review*, October 1962.

17. *Battle Flight To Arnhem, RAF Flying Review*, October 1962.

4. The British Lift Continues

1. Blakehill Farm airfield was near Chelsworth north of Swindon. 22 Dakotas of 233 Squadron took off towing Horsa gliders carrying 308 troops. Twelve Dakotas of 437 Squadron took 146 men to Arnhem.

2. Lieutenant Maltby's original Field Burial was near the roadside north of Reijerskamp Farm at Wolfhezen before he was interned at Oosterbeek War Cemetery, Arnhem. He left a widow, Jean Felicity Maltby.

3. Quoted in *Paras: Voices of The British Airborne Forces in the Second World War* by Roger Payne OAM (Amberley Publishing 2014).

4. *Air Battle for Arnhem* by Alan W. Cooper (Pen & Sword 2012)

5. The Horsas which broke loose over England included some of those carrying the Reconnaissance Squadron which was to have reconnoitred the route from the LZs into Arnhem. The loads of 21 gliders were delivered to Arnhem on the second lift. Four other gliders ditched; two with broken tow ropes and two as a result of tug engine trouble. In all, eight gliders ditched safely during this first lift and air-sea rescue service saved nearly all crews and passengers. Of the eight gliders, five were Arnhem-bound. Two gliders landed

near Drunen in Holland because of tug engine failure. Within minutes Dutch Resistance members had taken charge of the situation and the crews and passengers, totalling 34, were in hiding. For the next 34 days the Resistance risked not only their lives, but those of their families in concealing their British 'guests'. Eventually the party was found shelter in part of a lunatic asylum, being joined by the occupants of an American glider, making the total now 47. German soldiers then occupied the ground floor of the asylum for two days. The Resistance then found safer quarters and eventually the allied troops made their way to the village of Boxtel and safety. *The History of the Glider Pilot Regiment* by Claude Smith (Leo Cooper 1992).

6. The only previous experience of air insertion of radar units was in the Middle East where an AMES Type 6 radar, otherwise known as a Light Warning Set (LWS), had been modified to be carried in a Hudson or Bombay aircraft and was deployed to 'Marble Arch' in the Western Desert on 18 December 1942 where it became operational only 45 minutes after landing. All in all it was a remarkable achievement to modify the radars and form and train the two mobile radar units for use at Arnhem in such a short timescale.

7. The pontoon bridge was already unusable. The Germans had removed the centre portion a day or two before.

5. 'Market' Sunday 17 September 'D-Day' - The American Lift

1. *All The Way To Berlin* by James Megellas, (Presidio Press, 2003).

2. After passing their zones the American troop carriers were to turn 1800 to left or right, depending on the position of the zone and return by the way they had come. They were to fly at 1,500 feet on the trip out, descend to 500 feet to make their drop or release and return at 3,000 feet to avoid the incoming traffic. American paratroop formations would be the usual 9-plane 'V of V's in serials of from 27 to 45 aircraft. American glider formations again would be columns made up of pairs of pairs in echelon to the right in serials of from 30 to 50. RAF tow-planes and gliders would proceed in a loose column of pairs at 10-second intervals, flying at 2,500 feet on the way to their zones and returning at 5,000-7,000 feet.

3. Powerful and highly directional electric light used to mark routes and drop zones.

4. *All The Way To Berlin* by James Megellas (Presidio Press, 2003).

5. *All The Way To Berlin* by James Megellas (Presidio Press, 2003).

6. In part, from Walter Cronkite's foreword to John Lowden's *Silent Wings at War*.

7. *All The Way To Berlin* by James Megellas (Presidio Press, 2003).

8. *Shot Down Behind Enemy Lines: An 82nd Airborne Stick's Survival at Market-Garden* by Jan Bos.

9. *All The Way To Berlin* by James Megellas (Presidio Press, 2003). 'Maggie' Megellas was the most decorated member of the 82nd Airborne, and was proposed for the Medal of Honor. In 2018 Lieutenant Colonel Megellas celebrated his 101st birthday.

10. Ten or 15 minutes after the attack began all but one unlocated 88mm flak battery had stopped firing. Sixteen multi-gun sites were claimed destroyed and thirty-seven more damaged.

11. Possibly mechanic, Tech Sergeant Ralph Zipf and radio operator Staff Sergeant Roger Gullixon; both of whom survived.

12. In an article he wrote for the 26 March 1961, issue of *Family Weekly*.

13. Lowden, *Silent Wings of War*.

14. *Little One and His Guardian Angel: One man's story of the 440th Troop Carrier Group During WWII* by Charles E. Bullard (Williams Associates 2001).

15. On 16 February 1947 Mantell returned to Louisville, joining the newly formed Kentucky Air National Guard. He became an F-51D Mustang pilot in the 165th Fighter Squadron. On 7 January 1948, 25-year-old Captain Thomas F. Mantell died in the crash of his F-51 Mustang, after being sent in pursuit of an UFO. He may have died chasing a Skyhook balloon, which in 1948 was a top-secret project that Mantell would not have known about. Mantell pursued the object in a steep climb and disregarded suggestions to level his altitude. At high altitude he blacked out from a lack of oxygen. His relative inexperience with the F-51 may have been a contributing factor.

16. Two C-47s made emergency landings at Ghent and a third piloted by Major Ken Glassburn the 26-year old 304th Squadron commander was forced to land at Brussels with an injured paratrooper on board. On D-Day, 6th June, Glasswell had to ditch his aircraft in the Channel of 'Utah' beach after dropping men of the 82nd Airborne. *See Deliver Us From Darkness: The Untold Story of the Third Battalion, 506th PIR* by Ian Gardner.

17. *Market-Garden A Glider Pilot's Story by George E. 'Pete' Buckley.*

18. *Market-Garden A Glider Pilot's Story by George E. 'Pete' Buckley.*

6. 'D+1' 18 September - One Way Ticket To War

1. *The Pegasus Archive.*

2. Eleven airmen in the two Light Warning Units and Staff Sergeants' Kennedy, Ferguson and McInnes were taken into captivity. On 6080 LWU Squadron Leader Coxon and 1st Lieutenant Bruce Davis an American volunteer from the US 9th Air Force escaped, as did Squadron Leader Wheeler and Flight Lieutenant Richardson on 6341 LWU. Staff Sergeant Edwards and Sergeant Watson of the Glider Pilot Regiment also escaped.

3. Making up the rest of the British contingent were a C-47 with Advance Party from Barkston Heath, vehicles in seven Horsas from Keevil and a Hamilcar from Tarrant Rushton and Major Aeneas Perkins' 4th Parachute Squadron Royal Engineers and Squadron Headquarters at Uppingham flew in nine C-47s from Spanhoe and four Horsas from Keevil. Lieutenant Colonel W. Alford's133 Parachute Field Ambulance RAMC at Barleythorpe Hall flew in six C-47s from Spanhoe and Saltby and six Horsas from Keevil.

4. *Arnhem Doctor* by Stuart Mawson (Orbis Publishing Ltd London 1981).

5. Quoted in *Arnhem 1944: The Airborne Battle* by Martin Middlebrook (Viking 1994 and Pen & Sword 2009).

6. At Arnhem Waddy was wounded in fighting at Johanna Hoeve woods. He was subsequently wounded twice more while at a Main Dressing Station and eventually taken prisoner. In spring 1945 he was liberated by General Patton's army from Stalag VIIA in Bavaria and was able to return to the UK to marry his fiancée, Ann. He is a published author (*Tour of the Arnhem Battlefields*) and a recognised authority on Arnhem. From 1982 to 1996 he led a team of Arnhem veterans to talk to the students of the Army Staff College on their battlefield tours at Arnhem.

7. C-47 43-15180. One more C-47 with the Advance Party flew from Barkston Heath, the vehicles being carried in seven Horsas from Keevil and a Hamilcar from Tarrant Rushton.

8. One of them was later killed. The other was tried by a Dutch court for murder and was sentenced to 20 years but was out in 12.

9. Captain King was wounded and taken prisoner. General Sir Frank Douglas King GCB MBE died on 30 March 1998.

10. Quoted in *Arnhem 1944: The Airborne Battle* by Martin Middlebook (Viking 1994 and Pen & Sword 2009).

11. On 17 October 1946 by Royal Decree, Fulmer was knighted by Queen Wilhelmina of the Netherlands, receiving the Knight fourth class of the Military William Order. The Order is the highest and oldest military honour of the Kingdom of the Netherlands, bestowed for "performing excellent acts of Bravery, Leadership and Loyalty in battle" As of February 2015 Fulmer was one of only four knights still living.

12. The champagne was finally handed over in 1989.

13. Lieutenant Arnold, Staff Sergeant Quick, Technical Sergeant Broga, Lieutenant Colonel Kross and Major Cannon.

14. In order to bring in the loads of gliders aborting on the previous day the number dispatched was increased from 270 to 296. One crashed on take-off because of an engine failure.

15. Henk Welting on the RAF Air Force Commands/archive website.

16. Quoted in *The Elastic Band Called Arnhem - Paras: Voices of The British Airborne Forces in the Second World War* by Roger Payne OAM (Amberley Publishing 2014).

17. Quoted in *Like Flotsam from the Sky: Voices of The British Airborne Forces in the Second World War* by Roger Payne OAM (Amberley Publishing 2014).

18. Arie-Jan van Hees Eijden. Dereck Boyer DFC died in a boating accident in Guernsey on 7 January 2001.

19. For his courage, leadership and devotion to duty, holding together the men in his sector against the most enormous odds, beating off attacks time and again with a handful of men, he was awarded the Military Cross. In part his citation read: 'He never troubled about his own safety. He was never to be found in a trench at a time when the fire was heavy. He was always going round his positions steadying and cheering his men. For five days and nights without rest he held his sector and whether he was beating off attacks by day or leading patrols by night, he always showed himself to be a leader of the highest order.'

20. *The History of the Glider Pilot Regiment* by Claude Smith (Leo Cooper 1992).

21. *Arnhem Doctor* by Stuart Mawson (Orbis Publishing Ltd London 1981).

22. He survived and later wrote the introduction to Stuart Mawson's book *Arnhem Doctor*.

23. Quoted in *Arnhem 1944: The Airborne Battle* by Martin Middlebrook (Viking 1994 and Pen & Sword 2009).

24. Quoted in *A Tour of the Arnhem Battlefields* by John Waddy (Pen & Sword 199, 2001).

25. 'Bill' Higgs was incarcerated for ten grim months at Stalag 11B, Fallingbostel. Life in the camp was terrible, food was disgusting, all the prisoners became lousy as it was running with lice; there was so much filth about. The food was very basic, a piece of black bread and three 'spuds' cooked in their jackets which the PoWs lined up for in the freezing snow. On release and after his 40 days' leave was finished he had to report to Midhurst Sanatorium where he stayed for two years. He was operated on by Sir Thomas Price, an expert on lung aneurism, who was at that time the physician to King George VI. 'Bill' was finally demobbed in 1947, fit enough only for 'a light job in the open air.' 'Bill' has the honour of holding the altitude record in a Horsa glider. He was towed by a Short Stirling tug and released at an altitude of 15,000 feet. It is an all time record which has never been broken in the type of aircraft which was being used. See *Wiltshire at War* by Harry Angier.

7. 'D+1' The American Lift

1. *Valor Without Arms: A History of the 316th Troop Carrier Group 1942-1945* by Michael N. Ingisano Jr. (Merriam Press 2012).

2. On the 19th and 20th poor weather largely grounded the Allied and German air forces although on the 20th the 78th Fighter Group was dispatched to Holland. The Group patrolled the Hertogenbosch area but could find no suitable targets so Major Richard E. Conner led the P-47s north of Arnhem where they bombed five light flak positions and six more west of Nijmegen. Along the route they strafed a German troop convoy. Flak claimed several RAF Stirling glider tugs and many C-47s but all the Thunderbolts returned safely.

3. Quoted in *September Hope: The American Side of a Bridge Too Far* by John C. McManus.(Penguin, 2012).

4. McCormick, who suffered bruises and lacerations on right leg; Atterbury and SSgt Nichalos J. Carone, engineer who were uninjured and Powell who suffered burns on left hand and forearm, were rescued. McCormick's crew had flown C-47A-80-DL 43-15139 'Chalk 45' on 'D-Day', 6 June 1944.

8. The Third Lift - Tuesday 19 September ('D+2')

1. *Stirling Wings: The Short Stirling Goes To War* by Jonathan Falconer (Sutton Publishing Ltd 1995).

2. Quoted in *There Shall be Wings; The RAF from 1918 to the Present by* Max Arthur (Hodder & Stoughton 1993).

3. Quoted in *There Shall be Wings; The RAF from 1918 to the Present by* Max Arthur (Hodder & Stoughton 1993).

4. Quoted in *Stirling Wings: The Short Stirling Goes To War* by Jonathan Falconer (Sutton Publishing Ltd 1995).

5. Thanks are due to Keith and Ken Prowd and also to Arie-Jan van Hees, author of *Green On!*

6. Quoted in *Arnhem 1944: The Airborne Battle* by Martin Middlebrook (Viking 1994 and Pen & Sword 2009).

7. On the 24th they were able to get to the medical centre. Geoff Liggins had burns to his hands and face. He had also injured his back in the crash landing. Flight Sergeant Humphrey had a badly cut left leg, Rugsdale had a broken back and Sergeant Gaskin a broken leg. On the 24th the wounded were taken by ambulance to Nijmegen and put into a Casualty Clearing Station, all three, Braid, Prior and Simpson were taken by jeep to Nijmegen and stayed there for two days. They were taken to the Reichswald Forest for three days under canvas. They then ran the gauntlet on a transport column down a two-mile corridor known as 'Hell's Highway'. They finally arrived in Brussels and MI9. *Air Battle For Arnhem* by Alan W. Cooper (Pen & Sword 2012).

8. Quoted in *Winged Victory; The Story of a Bomber Command Air Gunner* by Jim Davis (R. J. Leach & Co, London, 1995). On the 29th 'Wally' Simpson arrived back home in Coventry. After Geoff Liggins visited his old airfield at RAF Keevil and had given his version of events, Walter was recommended for the Conspicuous Gallantry Medal (Flying), an inappropriate decoration as all the action was on the ground so the air officer commanding 38 Group deemed the Military Medal a more fitting award. Geoff Liggins was killed in a car crash in 1955.

9. Quoted in *Experiences of War: The British Airman* by Roger A. Freeman (Arms & Armour 1989). Flight Lieutenants W. J. Auld; W. R. Chalk and J. Francis and Driver E. H. Shovell, 63 Airborne RASC, who was wounded, were taken prisoner. *Air Battle For Arnhem* by Alan W. Cooper (Pen & Sword 2012).

10. *Arnhem: The Battle for Survival* by John Nichol and Tony Rennell (Penguin 2012).

11. General Sir Kenneth Thomas Darling KCB DSO CBE MBE died on 31 October 1998.

12. Quoted in *Out of the Blue: The Role of Luck in Air Warfare 1917-1966,* edited by Laddie Lucas (Hutchinson & Co Publishers Ltd 1985).

13. In 1984 'Len' Wilson's wedding was found in the area where he crashed and it was sent to his widow. See *Air Battle for Arnhem* by Alan W. Cooper (Pen & Sword Aviation, 2012).

14. Quoted in *There Shall be Wings; The RAF from 1918 to the Present by* Max Arthur (Hodder & Stoughton 1993).

15. Harry King spent the rest of the war in Stalag Luft I at Barth. Following the release of King from prison camp, full details of the action became known and pilot Lord received a posthumous VC, the only one awarded to any member of Transport Command during the Second World War. In May 1949 the Dutch Government awarded Harry King the *Bronzen Leeuw* (Netherlands Bronze Cross).

16. *Handley Page Halifax: From Hell to Victory and Beyond* by K. A. Merrick (Chevron Publishing Ltd 2009).

17. *Handley Page Halifax: From Hell to Victory and Beyond* by K. A. Merrick (Chevron Publishing Ltd 2009). An experienced glider pilot, Halsall's operational flying career had begun in Operation 'Husky' in June 1943 as co-pilot of a Waco glider flown by American pilot, Captain Tom McMillen and on 6 June 1944 had taken part in the 'D-Day' landings. Born at Southport on 18 March 1921 into a moderately well-off Lancastrian family, at school Halsall had excelled at medium- and long-distance running. His final operational flight was at the controls of ma Hamilcar carrying a 17 pounder anti-tank gun and its Dodge Limber in Operation 'Varsity'.

18. Quoted in *There Shall be Wings; The RAF from 1918 to the Present by* Max Arthur (Hodder & Stoughton 1993).

19. 'In and around Arnhem there are many memorials to various Para units, Glider Pilots, Air Dispatchers, Airborne units, but not one to the 175 RAF aircrews who gave their lives on these suicidal re-supply missions, which in my estimation was the bravest flying of the war.'

9. 'Bloody Tuesday' 'D+2' 19 September - The American Lift

1. *Market-Garden A Glider Pilot's Story by George E. 'Pete' Buckley.*

2. Escort duty between Hertogenbosch and Arnhem had originally been delegated to the Ninth Air Force, but on the morning of the 19th all responsibility for protection of the troop carriers from air action beyond Gheel was given to Eighth Air Force.

3. *Market-Garden A Glider Pilot's Story by George E. 'Pete' Buckley.*

4. *Market-Garden A Glider Pilot's Story by George E. 'Pete' Buckley.*

10. Wednesday 20 September - The Fourth Lift

1. Two P-51s and one P-47 got back but had to be salvaged.

2. In November Townshend was the sole British correspondent in a Royal Marine landing craft in the assault on Westkapelle, Walcheren Island, near Antwerp. He helped to haul wounded survivors out of the sea and veterans told him that the opposition was fiercer than at Dieppe. His night editor however, toned down his prose: 'Too much blood and guts. Might upset the readers at breakfast.' Townshend was next sent to the Far East. He reported from a forward fighter airstrip at Tolungoo in Burma; wrote an account of flying in a Dakota over the 'Hump' into China, which a professor of geography complained could only have been a subsidiary mountain range; and described from the island of Diego Garcia flying boats searching for Japanese submarines.

3. The pilot was subsequently awarded the DFC and Flight Sergeant Thompson received the DFM. Robertson and Thompson were killed on 10 May 1945 when taking the Air Officer Commanding of 38 Group, Air Vice Marshal Scarlet-Streatfield CBE and thirty men of the 1st Border Regiment and 1st Airborne, to Norway. Flight Lieutenant Rosedale was awarded the DFC in February 1945 having taken part in 'D-Day' operations in June 1944 and on his second tour as a bombing leader.

4. Marshall was killed on 3 April 1945.

5. Quoted in *Arnhem 1944: The Airborne Battle* by Martin Middlebrook (Viking 1994 and Pen & Sword 2009).

6. All of Lee's crew were reported safe and returned on the 25th. Thanks are due to Maurice McHugh's nephew, Peter John McHugh. It took nearly nine more months of uncertainty until 15 June 1945 for McHugh's family to receive official confirmation that Maurice was presumed dead. Later in March 1950 the family received official advice that Maurice had been reburied at Canadian War Cemetery at Groesbeek on the Dutch/German border.

7. Apart from those already mentioned the following Stirlings were also failed to return: On 196 Squadron LJ988 flown by Warrant Officer1 W. R. Tait RCAF. He and seven of his crew were killed when the Stirling crashed at Natuurbad, Doorwerth. One dispatcher survived. On 196 Squadron LJ840 piloted by Flight Sergeant J. P. Averill crashed while on fire at Betwe south of the Rhine having been hit by flak. All bailed out and returned. On 196 Squadron LJ851 (known to the ground crew as 'E-Elephant' (Never Forgets) piloted by Warrant Officer George R. Oliver crash landed at Vessum having been hit by a fighter. before reaching the DZ. All eight crew evaded. A Halifax flown by Flight Sergeant Goldsmith on 298 Squadron crash-landed in the water; two PR Spitfires on 16 Squadron were also lost; Flight Lieutenant Gerry Bastow and Flying Officer Brodby. One Mustang from 315 Squadron crashed near Jutphass. On the ground Lieutenant Air Commander Roffer Eden, age 31, a member of the Radar Unit and dropped on the 18th, was killed when a shell exploded at the Hartenstein HQ, Oosterbeek while he was repairing a wireless in an attempt to make contact with outside air support.

8. One additional aircraft towed a Waco, which had been on call, with a ton and half of supplies, making the total despatched 311.

9. This figure represents an average for several categories of supplies, a few items in one category being counted as equal to tons in another. It is further distorted by the fact that hardly any of the rations which were dropped were reported as collected.

10. This unit had been on its way from East Prussia to Aachen by rail on 17 September but had been diverted to Venlo for use against the 101st Division.

11. Thursday 21 September ('D+4')

1. See *Air Battle for Arnhem* by Alan W. Cooper (Pen & Sword, 2012).

2. Lance Corporal George Chisholm (26) and Drivers' Lionel Abbott (19) and Roy Abbott (22) of 223 Air Despatch Company were killed.

3. Jimmy received an immediate DFC to add to his King George V Jubilee medal which he had received in 1935 as a chorister at St. Paul's Cathedral. (When he joined the RAF and under 'square bashing', he wore the ribbon of this medal which his drill corporal took some umbrage, obviously not

himself having a medal). Because of the nature of his burns Jimmy was sent to RAF Wroughton near Swindon and then on to RAF Ely for further treatment and became a member of the 'Guinea Pig Club'. He would later conceal his substantial facial scars with his oversized handlebar moustache. He was a feature of London theatre in the immediate post-war years, debuting at London's Windmill Theatre in 1946 and on BBC radio the same year. He was married to Valerie Seymour for eleven years. During the 1970s however, he was publicly outed as a lifelong homosexual, much to his annoyance. He died in London on 7 July 1988 at the age of 68 from pneumonia.

4. Thanks are due to Steve Dyer ss.dyer@hotmail.com.

5. Thanks to the efforts of Messrs. Lex Roell and Jan Hey who both supplied information to the Commonwealth War Graves Commission, enough substantial evidence was produced which eventually led to identification of the unknown airman. Flying Officer Cressman received his own gravestone on 24 August 1998.

6. 'Ginger' Greenwell had flown thirty operations as a navigator on 196 Squadron and on the 2 August had navigated his aircraft on two engines and the third failing, back from the Brest Peninsula to Colerne; his aircraft had been hit on the final run into the DZ.

7. In total 295 Squadron flew 106 six sorties to Nijmegen and Arnhem, resulting in the loss of three aircraft, seven aircrew, two dispatchers and seven men taken prisoner.

8. Thanks are due to Roy Wilcock for biographical details in *Aircrew Remembered*.

9. Following the Arnhem tragedy Frank Corbett was drafted to the Far East and joined the aircraft carrier *Unicorn* in Sydney Australia and served in her for the remainder of the war.

10. 299 Squadron's final sorties in the Operation came on Saturday 23rd with fourteen Stirlings delivering supplies, three of which limped back to Keevil with serious damage. 299, equal with its neighbour at Keevil, 196 Squadron, flew a total of 112 sorties in 'Market-Garden'; more than any other squadron involved in the Operation.

11. Quoted in *Arnhem: The Battle for Survival* by John Nichol and Tony Rennell (Penguin 2011).

12. Quoted in *Arnhem 1944: The Airborne Battle* by Martin Middlebrook (Viking 1994 and Pen & Sword 2009).

13. Ibid.

14. Quoted in *Paras: Voices of The British Airborne Forces in the Second World War* by Roger Payne OAM (Amberley Publishing 2014).

NOTES

12. Thursday 21 September ('D+4') The Polish Lift

1. The 500 Polish paratroopers in these aircraft endured a further delay of 48 hours before, at last, they were dropped near Grave, deep into the 82nd Airborne Division's area, on Saturday 23rd September; the drop zones closer to the Rhine being considered too hazardous at this time.

2. On the 24th came the welcome news that 'Moose' Worley and the rest of Dawkins crew were safe and in the hands of the 82nd Airborne Infantry Division in Holland. Then came the report that Lieutenant Boon and his crew were also safe and Boon returned with a thrilling story of having been thoroughly taken care of by the underground in Holland. He had been behind the German lines for two days.

3. By A. Szmid, writing on the BBC Peoples War website.

4. By 25 September, when the order was given for an Allied evacuation he was able to escape unharmed and by boat he still carried his radio. His unit suffered the greatest proportional loss of men from any Polish unit involved in the battle: 37% of the Battery were dead or missing, a further 22% were wounded and Captain Jan Kanty Wardzała the commanding officer was taken prisoner.

5. On 2 May 2017, they all came home, thanks to the Department of Defense's POW/Missing Personnel Office (DPMO), whose motto is 'Promise Kept' and whose mission is to recover and repatriate the remains of military troops from five wars.

13. 'D+6' Saturday 23 September

1. On 25 September another 25th Bomb Group Mosquito 'Bluestocking' mission was launched as evacuation of the surviving paratroops from Arnhem began. 1st Lieutenant Clayborne O. Vinyard and his navigator, 1st Lieutenant John J. O'Mara, flew beyond their Netherlands objective, reaching the outskirts of Frankfurt before turning back. They descended to 18,000 feet where a Luftwaffe night-fighter shot them down. They were taken prisoner and sent to Stalag Luft I.

2. Darvall also suggested to Horrocks, Browning and Air Vice-Marshal Broadhurst, commanding 83 Group of the 2nd Tactical Air Force, that fighters might be used for supply dropping in place of the more vulnerable Dakotas and Stirlings. It appears that there was some measure of unanimity about the advisability of such a move, but no fighters joined in re-supply missions over Arnhem.

3. *Arnhem Lift* by Louis Hagen.

4. 190 Squadron flew 98 sorties during Operation 'Market Garden' and had suffered the heaviest losses of any of the sixteen squadrons in 38 and 46 Groups. Twelve Stirlings had been lost, thirty-nine aircrew and twelve

RASC dispatchers were dead and fifteen aircrew had been taken prisoner. A further twenty-five personnel who had been shot down over Arnhem had been able to return to the Allied lines when the 1st Airborne Division withdrew.

5. Ken Cranefield died aged 94 on the anniversary of his first sortie to Arnhem on 17 September 2016, the same year that BBMF Dakota ZA947 was painted to represent FZ692.

6. Quoted in *Arnhem 1944: The Airborne Battle* by Martin Middlebrook (Viking 1994 and Pen & Sword 2009).

7. 'Market-Garden' cost 38 and 46 Groups 55 aircraft lost with a further 320 damaged by flak and 7 by fighters. The Second Tactical Air Force, though fully conversant with the situation in Holland, was unaware of the immediate changes of plan necessitated by the exigencies of the situation. It could not and did not therefore, provide the full air cover of which it was capable.

8. *Two Brave Bond Uncles* by Paul Brooker writing on the *WW2 Peoples War* web site.

9. *I Was At Arnhem* by Flight Lieutenant A. A. Williams.

Index

INDEX

INDEX